ANALYSIS OF
ALGORITHMS AND
DATA STRUCTURES

INTERNATIONAL COMPUTER SCIENCE SERIES

Consulting editors   **A D McGettrick**   University of Strathclyde

J van Leeuwen   University of Utrecht

SELECTED TITLES IN THE SERIES

Programming Language Translation: A Practical Approach   *P D Terry*

Data Abstraction in Programming Languages   *J M Bishop*

The Specification of Computer Programs   *W M Turski and T S E Maibaum*

Syntax Analysis and Software Tools   *K J Gough*

Functional Programming   *A J Field and P G Harrison*

The Theory of Computability: Programs, Machines, Effectiveness and Feasibility
  R Sommerhalder and S C van Westrhenen

An Introduction to Functional Programming through Lambda Calculus
  G Michaelson

High-Level Languages and their Compilers   *D Watson*

Programming in Ada (3rd Edn)   *J G P Barnes*

Elements of Functional Programming   *C Reade*

Software Development with Modula-2   *D Budgen*

Program Derivation: The Development of Programs from Specification
  R G Dromey

Object-Oriented Programming with Simula   *B Kirkerud*

Program Design with Modula-2   *S Eisenbach and C Sadler*

Real Time Systems and Their Programming Languages   *A Burns and A Wellings*

Fortran 77 Programming (2nd Edn)   *T M R Ellis*

Prolog Programming for Artificial Intelligence (2nd Edn)   *I Bratko*

Logic for Computer Science   *S Reeves and M Clarke*

Computer Architecture   *M De Blasi*

The Programming Process   *J T Latham, V J Bush and I D Cottam*

ANALYSIS OF ALGORITHMS AND DATA STRUCTURES

Lech Banachowski Antoni Kreczmar

Wojciech Rytter

Institute of Informatics, Warsaw University

ADDISON-WESLEY
PUBLISHING
COMPANY

Wokingham, England · Reading, Massachusetts · Menlo Park, California · New York
Don Mills, Ontario · Amsterdam · Bonn · Sydney · Singapore
Tokyo · Madrid · San Juan · Milan · Paris · Mexico City · Seoul · Taipei

The programs in this book have been included for their instructional
value. They have been tested with care but are not guaranteed for any
particular purpose. The publisher does not offer any warranties or
representations, nor does it accept any liabilities with respect to
the programs.

Many of the designations used by manufacturers and sellers to
distinguish their products are claimed as trademarks. Addison-Wesley
has made every attempt to supply trademark information about
manufacturers and their products mentioned in this book.

Cover designed by Crayon Design of Henley-on-Thames and
printed by The Riverside Printing Co. (Reading) Ltd.
Typeset by Macmillan India Ltd, Bangalore 25.
Printed in Great Britain by T. J. Press (Padstow) Ltd, Cornwall.

First printed 1991.

British Library Cataloguing in Publication Data available

Library of Congress Cataloging in Publication Data
Banachowski, Lech.
    Analysis of algorithms and data structures/Lech Banachowski,
Antoni Kreczmar, Wojciech Rytter.
       p. cm. — (International computer science series)
    Includes bibliographical references and index
    ISBN 0-201-41693-X
    1. Computer algorithms.   2. Data structures (Computer science)
I. Kreczmar, Antoni. II. Rytter, Wojciech. III. Title.
IV. Series.
QA76.9.A43B36   1991   91-10971
005.7'3—dc20   CIP

To our wives

Preface

Approach

The analysis of algorithms is one of the central domains of theoretical computer science. The main objects in this domain are algorithms whose structure and properties are investigated from different viewpoints and on different levels of abstraction.

This book presents a variety of approaches to the analysis of algorithms and data structures. However it differs in various respects from the others. On the one hand, it contains a smaller variety of algorithms than *The Design and Analysis of Computer Algorithms* by Aho *et al.* (1974) or *Algorithms* by Sedgewick (1988), but on the other hand the analysis goes much deeper. Moreover the book covers some important fields which are not covered by any other textbook, such as embeddings between data structures, the pointer machine model of computations, self-organizing data structures, pebble games modelling space-efficient computations, speeding up of algorithms by transformations (methods of dynamic and algebraic simulation) and combinatorics of parallel operations on trees.

Another distinctive feature of the book is the systematic way in which algorithms are treated. Specifically, we concentrate on three basic aspects of analysis:

- *probabilistic* probabilistic models, generating functions;
- *structural* optimality of data structures, lower bounds, tree techniques, embeddings between data structures, pebble games, a structural approach to space complexity;
- *transformational* reduction of complexity using analysis of algorithms, various types of simulations, analysis 'at work' during the construction of algorithms.

The exposition of the material goes smoothly from an elementary level to a more and more advanced level. However, from the very beginning we emphasize the mathematical aspects of the algorithmic material to prepare the reader for the 'philosophy' of the more advanced second part.

Use in the curriculum

All the features mentioned above make the book attractive for courses on analysis of algorithms aimed at advanced undergraduate or graduate students of computer science and mathematics. Chapter 1 can also be used as a basis for an elementary introduction to algorithms and data structures. The book can serve as a reference for advanced courses on analysis of algorithms and data structures instead of the number of separate papers to which students are usually referred.

Outline of contents

Chapter 1 presents the concept of an algorithm and its properties. It introduces central topics such as the correctness and complexity of an algorithm as well as some necessary material concerning data types. The chapter ends with the presentation of some models of computation.

All the algorithms appearing in this introductory chapter are written in pure Pascal and may be run on a computer. The remaining chapters (the main part of the book) focus more on conceptual aspects than on programming itself. Thus the algorithms presented in the next chapters will be described less formally, sometimes using narrative English.

Chapter 2 is devoted to probabilistic methods, which are used to characterize the average cost of typical sorting and searching algorithms. We present these analyses as completely as possible.

Optimality considerations in data structures are the subject of Chapters 3 and 4. These include self-organizing lists and trees, implicit data structures, the pointer machine model, the lowest common ancestor problem, data structure embeddings and the pebbling problem.

Chapters 5 and 6 bring together the simulation techniques that make the design of efficient algorithms easier. They cover such topics as dynamic and algebraic simulation, composition systems and the tabulation method.

Chapter 7 is devoted to the design of efficient parallel algorithms. Parallel versions of sequential algorithms from Chapter 6 are presented. The emphasis is upon the combinatorics of trees related to fast parallel algorithms.

Exercises

Each chapter ends with a number of exercises (the more difficult ones are starred). Some of them refer directly to the material presented in the chapter, while others present new related topics.

Prerequisites

A certain maturity in computer science and mathematics is needed, equivalent to senior undergraduate level in computer science. Computer science prerequisites include undergraduate courses on data structures and the design and analysis of computer algorithms. Some practice in programming in a high-level programming language like Pascal or PL1 is also required. Mathematical prerequisites include elementary parts of probability theory, analytical calculus, set calculus and algebra.

Acknowledgements

We are pleased to express our thanks to the following reviewers and advisors who helped us to improve the book: K. Diks, P. Findeisen, P. Gburzyński, M. Lissowska, W. Plandowski, T. Radzik, A. Salwicki, W. M. Turski, W. Wyglądała from Warsaw University. Special thanks are also due to the referees whose comments contributed greatly to the present overall shape of the book.

This book is based on two others which were written in Polish and were published in 1980 and 1984 by the Polish Scientific–Technical Publishing Company, Warsaw. Without the support of our Polish publishers this English version would never have appeared.

We also wish to emphasize the aid of our students at the Warsaw University who were the first critical recipients of the material in this book and the aid of Mr J. Trzeciak who helped us to correct the English version.

Lech Banachowski
Antoni Kreczmar
Wojciech Rytter

Warsaw, October, 1990

Contents

Chapter 1
Algorithms and Their Properties

This is an introductory chapter which aims not only to acquaint the reader with the analysis of algorithms and data structures, but also to demonstrate the style of the book. First, we shall illustrate, by means of several examples, the concepts of the algorithm and the data structure as well as how to implement them in Pascal. Second, we shall formally define related notions such as algorithm correctness, time and space complexity, worst-case and average-case cost of an algorithm, asymptotic complexity, logarithmic and uniform cost criteria and decision trees. Finally, we present some of the mathematical background and tools that will be used in the analysis of algorithms and data structures throughout the book.

1.1 The algorithm and data types

An **algorithm** is a prescription for a systematic method which solves a given problem. Such a prescription should be precise enough to be used in a completely automatic manner. Moreover, to apply an algorithm, one should specify the **data types** in which it is to work.

Let us consider two simple examples. Euclid's algorithm for finding the greatest common divisor of two positive integers works in the data type integer and uses one elementary operation (integer division), and one elementary relation (equal to). The well-known textbook algorithm for solving a quadratic equation works in the data type of real numbers endowed with five elementary operations (addition, subtraction, multiplication, division and taking the square root of a non-negative real number), and with two relations (equal to and greater than).

The two data types presented above are abstract, in the sense that they are mathematical objects which do not appear in computer practice since instead of abstract numbers discrete representations are used. This leads to many problems and misunderstandings. For instance, the set of integers is reduced to its finite subset (symmetric or nearly symmetric around zero) and so the elementary operations are partial (the result of an operation may fall outside the represented subset). A more fundamental problem concerns real numbers. While the admissible integers are represented precisely, real numbers are approximated by their finite expansions in some base, and therefore the results of elementary operations are merely approximations of the results of the corresponding operations in the data type. This property of the data type of real numbers makes the analysis of algorithms in this structure much more complex. These aspects of the analysis of algorithms, although very important from a practical point of view, will not be considered in this book.

To define algorithms we shall use a programming language. The syntax of the language will make the methods of expressing algorithms precise, while its semantics will establish the way of interpreting these syntactic forms in the given data types.

Many criteria were applied in choosing the appropriate programming language for this book. The first issue was the popularity of the language and the clearness of its semantics. Second, the language had to be equipped with a broad set of programming constructs able to define quite complex algorithms. And last, but not least, was the fact that the programs defining the algorithms had to be easy to run on a computer. Taking all these issues into account we decided to choose Pascal, although it does have some drawbacks (for example, it sometimes has awkward control structures, it limits the structuring of data, and so on).

To begin the presentation of algorithms implemented in Pascal let us try to put down the two algorithms mentioned above: Euclid's algorithm and the textbook algorithm for solving a quadratic equation.

EXAMPLE 1.1

On input we have the representations of two positive integers. Denote them by n and m. We want to compute their greatest common divisor (gcd). It is, by definition, the largest positive integer which divides n and m.

n	m	r
420	825	420
825	420	405
420	405	15
405	15	0

Figure 1.1 Example of a computation of *GCD*.

Let q be the quotient and r the remainder of the division of n by m, so $n = q*m + r$, where $0 \leqslant r < m$. Now, if $r = 0$, then the greatest common divisor of n and m is m, since m divides n. If $r > 0$, then any common divisor of n and m divides r, but also any common divisor of m and r divides n. Hence n and m have the same common divisors as m and r, and in particular, both pairs have the same greatest common divisor. We can reduce the problem of computing the gcd of n and m to that of computing the gcd of m and r. Why is this new problem an easier one? Since $m > r$ we have a 'smaller problem' to solve in the sense that the second elements of pairs thus computed form a strictly decreasing sequence of positive integers. No such sequence may be infinite. Thus after a finite number of steps we must get $r = 0$ and the required greatest common divisor equals m.

A program in Pascal implementing the algorithm described above may have the following form:

```
program GCD;
  var r, n, m: integer;
begin
  read(n); read(m);
  r := n mod m;
  while r <> 0 do
  begin
    n := m; m := r; r := n mod m
  end;
  write(m)
end.
```

Since variables r, n and m are declared as integer variables the *GCD* program is to be interpreted in the set of integers. Moreover we assume that the initial values of n and m are strictly positive.

An example of a computation of the above algorithm for the initial values $n = 420$ and $m = 825$ is presented in Figure 1.1.

In Pascal algorithms may be defined by functions and procedures. The example below presents the textbook algorithm for solving a quadratic equation in a form of a procedure.

EXAMPLE 1.2

```
procedure quadraticequation(a, b, c: real; var x1, x2: real);
  var delta: real;
begin
  if a = 0 then
    writeln('not a quadratic equation')
  else
  begin
    delta := b * b − 4.0 * a * c;
    if delta < 0 then
    writeln('no real roots')
    else
    begin
      delta := sqrt(delta);
      x1 := (−b + delta)/a/2.0;
      x2 := (−b − delta)/a/2.0
    end
  end
end
```

Procedure *quadraticequation* has three input parameters a, b and c representing the coefficients of the equation:

$$ax^2 + bx + c = 0$$

and two output parameters $x1$ and $x2$ representing the computed values of its roots. An auxiliary variable *delta* is a local variable of the procedure. All these parameters, as well as variable *delta*, are interpreted in the data type of real numbers, according to their declarations.

1.2   Recursive algorithms

A powerful method for algorithm design is provided by a recursive approach. The general idea is as follows. Having been given an instance of a problem, it is then reduced to a number of instances of the same problem, each of the instances being of a 'smaller size' than the original one. If this process of problem-size reduction leads eventually to problem instances that are easily solved by some other methods, then we are able to solve the original instance of our problem.

Functions and procedures in Pascal may be called recursively (that is, they may be called in their own bodies), thus they may be used directly for implementing recursive algorithms. However, this should be done with due care, since each recursive call of the function (procedure) requires additional memory, and the programmer should be aware of that fact.

In spite of this technical problem recursive functions and procedures are extensively used in designing algorithms. The following examples illustrate the technique.

EXAMPLE 1.3 _____

Let us consider Euclid's algorithm as described in Example 1.1. According to the definition of the algorithm we can apply it recursively for m and r while the remainder r of the division of n by m is not 0. If $r = 0$ the algorithm halts with the result m. Thus the following declaration of a recursive function *Euclid* with two input parameters n and m gives the Pascal implementation of the recursive algorithm.

```
function Euclid(n, m:integer):integer;
   var r:integer;
begin
   r:= n mod m;
   if r = 0 then
      Euclid:= m
   else
      Euclid:= Euclid(m, r)
end
```

It might be said that there is no need to design a recursive algorithm when there is a non-recursive counterpart. Indeed, as was already mentioned, recursive functions and procedures usually require more time and memory than non-recursive ones. On the other hand, there are some problems which can be easily solved by a recursive algorithm and which have no simple and direct non-recursive solution. Let us look at the following example.

EXAMPLE 1.4 _____

We want to generate all permutations of the set $\{1, \ldots, n\}$. We shall use an array $P[1 .. n]$ with integer entries to represent a permutation. At the beginning, all n entries of the array $P[1 .. n]$ are free (a free entry will be denoted by 0). Let us design an algorithm which for a given argument i generates all possible permutations of the set $\{1, \ldots, i\}$ in all i free entries of array $P[1 .. n]$. (Thus for $i = n$ it will generate all permutations of $\{1, \ldots, n\}$.) This algorithm works as follows. There are i free entries in the array $P[1 .. n]$. Thus we can put the value i at each free entry and each time apply the algorithm recursively for the argument $i - 1$. The following Pascal program implements this idea:

```
program permutations;
   const n = 5;
   var P: array [1 .. n] of integer; k: integer;
   procedure perm(i: integer);      {i = the number of free entries}
      var j: integer;
   begin
      if i = 0 then
      begin
         for j := 1 to n do write(P[j], ' ' );
         writeln
      end else
      for j := 1 to n do
      if P[j] = 0 then
      begin
         P[j] := i; perm(i - 1); P[j] := 0
      end
   end;
begin
   for k := 1 to n do P[k] := 0;      {initialize P[1 .. n]}
   perm(n);
end.
```

The procedure *perm* declared in the program implements a recursive algorithm for permutation generation. If the value of parameter i equals 0, then it means that *perm* was recursively called for all consecutive values $n, \ldots, 1$, so array $P[1 .. n]$ has no free entries and represents a permutation of $\{1, \ldots, n\}$. Thus we can write it out. For the value of parameter i greater than 0, by the inductive assumption we know that the values $i + 1, \ldots, n$ are already assigned to some entries of array $P[1 .. n]$. Thus using an auxiliary variable j we search for all free entries in array $P[1 .. n]$. When such a free entry is found we assign to it the value i and we call the procedure *perm* recursively with the value of the actual parameter equal to $i - 1$. After the recursive call we must reconstruct the state of array $P[1 .. n]$. (Compare with assignment $P[j] := 0$.)

1.3   The semantic correctness of algorithms

At the same time as designing and using programs on computers we try to learn their properties. We want to know, for example, whether a program really is a solution to the problem under study, and whether the execution of the program will fit into the amount of time and computer memory that we can allot to it. In the following sections we shall briefly describe methods for the analysis of algorithms that are helpful in finding the answers to such questions. First we shall deal with the semantic correctness of algorithms. We start with some basic definitions.

The data supplied to an algorithm from the outside environment is called **input data** (or **input** for short). The values that an algorithm communicates to the outside environment are **output data** (or **output** for short). With each algorithm we associate two conditions. The first, called an **input condition**, describes restrictions imposed on input data for the algorithm. The second, called an **output condition**, describes the desired properties of output data and its relation to the input data.

Let us assume that we are given an algorithm K along with two conditions: an input condition α and an output condition β. A fundamental property of algorithms is their semantic correctness. We say that K is **semantically correct** (or simply **correct**) with respect to input condition α and output condition β if, for every input satisfying α, the computation of algorithm K terminates and the output satisfies β. An equivalent term for 'semantically correct' which is also commonly used is **totally correct**.

Notice that for each algorithm one can find conditions (for example *false* and *true*) with respect to which the algorithm is correct, and there are conditions (for example *true* and *false*) for which it is incorrect. Input and output conditions are not determined solely by the algorithm itself but also by our requirements regarding the algorithm.

EXAMPLE 1.5

Consider the following algorithm for integer division:

```
       procedure intdiv(x, y: integer; var q, r: integer);
       label 1, 2, 3;
       begin
1:        q := 0; r := x;
2:        while y <= r do
          begin
              q := q + 1;
              r := r - y
          end;
3:     end
```

As an input we take the values of x and y, and as an output the final values of q and r. Algorithm *intdiv* is correct with respect to the following pair of conditions which express its intended meaning:

(1) $x \geqslant 0 \wedge y > 0$ and $x = q * y + r \wedge 0 \leqslant r < y$;

but it is incorrect with respect to the following pairs of conditions:

(2) $x \geqslant 0 \wedge y \geqslant 0$ and $x = q*y + r \wedge 0 \leqslant r < y$; (because it may not terminate)

(3) $x \geqslant 0 \wedge y > 0$ and $x = q*y + r \wedge 0 < r < y$; (the output may not satisfy the output condition).

The incorrectness of an algorithm may be of one of the following three types:

- For some input the computation terminates but the output does not satisfy the output condition; or
- The computation is aborted without reaching the end of the algorithm (because of the execution of an undefined operation like division); or
- The computation never terminates.

Therefore, the correctness of an algorithm with respect to an input condition α and an output condition β is established by showing separately the following three properties:

(1) **Partial correctness**   For every input satisfying α, if the computation terminates (that is, it reaches the end of the algorithm) then the output satisfies β.

(2) **Definiteness property**   For every input satisfying α, each partial operation during the computation is executable (that is, the computation is not aborted).

(3) **Stop property**   For every input satisfying α the computation terminates (it is finite).

The properties of partial correctness, definiteness and stop may be proved using mathematical induction on the length of a computation. The cases of a loop and a recursive procedure are handled in a slightly different way.

EXAMPLE 1.6

Let us prove that algorithm *intdiv* (see Example 1.5) is correct with respect to the conditions

$$\alpha(x, y): x \geqslant 0 \wedge y > 0$$

and

$$\beta(x, y, q, r): x = q*y + r \wedge 0 \leqslant r < y$$

We have to show that each computation of *intdiv* starting (at label 1) with an input satisfying α terminates and the final values of x, y, q and r satisfy β. In order to do this we have to make use of what happens in the algorithm between labels 1 and 3. We look for a condition which is satisfied by the values of x, y, q and r at the intermediate label 2 every time the test $y \leqslant r$ controlling the loop takes place. Such a condition is called a **loop invariant**. We define:

$$\gamma(x, y, q, r): x = q*y + r \wedge r \geqslant 0 \wedge y > 0$$

We shall show that whenever the computation of *intdiv* starts with values of the variables satisfying α and reaches the test $y \leqslant r$, the current values of the variables satisfy γ.

The computation can reach label 2 directly from label 1. Then $q = 0$, $r = x$ and γ is satisfied since α holds. The computation can reach label 2 from label 2 itself. Then the test condition $y \leqslant r$ holds and the iterated compound statement is executed. Let us assume that before the execution of the iterated compound statement the values of the variables satisfy γ. Execution of the iterated compound statement changes the value of q to $q' = q + 1$ and that of r to $r' = r - y$. Let us verify whether γ still holds. We obtain

$$\gamma(x, y, q', r') \equiv x = q'*y + r' \wedge r' \geqslant 0 \wedge y > 0$$

$$\equiv x = (q + 1)*y + (r - y) \wedge r - y \geqslant 0 \wedge y > 0$$

Since $(q + 1)*y + (r - y) = q*y + r = x$ the first conjunct is true. So is the second, $r - y \geqslant 0$, because we have assumed the test condition $y \leqslant r$ to be satisfied. Finally, $y > 0$ holds because the value of y has not changed. Applying induction on the number of times the test condition γ is evaluated (that is, the number of passes through label 2) we infer that γ holds whenever the computation reaches label 2.

If the computation eventually terminates, the loop test has to be false, that is, $y > r$. Since γ is satisfied and $y > r$ we see that the condition β holds. We have thus established the partial correctness of *intdiv* with respect to α and β.

To prove the stop property we notice that the variable q is a loop count (it counts the number of times the loop is repeated) and that the loop invariant γ implies

$$q = \frac{x}{y} - \frac{r}{y} \leqslant \frac{x}{y}$$

Since *intdiv* does not contain any partial operations it also has the definiteness property. If partial operations were present, we would have to use information collected in a loop invariant to show that any time a partial operation is to be performed the result is defined.

The correctness of recursive algorithms is usually demonstrated by applying induction on the size of inputs (which usually corresponds to the length of a computation). There is no need for separate proofs of partial correctness, definiteness and stop properties.

EXAMPLE 1.7 _____

Consider the function *Euclid* from Example 1.3 which recursively computes the greatest common divisor of positive integers *n* and *m*. Let us put the relevant input and output conditions in the declaration of this function.

```
function Euclid(n, m : integer): integer;
  var r : integer;
begin                              {α: n > 0 ∧ m > 0}
  r := n mod m;
  if r = 0 then
    Euclid := m
  else
    Euclid := Euclid(m, r)     {β: Euclid(n, m) = gcd(n, m)}
end
```

We shall prove that the function *Euclid* is correct with respect to the stated input condition α and output condition β. To do this we shall show that for any positive integers *n* and *m* the computation of the call $Euclid(n, m)$ terminates with the final value $Euclid = \gcd(n, m)$. We apply induction on the value of *m*. Let *n* be a positive integer. Assume that for all pairs $n1$, $m1$ such that $n1 > 0$, $m1 > 0$ and $m1 < n$ the computation of the call $Euclid(n1, m1)$ terminates with the final value $Euclid = \gcd(n1, m1)$. Let *n*, *m* be a pair of positive integers such that $m = n$. Since $m > 0$, the value $r = n \bmod m$ is defined. There are two possible cases. If $r = 0$ then the computation of $Euclid(n, m)$ terminates with $Euclid = m = \gcd(n, m)$. If $r > 0$ then the computation proceeds to the recursive call $Euclid(m, r)$. By the definition of integer division we have $r < m = n$ and by the induction hypothesis we reach the conclusion that the computation of $Euclid(m, r)$ terminates with the final value equal to $\gcd(m, r)$. Hence the computation of the main call $Euclid(n, m)$ also terminates with $Euclid = \gcd(m, r)$, which is equal to $\gcd(n, m)$ by elementary arithmetic.

Examples 1.6 and 1.7 show how to prove the correctness of algorithms in a formal way. Now that we know what constitutes a correctness proof, we will proceed more informally, with the understanding that the informal justifications that are presented can be expanded into formal proofs. It can be seen that correctness proofs are usually related more to an underlying algorithmic method than to a specific program implementing the method.

1.4   Good and better algorithms

We design algorithms with the intention of using them. Thus, most important of all, they must be correct. However, if possible, we should always try to improve them. The two following examples illustrate this way of thinking about algorithm design.

EXAMPLE 1.8 _____

Consider two numbers, real x and integer $n \geqslant 1$. Our aim is to design an algorithm for the computation of x^n. The question seems to be easy, since it is sufficient to multiply x by itself $(n - 1)$ times. However, for $n = 8$, for example, this would be a wasteful: we can easily compute x^2, x^4 and x^8 by successive squaring, which requires only three multiplications. Let us generalize this observation.

Denote by $a_k a_{k-1} \ldots a_1 a_0$ the binary representation of n. In order to explain the structure of our algorithm let us assume that the value of some real variable z equals x^{2^k}, while the value of some other real variable y equals x^n. For a new natural number with the binary representation $a_{k+1} a_k a_{k-1} \ldots a_1 a_0$ we shall show how to compute new values of the variables z and y. The new value of z should be equal to $x^{2^{k+1}}$. If $a_{k+1} = 0$, the new value of y should be $x^n * x^{2^{k+1}}$ and if $a_{k+1} = 1$ then the new value of y should be x^n. Now consider a function:

```
function binarypower (x: real; n: integer): real;
    var y, z: real; m: integer;
begin
    z := x; y := 1.0; m := n;
    repeat                    {z^m y = x^n}
      if m mod 2 = 1 then
        y := y * z;
      m := m div 2; z := z * z
    until m = 0;
    binarypower := y;
end
```

We can easily show using the repeat loop invariant $z^m y = x^n$ that the function _binarypower_ implements our algorithm. An example of a

m	y	z
23	1.0	x
11	x	x^2
5	x^3	x^4
2	x^7	x^8
1	x^7	x^{16}
0	x^{23}	x^{32}

Figure 1.2   Example of a computation of *binarypower*.

computation of *binarypower* for $n = 23$ and arbitrary x is presented in Figure 1.2.

We now introduce two important functions used extensively in the analysis of algorithms: **floor** and **ceiling**. Floor for any real number x gives the greatest integer i such that $i \leqslant x$ and is denoted by $\lfloor x \rfloor$. Ceiling gives the smallest integer i such that $i \geqslant x$ and is denoted by $\lceil x \rceil$.

Using this notation we have $k = \lfloor \log n \rfloor$ (in this book log will always denote logarithm to the base 2) when the binary representation of n is $a_k a_{k-1} \ldots a_1 a_0$, $a_k \neq 0$. In the function *binarypower* the assignment statement $z := z * z$ is executed as many times as the iteration statement. Since this iteration is performed $k + 1$ times, the number of multiplications $z * z$ is $\lfloor \log n \rfloor + 1$. What about the multiplications $y * z$ in the conditional statement? They are performed as many times as there are 1s in the binary representation of n; denote that number by $s(n)$ (for instance, $s(23) = 4$, since 23 has the binary representation 10111). Thus the total number of multiplications performed in *binarypower* equals $s(n) + \lfloor \log n \rfloor + 1$. For $n = 23$ the natural algorithm for computing x^n requires 22 multiplications, while *binarypower* calculates x^n in only 9 multiplications.

EXAMPLE 1.9

For a finite sequence $a_1, \ldots, a_n$ of integers ($n \geqslant 2$) we want to find its maximal and minimal value. We could do it by comparing each element a_i, $i = 2, \ldots, n$, of our sequence with the already found maximal *Max* and minimal *min* value (initially $Max = min = a_1$). If a_i is greater than *Max*, we update *Max*, if a_i is smaller than *min*, we update *min*. This algorithm does, however, $2n - 2$ comparisons, since we compare each element a_i, $i = 2, \ldots, n$ with *Max* and *min* independently.

Is it possible to design a better algorithm? Yes, suppose that we pair up the elements of a sequence $a_1, \ldots, a_n$ as follows: $(a_1, a_2), (a_3, a_4), \ldots$ with the last pair not complete if n is odd. We first compare the elements of each pair. The greater element need not be compared with *min*, nor the smaller with *Max*. So we update *Max* and *min* comparing each with only one half of the sequence $a_1, \ldots, a_n$. The number of comparisons within pairs is only $n/2$, thus in total approximately $\frac{3}{2}n$ comparisons are performed. We leave a complete definition of this algorithm as an exercise (see Exercise 1.14).

It is worth mentioning that the above algorithm finds the maximal and minimal values in a sequence of length n in exactly $\lceil \frac{3}{2}n \rceil - 2$ comparisons, and moreover, this is the minimal number of comparisons necessary to solve this problem (see Exercise 1.15).

1.5 The complexity of algorithms

Execution of an algorithm on a computer requires a certain amount of time as well as a certain amount of memory. Before we encode our algorithm in a form acceptable to a computer and start testing and using it, we should check whether it is at all feasible to use our algorithm on a computer with the expected input data. It often turns out that for many known algorithms the execution time (and sometimes the amount of memory needed) grows too quickly as the size of the input increases.

Assume, for example, that we are given an algorithm whose input is a natural number n and whose computation consists of $n!$ steps. Assuming that a computer performs 10^5 single operations per second and that we have it at our exclusive disposal for a period of 24 hours, the algorithm can be executed for one input only of size $n \leqslant 13$. It follows that algorithms which require some operations to be performed for each permutation of n elements are practically intractable on computers. Assuming that for inputs of size n the computation of an algorithm takes 2^n steps, the overall situation hardly improves. Now the computer running without interruptions for 24 hours can cope with only one input of size $n \leqslant 33$.

The situation changes substantially when we move on to algorithms for which the number of computation steps (and hence the actual time of execution) is a polynomial function of n. For example, the largest size n of inputs for algorithms which require n^3, n^2, $n\log n$ and $20n$ computation steps equals about 2×10^3, 9×10^4, 2.5×10^6 and 4.32×10^8 respectively (under the same assumptions about the computer as before).

There is no hope of achieving significant progress by designing faster machines instead of faster algorithms. Assuming that our algorithm requires 2^n steps, the largest size n increases only by $\log k$ while the machine speed increases k times!

The above analysis shows that knowledge of estimates of the running time of an algorithm is indispensable in ensuring that the algorithm can actually be used on a computer (now and in the future). Knowledge of the running time is also advantageous when we want to select the most efficient algorithm from those at our disposal. Suppose, for example, that we are to solve a problem for an input of size $n = 10\,000$ on a computer which performs 10^5

elementary operations per second. Suppose also that we have four algorithms performing n^3, n^2, $10n \log n$ and $20n$ elementary operations per second respectively, for an input of size n. To process the input the first algorithm takes about 115 days, the second about 17 minutes, the third about 13 seconds and the fourth only about 2 seconds.

To estimate the running time of an algorithm we estimate the overall number of **unit operations** performed during the execution of an algorithm. Multiplying this number by the average execution time of a unit operation on a computer, we can obtain an approximation of the actual time of the execution of the algorithm.

The following Pascal operations can be treated as unit operations:

(1) Assigning a value to a variable of simple or pointer type.
(2) Evaluation of a component variable (an indexed variable or a record field selector) which is of simple or pointer type.
(3) Execution of an arithmetic, boolean or relational operator.
(4) Execution of an empty, input or output statement.
(5) Initialization or termination of a procedure or function call.

We shall restrict our attention to algorithms whose computation can be decomposed into the unit operations listed above.

Let us assume that we are given an algorithm K and a set D of inputs such that K has the definiteness and stop properties on the set D. By $t(d)$ we denote the number of unit operations performed by K for input d in D. The function t from D to the set of natural numbers is called the **full cost function** of K.

EXAMPLE 1.10

Consider the following algorithm which checks if a positive integer n is a prime number.

```
        function prime (n: integer): Boolean;
        label 1, 2, 3, 4;
        var p: integer; b: Boolean;
        begin              {α: n > 1}
   1:       p := 2; b := true;
   2:       while (p * p <= n) and b do
                        {b is true ≡ n mod q ≠ 0 for each 2 ≤ q < p}
                begin
   3:            if n mod p = 0 then b := false;
                p := p + 1
                end;
   4:       prime := b
                        {β: prime ≡ n mod q ≠ 0 for each 2 ≤ q < n}
        end
```

We shall analyze the number of unit operations performed by *prime*. The input is a positive integer $n > 1$. The following number of unit operations are performed in the labelled lines of the algorithm:

- Line 1 exactly 2 unit operations.
- Line 2 at most $3\lfloor\sqrt{n}\rfloor$ unit operations.
- Line 3 at most $4(\lfloor\sqrt{n}\rfloor - 1) + 1$ unit operations.
- Line 4 exactly 1 unit operation.

In total at most $7\lfloor\sqrt{n}\rfloor$ unit operations are performed. More precisely, if n is a prime number we have exactly $t(n) = 7\lfloor\sqrt{n}\rfloor - 1$, and if n is the square of a prime number then $t(n) = 7\lfloor\sqrt{n}\rfloor$. On the other hand if n is even then $t(n) = 14$. The function $t(n)$ is difficult to express by means of one formula. This is typical of the full cost functions of algorithms. Therefore we usually content ourselves with finding the order of magnitude of a full cost function.

Now we introduce the definition of the order of magnitude of a function. Let X be a set, with f and g functions from X to the set of real numbers. We say that f is **at most of the order** of g, written $f = O(g)$, if there is a positive constant such that

$$|f(x)| \leqslant c|g(x)|$$

for almost all x in X (that is, all except for a finite number). We say that f is **at least of the order** of g, written $f = \Omega(g)$, if there is a positive constant such that

$$|f(x)| \geqslant c|g(x)|$$

for almost all x in X. We say that f is **exactly of the order** of g, written $f = \Theta(g)$, if both $f = O(g)$ and $f = \Omega(g)$.

The full cost function $t(n)$ of *prime* is at most of the order of $\sqrt{n}$ that is, $t(n) = O(\sqrt{n})$, but it is not exactly of that order since for infinitely many n, $t(n) = 14$. On the other hand, the function $7\lfloor\sqrt{n}\rfloor$ is exactly of the order of $\sqrt{n}$ since

$$7\lfloor\sqrt{n}\rfloor \leqslant 7\sqrt{n}$$

and for $n \geqslant 4$

$$7\lfloor\sqrt{n}\rfloor \geqslant 7(\sqrt{n} - 1) \geqslant 7(\sqrt{n} - \tfrac{1}{2}\sqrt{n}) = 3.5\sqrt{n}$$

Note that the orders of magnitude have the following simple properties (f, g, h denote functions from X to the set of real numbers):

(1) if $f = O(g)$ and $g = O(h)$ then $f = O(h)$

(2) if $f = \Omega(g)$ and $g = \Omega(h)$ then $f = \Omega(h)$

(3) if $f = \Theta(g)$ and $g = \Theta(h)$ then $f = \Theta(h)$

(4) if $f = O(g)$ then $g = \Omega(f)$

(5) if $f = \Theta(g)$ then $g = \Theta(f)$

The dependence of the full cost function of an algorithm on all constituent elements of input data essentially complicates the estimation and comparison of the total number of unit operations performed by the algorithm. Therefore it is convenient to distinguish only that part of the input which has the greatest impact on the full cost function. For example, in the straightforward algorithm for matrix multiplication an input consists of three natural numbers n, m, k and two matrices A and B of size $n \times m$ and $m \times k$, respectively. The value of the full cost function depends only on the values of n, m and k. The distinguished part (or, more generally, some characteristic) of the input will be called its **size**. The growth of the full cost function of the algorithm will be presented as a function of the size rather than of the input itself.

More formally, with each algorithmic problem whose set of inputs is D we associate a set W of sizes of inputs and a function transforming D into W called a size **function** of inputs in D. The value of this function for an input d in D is denoted by $|d|$ and called a **size** of d. Usually the set D of inputs is a subset of the Cartesian product of some data types, $D = D_1 \times D_2 \times \ldots \times D_m$; the set W is the projection of D on to some singled-out components; and the size function is the projection map. For example, in the problem of matrix multiplication the size of $d = (n, m, k, A, B)$ is defined as $|d|_1 = (n, m, k)$ or alternatively as $|d|_2 = \max(n, m, k)$.

Our next problem is how to transform the full cost function of an algorithm into a function depending only on the sizes of inputs instead of the inputs themselves. For a given size there may be many inputs of this size with possibly different values of the full cost function. The two solutions we consider are to take the worst-case cost and the average of costs for inputs of the same size.

Using the notation introduced earlier, the **cost function** of the algorithm K means the partial function

$$T(w) = \sup\{t(d) : d \in D, |d| = w\}$$

mapping the set W of sizes to the set of natural numbers. Notice that $T(w)$ is undefined if and only if the set $\{t(d) : d \in D, |d| = w\}$ is infinite. Instead of the term 'cost function' the following terms are also used: **worst-case cost function, time complexity** and **worst-case time complexity**.

We shall make one more important observation here. Instead of counting all unit operations performed by an algorithm, it is easier to distinguish and count only some characteristic operations, called **basic operations**, with the following property: the total number of unit operations performed is exactly of the order of the number of basic operations. For example, the multiplication operation in line 2 is a basic operation for the algorithm *prime* (see Example 1.10).

The equal order of magnitude of the numbers of all unit and basic operations implies the equal order of the corresponding worst-case cost functions. More precisely, let $t'(d)$ be the number of basic operations performed by K for input d, and let $T'(w)$ be the counterpart of $T(w)$, that is

$$T'(w) = sup\{t'(d) : d \in D, |d| = w\}$$

It is straightforward to show that if for each size w of inputs the set

$$\{t(d) : d \in D, |d| = w\}$$

is finite then the asymptotic equality

$$t(d) = \Theta(t'(d))$$

implies the asymptotic equality

$$T(w) = \Theta(T'(w))$$

EXAMPLE 1.11

We shall carry out the analysis of the time complexity for an algorithm which sorts sequences of elements. Let L be a data type linearly ordered by a relation '$\leqslant$'. Let $a_1, a_2, \ldots, a_n$ be a sequence of elements of L. The **sorting problem** is to find a permutation

$$\sigma : \{1, 2, \ldots, n\} \rightarrow \{1, 2, \ldots, n\}$$

such that

$$a_{\sigma(1)} \leqslant a_{\sigma(2)} \leqslant \ldots \leqslant a_{\sigma(n)}$$

that is, the given elements are to be arranged in non-decreasing order. We assume that the input elements are stored in an array

$$a : \textbf{array } [1 \ldots n] \textbf{ of } L$$

At the completion of the algorithm the sorted sequence is to be stored in the same array a.

Let us consider the algorithm for sorting by consecutive insertions. Its construction is based on the following inductive reasoning. If $2 \leqslant i \leqslant n$ and the elements $a[1] \leqslant a[2] \leqslant \ldots \leqslant a[i-1]$ have already been sorted, then we take the next element $a[i]$ and put it in its proper place. Specifically, we compare $a[i]$ to consecutive elements $a[i-1]$, $a[i-2]$, ... If the subsequent element is greater than $a[i]$ we interchange it with $a[i]$; otherwise we end the insertion of $a[i]$. (Note that a special case appears when $a[i]$ is smaller than $a[1]$.) We define this algorithm by the following procedure *Insertionsort* with one parameter n, and for which array $a[1 .. n]$ of type L is a non-local variable.

```
      procedure Insertionsort (n:integer);
      label 1, 2;
      var i, j:integer; v:L; b: Boolean;
      begin                      {α:n ⩾ 1}
        for i:= 2 to n do        {2 ⩽ i ⩽ n + 1 ∧ a[1] ⩽ ··· ⩽ a[i − 1]}
  1:      if a[i − 1] > a[i] then
        begin
          v:= a[i];
          j:= i − 1;
          b:= false;
          repeat               {a[1] ⩽ ... ⩽ a[j] ⩽ a[j + 2] ⩽ ··· ⩽ a[i]}
            a[j + 1]:= a[j];
            j:= j − 1;
            if j = 0 then       {v < a[1], end inner loop}
              b:= true
            else
  2:          if a[j] <= v then   {a[j] ⩽ v < a[j + 2], end inner loop}
              b:= true;
          until b;
          a[j + 1]:= v          {a[1] ⩽ ... ⩽ a[j] ⩽ a[j + 1] ⩽ ··· ⩽ a[i]}
        end
      end                        {β: a[1] ⩽ a[2] ⩽ ... ⩽ a[n]}
```

Note that the input condition α and output condition β are given as comments. In addition, some important invariants are also enclosed in comments.

An input for the sorting problem is a pair (n, a) where $n \geqslant 1$ and a is an array, a: **array** $[1 .. n]$ **of** L, of elements of type L. The value n is regarded as the size of the input, $|(a, n)| = n$. Let $t(n, a)$ and $T(n)$ denote the full cost function and the cost function for *Insertionsort* respectively. By definition,

$$T(n) = sup\{t(n, a):a \text{ is an array as above}\}$$

We shall show that $T(n) = \Theta(n^2)$. Observe that the total number of unit operations performed by *Insertionsort* is exactly of the order of the number of comparisons between elements of a (in the lines labelled 1 and 2). Therefore comparisons are basic operations for *Insertionsort*. The comparison in line 1 is repeated exactly $n - 1$ times. For fixed i the loop controlling comparison $a[j] \leqslant v$ is performed at most $i - 1$ times (for j ranging from $i - 2$ to 1). Hence the total number of comparisons performed for an input d of size n is at most

$$(n - 1) + \sum_{i=2}^{n} (i - 2) = \frac{n(n - 1)}{2} = 0.5n^2 - 0.5n - 1$$

Notice that if the entries of the array a are initially arranged in decreasing order (for example, $a[i] = n - i + 1$ for $1 \leqslant i \leqslant n$ where type L is integer) then *Insertionsort* performs exactly that number of comparisons. We conclude that

$$T(n) = \Theta(n^2)$$

Besides the time complexity we shall also consider the so-called **space complexity** of algorithms. We shall adopt the notation introduced earlier to define time complexity. In addition, let $s(d)$ be the maximum number of memory cells occupied by all data during the execution of an algorithm K. We assume that each constant or variable of simple or pointer type (component variables included) occupies exactly one memory cell. The function s from the set D of inputs into the set of natural numbers is called the **full space complexity function** of K. The **space complexity** is the partial function

$$S(w) = sup\{s(d) : d \in D, |d| = w\}$$

from the set W of sizes of inputs to the set of natural numbers. For example, the algorithm *prime* uses three variables p, n and B, therefore its space complexity is $\Theta(1)$.

1.6   The average-case complexity of algorithms

The worst-case time complexity is obtained from the full cost function of an algorithm by taking the supremum over the values of the full cost function for all inputs of the same size. Another obvious alternative is to take the average value. If our algorithm is to be used many times and we know the probability distribution with which different inputs of the same size occur, then this 'average' approach may provide a more realistic characterization of the performance of our algorithm than the 'worst-case' approach.

Assume as before that we are given an algorithm K with a set D of inputs such that K has the definiteness and stop properties on D. Let W be a set of sizes of inputs and let $|\cdot|$ be a size function of inputs in D. Let t and s be the full cost function and the full space complexity function for K, respectively. In addition we shall assume that for each size w in W the following two conditions hold:

(1) the set $\{d \in D: |d| = w\}$ is finite;
(2) a probability function is defined on the set of inputs of size w and is denoted by Pr_w.

By definition

$$\sum_{|d| = w} Pr_w(d) = 1$$

For example, let

$$D = \{(n, a): n \geqslant 1 \text{ and } a \text{ is a permutation of } 1, 2, \ldots, n\}$$
$$|(n, a)| = n$$

$$Pr_n(d) = \frac{1}{n!} \quad \text{(which means that each permutation is equally likely to occur)}$$

By the **average time complexity** we mean the following function

$$T_{ave}(w) = \sum_{|d| = w} Pr_w(d) t(d)$$

from the set W of sizes of inputs into the set of real numbers. Similarly, by the **average space complexity** we mean the function

$$S_{ave}(w) = \sum_{|d| = w} Pr_w(d) s(d)$$

from W to the set of real numbers. For algorithms considered in this book the full space complexity function depends only on the size of inputs and therefore the situation is trivial: the average space complexity is equal to the space complexity.

Before we consider an example of the analysis of the average time complexity of an algorithm, we shall give several general definitions and facts. As for the time complexity the same technique of counting only basic operations can be applied to the analysis of the average time complexity.

For each size w in W the restriction of the full cost function t to inputs of size w is a random variable; it is denoted by t_w. The random variable t_w assumes natural numbers as values. The probability distribution of t_w is denoted by p_{wk}, that is, the probability that for an input d of size w, $t_w(d)$ is equal to k. Notice that

$$T_{ave}(w) = \sum_{|d| = w} Pr_w(d)t(d)$$

$$= \sum_{k \geqslant 0} k \left(\sum_{|d| = w, t(d) = k} Pr_w(d) \right)$$

$$= \sum_{k \geqslant 0} kp_{wk} \tag{1.1}$$

for each size w in W, that is, the average time complexity of K for input size w is equal to the mean value $E(w)$ of the random variable t_w. Apart from the function $E(w)$ the statistical properties of the running time of K are also characterized by two other functions: *variance* $V(w)$ and *standard deviation* $D(w)$ of t_w with w ranging over W. These quantities determine how much the random variables t_w are concentrated around their mean values. The smaller the standard deviation the better concentration of t_w around its mean value.

Recall that by definition the variance of t_w is

$$V(w) = \sum_{k \geqslant 0} (k - T_{ave}(w))^2 \, p_{wk}$$

and the standard deviation of t_w is

$$D(w) = \sqrt{V(w)}$$

To find the statistical quantities $E(w)$, $V(w)$ and $D(w)$ we shall use the method of generating functions. By the **generating function** for random variables t_w we mean the function

$$P_w(z) = \sum_{k \geqslant 0} p_{wk} z^k$$

with arguments and values being real numbers. From the assumption that the set of inputs of size w is finite, it follows that the series above is finite, that is, from some k onwards, all p_{wk} are 0. Thus, the definition of $P_w(z)$ is sound. By the definition of probability it follows that for each size w in W

$$P_w(1) = 1 \tag{1.2}$$

Let us take the first derivative of the generating function P_w at $z = 1$. We obtain

$$P'_w(1) = \left(\sum_{k \geqslant 1} kp_{wk} z^{k-1} \right)(1) = \sum_{k \geqslant 0} kp_{wk}$$

that is, for each size w in W we have

$$E(w) = P'_w(1) \tag{1.3}$$

Next, consider the second derivative of $P_w(z)$ at $z = 1$. We obtain

$$P''_w(1) = \left(\sum_{k \geq 2} k(k-1)p_{wk} z^{k-2} \right)(1) = \sum_{k \geq 1} k(k-1)p_{wk} \tag{1.4}$$

Applying (1.2), (1.3) and (1.4) we obtain the following formula for the variance of the random variable t_w:

$$
\begin{aligned}
V(w) &= \sum_{k \geq 0} (k - P'_w(1))^2 p_{wk} \\
&= \sum_{k \geq 0} k^2 p_{wk} - 2P'_w(1) \sum_{k \geq 0} kp_{wk} + P'_w(1)^2 \sum_{k \geq 0} p_{wk} \\
&= \sum_{k \geq 1} k(k-1)p_{wk} + \sum_{k \geq 0} kp_{wk} - 2P'_w(1)^2 + P'_w(1)^2 \\
&= P''_w(1) + P'_w(1) - P'_w(1)^2
\end{aligned}
\tag{1.5}
$$

Formulas (1.3) and (1.5) make it possible to compute the mean value and the variance of the random variable t_w without knowing explicit formulas for the probability distribution p_{wk}. Now we shall illustrate the method of generating functions by a simple example.

EXAMPLE 1.12

We shall carry out the probabilistic analysis of the linear search in an unordered array a: **array**$[1 \, . . \, n]$ **of** *integer*:

```
function Linsearch (x: integer): Boolean;
    var i: integer; b: Boolean;
begin
    b := true; i := 1; Linsearch := false;
    while (i <= n) and b do
    begin
        if a[i] = x then
        begin
            b := false; Linsearch := true
        end else
            i := i + 1
    end;
end
```

under the following two assumptions:

(1) The set of inputs consists of triples $d = (n, a, x)$ where n is a positive integer, a is a permutation of $1, 2, \ldots, n$ and x is an integer from 1 through n, and the size of $d = (n, a, x)$ is n.

(2) For every n all occurrences of inputs of size n are equally likely.

As a basic operation we take the number of comparisons '$a[i] = x$' made by *Linsearch*. Let t_n be the random variable equal to the number of basic operations performed by *Linsearch* for an input of size n. Our aim is to find the quantities $E(n)$, $D(n)$ and $V(n)$.

From assumptions (1) and (2) it follows that

$$Pr_n(d) = \frac{1}{n!} \quad \text{and} \quad p_{nk} = \frac{1}{n}$$

for each input d of size n and each k from 1 through n. Let

$$P_n(z) = \sum_{k \geqslant 0} p_{nk} z^k = \frac{1}{n} \sum_{k=1}^{n} z^k$$

be the generating function for t_n, $n \geqslant 1$. By differentiating we get

$$P_n'(z) = \frac{1}{n} \sum_{k=1}^{n} k z^{k-1} \quad \text{and} \quad P_n''(z) = \frac{1}{n} \sum_{k=1}^{n} k(k-1) z^{k-2}$$

Hence

$$P_n'(1) = \frac{1}{n} \sum_{k=1}^{n} k = \frac{1}{n} \frac{n(n+1)}{2} = \frac{n+1}{2}$$

and

$$P_n''(1) = \frac{1}{n} \sum_{k=1}^{n} k(k-1) = \frac{1}{n} \left(\sum_{k=1}^{n} k^2 - \sum_{k=1}^{n} k \right)$$

$$= \frac{1}{n} \left(\frac{n(n+1)(2n+1)}{6} - \frac{n(n+1)}{2} \right)$$

$$= \frac{n+1}{6} (2n + 1 - 3) = \frac{(n+1)(n-1)}{3}$$

Applying (1.3) and (1.5) we obtain

$$E(n) = \frac{n+1}{2}$$

and

$$V(n) = \frac{(n+1)(n-1)}{3} + \frac{n+1}{2} - \frac{(n+1)^2}{4}$$

$$= \frac{n+1}{12}(4n - 4 + 6 - 3n - 3) = \frac{(n+1)(n-1)}{12}$$

Finally,

$$D(n) = \sqrt{\frac{(n+1)(n-1)}{12}} \cong 0.29n$$

1.7 Abstract data types

We shall assume that the reader is familiar with Pascal data types such as arrays and records. The purpose of this section is to present a way of defining more abstract data types in terms of those elementary ones provided by the language.

EXAMPLE 1.13

We want to build up a store of elements called a **queue**. At the beginning the queue is empty. We can freely add new elements to a queue and we can delete elements from a queue, but every deletion removes the 'oldest' remaining element. Such a store is also called **FIFO**, because it works according to the rule First-In First-Out.

We can implement a queue in an array with two indices *head* and *tail* pointing to the front and back of queue respectively, and one variable *counter* whose value is the current queue length, as in Figure 1.3. The indices *head* and *tail* go through this array in a cyclic manner.

The following declarations implement this idea in the case of a queue with positive integer elements. Type *queue* is a record type which defines the structure shown in Figure 1.3. This structure consists of an integer array *contents* of length N and of three integer values *head*, *tail* and *counter*. The procedure *initialize* is used for preparing the initial state of this structure. The procedure *into* adds a new element i to a queue Q. The

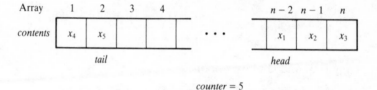

Figure 1.3 Queue implemented in an array.

procedure *out* deletes the oldest remaining element from a non-empty queue *Q*. Finally, the function *first* returns the value of the oldest remaining element.

```
type
  queue = record
                contents: array [1 .. n] of integer;
                    {where N is a constant defined in a program}
                    head, tail, counter: integer
              end

procedure initialize (var Q: queue);
begin
    Q. head := 1;          {for head = 1, tail = n}
    Q. tail := n;          {contents[head .. tail] represents}
    Q. counter := 0;       {the empty queue}
end

procedure into(i: integer; var Q: queue);
begin
    if Q. counter = n then           {no more space in contents}
       writeln('queue overflow')      {terminate computation}
    else
    begin
        Q. counter := Q. counter + 1;      {advance counter}
        if Q. tail = n then                 {advance tail cyclically}
           Q. tail := 1
        else
           Q. tail := Q. tail + 1;
        Q. contents[Q. tail] := i           {add i}
    end
end

procedure out(var Q: queue);
begin
    if Q. counter = 0 then
       writeln('queue empty')
    else
    begin
        Q. counter := Q. counter − 1;      {decrease counter}
        if Q. head = n then                 {advance head cyclically}
           Q. head := 1
        else
           Q. head := Q. head + 1
    end
end
```

```
function first(Q : queue) : integer;
begin
  if Q. counter = 0 then
    writeln('queue empty')
  else
    first := Q. contents[Q. head]
end
```

This example presents an implementation of a queue using a data structure in which the number of elements is determined solely by its declaration (the number of queue elements is bounded by the constant n). Thus when the number of stored elements exceeds n, the computation of this algorithm must be terminated (compare this with the procedure *into*). This may not always be very practical. What we need in this case is the possibility of dynamically allocated memory for data structures. To meet this need Pascal introduces a construct called **pointer type**. We shall illustrate this tool in the next example.

EXAMPLE 1.14

Let us consider a store with three available operations: *push*, *pop* and *top*. Operation *push* inserts a new element into the store, *pop* removes the most recently inserted element and *top* returns the value of the most recently inserted element. Such a store is called a **stack** or **LIFO**, because it works according to the principle Last-In First-Out. We arrange this store in the form of a **list**, that is, a sequence of values linked by pointers (see Figure 1.4).

To *push* a new element into the store one adds it to the front of the list pointed to by *head*. To perform *pop* one can simply move the value of *head* to the next list element. The function *top* returns the value pointed to by *head*. The declarations given below implement these ideas in the case of a stack with integer elements.

```
type
  listelem = ^ element;
  element = record
              a:     integer;
              next:  listelem
            end
```

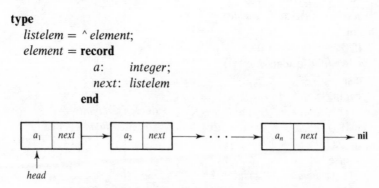

Figure 1.4 One-way list structure.

```
procedure push(i: integer; var head: listelem);
var p: listelem;
begin
  new(p);                    {generate a new element}
  p^.a := i;
  p^.next := head;           {append i}
  head := p
end

procedure pop(var head: listelem);
var p: listelem;
begin
  if head = nil then
    writeln ('stack empty')
  else
  begin
    p := head;
    head := head^.next;
    dispose(p)               {deallocate p}
  end
end

function top(head: listelem): integer;
begin
  if head = nil then
    writeln('stack empty')
  else
    top := head^.a
end
```

The statement *dispose*(*p*) used in the function *pop* releases the variable pointed to by *p*. In this way such a location may be immediately reused by another variable (when for instance *new*(*p*) is called).

1.8 Trees

In Example 1.14 for stack implementation we used a list structure. Another structure often encountered is a tree, for which we shall now give an algorithmic definition. Let *L* denote any type and let us consider new types to be defined as follows:

```
type refnode = ^node;
     node = record
                 a:   L;
                 up:  refnode
             end
```

Consider now a collection of variables of type *node* with one distinguished variable pointed to by a variable *root* of type *refnode* such that for a variable *p* of type *refnode* pointing to any element of this collection the statement

while $p <> root$ **do** $p := p^\wedge . up;$

always has a finite computation. Such a collection is called a **tree**. An example of a tree is given in Figure 1.5.

The node pointed to by the variable *root* is called a **tree root**. For any node of a tree except the tree root, the pointer *up* points to another node called its **father**. Thus the tree root is the only node which has no father. Similarly, a node is called a **son** of another node, if its pointer *up* points to it. A node which has no sons is called a **leaf**. The length of a path from a node to the tree root is called the **depth** of the node, for instance, the depth of the tree root is always 0. The **height** of a tree is the maximal depth of its nodes. A **subtree** is a subcollection of nodes that form a tree with one node being its root.

The tree, as defined above, is a simple structure that can be used for storing elements of type *L* in a way different from that of a list structure, although a list is a special kind of a tree. It is evident that with the use of the pointer *up* we can climb up a tree towards its root, just as we were able to go over a list using the pointer *next*. However, this time we are not able to pass through the whole tree since there is no way to go down. One structure that makes it possible to do this is a **binary tree**. This is a tree whose *node* structure is

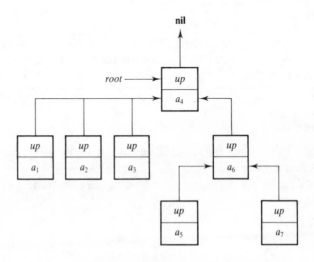

Figure 1.5   An example of a tree.

extended as follows:

```
type refnode = ^node;
     node = record
               a: L;
               up, left, right: refnode
            end
```

A binary tree satisfies the same condition as a tree. Additionally, for any p and q pointing to a tree node the following conditions hold:

(1) if $q^\wedge . left <> $ **nil**, then $q^\wedge . left^\wedge . up = q$

(2) if $q^\wedge . right <> $ **nil**, then $q^\wedge . right^\wedge . up = q$

(3) if $q^\wedge . left <> $ **nil** and $q^\wedge . right <> $ **nil**, then $q^\wedge . left <> q^\wedge . right$.

(4) if $q^\wedge . up = p$ and $p <> $ **nil**, then $p^\wedge . left = q$ or $p^\wedge . right = q$

Conditions (1) and (2) say that the pointers *left* and *right* point to sons, (3) says that these sons (if they exist) are different, and finally (4) says that there are no sons other than those pointed to by *left* and *right*. An example of a binary tree is presented in Figure 1.6.

One important case of a binary tree is when the selector a takes values from a linearly ordered type L. Suppose that for any node p belonging to such a

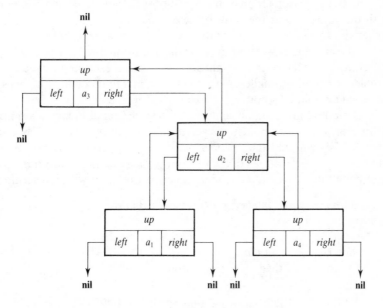

Figure 1.6   An example of a binary tree.

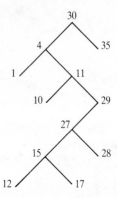

Figure 1.7   Example of a binary search tree.

tree, the following conditions hold:

(1) if q belongs to the left subtree of p, then $q^\wedge.a < p^\wedge.a$

(2) if q belongs to the right subtree of p, then $q^\wedge.a > p^\wedge.a$

This type of tree is called a **binary search tree**. An example of a binary search tree is given in Figure 1.7.

EXAMPLE 1.15

Binary search trees have many important properties. First of all it is an easy matter to search for an element x of type L. Indeed, we first compare x with the value of a at the root. If these values are equal, then x is found. Otherwise there are two possibilities: x is either smaller or greater than the value of a at the root. Accordingly, by the definition of a binary search tree, x is either in the left or in the right subtree. Thus at each step we reduce the problem to another smaller one, and clearly, in a finite number of steps we either check that x is not in the tree or find it in a certain node.

This method gives an efficient way of searching in a binary search tree. Moreover, it is also an easy matter to add new elements to such a tree, because they will find their proper places at new leaves of the tree. Let us put down the declarations of the function *member* and the procedure *insert* specifying these ideas in the case of binary search trees with integer nodes.

```
function member(i: integer; root: refnode): Boolean;
begin
    member := false;           {assume i is not in the tree}
    while root <> nil do
    if root^.a = i then        {i is found}
    begin
        member := true;        {change the assumption}
        root := nil            {terminate loop}
    end
```

```
    else                           {continue search in a subtree}
      if root^.a > i then
        root := root^.left
      else
        root := root^·right
end


procedure insert(i: integer; var root: refnode);
    var p:refnode;
    {addnode is an auxiliary function declared inside insert}
    function addnode(i: integer): refnode;
        var q:refnode;
    begin
      new(q);                  {generate a new node}
      q^.a := i;               {put i at this node}
      q^.left := nil;          {without sons}
      q^.right := nil;
      addnode := q
    end;


    begin
      if root = nil then               {tree is empty}
        root := addnode (i)            {place i in the root}
      else
      begin
      p := root;
      while p^.a <> i do               {terminate when i is in p}
      begin
        if p^.a > i then
        begin
          if p^.left = nil then        {add i as a new left leaf}
            p^.left := addnode (i);
          p := p^.left
        end
        else
        begin
          if p^.right = nil then       {add i as a new right leaf}
            p^.right := addnode (i)
          p := p^.right
        end
      end
    end
end
```

1.9 Linear selection

In this section we shall show an example of an algorithm whose complete implementation is rather difficult but instructive. Our target is the interesting algorithm which solves the selection problem in linear time (Blum *et al.*, 1972). It is based on the divide-and-conquer technique which consists in designing an algorithm by dividing a problem into a number of smaller instances of the same problem, and then, in solving these instances by the same algorithm.

To begin with let us first define the selection problem. It consists in finding the kth greatest element in a sequence represented by an array $a[1 .. n]$ with elements belonging to a linearly ordered type L. Thus as input we have a pair $(a[1 .. n], k)$, where $1 \leqslant k \leqslant n$. For any x in the sequence $a[1 .. n]$ denote by $a_>(x)$ the set $\{i \in 1 .. n: a[i] > x\}$ and by $a_\geqslant(x)$ the set $\{i \in 1 .. n: a[i] \geqslant x\}$. The algorithm must find x such that the number of indices in $a_>(x)$ is smaller than k, and the number of indices in $a_\geqslant(x)$ is no smaller than k. Indeed, such an x is the kth greatest element in $a[1 .. n]$ since there are at most $k - 1$ elements greater than x and at least k elements greater than or equal to x.

A simple way to tackle the problem is based on the divide-and-conquer technique. Let us choose $v = a[1]$ and rearrange $a[1 .. n]$ so that $a[1 .. i]$, $a[i + 1 .. j]$ and $a[j + 1 .. n]$ consist of elements equal to v, greater than v and smaller than v respectively. Now, if $j - i$ (the number of indices in $a_>(v)$) is greater than or equal to k, then the kth greatest element in $a[1 .. n]$ is the kth greatest element in $a[i + 1 .. j]$ and the problem reduces to the subproblem $(a[i + 1 .. j], k)$. If j (the number of indices in $a_\geqslant(v)$) is smaller than k, then the kth greatest element in $a[1 .. n]$ is the $(k - j)$th greatest element in $a[j + 1 .. n]$ and the problem reduces to the subproblem $(a[j + 1 .. n], (k - j))$. Otherwise v is the required element.

Let us start the precise definition of this algorithm from a procedure *Rearrange* used for rearranging the given array. Inside *Rearrange*, array $a[1 .. n]$ with elements of type L is a non-local variable. Input parameters l and r define the part $a[l .. r]$ of array $a[1 .. n]$ under consideration. Upon the exit from the procedure *Rearrange*, the output parameters i and j satisfy the relevant output condition: that is, that $l \leqslant i \leqslant j \leqslant r$, $a[l], \ldots, a[i] = v$, $a[i + 1], \ldots, a[j] > v$ and $a[j + 1], \ldots, a[r] < v$.

```
procedure Rearrange(l, r: integer; var i, j: integer);
   {rearrange a[l .. r] with respect to a[l]}
      var v: L;
            p: integer;
   begin
      v := a[l]; p := l + 1;
      i := l; j := r;
      while j >= p do          {a[l .. i] = v, a[i + 1 .. p − 1] > v,
                                a[j + 1 .. r] < v}
```

```
if a[p] = v then          {swap a[p] with a[i + 1], advance i, p}
begin
    i := i + 1;
    swap(a[p], a[i]);
    p := p + 1
end
else
if a[p] > v then          {advance p}
    p := p + 1
else                      {a[p] < v}
begin                     {swap a[p] with a[j], decrease j}
    swap(a[j], a[p]);
    j := j − 1
end
end                       {a[l .. i] = v, a[i + 1 .. j] > v,
                           a[j + 1 .. r] < v}
```

The procedure *swap* declared below is used for exchanging two different entries of the array $a[1 .. n]$:

```
procedure swap(var x, y: L);
    var z: L;
begin
    z := x; x := y; y := z
end
```

The way in which the procedure *Rearrange* works follows from a natural invariant of its main loop, that is, $a[l], \ldots, a[i] = v$, $a[i + 1], \ldots, a[p − 1] > v$ and $a[j + 1], \ldots, a[r] < v$.

Now we can define the main algorithm. It will be given in the form of a function *Select* for which array $a[1 .. n]$ is a non-local variable. The returned value is an index in the array $a[1 .. n]$ of the kth greatest element of the original array $a[1 .. n]$ (note that $a[1 .. n]$ is permuted during this process). Although the informal definition of the algorithm was recursive, the function *Select* is not recursive. In its main loop we use two indices l and r to define the part $a[l, .. r]$ of the array $a[1 .. n]$ under consideration. Thus to reduce a problem to one of its subproblems, it is sufficient to update these two indices and the value of k.

```
function Select(n, k: integer): integer;
    {solve the problem (a[1 .. n], k)}
    var l, r, i, j: integer;
begin
    l := 1; r := n;              {(a[1 .. n], k) is the given problem}
    while r > l do               {solve the problem (a[l .. r], k)}
```

```
begin
    Rearrange(l, r, i, j);        {a[l .. i] = v, a[i + 1 .. j] > v,
                                   a[j + 1 .. r] < v}
    if j − i >= k then            {reduce to (a[i + 1 .. j], k)}
    begin
        l := i + 1; r := j
    end else
    if k > j + 1 − l then         {reduce to (a[j + 1 .. r], k − j − 1 + l)}
    begin
        k := k − j − 1 + l;
        l := j + 1
    end else
        r := l                    {terminate the algorithm}
    end;
    Select := l
end
```

It can be easily shown that the worst-case time complexity of this algorithm is $\Theta(n^2)$ (see Exercise 1.25), and that its average time complexity is $\Theta(n)$ (see Exercise 2.3). Such a disparity is, of course, not very encouraging. However, there is a technique which may speed up the selection process substantially. The idea is based on the good selection of the element v with respect to which $a[l .. r]$ is rearranged.

Consider an array $a[1 .. n]$ and try to find v such that at least $n/4$ elements will be eliminated in the reduction phase, that is, the new subproblem will have no more than $3n/4$ elements. How to do this? Imagine the elements of $a[1 .. n]$ arranged in a rectangular matrix with columns already sorted (see Figure 1.8). Choose v to be the median of the central row in this matrix. Then at least one-quarter of the entries of this matrix will be no greater than v, and at least one-quarter will be no smaller than v. Moreover, note that the search for v is also a selection problem. So we may apply recursively the same algorithm for the central row of our matrix with k one-half of its length.

Denote the worst-case time complexity of the above algorithm by $T(n)$. This is the sum of $T_1(n)$, $T_2(n)$, $T_3(n)$ and $T_4(n)$, where $T_1(n)$ is the cost of sorting the columns of the matrix, $T_2(n)$ the cost of searching for v, $T_3(n)$ the

Figure 1.8 Matrix for selecting a median element v.

cost of rearranging the array with respect to that for v and $T_4(n)$ is the cost of eliminating the elements no smaller than v or no greater than v. Thus

$$T(n) = T_1(n) + T_2(n) + T_3(n) + T_4(n) \qquad (1.6)$$

We have already shown that $T_4(n)$ may be estimated by $T(3n/4)$. If the matrix constructed has a fixed column length, that is, it is independent of n, then the cost of column sorting will be linear in n. The cost $T_3(n)$ is also linear in n. Thus we can assume that $T_1(n) \leqslant dn$ and $T_3(n) \leqslant en$ for some constants $d > 0$ and $e > 0$. Finally, $T_2(n)$ is estimated by $T(n/x)$, where x is the column length, since we search for the median element in a row of length n/x. Thus from (1.6) we obtain

$$T(n) \leqslant (d + e)n + T\left(\frac{n}{x}\right) + T\left(\frac{3}{4}n\right) \qquad (1.7)$$

The smallest x for which $T(n)$ may be estimated by a linear function is $x = 5$. This follows from (1.7) and from the fact that $n/5 + 3n/4 < n$, and $n/x + 3n/4 \geqslant n$ for $x \leqslant 4$. Later on we shall show precisely that $T(n)$ is $O(n)$, if $x = 5$. Now we shall define the algorithm described above in the form of a function *Linearselect*.

Linearselect will be based upon *Select*, but will include a declaration of a recursive function *Rs*. The latter arranges the columns of a matrix as consecutive segments of an array $a[1 .. n]$ of length 5, that is, $a[1 .. 5]$, $a[6 .. 10], \ldots$ Since *Rs* will be called recursively to find the median in the central row of the constructed matrix, the next subproblem will have as input the sequence $a[3], a[8], \ldots$ Thus, in general, *Rs* solves the problem of searching for the kth greatest element in the sequence $a[l], a[l + s], \ldots,$ $a[l + (i - 1) * s]$, where s is a power of 5, i is the greatest value such that $l + (i - 1) * s \leqslant r$ and $1 \leqslant k \leqslant i$. Let us denote a sequence $a[l], a[l + s], \ldots,$ $a[r]$ by $a[l .. r:s]$ and a generalized problem by the pair $(a[l .. r:s], k)$.

First, as before, we should put down a declaration of the modified procedure *Rearrange* with one additional input parameter s specifying the step of the considered sequence $a[l], a[l + s], \ldots, a[r]$. However, since this modification is trivial we can go directly to the declaration of function *Linearselect*.

```
function Linearselect (n, k: integer): integer;
    {solve the problem (a[1 .. n: 1], k)}
    procedure Sortcolumns (l, r, s: integer);
    {sort the columns of a[l .. r:s] by Insertionsort}
        var i, j, t, p, q: integer;
            b: Boolean; x: L;
    begin
        t := 5 * s;                    {t is the column span}
        i := l - t; j := l - s;
```

```
repeat
    i := i + t; j := j + t;        {a[i..j:s] is the next column}
    if j > r then j := r;          {adjust j for the last column}
    p := i + s;                    {start from inserting a[i + s]}
    while p <= j do
    begin
        x := a[p];                 {x = a[p] inserted element}
        q := p;                    {a[q] is expected position for x}
        b := false;                {b defines the until condition}
        repeat
            if q = i then          {the end of column, exit}
                b := true
            else
            if a[q − s] <= x       {a[q] is the position of x, exit}
            then
                b := true
            else                   {move a[q − s] to the right}
            begin
                a[q] := a[q − s];
                q := q − s         {update q}
            end;
        until b;
        a[q] := x;                 {insert x at a[q]}
        p := p + s                 {a[p] the next element}
    end                            {a[i] ⩽ a[i + s] ⩽ ··· ⩽ a[j]}
    until (j >= r);
end;


function Rs(p, q, s, k : integer) : integer;
{solve the problem (a[p .. q:s], k)}
    var l, r, i, j, t : integer;
begin
    l := p; r := q; t := 5 * s;    {initialize l, r, t}
    while r > l do                 {consider a[l .. r:s]}
    begin
        Sortcolumns (l, r, s);     {sort the columns}
        i := (r − l + s) div t;    {i is the number of columns}
        if i > 1 then              {call function Rs recursively}
        begin
            p := l + 2 * s;        {a[p] first central element}
            q := p + (i − 1) * t;  {a[q] last central element}
            i := Rs(p, q, t, i div 2)  {solve (a[p .. q:t], i/2)}
        end
```

```
      else
          i := l;                          {there is only one row}
      swap(a[i], a[l]);
      Rearrange (l, r, s, i, j);           {rearrange a[l .. r:s]}
      if (j − i) div s >= k then           {reduce to}
      begin                                {(a[i + s .. j:s], k)}
          l := i + s; r := j
      end
      else
      if k > (j + s − l) div s then        {reduce to}
      begin                                {(a[j+s .. r:s], ⌊k−(j+s−l)/s⌋)}
          k := k − (j + s − l) div s;
          l := j + s
      end
      else r := l                          {terminate the main loop}
    end;
      Rs := l                              {return a[l]}
  end;                                     {end of function Rs}
begin
  Linearselect := Rs(1, n, 1, k)
end
```

Theorem 1.1

The worst-case time complexity of *Linearselect* is $\Theta(n)$.

Proof   The cost of sorting the columns may be bounded by dn, where $d > 0$ is a constant. The recursive call has a cost of at most $T(\lfloor n/5 \rfloor)$, since the central row has length $\lfloor n/5 \rfloor$. The selected element $v = a[p]$ is the median of the central row. Thus at least $3\lfloor \lfloor n/5 \rfloor/2 \rfloor$ elements are no smaller than v and the same number of elements are no greater than v. But for $n \geqslant 90$ we have

$$3\left\lfloor \left\lfloor \frac{n}{5} \right\rfloor \Big/ 2 \right\rfloor \geqslant \frac{n}{4}$$

Thus for $n \geqslant 90$ the number of elements no smaller than v is at least $n/4$, as is the number of elements no greater than v. The cost of rearranging may be bounded by en, for a constant $e > 0$. Since the first loop eliminates in each pass either the elements no smaller than v or the elements no greater than v, the next pass will operate on a sequence of length at most $\lfloor 3n/4 \rfloor$. For $n \geqslant 90$ we obtain

$$T(n) \leqslant (d + e)n + T\left(\left\lfloor \frac{n}{5} \right\rfloor\right) + T\left(\left\lfloor \frac{3}{4}n \right\rfloor\right)$$

For $n < 90$ we can bound $T(n)$ by fn for some constant $f > 0$. Now let c be $max((d + e), f)$, then

$$T(n) \leqslant cn \qquad\qquad \text{for } n < 90 \qquad\qquad (1.8)$$

$$T(n) \leqslant cn + T\left(\left\lfloor \frac{n}{5} \right\rfloor\right) + T\left(\left\lfloor \frac{3}{4}n \right\rfloor\right) \qquad \text{for } n \geqslant 90 \qquad (1.9)$$

Now we shall show by induction that $T(n) \leqslant 20cn$. For $n < 90$ this follows immediately from (1.8). Suppose that the claim holds for all $90 \leqslant m < n$. From (1.9) we get

$$T(n) \leqslant cn + 20c\left(\frac{n}{5} + \frac{3}{4}n\right) \leqslant 20cn$$

which proves that $T(n) = \Theta(n)$ (the lower bound is trivial). ∎

1.10 Models of computation

So far the analysis of algorithms has been carried out under two assumptions:

(1) Unit Pascal operations (such as assigning a value to a variable or executing operators) are performed in a constant time regardless of the values of the arguments involved.

(2) Each value of a simple or pointer type occupies one cell of memory regardless of its actual size.

These assumptions about the way the computational complexity is measured are known as the **uniform cost model**. This is commonly used in the analysis of computational complexity: in the remainder of this book complexity will also be measured according to this model.

Now we shall briefly look at another way of measuring complexity, the so-called **logarithmic cost model**. It is based on the following two assumptions:

(1) Unit Pascal operations take time proportional to the binary length of their arguments.

(2) Each value of a simple or pointer type occupies an area of memory whose size is proportional to the binary length of the value.

Recall that the binary length of a positive integer n is $\lfloor \log n \rfloor + 1$. Observe that if the size of the input is a natural number, say n, and if the binary lengths of all values dealt with in the computation of an algorithm are bounded from above by

$$c \log n, \quad \text{for some constant } c > 0 \qquad\qquad (1.10)$$

then denoting by $T(n)$ and $T_{\log}(n)$ the cost functions of the algorithm counted on the basis of the uniform cost criterion and the logarithmic cost criterion, respectively, we obtain

$$T(n) \leqslant T_{\log}(n) \leqslant c' T(n) \log n$$

where $n > 1$ and c' is a constant greater than 1.

Sometimes the difference in the orders of magnitude of both cost functions may be greater. For the algorithm presented below the cost function measured on the basis of the uniform cost model is polynomial; on the other hand, the cost function measured on the basis of the logarithmic cost model is exponential.

EXAMPLE 1.16 ───

Consider the following algorithm PP:

```
begin {n ⩾ 0}
    i := 0; k := 2;
    while i < n do {0 ⩽ i ⩽ n ∧ k = 2^{2^i}}
    begin k := k * k; i := i + 1 end
    {k = 2^{2^n}}
end
```

where n, i and k are integer variables.

As a basic operation we shall consider multiplication. For an input n the algorithm performs n multiplications. Therefore the time complexity and the space complexity of PP measured on the basis of the uniform cost model are $O(n)$ and $O(1)$, respectively. Under the logarithmic cost model the cost of multiplying $k = 2^{2^i}$ by itself (see the enclosed invariant) is $2 \log 2^{2^i} + 2 = 2^{i+1} + 2$. Therefore the time complexity of PP measured on the basis of the logarithmic cost model is

$$\Theta\left(\sum_{i=0}^{n-1} 2^{i+1}\right) = \Theta(2^n)$$

The largest integer stored in the memory is $k = 2^{2^n}$; its binary length is $2^n + 1$. Therefore the space complexity of PP measured according to the logarithmic cost model is also $\Theta(2^n)$.

───

Following this we shall consider only algorithms which satisfy the condition (1.10) under which the difference in results given by the uniform cost criterion and the logarithmic cost criterion is inconsequential.

It should be mentioned that there is (mainly from the theoretical point of view) at least one more important criterion for measuring the cost of an algorithm, namely the number of steps (the number of memory cells) of the Turing machine implementing the algorithm (see Aho *et al.* (1974)). However, this will not be discussed further here.

Apart from the notion of the complexity of an algorithm there is one more notion which plays an important role in the analysis of algorithms, namely the **complexity of an algorithmic problem**. Assume that a cost measuring criterion is fixed. Let P be an algorithmic problem with a set D of inputs, a set W of sizes of inputs, a size function $| \, . \, |: D \to W$ of inputs in D, and f a function from the set W into the set of real numbers. P has **time complexity** $O(f)$ if there is an algorithm solving P whose time complexity is $O(f)$. P has **time complexity** $\Omega(f)$ if the time complexity of every algorithm solving P is $\Omega(f)$. Finally, P has **time complexity** $\Theta(f)$ if its time complexity is both $O(f)$ and $\Omega(f)$. In a similar way the corresponding notions for the average and space complexity are defined.

Mainstream research in the analysis of algorithms is directed towards establishing the exact orders of the complexity for known algorithmic problems. Up to now the majority of results provide upper bounds on the complexity simply by constructing an algorithm solving the problem under consideration. To prove a lower bound (that P has time complexity $\Omega(f)$ for some f) is much harder. No model of computation has been proposed so far that includes algorithms developed in programming languages that simultaneously would be useful in constructing proofs of lower bounds for algorithmic problems. To date, lower bounds have been obtained only within severely restricted models of computation.

We shall present one such class of special algorithms called **decision trees**. By a decision tree (or **comparison tree**) we mean a binary tree satisfying the following two conditions:

(1) Each node of the tree which is not a leaf is assigned a test of the form $a < b$, where a and b are two variables of a simple type.

(2) Each node of a tree which is a leaf is assigned an output statement communicating the results.

The computation starts at the root of the tree and consists of consecutive executions of tests stored in the nodes of the tree. At an internal node we would leave it for the left son if the test yielded *true*, and for the right son otherwise. The computation eventually reaches a leaf and ends with outputting the results. As a basic operation we choose comparison. Observe that the number of comparisons executed is equal to the length of the computation path from the root to a leaf, which in the worst case is equal to the height of the tree. Figure 1.9 shows an example of a decision tree which sorts three-element sequences stored in variables a, b and c.

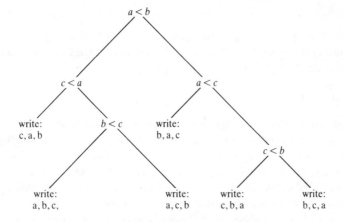

Figure 1.9   A decision tree sorting a sequence a, b, c.

Assume that we are given an algorithmic problem P with a set D of inputs, a set W of input sizes and a size function $|\,.\,|: D \to W$. Let $\{A_w\}_{w \in W}$ be a collection of decision trees such that for each size w in W the decision tree A_w solves P for all inputs of size w. We say then that the sequence $\{A_w\}_{w \in W}$ *solves* P. By the time complexity of $\{A_w\}_{w \in W}$ we mean the function that with each size w in W associates the height of the decision tree A_w. Below we shall present two simple general criteria allowing the derivation of lower bounds on time complexity in the decision tree model.

Since every binary tree with l leaves is of height at least $\log l$ we get the following theorem:

Theorem 1.2

If an algorithmic problem P, for inputs of size w, yields $l(w)$ distinct results then the time complexity of P in the decision tree model is $\Omega(\log l(w))$.

EXAMPLE 1.17 _____

Consider the sorting problem. For an input $d = (n, a)$ consisting in a positive integer n and a sequence $a = a_1, a_2, \ldots, a_n$ of elements of a linearly ordered set L, the result is a permutation $\sigma: \{1, 2, \ldots, n\} \to \{1, 2, \ldots, n\}$ such that $a_{\sigma(1)} \leqslant a_{\sigma(2)} \leqslant \ldots \leqslant a_{\sigma(n)}$. For each size n of inputs there are $n!$ possible distinct results. Applying Theorem 1.2 and Stirling's formula $\log n! = \Theta(n \log n)$ (see Knuth (1968)) we infer that the time complexity of the sorting problem in the decision tree model is $\Omega(n \log n)$.

Similarly since every binary tree with m nodes is of height at least $\lceil \log(m + 1) \rceil$ we obtain the following theorem:

Theorem 1.3

If for any sequence $\{A_w\}_{w \in W}$ of decision trees solving an algorithmic problem P the number of nodes in the tree A_w is at least $m(w)$, then the time complexity of P in the decision tree model is $\Omega(\log m(w))$.

EXAMPLE 1.18 _____

Consider the searching problem in the following form. For an input $d = (n, a, x)$ consisting of a positive integer n, a sorted sequence $a = a_1 < a_2 < \ldots < a_n$ of distinct elements of a linearly ordered set L and an element x in L, the result is 'yes' if x is among the elements in a and 'no' otherwise. We define $|(n, a, x)| = n$. Each decision tree solving this problem for inputs of size n has to contain a node with the test comparing a_i and x for each $1 \leqslant i \leqslant n$. Indeed, if such a test is missing for some i then consider two inputs differing only in x, namely in the first input $x = a_i$ and in the second $x = c$ where $c \neq a_i$ and $a_{i-1} < c < a_{i+1}$ ($c < a_1$ if $i = 1$; $c > a_n$ if $i = n$). Such assignments can always be found because L is infinite. The decision tree would give the same result for both inputs though the results are clearly different. Therefore the decision tree for size n has to have at least n nodes. Applying Theorem 1.3 we infer that the time complexity of the searching problem under study is $\Omega(\log n)$.

There are many books on the analysis of algorithms and data structures that may be used for further studies, for example, Aho *et al.* (1974), Baase (1983), Horowitz and Sahni (1978), Knuth (1968, 1973), Manber (1989) and Sedgewick (1988).

Manna (1974) provides an excellent introduction to the methods of proving program correctness as well as to some other logical aspects of the analysis of algorithms.

All the examples of algorithms and data structures presented in this introductory chapter also appear in the other textbooks. Perhaps one exception is the example of the recursive algorithm *permutations* (Section 1.2), the idea for which was suggested to us by P. Gburzyński (private communication).

SUMMARY

Key points covered in this chapter include:

- the algorithm as a program in Pascal
- recursive algorithms
- total and partial correctness
- time and space complexity
- the probabilistic analysis of algorithms

- implementation of abstract data structures
- the selection problem
- uniform and logarithmic cost criteria
- the complexity of a problem.

EXERCISES

1.1 Write a program which computes the greatest common divisor using only the operations of addition and subtraction.

1.2 Apply Euclid's algorithm to find, for given integers n and m, integer coefficients x and y such that $xn + ym = \gcd(n, m)$, where gcd denotes the greatest common divisor.

1.3 Write a recursive function for computing the nth Fibonacci number F_n defined as follows:

$$F_0 = 1, F_1 = 1, F_{n+1} = F_n + F_{n-1} \quad \text{for } n \geqslant 1$$

1.4 Write a non-recursive function which computes the nth Fibonacci number F_n.

1.5 Prove that Euclid's algorithm for $n, m \leqslant N$ performs the maximal number of divisions when $n = F_k, m = F_{k+1}$ are the greatest Fibonacci numbers not exceeding N.

1.6 Write a program that generates all permutations of the set $\{1, \ldots, n)$ in a reverse order to that produced by the program *permutations*.

1.7 Modify algorithm *permutations* so that it generates all k possible combinations of the set $\{1, \ldots, n\}$.

1.8 Using the formulas

$$F_{2n} = F_n^2 + F_{n-1}^2 \quad \text{and} \quad F_{2n+1} = F_n^2 + 2F_n F_{n-1}$$

write a non-recursive function which computes F_n in approximately $\log n$ arithmetic operations.

1.9 Let x, a, b, p, q and r be integer variables. Prove that the algorithms (a)–(e) below are correct with respect to the input condition

$$\alpha: x \geqslant 0$$

and the output condition

$$\beta\colon a^2 \leqslant x < (a + 1)^2$$

(a) **begin**
    $a := 0;$
    while $(a + 1) * (a + 1) <= x$ **do** $a := a + 1$
    end

(b) **begin**
    $a := 0;\ p := 1;\ r := 1;$
    while $p <= x$ **do**
    begin $a := a + 1;\ r := r + 2;\ p := p + r$ **end**
    end

(c) **begin**
    $a := 0;\ b := x + 1;$
    while $a + 1 <> b$ **do**
    begin
      $p := (a + b)$ **div** $2;$
      if $p * p > x$ **then** $b := p$ **else** $a := p$
    end
    end

(d) **begin**
    $q := 1;$
    while $x >= q * q$ **do** $q := 2 * q;$
    $a := 0;$
    while $q > 1$ **do**
    begin
      $q := q$ **div** $2;$
      if $(a + q) * (a + q) <= x$ **then** $a := a + q$
    end
    end

(e) **begin**
    $q := 1;$
    while $x >= q$ **do** $q := 4 * q;$
    $r := x;$
    $a := 0;$
    while $q > 1$ **do**
    begin
      $q := q$ **div** $4;$
      $a := a$ **div** $2;$
      if $2 * a + q <= r$ **then**
      begin $r := r - 2 * a - q;\ a := a + q$ **end**
    end
    end

1.10 Using the methods applied in the algorithms in Exercise 1.9(a)–(e) write the corresponding algorithms for finding the quotient and the remainder of the division of the natural numbers x and y. Prove the correctness property for those algorithms with respect to the input condition

$$\alpha: x \geqslant 0 \land y > 0$$

and the output condition

$$\beta: x = q * y + r \land 0 \leqslant r < y$$

1.11 Prove the correctness of the program *permutations*.

1.12 Prove the correctness of the function *binarypower*.

1.13 Write a program which finds the maximal element in an array $A[1..n]$ of integers. Prove that at least $n - 1$ comparisons must be performed to solve this problem.

1.14 Write a program which implements the algorithm described in Example 1.9.

1.15* Prove Pohl's theorem (Pohl, 1972), that is, that the algorithm described in Example 1.9 is optimal with respect to the number of performed comparisons.

1.16 Suppose that an array $A[1..n]$ of integers is ordered, that is, $A[1] < A[2] < \ldots < A[n]$. Write a program which in approximately $\log n$ comparisons verifies whether an integer i is an element of the array.

1.17 Estimate the time complexity for the algorithms in Exercise 1.9, defining the size of an input x first as $|x|_1 = x$, then as $|x|_2 = \lfloor \log x \rfloor + 1$ (assuming $|0|_2 = 0$).

1.18 Design a non-recursive algorithm computing the values of the function

$$\begin{cases} F(0) = 0 \\ F(n) = 2^{F(n-1)} & \text{for } n \geqslant 1 \end{cases}$$

Setting $|n| = n$, estimate the time complexity of the designed algorithm applying first the uniform cost criterion, and then the logarithmic cost criterion.

1.19 Let $T(n)$ be a non-decreasing function from the set of natural numbers into itself. Let $f(x)$ be a non-decreasing function from the set of real numbers into itself. Let d be a constant greater than 1. Prove that if

(1) $T(d^k) = \Theta(f(d^k))$ and

(2) there are real constants x_0 and $c > 0$ such that for all $x \geqslant x_0$, $|f(dx)| \leqslant c|f(x)|$, then $T(n) = \Theta(f(n))$.

Verify which functions given below satisfy condition (2):
(a) x
(b) $x \log x$ $(x > 0)$
(c) x^w (w is a positive integer)
(d) d^x

1.20 (Aho *et al.* (1974)). Let a, b and c be non-negative constants. Prove that the solution to the recurrence

$$T(n) = \begin{cases} b & \text{for } n = 1 \\ aT(n/c) + bn & \text{for } n > 1 \end{cases}$$

for n being a power of c is

$$T(n) = \begin{cases} O(n) & \text{if } a < c \\ O(n \log n) & \text{if } a = c \\ O(n^{\log_c n}) & \text{if } a > c \end{cases}$$

1.21 Prove that the generating function of the sum of two independent random variables is the product of their generating functions.

1.22 Prove that the mean value of the sum of two independent random variables is equal to the sum of their mean values.

1.23 Write a program which computes the height of a binary tree.

1.24 Write a program which deletes an element from a binary search tree.

1.25 Prove that the algorithm *Select* has the worst-case time complexity $\Theta(n^2)$.

1.26 In procedure *Rearrange*, when $a[p] < v$, we swap this element with $a[j]$, then we update j and continue the loop with the testing of $a[p]$. But $a[j]$ could be already smaller than v which means that some swaps are redundant. Write another version of procedure *Rearrange* that avoids these redundant swaps.

1.27 Write a complete version of function *Linearselect* and run it on a computer.

1.28* The length of columns ($x = 5$) in the algorithm *Linearselect* is the smallest one for which *Linearselect* has linear time complexity. Thus for $x > 5$ this cost will be linear as well, but the number of comparisons needed for sorting will increase. Find the optimal value for x, such that the coefficient in the linear cost of a selection process will be the smallest one.

1.29 Estimate the space complexity of *Linearselect* and design its non-recursive version.

Chapter 2
Probabilistic Analysis of Algorithms

In this chapter we present a methodology for the probabilistic analysis of algorithms. To aid the presentation we have selected a small set of characteristic examples of sorting and searching algorithms. The analysis we perform sometimes goes quite deep but it is not our intention to present either of these problems in an exhaustive way.

2.1 *Insertionsort*

Worst-case time complexity concerns the analysis of a function $T(n)$ whose value is the maximum number of steps performed by an algorithm for input of size n. Thus T may be treated as a function from N into N, where N denotes the set of positive integers.

Probabilistic analysis of algorithms is more complicated. It focuses on the characterization of a random variable $T(n)$ whose value is the cost of an algorithm when the input ranges over some probabilistic space of data of size n. Thus first a definition of this probabilistic space must be given, and then the characteristic values of a random variable $T(n)$ such as $E(n)$, its mean value, $V(n)$, its variance and $D(n)$, its standard deviation, may be estimated. An example of the probabilistic analysis of algorithms has already been presented in Section 1.5. This chapter is devoted to the probabilistic analysis of typical sorting and searching algorithms. Most of the results contained herein can also be found in Knuth (1973), however we shall try to present them in a more systematic way. We shall start with the study of the algorithm *Insertionsort* already defined in Section 1.5, whose probabilistic analysis may be used as a model example.

Let us begin with the definition of a probabilistic space for the sorting problem. As input data we have an array $a[1 . . n]$ with elements from a linearly ordered set. Upon exit, the elements of $a[1 . . n]$ must satisfy the condition

$$a[1] \leqslant a[2] \leqslant \cdots \leqslant a[n]$$

We shall carry out the analysis of the average time complexity for the sorting algorithm under the following two assumptions:

(1) The set of inputs consists of pairs $d = (n, a)$ where n is a positive integer, a is a permutation of $1, 2, \ldots, n$ and the size of $d = (n, a)$ is n.
(2) For every n all occurrences of inputs of size n are equally likely.

From these assumptions it follows that

$$Pr_n(d) = \frac{1}{n!}$$

for each input d of size n.

Now let us analyse the algorithm *Insertionsort*. Remember that its construction is based on the following inductive reasoning. If $2 \leqslant i \leqslant n$ and the elements $a[1] \leqslant a[2] \leqslant \cdots \leqslant a[i-1]$ have already been sorted, then we take the next element $a[i]$ and put it in its proper place. Specifically, we compare $a[i]$ to consecutive elements $a[i-1]$, $a[i \doteq 2]$, $\ldots$, $a[1]$. If the subsequent element is greater than $a[i]$ we interchange it with $a[i]$; otherwise we complete the insertion of $a[i]$.

We obtain the following procedure *Insertionsort* for which array $a[0 . . n]$ of elements of type L is a non-local variable. Element $a[0]$ is introduced to make the insertion process simpler. Namely, if we assign $a[0] = min$, where *min* is a constant whose value is the smallest element of type L that can be represented on a computer, then there is no need to distinguish the particular case when $a[i]$ is smaller than all $a[i-1]$, $a[i-2]$, $\ldots$, $a[1]$, in other words $a[0]$ works as a sentinel in the process of inserting.

```
procedure Insertionsort (n: integer);
    var i, j: integer; v: L;
begin
    for i := 2 to n do
    if a[i - 1] > a[i] then
```

```
begin
    v := a[i];  j := i − 1;
    repeat
        a[j + 1] := a[j];  j := j − 1;
    until a[j] <= v;
    a[j + 1] := v
end
end
```

Recall that comparisons are basic operations for *Insertionsort*. In the conditional statement $n − 1$ comparisons are performed regardless of the permutation $a[1 .. n]$. Therefore it is sufficient to restrict our attention to the comparisons $a[j] \leqslant v$. Denote by $E(n)$, $V(n)$ and $D(n)$ the mean value, variation and standard deviation, respectively, of the random variable $T(n)$ equal to the number of comparisons $a[j] \leqslant v$ for inputs of size n.

Let $p(n, k)$ be the probability distribution of the random variable $T(n)$, that is, $p(n, k)$ is the probability that for an input of size n exactly k comparisons are performed. Notice that

$$p(1, 0) = 1 \qquad \text{and} \qquad p(1, k) = 0 \qquad \text{for } k > 0$$

Assume now that $n > 1$. Observe that for fixed i the number of comparisons $a[j] \leqslant v$ is equal to the number of elements greater than $a[i]$ among $a[1], a[2], \ldots, a[i − 1]$.

Let us write a formula for the number of permutations a of $\{1, \ldots, n\}$ for which exactly $k \geqslant 0$ comparisons $a(j) \leqslant v$ are done. By the definition of $p(n, k)$ that number is $p(n, k)n!$. The same number can also be expressed in the following way. Each number $l = 1, 2, \ldots, n$ can be the nth entry $a[n]$ in the input permutation a. Assume for a moment that $a[n] = l$. Then for $i = n$ exactly $n − l$ comparisons $a[j] \leqslant v$ are done leaving $k − (n − l)$ comparisons for the iterations $i = 2, \ldots, n − 1$. Therefore the number of permutations for which in total k comparisons $a[j] \leqslant v$ are done and, in addition, for which $a[n] = l$ is

$$(n − 1)! \, p(n − 1, k − n + l)$$

provided that $k − n + l \geqslant 0$, otherwise there are no such permutations. Summing up we obtain

$$n! \, p(n, k) = (n − 1)! \sum_{l=\max(1, n-k)}^{n} p(n − 1, k − n + l)$$

$$= (n − 1)! \sum_{i=0}^{\min(n − 1, k)} p(n − 1, k − i)$$

Hence

$$p(n, k) = \left(\sum_{0 \leqslant i \leqslant n-1, \, i \leqslant k} p(n − 1, k − i) \right) \Big/ n \qquad (2.1)$$

Let

$$P_n(z) = \sum_{k \geq 0} p(n, k) z^k$$

be the generating function for $T(n)$, $n \geq 1$. Notice that

$$P_1(z) = 1$$

hence by (1.3) and (1.5) from Section 1.6 we obtain

$$E(1) = 0 \qquad \text{and} \qquad V(1) = 0$$

Assume now that $n > 1$. We shall show that

$$P_n(z) = \frac{1}{n} P_{n-1}(z) \sum_{0 \leq i \leq n-1} z^i \tag{2.2}$$

We transform the right-hand side of (2.2) using (2.1):

$$\frac{1}{n} P_{n-1}(z) \sum_{0 \leq i \leq n-1} z^i = \frac{1}{n} \left(\sum_{m \geq 0} p(n-1, m) z^m \right) \left(\sum_{0 \leq i \leq n-1} z^i \right)$$

$$= \frac{1}{n} \sum_{m \geq 0} \sum_{0 \leq i \leq n-1} p(n-1, m) z^{m+i}$$

$$= \frac{1}{n} \sum_{k \geq 0} \left(\sum_{0 \leq i \leq n-1, \, i \leq k} p(n-1, k-i) \right) z^k$$

$$= \sum_{k \geq 0} p(n, k) z^k = P_n(z)$$

By differentiating both sides of (2.2) we obtain

$$P_n'(z) = \frac{1}{n} P_{n-1}'(z) \sum_{0 \leq i \leq n-1} z^i + \frac{1}{n} P_{n-1}(z) \sum_{1 \leq i \leq n-1} i z^{i-1}$$

and

$$P_n''(z) = \frac{1}{n} P_{n-1}''(z) \sum_{0 \leq i \leq n-1} z^i + \frac{2}{n} P_{n-1}'(z) \sum_{1 \leq i \leq n-1} i z^{i-1}$$

$$+ \frac{1}{n} P_{n-1}(z) \sum_{2 \leq i \leq n-1} i(i-1) z^{i-2}$$

Hence

$$P_n'(1) = \frac{1}{n} P_{n-1}'(1) n + \frac{1}{n} P_{n-1}(1) \sum_{1 \leq i \leq n-1} i$$

$$= P_{n-1}'(1) + \frac{n-1}{2} \tag{2.3}$$

and

$$P_n''(1) = \frac{1}{n}P_{n-1}''(1)n + \frac{2}{n}P_{n-1}'(1) \sum_{1 \leq i \leq n-1} i + \frac{1}{n}P_{n-1}(1) \sum_{2 \leq i \leq n-1} i(i-1)$$

$$= P_{n-1}''(1) + (n-1)P_{n-1}'(1) + \frac{1}{n}\left(\frac{n(n-1)(2n-1)}{6} - \frac{n(n-1)}{2}\right)$$

$$= P_{n-1}''(1) + (n-1)P_{n-1}'(1) + \frac{2n^2 - 6n + 4}{6} \qquad \textbf{(2.4)}$$

Now it is possible to obtain recursive formulas for $E(n)$ and $V(n)$. Using (1.3) and (2.3) we obtain

$$E(n) = E(n-1) + (n-1)/2$$

for each size $n > 1$. Unfolding the recursion for $E(n-1)$, $E(n-2)$, ..., $E(2)$ and taking into account that $E(1) = 0$ we obtain

$$E(n) = (n-1)/2 + (n-2)/2 + \ldots + 1/2 + E(1) = \frac{n(n-1)}{4} \qquad \textbf{(2.5)}$$

for each size $n > 0$.

Next, substituting (2.3) and (2.4) for $P_n'(1)$ and $P_n''(1)$, respectively, in (2.5), we obtain

$$
\begin{aligned}
V(n) &= P_n''(1) + P_n'(1) - P_n'(1)^2 \\
&= P_{n-1}''(1) + (n-1)P_{n-1}'(1) + (2n^2 - 6n + 4)/6 \\
&\quad + P_{n-1}'(1) + (n-1)/2 - (P_{n-1}'(1) + (n-1)/2)^2 \\
&= (P_{n-1}''(1) + P_{n-1}'(1) - P_{n-1}'(1)^2) + (n^2 - 1)/12 \\
&= V(n-1) + (n^2 - 1)/12
\end{aligned}
$$

Unfolding the recursion for $V(n-1)$, $V(n-2)$, ..., $V(2)$ and taking into account that $V(1) = 0$ we obtain

$$
\begin{aligned}
V(n) &= \frac{n^2 - 1}{12} + \frac{(n-1)^2 - 1}{12} + \ldots + \frac{2^2 - 1}{12} + V(1) \\
&= \frac{1}{12}\left(\sum_{i=1}^{n} i^2 - n\right) \\
&= \frac{1}{12}\left(\frac{n(n+1)(2n+1)}{6} - n\right) \\
&= \frac{n(n-1)(2n+5)}{72} \qquad \textbf{(2.6)}
\end{aligned}
$$

and

$$D(n) = \sqrt{\frac{n(n-1)(2n+5)}{72}} \qquad\qquad (2.7)$$

for the random variable 'the number of comparisons $a[j] \leqslant v$ performed by *Insertionsort*'. These formulas remain the same for the random variable 'the total number of comparisons performed by *Insertionsort*' except that the mean value $E(n)$ should also include $n - 1$ comparisons which are always performed in the conditional statement:

$$E(n) = (n-1) + \frac{n(n-1)}{4} = \frac{1}{4}n^2 + \frac{3}{4}n - 1$$

Since comparisons are basic operations for *Insertionsort* we conclude that the average time complexity of *Insertionsort* is

$$E(n) = \Theta(n^2)$$

that is, it is of the same order of magnitude as the worst-case time complexity. The standard deviation is $\Theta(n^{3/2})$ which means moderate concentration of the cost around the average time complexity ($\Theta(n)$ would mean good concentration, $\Theta(n^2)$ poor concentration).

The results of testing show that *Insertionsort* is a fast algorithm in comparison to other sorting algorithms for small sizes of inputs, say $n \leqslant 20$. For larger sizes it becomes slower and slower.

2.2   Quicksort

The first theoretically interesting and practically useful algorithm for internal sorting was invented by C. A. R. Hoare in 1962. This algorithm is called *Quicksort*. Its idea is based on the divide-and-conquer technique.

For an input array $a[1 .. n]$, set $v = a[1]$ and rearrange $a[1 .. n]$ so that to the left of v there are elements smaller than or equal to v and to the right those greater than or equal to v. Thus such a rearranged array will satisfy:

$$a[1], \ldots, a[j-1] \leqslant v \leqslant a[j+1], \ldots, a[n]$$

where $v = a[j]$ for some j, $l \leqslant j \leqslant n$. This way the sorting of $a[1 .. n]$ is reduced to the sorting of $a[1 .. j-1]$ and the sorting of $a[j+1 .. n]$. If the length of an input array is smaller than 2, then there is nothing to do. Otherwise the algorithm is applied recursively to the sequences of smaller sizes.

We shall present this algorithm in the form of a recursive procedure Qs which has two formal parameters l and r, the bounds of the considered part $a[l \mathinner{\ldotp\ldotp} r]$ of $a[1 \mathinner{\ldotp\ldotp} n]$. The whole algorithm will be a procedure *Quicksort* inside which Qs will be declared and called. For technical reasons we want to have upon entrance to *Quicksort* an array a satisfying $a[n + 1] \geqslant a[i]$, that is, a with one additional element $a[n + 1]$ no smaller than all other elements. This way a rearranging phase of the algorithm will be simpler. Moreover, inside *Quicksort*, array $a[1 \mathinner{\ldotp\ldotp} n + 1]$ of type L is a non-local variable.

```
procedure Quicksort;              {n ⩾ 1 and a[n + 1] ⩾ a[i] for 1 ⩽ i ⩽ n}

  procedure Qs(l, r: integer);    {l ⩽ r and a[r + 1] ⩾ a[i] for l ⩽ i ⩽ r}
  var i, j: integer;
      x, v: L;
  begin
  v:= a[l]; i:= l; j:= r + 1;     {rearrange with respect to v}
    repeat                        {a[l], ..., a[i] ⩽ v ⩽ a[j], ..., a[r + 1]}
      repeat
        i:= i + 1
      until a[i] >= v;
      repeat
        j:= j - 1
      until v >= a[j];
      if i < j then
        swap(a[i], a[j])
    until i >= j;
    swap(a[l], a[j]);
                                  {a[l], ..., a[j - 1] ⩽ a[j]}
                                  {a[j] ⩽ a[j + 1], ..., a[r + 1]}
    if j - 1 >= l then            {sort a[l .. j - 1]}
      Qs(l, j - 1);
    if r >= j + 1 then            {sort a[j + 1 .. r]}
      Qs(j + 1, r)
  end;                            {a[l] ⩽ ... ⩽ a[r] ⩽ a[r + 1]}
begin
  Qs(l, n)
end
```

Theorem 2.1

Let $E(n)$ and $D(n)$ denote the mean value and the standard deviation of the random variable designating the cost of *Quicksort* in the permutation model. Then

(1) $E(n) = \Theta(n \log n)$

(2) $D(n) = \Theta(n)$

Proof First we claim that a random permutation given upon entrance to procedure Qs is transformed so that two recursive calls of Qs are also applied to random permutations.

Let s denote the first element of a given permutation of length n entering Qs. The rearranging phase produces a permutation of $\{1, \ldots, s - 1\}$ on the left of s and a permutation of $\{s + 1, \ldots, n\}$ on the right of s. The number of all possible results is therefore $(s - 1)!(n - s)!$, that is, the number of permutations of $\{1, \ldots, s - 1\}$ multiplied by the number of permutations of $\{s + 1, \ldots, n\}$. The number of all the possible inputs is $(n - 1)!$, since there are $(n - 1)!$ permutations of $\{1, \ldots, n\}$ with first element fixed, equal to s. To prove that two permutations obtained after the rearranging phase are random it is sufficient to prove that the $(n - 1)!$ inputs are uniformly distributed among the $(s - 1)!(n - s)!$ outputs, that is, for each of them there are exactly

$$\frac{(n - 1)!}{(s - 1)!(n - s)!} = \binom{n - 1}{s - 1}$$

different inputs.

Let $a_1, \ldots, a_n$ be a permutation obtained after the rearranging phase in Qs. We want to construct $\binom{n - 1}{s - 1}$ different permutations which, given upon entrance to Qs, are transformed into $a_1, \ldots, a_n$.

Let $b(i)$ be 0 for $i \leqslant s$ and 1 for $i > s$. Thus the sequence $b(a_1), \ldots, b(a_n)$ consists of s zeros followed by $n - s$ ones. Let $c_1, \ldots, c_n$ denote any input permutation leading to $a_1, \ldots, a_n$. The sequence $b(c_1), \ldots, b(c_n)$ consists of s zeros and $n - s$ ones, where $b(c_1) = 0$, since $c_1 = s$. When transforming $c_1, \ldots, c_n$ into $a_1, \ldots, a_n$, Qs swaps elements greater than s with those smaller than s going from both ends of a permutation. Such a transformation may be treated as a set of interchanges between 1 and 0 in the sequence $b(c_1), \ldots, b(c_n)$ (see Figure 2.1).

The number of all 0–1 sequences of length $n - 1$ with $s - 1$ zeros and $n - s$ ones is $\binom{n - 1}{s - 1}$. Since each such sequence gives different $c_1, \ldots, c_n$, this proves the claim.

We now proceed to the estimation of $E(n)$ and $D(n)$. We introduce the following notation. Let p_{nks} denote the probability that Qs does exactly k

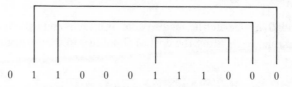

Figure 2.1 Example of the sequence of exchanges for a 0–1 array.

comparisons assuming that the first element of the given permutation is s, and let p_{nk} denote the probability that Qs does exactly k comparisons, for an arbitrary permutation. The generating function for the number of comparisons is

$$P_n(z) = \sum_{k \geq 0} p_{nk} z^k \tag{2.8}$$

For a permutation $a_1, \ldots, a_n$ with $a_1 = s$, in the main loop Qs does exactly $n + 1$ comparisons. Thus this step has a generating function z^{n+1}. The number of comparisons in the two recursive calls of Qs is determined by the generating functions $P_{s-1}(z)$ and $P_{n-s}(z)$. This follows from the fact that after the transformation made by the main loop the algorithm produces two random permutations of length $s - 1$ and $n - s$. Multiplying these three functions we get

$$z^{n+1} P_{s-1}(z) P_{n-s}(z) = \sum_{k \geq 0} p_{nks} z^k$$

Summing the above equations for $s = 1, \ldots, n$ and dividing by n we obtain the following recursive equation for $n \geq 1$:

$$\frac{1}{n} z^{n+1} \sum_{s=1}^{n} P_{s-1}(z) P_{n-s}(z) = \sum_{k \geq 0} \frac{1}{n} \sum_{s=1}^{n} p_{nks} z^k = \sum_{k \geq 0} p_{nk} z^k = P_n(z)$$

Since for $n = 0$ we can assume that the cost of *Quicksort* is 0, we obtain the following recursive formula for the generating function $P_n(z)$:

$$P_n(z) = \frac{1}{n} z^{n+1} \sum_{s=1}^{n} P_{s-1}(z) P_{n-s}(z) \quad \text{for} \quad n \geq 1 \quad \text{and} \quad P_0(z) = 1 \tag{2.9}$$

The first five elements of the sequence $P_n(z)$, $n = 0, 1, 2, \ldots$, are

$$1, z^2, z^5, \tfrac{1}{3} z^8 + \tfrac{2}{3} z^9, \tfrac{1}{2} z^{12} + \tfrac{1}{6} z^{13} + \tfrac{1}{3} z^{14}, \ldots$$

Thus, for instance, for $n = 4$ the algorithm does 12 comparisons with probability $\frac{1}{2}$, 13 comparisons with probability $\frac{1}{6}$, and 14 comparisons with probability $\frac{1}{3}$.

If we can calculate $P_n'(1)$ and $P_n''(1)$ using (2.9), then we shall also be able to calculate $E(n)$ and $D(n)$ (see Section 1.6). Denote $P_n'(1)$ by f_n and $P_n''(1)$ by g_n and introduce the respective generating functions. That is

$$f(x) = \sum_{n \geq 0} f_n x^n \quad g(x) = \sum_{n \geq 0} g_n x^n$$

Now from (2.9) we want to find explicit formulas for $f(x)$ and $g(x)$. So let us differentiate both sides of (2.9) and set $z = 1$. We obtain

$$f_n = (n + 1) + \frac{1}{n} \sum_{s=1}^{n} f_{s-1} + \frac{1}{n} \sum_{s=1}^{n} f_{n-s} = (n + 1) + \frac{2}{n} \sum_{s=1}^{n} f_{s-1}$$

and similarly, differentiating (2.9) twice and setting $z = 1$, we obtain

$$g_n = n(n + 1) + \frac{4}{n}(n + 1) \sum_{s=1}^{n} f_{s-1} + \frac{2}{n} \sum_{s=1}^{n} f_{s-1} f_{n-s} + \frac{2}{n} \sum_{s=1}^{n} g_{s-1}$$

The recursive equation for f_n is easy to solve by various methods (see Knuth (1973)), while the similar but more complicated recursive equation for g_n usually causes a great deal of trouble. We now must apply a certain analytic method for estimating f_n and then repeat for g_n, using more sophisticated techniques.

Multiplying the above two recursive equations by n we obtain

$$n f_n = n(n + 1) + 2 \sum_{s=1}^{n} f_{s-1} \tag{2.10}$$

$$n g_n = n^2(n + 1) + 4(n + 1) \sum_{s=1}^{n} f_{s-1} + 2 \sum_{s=1}^{n} f_{s-1} f_{n-s}$$
$$+ 2 \sum_{s=1}^{n} g_{s-1} \tag{2.11}$$

Both sides of (2.10) are sequences that can be expressed in terms of the generating function $f(x)$, and some other well-known expansions. First, $n(n + 1)$ has generating function $2x/(1 - x)^3$. Next, taking the expansion of $x f(x)/(1 - x)$ we see that

$$x f(x) \frac{1}{1 - x} = \sum_{n \geqslant 0} f_n x^{n+1} \sum_{n \geqslant 0} x^n = \sum_{n \geqslant 0} \left(\sum_{s=1}^{n} f_{s-1} \right) x^n \tag{2.12}$$

and doing the same for the expansion of $x f'(x)$ we see that

$$x f'(x) = x \sum_{n \geqslant 0} n f_n x^{n-1} = \sum_{n \geqslant 0} n f_n x^n$$

These expansions allow us to express (2.10) in a compact analytic form:

$$x f'(x) = \frac{2x}{(1 - x)^3} + 2x \frac{f(x)}{1 - x} \tag{2.13}$$

Multiplying (2.13) by $(1 - x)^2/x$ and then integrating both sides we obtain

$$\int (1 - x)^2 f'(x) dx = \int \frac{2}{1 - x} dx + \int 2(1 - x) f(x) dx$$

Now the left-hand side can be integrated by parts, which eliminates the last term of the right-hand side and gives

$$(1 - x)^2 f(x) = \int \frac{2}{1 - x} dx = -2\ln(1 - x)$$

and finally, we obtain the following simple formula for $f(x)$

$$f(x) = -\frac{2\ln(1 - x)}{(1 - x)^2} \tag{2.14}$$

From

$$-\ln(1 - x) = \sum_{n \geqslant 1} \frac{x^n}{n} \quad \text{and} \quad \frac{1}{(1 - x)^2} = \sum_{n \geqslant 0} (n + 1)x^n$$

we have

$$f(x) = 2 \left(\sum_{n \geqslant 1} \frac{x^n}{n} \right) \left(\sum_{n \geqslant 0} (n + 1)x^n \right) = 2 \sum_{n \geqslant 0} \left(\sum_{s=1}^{n} \frac{n + 1 - s}{s} x^n \right)$$

$$= 2 \sum_{n \geqslant 0} ((n + 1)H_n - n)x^n \tag{2.15}$$

where

$$H_n = 1 + \frac{1}{2} + \frac{1}{3} + \cdots + \frac{1}{n}$$

is a harmonic number equal asymptotically to $\ln n$. Thus (2.15) proves conclusion (1) of our theorem, since

$$E(n) = P'_n(1) = f_n = 2((n + 1)H_n - n) = \Theta(n \log n)$$

Now we shall try to apply the same technique for the calculation of $P''_n(1)$. To begin with we must find the corresponding analytic forms for all sequences appearing in (2.11). By easy calculation one can verify that $n^2(n + 1)$ has a generating function $x(2 + 4x)/(1 - x)^4$. Next, using (2.12), we have

$$\left(\frac{x^2 f(x)}{(1 - x)} \right)' = \left(\sum_{n \geqslant 0} \left(\sum_{s=1}^{n} f_{s-1} \right) x^{n+1} \right)' = \sum_{n \geqslant 0} (n + 1) \left(\sum_{s=1}^{n} f_{s-1} \right) x^n$$

and finally, multiplying $f(x)$ by itself we obtain

$$xf(x)f(x) = x \sum_{n \geqslant 0} f_n x^n \sum_{n \geqslant 0} f_n x^n = x \sum_{n \geqslant 0} \left(\sum_{s=0}^{n} f_s f_{n-s} \right) x^n$$

$$= \sum_{n \geqslant 0} \left(\sum_{s=1}^{n} f_{s-1} f_{n-s} \right) x^n$$

From these expansions and (2.11) we obtain a differential equation for $g(x)$, similar to (2.13):

$$xg'(x) = x \frac{2 + 4x}{(1 - x)^4} + 4 \left(\frac{x^2 f(x)}{(1 - x)} \right)' + 2xf^2(x) + 2x \frac{g(x)}{1 - x} \qquad \textbf{(2.16)}$$

Multiplying (2.16) by $(1 - x)^2/x$ and using (2.13) we transform it in the same manner as (2.13) to obtain

$$(1 - x)^2 g'(x) = \frac{2 + 12x}{(1 - x)^2} + 8f(x) + 4xf(x) + 2(1 - x)^2 f^2(x)$$

$$+ 2(1 - x)g(x) \qquad \textbf{(2.17)}$$

Now we would like to integrate both sides of equation (2.17). This would give a similar effect to that in the case of (2.13), that is, the term $2(1 - x)g(x)$ would vanish. However, much more work must be done in order to integrate the other terms. The major problem concerns the term $2(1 - x)^2 f^2(x)$. To integrate it quickly let us use (2.13) once again, namely, multiplying it by $f(x)(1 - x)^3/x$ and integrating, to obtain

$$\int (1 - x)^3 f'(x)f(x) \, dx = 2 \int f(x) \, dx + 2 \int (1 - x)^2 f^2(x) \, dx \qquad \textbf{(2.18)}$$

Integrating the left-hand side by parts, we have

$$(1 - x)^3 f^2(x) + 3 \int (1 - x)^2 f^2(x) \, dx - \int f(x)(1 - x)^3 f'(x) \, dx$$

$$= 2 \int f(x) \, dx + 2 \int (1 - x)^2 f^2(x) \, dx \qquad \textbf{(2.19)}$$

and again substituting (2.18) in (2.19) from (2.17) we finally obtain

$$(1 - x)^2 g(x) = \int \frac{2 + 12x}{(1 - x)^2} \, dx + \int 4xf(x) \, dx + 2(1 - x)^3 f^2(x) \qquad \textbf{(2.20)}$$

The integrals in (2.20) now pose no problem:

$$\int \frac{2 + 12x}{(1 - x)^2}\, dx = \int (2 + 12x)\, d\,\frac{1}{1 - x} = \frac{2 + 12x}{1 - x} - \int \frac{12}{1 - x}\, dx$$

$$= \frac{2 + 12x}{1 - x} + 12\ln(1 - x)$$

and

$$-\int \frac{8x\ln(1 - x)}{(1 - x)^2}\, dx = -8 \int x\ln(1 - x)\, d\,\frac{1}{1 - x}$$

$$= \frac{-8x\ln(1 - x)}{1 - x} + 8 \int \left(\frac{\ln(1 - x)}{1 - x} - \frac{x}{(1 - x)^2} \right) dx$$

$$= \frac{-8x\ln(1 - x)}{1 - x} - 4\ln^2(1 - x)$$

$$- \frac{8x}{1 - x} - 8\ln(1 - x)$$

From (2.20), we obtain

$$g(x) = \frac{6x}{(1 - x)^3} - \frac{8\ln(1 - x)}{(1 - x)^3} + \frac{8\ln^2(1 - x)}{(1 - x)^3}$$

$$+ \frac{12\ln(1 - x)}{(1 - x)^2} - \frac{4\ln^2(1 - x)}{(1 - x)^2}$$

because the integration constant is -2 by $g(0) = 0$. Since the third term in the above formula has a complicated expansion, we prefer the following equivalent expression:

$$g(x) = \frac{6x}{(1 - x)^3} + x\left(\frac{4\ln^2(1 - x)}{(1 - x)^2} \right)'$$

$$+ \frac{4\ln(1 - x)}{(1 - x)^2} + \frac{4\ln^2(1 - x)}{(1 - x)^2} \tag{2.21}$$

To expand the terms occurring in (2.21) we shall need not only the harmonic numbers H_n, but also the second harmonic numbers

$$H_n^{(2)} = 1 + \frac{1}{4} + \frac{1}{9} + \cdots + \frac{1}{n^2}$$

which are estimated by a constant, since the corresponding series is convergent to $\pi^2/6$. The following two summation formulas will also be very useful:

$$\sum_{s=1}^{n} H_{s-1} = \sum_{s=1}^{n} \sum_{j=1}^{s-1} \frac{1}{j} = \sum_{j=1}^{n} \sum_{s=j+1}^{n} \frac{1}{j} = \sum_{j=1}^{n} \frac{n-j}{j} = nH_n - n \qquad (2.22)$$

$$H_n^2 = \left(\sum_{i=1}^{n} \frac{1}{i}\right)\left(\sum_{j=1}^{n} \frac{1}{j}\right) = \sum_{i=1}^{n} \sum_{j=1}^{n} \frac{1}{i \cdot j} = \sum_{i=1}^{n} \frac{1}{i^2} + 2 \sum_{i=1}^{n} \sum_{j=i+1}^{n} \frac{1}{i \cdot j}$$

$$= H_n^{(2)} + 2 \sum_{j=1}^{n} \sum_{i=1}^{j-1} \frac{1}{i \cdot j} = H_n^{(2)} + 2 \sum_{j=1}^{n} \frac{H_{j-1}}{j} \qquad (2.23)$$

Using (2.22) and (2.23) we can expand the last term in (2.21):

$$\frac{\ln^2(1-x)}{(1-x)^2} = 2 \frac{1}{(1-x)^2} \int -\frac{\ln(1-x)}{1-x} dx$$

$$= 2 \sum_{n \geq 0} (n+1)x^n \int \left(\sum_{n \geq 1} \frac{x^n}{n}\right)\left(\sum_{n \geq 0} x^n\right) dx$$

$$= 2 \sum_{n \geq 0} (n+1)x^n \int \sum_{n \geq 0} H_n x^n dx$$

$$= 2 \left(\sum_{n \geq 0} (n+1)x^n\right)\left(\sum_{n \geq 0} \frac{H_n}{n+1} x^{n+1}\right)$$

$$= 2 \sum_{n \geq 0} \left(\sum_{s \geq 0}^{n} \frac{H_{s-1}}{s}(n+1-s)\right) x^n$$

$$= 2 \sum_{n \geq 0} \left((n+1) \sum_{s=1}^{n} \frac{H_{s-1}}{s}\right) x^n - 2 \left(\sum_{n \geq 0} \sum_{s=1}^{n} H_{s-1}\right) x^n$$

$$= \sum_{n \geq 0} (n+1)(H_n^2 - H_n^{(2)})x^n - 2 \sum_{n \geq 0} (nH_n - n)x^n \qquad (2.24)$$

We are now ready to expand $g(x)$ using (2.21). First we shall neglect the last two terms. Note that $6x/(1-x)^3$ has a simple expansion into a series $\sum 3n(n+1)x^n$, so it has coefficients of order $\Theta(n^2)$. The last term $\ln^2(1-x)/(1-x)^2$ expanded in (2.24) has coefficients of order $\Theta(n\log^2 n)$ and the next-to-last term was already expanded in (2.15) and gives coefficients of order $\Theta(n \log n)$. Now by differentiating (2.24) from (2.21) we have:

$$P_n''(1) = 4n(n+1)(H_n^2 - H_n^{(2)}) - 8n^2 H_n + 8n^2 + 3n(n+1)$$
$$+ \Theta(n\log^2(n))$$

Using the fact that $H_n^{(2)} \cong \pi^2/6$ and (2.15) we get:

$$D^2(n) = P_n''(1) + P_n'(1) - (P_n'(1))^2 = (7 - \tfrac{2}{3}\pi^2)n^2 + \Theta(n\log^2(n))$$

From the above we see that $D(n) \simeq 0.648n$ and conclusion (2) of our theorem is proved.   ∎

Theorem 2.1 shows that the average time complexity of *Quicksort* is of the order $\Theta(n \log n)$. Its worst-case time complexity is of order $\Theta(n^2)$ (see Exercise 2.4). The standard deviation is of the order $\Theta(n)$ which means good concentration of the cost around the average time complexity.

2.3   Searching in ordered sets

Let us consider an arbitrary set U linearly ordered by a relation '$\leqslant$'. Elements of U will be denoted by lower-case italic letters x, y, z, while subsets of U will be denoted by upper-case italic letters A, B, C.

The problem of searching in an ordered set may be defined as follows. Let A be any finite subset of U and let x be an element of U. First of all we want to know whether x belongs to A or not. Let us call this operation *member*. Its definition is as follows:

$$member(x, A) = \begin{cases} true & \text{if } x \in A \\ false & \text{if } x \notin A \end{cases}$$

We say that a search for x in A is successful if $member(x, A)$ returns *true* and unsuccessful if $member(x, A)$ returns *false*.

Another operation concerning searching in ordered sets is the operation of adding a new element to A. For given x and A we augment A with x, if $x \notin A$. Let us call this operation *insert*. Operation $insert(x, A)$ may be defined using the notation of set theory, that is, it changes A according to the assignment statement

$$A := A \cup \{x\}$$

The last operation considered in this chapter is $delete(x, A)$. It eliminates an element x from a set A if $x \in A$, so it may be defined by the assignment statement

$$A := A - \{x\}$$

A set A on which the three operations *member*, *insert* and *delete* are performed will be called a **dictionary**. Initially dictionary A is empty. Each time $insert(x, A)$ is performed, an element x is added to A if $x \notin A$, each time $delete(x, A)$ is performed, an element x is removed from A if $x \in A$. Operation $member(x, A)$ is used for testing whether x belongs to A or not.

We now define a probabilistic model for this searching process by answering two questions: 'What is meant by a random dictionary A?' and 'What is meant by a random element x?'

To answer the first question we assume that a random dictionary $A = \{x_1, \ldots, x_n\}$ is obtained from an empty one as the result of executing $insert(x_1, A), \ldots, insert(x_n, A)$. Thus we can assume that the sequence $\langle x_1, \ldots, x_n \rangle$ from which we build up A is random. Denote by $Pr(\langle x_1, \ldots, x_n \rangle)$ the probability that a sequence $\langle x_1, \ldots, x_n \rangle$ occurs. Since our set U is linearly ordered, it is natural to assume the permutation model for this distribution (see Section 1.6), that is, $\langle x_1, \ldots, x_n \rangle$ is a random permutation of $\{1, \ldots, n\}$ and $Pr(\langle x_1, \ldots, x_n \rangle) = 1/n!$.

To answer the latter question we must consider two cases, first when $x \notin A$ and second when $x \in A$. If $x \notin A$, then the randomness of x is settled by the randomness of $A \cup \{x\}$, that is, we can treat $\langle x_1, \ldots, x_n, x \rangle$ as a random permutation of $\{1, \ldots, n + 1\}$. If $x \in A$, $A = \{x_1, \ldots, x_n\}$ then we can assume that $x = x_i$ with the same probability for each $i = 1, \ldots, n$, that is, $Pr(x = x_i) = 1/n$.

Suppose that we have an algorithm-implementing operation $member(x, A)$ and let $|A| = n$. Since the execution of $member(x, A)$ may be successful or unsuccessful, it is convenient to define its complexity in these two cases separately. So let $T^-(n)$ and $T^+(n)$ denote the random variables whose values are equal to the number of steps performed by the considered algorithm in the case of $x \notin A$ and $x \in A$ respectively. According to our notation we can designate by $E^-(n)$, $V^-(n)$ and $D^-(n)$ the mean value, variance and standard deviation of $T^-(n)$, and similarly by $E^+(n)$, $V^+(n)$ and $D^+(n)$ the mean value, variance and standard deviation of $T^+(n)$. The generating function of $T^-(n)$ and $T^+(n)$ will be denoted by $P_n^-(z)$ and $P_n^+(z)$, respectively.

We start the presentation of various searching algorithms with the simplest one called **search in an ordered list**. The elements belonging to a dictionary $A = \{x_1, \ldots, x_n\}$ are arranged in a list such that $x_1 < x_2 < \ldots < x_n$ (see Figure 2.2).

Operation $member(x, A)$ starts from the list head and passes through the links, testing each time whether x is smaller than, equal to, or greater than a stored element x_i. This process terminates successfully if x is found, and unsuccessfully if the list ends or a tested element x_i is already greater than x. Operation $insert(x, A)$ is similar to $member(x, A)$, however in a successful case the list remains unchanged, while in an unsuccessful case x is added at the appropriate position found during the searching process. Operation $delete(x, A)$ is a complement to $insert(x, A)$, in that it leaves the list unchanged in an unsuccessful case and eliminates x from the list in a successful

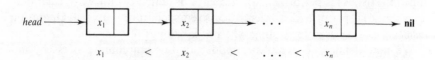

Figure 2.2   Linear list representing dictionary $A = \{x_1, \ldots, x_n\}$.

case. Formal definition of these algorithms are very simple so we leave them as exercises.

We begin the probabilistic analysis of this algorithm from an unsuccessful case. Since, according to the permutation model, a new element x may stand at each position, that is, before x_1, or between x_i and x_{i+1} for $i = 1, \ldots, n-1$, or after x_n, with the same probability equal to $1/(n+1)$, we immediately have

$$P_n^-(z) = \frac{1}{n+1} \sum_{k=1}^{n+1} z^k$$

Thus using (1.3) and (1.5) from Chapter 1 we have

$$E^-(n) = P_n^{-\prime}(1) = \frac{n+2}{2} = 0.5n + O(1)$$

$$V^-(n) = P_n^{-\prime\prime}(1) + P_n^{-\prime}(1) - (P_n^{-\prime}(1))^2 = \frac{n(n+2)}{12} \cong 0.08n^2 + O(n)$$

$$D^-(n) = \sqrt{V^-(n)} \cong 0.289n$$

In a successful case we have

$$P_n^+(z) = \frac{1}{n} \sum_{k=1}^{n} z^k$$

and

$$E^+(n) = P_n^{+\prime}(1) = \frac{n+1}{2} = 0.5n + O(1)$$

$$V^+(n) = P_n^{+\prime\prime}(1) + P_n^{+\prime}(1) - (P_n^{+\prime}(1))^2 = \frac{n^2-1}{12} \cong 0.08n^2 + O(n)$$

$$D^+(n) = \sqrt{V^+(n)} \cong 0.289n$$

The cost of $insert(x, A)$ is the same as $member(x, A)$ in an unsuccessful case, disregarding a term of order $O(1)$. Similarly, the cost of $delete(x, A)$ is the same as $member(x, A)$ in a successful case, also disregarding a term of order $O(1)$. This completes the probabilistic analysis of the searching algorithms in ordered lists.

As we can see from the above analysis such a sequential search is rather inefficient. The most popular technique which gives a substantial speed-up is based on the binary search tree structure. Remember (see Section 1.8) that for any node p in a binary search tree the following conditions hold:

(1) if q belongs to the left subtree of p, then $q^\wedge . a < p^\wedge . a$

(2) if q belongs to the right subtree of p, then $q^\wedge . a > p^\wedge . a$

where the selector a takes values in a linearly ordered set U. Thus a finite subset A of the set U may be represented by a binary search tree as the set of corresponding values of selector a. The operations $member(x, A)$ and $insert(x, A)$ were already defined in Example 1.15, the definition of $delete(x, A)$ and its analysis will be presented at the end of this section.

All three operations, $member(x, A)$, $insert(x, A)$ and $delete(x, A)$, perform searching for x. This searching is successful when x is found in a certain node of the binary search tree and is unsuccessful when this process ends at the value **nil**. Note that then, in the case of operation $insert(x, A)$, a new node with value x is created in the position corresponding to this value **nil**. We shall call such a position an **external node** of a binary search tree. To distinguish external nodes from normal nodes the latter will be called the **internal nodes** of a binary search tree.

An example of a binary search tree with internal and external nodes is given in Figure 2.3.

For binary search trees the cost $T^-(n)$ of the operation $member(x, A)$ in an unsuccessful case is practically the same as the cost of $insert(x, A)$. Indeed, as in the case of an ordered linear list, the latter cost differs from the first only by a term of order $O(1)$. Thus $T^-(n)$ corresponds to the cost of $insert(x, A)$ as well.

We begin the probabilistic analysis of the operation $insert$ in a binary search tree with Theorem 2.2.

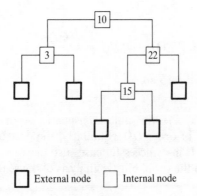

□ External node   ☐ Internal node

Figure 2.3 A binary search tree with external nodes.

Theorem 2.2

Denote by $r_{n,k}$ the number of permutations $\langle x_1, \ldots, x_{n+1} \rangle$ such that $T^-(n) = k$, that is, the cost of $insert(x_{n+1}, A)$ where A was generated by $insert(x_1, A), \ldots, insert(x_n, A)$ is equal to k. Then

$$r_{n,k} = 2r_{n-1,k-1} + (n-1)r_{n-1,k} \qquad \text{for} \quad n \geqslant 1, k > 0 \qquad \textbf{(2.25)}$$

$$r_{0,0} = 1, \qquad r_{0,k} = 0 \quad \text{for} \quad k > 0, \qquad r_{n,0} = 0 \quad \text{for} \quad n \geqslant 1 \qquad \textbf{(2.26)}$$

Proof It is easy to verify the boundary conditions (2.26). Indeed, there is only one permutation $\langle 1 \rangle$ for which we obtain an empty tree and the cost of inserting 1 is 0, thus $r_{0,0} = 1$. Moreover $r_{0,k}$ for $k > 0$ equals 0, since there is only one permutation of $\{1\}$. Finally $r_{n,0} = 0$ for $n \geqslant 1$, since any insertion to a non-empty tree must cost more than 0.

In order to prove (2.25) consider a permutation $\langle x_1, \ldots, x_n \rangle$ such that the cost of $insert(x_n, A)$ is $k - 1$. Now take all the sequences $\langle x_1', \ldots, x_{n-1}', y, x_n' \rangle$ such that y ranges over $\{1, \ldots, n+1\}$ and $x_j' = x_j$ for $x_j < y$ and $x_j' = x_j + 1$ for $x_j \geqslant y$, $j = 1, \ldots, n$. It is evident that there are $n + 1$ such sequences and that each one is a permutation of $\{1, \ldots, n+1\}$.

For $y = x_n$ the sequence $\langle x_1', \ldots, x_{n-1}', y \rangle$ produces a tree isomorphic to that produced by $\langle x_1, \ldots, x_n \rangle$, since the ordering between the input data remains unchanged. But then the execution of $insert(x_n', A)$, where $x_n' = x_n + 1$, costs one more than the execution of $insert(x_n, A)$, since element x_n' finds its position to the right of y. Thus the cost of $insert(x_n', A)$ is k. For $y = x_n + 1$ the sequence $\langle x_1', \ldots, x_{n-1}', y \rangle$ also produces a tree isomorphic to that produced by $\langle x_1, \ldots, x_n \rangle$, and then x_n' finds its position to the left of y. Thus the execution of $insert(x_n', A)$ costs k. For the other values of y, element x_n' finds its position at the same place as x_n. Thus the cost of $insert(x_n', A)$ remains unchanged.

The recursive relation (2.25) is now evident, since for two values of y, $1 \leqslant y \leqslant n + 1$, we have a permutation $\langle x_1, \ldots, x_{n+1} \rangle$ with the cost of $insert(x_{n+1}, A)$ equal to the cost of $insert(x_n, A)$ plus 1, and for the remaining $n - 1$ values of y we have a permutation $\langle x_1, \ldots, x_{n+1} \rangle$ with the cost of $insert(x_{n+1}, A)$ equal to that of $insert(x_n, A)$. ∎

From Theorem 2.2 we can easily calculate the generating function $P_n^-(z)$. Since $p_{n,k}^- = r_{n,k}/(n+1)!$ is the probability that $member(x, A)$ costs k steps in an unsuccessful case, multiplying $P_n^-(z)$ by $(n+1)!$ we obtain

$$(n+1)! \, P_n^-(z) = \sum_{k=0}^{\infty} r_{n,k} z^k = 2 \sum_{k=1}^{\infty} r_{n-1,k-1} z^k + (n-1) \sum_{k=1}^{\infty} r_{n-1,k} z^k$$

$$= (2z)n! \, P_{n-1}^-(z) + (n-1)n! \, P_{n-1}^-(z)$$

$$= (2z + n - 1)n! \, P_{n-1}^-(z)$$

Now by $P_0(z) = 1$ we immediately obtain

$$P_n^-(z) = \frac{1}{n+1} \prod_{k=1}^{n} (2z + k - 1) = \prod_{k=1}^{n} \frac{2z + k - 1}{k + 1}$$

The factor $(2z + k - 1)/(k + 1)$ in the above product is the generating function of a random variable, because its value at 1 is 1. Thus we can apply the results presented in Chapter 1 (see Exercises 1.21 and 1.22).

$$E^-(n) = \sum_{k=1}^{n} \left(\frac{2z + k - 1}{k + 1} \right)' \bigg|_{z=1} = \sum_{k=1}^{n} \frac{2}{k+1} = 2H_{n+1} - 2$$

$$= 2\ln(n) + O(1)$$

$$V^-(n) = \sum_{k=1}^{n} \left(\frac{2z + k - 1}{k + 1} \right)'' \bigg|_{z=1} + \sum_{k=1}^{n} \frac{2}{k+1} - \sum_{k=1}^{n} \left(\frac{2}{k+1} \right)^2$$

$$= 2H_{n+1} - 2 - 4H_{n+1}^{(2)} + 4$$

$$= 2\ln(n) + O(1)$$

$$D^-(n) = \sqrt{2\ln(n)} + O(1)$$

To calculate $E^+(n)$ and $V^+(n)$ we shall use the following theorem.

Theorem 2.3

Let $P_n^-(z)$ and $P_n^+(z)$ denote the generating functions for the cost of *member*(x, A) in an unsuccessful and a successful case, respectively. Then

$$(n + 1)zP_n^-(z) + nP_n^+(z) = z + 2nzP_n^+(z) \tag{2.27}$$

Proof   Consider a permutation $\bar{x} = \langle x_1, \ldots, x_n \rangle$ of $\{1, \ldots, n\}$. Denote by $w_k(\bar{x})$ the number of internal nodes at level k and by $v_k(\bar{x})$ the number of external nodes at level k in a tree produced from $\bar{x}$. Since it is a binary tree we have $v_k(\bar{x}) + w_k(\bar{x}) = 2w_{k-1}(\bar{x})$ for $k > 0$, because each internal node at level $k - 1$ has exactly two sons (including external nodes) at level k. Moreover $v_0(\bar{x}) + w_0(\bar{x}) = 1$. Thus

$$\sum_{\bar{x}} (v_k(\bar{x}) + w_k(\bar{x})) = \begin{cases} n! & \text{if } k = 0 \\ 2\sum_{\bar{x}} w_{k-1}(\bar{x}) & \text{if } k > 0 \end{cases} \tag{2.28}$$

where the sums are taken over all permutations of $\{1, \ldots, n\}$. On the other hand

$$n!(n+1)p_{n,k}^- = \sum_{\bar{x}} v_k(\bar{x}) \tag{2.29}$$

$$n!np_{n,k}^+ = \sum_{\bar{x}} w_{k-1}(\bar{x}) \tag{2.30}$$

From (2.28), (2.29) and (2.30) and the definitions of $P_n^-(z)$ and $P_n^+(z)$ we now obtain

$$
\begin{aligned}
(n+1)zP_n^-(z) + nP_n^+(z) &= (n+1)z\sum_{k=0}^{\infty} p_{n,k}^- z^k + n\sum_{k=0}^{\infty} p_{n,k}^+ z^k \\
&= z\frac{1}{n!}\sum_{k=0}^{\infty} z^k\sum_{\bar{x}} v_k(\bar{x}) + \frac{1}{n!}\sum_{k=1}^{\infty} z^k\sum_{\bar{x}} w_{k-1}(\bar{x}) \\
&= z\frac{1}{n!}\left(n! + \sum_{k=1}^{\infty} z^k\sum_{\bar{x}} (v_k(\bar{x}) + w_k(\bar{x}))\right) \\
&= z + z\frac{2}{n!}\sum_{k=1}^{\infty} z^k\sum_{\bar{x}} w_{k-1}(\bar{x}) \\
&= z + 2nz\sum_{k=0}^{\infty} p_{n,k}^+ \\
&= z + 2nzP_n^+(z)
\end{aligned}
$$

which proves (2.27).   ∎

Theorem 2.3 enables us to calculate $E^+(n)$ and $V^+(n)$ from $E^-(n)$ and $V^-(n)$. Let us differentiate (2.27) and set $z = 1$. We obtain

$$(n+1) + (n+1)P_n^{-\prime}(1) + nP_n^{+\prime}(1) = 1 + 2n + 2nP_n^{+\prime}(1)$$

and from $E^-(n) = P_n^{-\prime}(1)$, $E^+(n) = P_n^{+\prime}(1)$ we obtain

$$E^+(n) = \left(1 + \frac{1}{n}\right)E^-(n) - 1 = 2\ln(n) + O(1)$$

Differentiating (2.27) twice and setting $z = 1$ we have

$$2(n+1)P_n^{-\prime}(1) + (n+1)P_n^{-\prime\prime}(1) + nP_n^{+\prime}(1) = 4nP_n^{+\prime}(1) + 2nP_n^{+\prime\prime}(1)$$

Now, from

$$V^+(n) = P_n^{+\prime\prime}(1) + E^+(n) - (E^+(n))^2$$

we obtain

$$V^+(n) = \left(1 + \frac{1}{n}\right) V^-(n) - \frac{n+1}{n^2} (E^-(n))^2 + 2$$

$$= \left(1 + \frac{1}{n}\right)(2H_{n+1} - 4H_{n+1}^{(2)} + 2) - 4\frac{n+1}{n^2}(H_{n+1} - 2)^2 + 2$$

$$= 2\ln(n) + O(\ln^2(n)/n)$$

and

$$D^+(n) = \sqrt{2\ln(n)} + O(\ln(n)/n)$$

Probabilistic analysis of *member*(x, A) and *insert*(x, A) in binary search trees shows that their average cost is of order $\ln n$ and that the corresponding random variables are well concentrated about their mean values (the standard deviation in both cases is of order $\sqrt{\ln n}$). It is, of course, much better than in the case of a sequential search in an ordered list.

Now we shall describe briefly the way in which operation *delete*(x, A) can be performed. First we search for x in A using *member*(x, A). Suppose that x occurs at a node v. If v has no right son, then we extract v from the tree by reassigning a pointer so as to bypass the deleted node v. If v has a right son w, then we search for the leftmost element t in the subtree w. Element t is the smallest one in this subtree. Thus extracting t from subtree w (it is possible because t has no left son) and inserting it in the place of v we can eliminate x from A preserving simultaneously the invariants of binary search tree (see Figure 2.4). The formal definition of this operation we leave as an exercise.

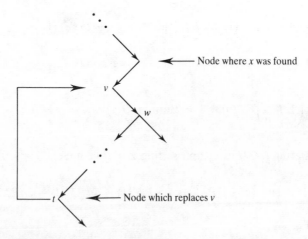

Figure 2.4 Operation *delete*(x, A) in binary search trees.

The cost of *delete*(x, A) is equal to the cost of searching for x plus the cost of searching for the node t. Let us try to estimate this latter cost.

The internal nodes of a binary search tree generated from a permutation $\bar{x} = \langle x_1, \ldots, x_n \rangle$ of $\{1, \ldots, n\}$ are enumerated in the natural order by the values situated in these nodes (it is the in-order enumeration). Let us enumerate the external nodes of this tree by consecutive natural numbers (see Figure 2.5). The cost of search for t (the leftmost node in subtree w) equals the length of a path going from v to t (see Figure 2.4). The value in t is $x + 1$, because $x + 1$ is the next to x value in this tree. Consider an external node s which is the left son of the node t. The number of external nodes to the left of s is exactly x since there are x values smaller than $x + 1$ in this tree. Thus the number of s is $x + 1$ in the enumeration of external nodes, and we see that the length of the path from v to t is equal to the depth of the external node $x + 1$ minus the depth of the internal node x.

Let us denote by $ind(\bar{x}, x)$ the depth of an internal node x in a binary search tree generated from $\bar{x}$. Similarly, denote by $exd(\bar{x}, x)$ the depth of an external node x in such a tree. Then for any $\bar{x}$ the following condition holds:

$$\sum_{x=1}^{n+1} exd(\bar{x}, x) - \sum_{x=1}^{n} ind(\bar{x}, x) = 2n \tag{2.31}$$

We shall prove (2.31) by induction on n. For $n = 1$ we have one internal node with depth 0 and two external nodes with depth 1, so (2.31) is satisfied. In the case of a tree with n internal nodes, replace one external node lying at depth k by an internal one. We obtain two new external nodes at depth $k + 1$ and one more internal node at depth k. Thus the first sum in (2.31) increases

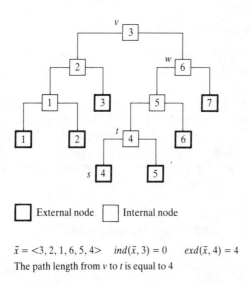

☐ External node   ☐ Internal node

$\bar{x} = \langle 3, 2, 1, 6, 5, 4 \rangle$ $ind(\bar{x}, 3) = 0$ $exd(\bar{x}, 4) = 4$

The path length from v to t is equal to 4

Figure 2.5 A binary search tree with external nodes.

by $k + 1 + k + 1 - k = k + 2$, while the second sum in (2.31) increases by k. Since the number of internal nodes is now $n + 1$ and the left-hand side of (2.31) increases by 2, we have proved (2.31).

From (2.31) we can easily estimate the average cost of search for t. It is equal to

$$\frac{1}{n!n} \sum_{\bar{x}} \sum_{x=1}^{n} (exd(\bar{x}, x + 1) - ind(\bar{x}, x)) = \frac{1}{n!n} \sum_{\bar{x}} (2n - exd(\bar{x}, 1))$$

which can easily be estimated by a constant. Thus the average cost of $delete(x, A)$ is the same as that of $insert(x, A)$ and $member(x, A)$. What remains unclear is the assumption that a random binary search tree is generated by a random permutation $\bar{x} = \langle x_1, \ldots, x_n \rangle$ when $delete$ comes into play. Note that our probabilistic model works properly only if among the admissible operations on a binary search tree there is no $delete(x, A)$. So let us complete this analysis with Hibbard's theorem (Knuth, 1973) which shows that the operation $delete$ does not disturb the randomness of binary search trees.

Operation $delete(x, A)$, where A is represented by a binary search tree generated from a permutation of $\{1, \ldots, n\}$, produces another binary search tree generated by a permutation of $\{1, \ldots, n - 1\}$. Thus, speaking in terms of permutations, $delete(x, A)$ has $nn!$ different inputs $(x, \bar{x})$, where $x \in \{1, \ldots, n\}$ and $\bar{x}$ is a permutation of $\{1, \ldots, n\}$, and $(n - 1)!$ different results $\bar{y}$, where $\bar{y}$ is a permutation of $\{1, \ldots, n - 1\}$. To prove that $delete$ does not disturb the randomness of a tree it is sufficient to show that $\bar{y}$ is obtained from exactly n^2 different inputs. This fact is provided by Hibbard's theorem.

Theorem 2.4   (Hibbard's Theorem)

Any permutation $\bar{y}$ that corresponds to a binary search tree obtained as a result of $delete(x, A)$ is obtained from exactly n^2 different inputs $(x, \bar{x})$.

Proof   Consider $x \in \{1, \ldots, n\}$ and $\bar{x} = \langle x_1, \ldots, x_n \rangle$ such that $x = x_i$, for some i, $1 \leqslant i \leqslant n$. If $x_i = n$ or $x_i + 1 = x_j$ for $1 \leqslant j < i$, it means that to the right of x_i there are no nodes in the tree generated from $\bar{x}$. Indeed, in the first case, x_i is the greatest element. In the latter, element x_j is inserted before x_i and all elements greater than x_i are also greater than x_j. The operation $delete(x, A)$ produces a new binary search tree with node x_i extracted. Thus the permutation $\bar{y} = \langle y_1, \ldots, y_{n-1} \rangle$ is obtained from $\bar{x} = \langle x_1, \ldots, x_n \rangle$ by the elimination of x_i. But to obtain a permutation of $\{1, \ldots, n - 1\}$ the values greater than x_i must be decreased. Thus

$$\bar{y} = \langle x'_1, \ldots, x'_{i-1}, x'_{i+1}, \ldots, x'_n \rangle \tag{2.32}$$

where $x'_k = x_k$ for $x_k < x_i$ and $x'_k = x_k - 1$ for $x_k > x_i$.

Consider the other case, that is, when $x_i + 1 = x_j$ for $i < j$. It means that x_j is the smallest in the right subtree of x_i. This corresponds to the situation when node t replaces node v (see Figure 2.4). Thus x_i should be eliminated and replaced by x_j. Again, to obtain a permutation of $\{1, \ldots, n-1\}$ the values greater than x_i must be decreased, that is, denoting as before $x'_k = x_k$ for $x_k < x_i$ and $x'_k = x_k - 1$ for $x_k > x_i$ we have

$$\bar{y} = \langle x'_1, \ldots, x'_{i-1}, x'_j, x'_{i+1}, \ldots, x'_{j-1}, x'_{j+1}, \ldots, x'_n \rangle \qquad (2.33)$$

In order to prove the theorem it is sufficient to show that each permutation $\bar{y}$ may be obtained from at least n^2 different inputs $(x, \bar{x})$. Let (i, j) be any pair of integers such that $1 \leqslant i \leqslant n$ and $1 \leqslant j \leqslant n$. There are n^2 such pairs and for each of them we shall construct a different input $(x, \bar{x})$ giving the same result $\bar{y}$.

We shall consider three cases: $i = j$, $i > j$ and $i < j$. For $i = j$ we take

$$\bar{x} = \langle y_1, \ldots, y_{i-1}, n, y_{i+1}, \ldots, y_{n-1} \rangle \text{ and } x = n$$

According to (2.32), the operation *delete* for such an input yields $\bar{y}$. For $i > j$ we take

$$\bar{x} = \langle y'_1, \ldots, y'_{j-1}, y_j + 1, y'_j, \ldots, y'_{i-1}, y_j, y'_i, \ldots, y'_{n-1} \rangle \text{ and } x = y_j$$

where $y'_k = y_k$ for $y_k < y_j$ and $y'_k = y_k + 1$ for $y_k > y_j$. According to (2.32) the operation *delete* also yields $\bar{y}$, since eliminating y_j from $\bar{x}$ and decreasing those components greater than y_j gives $\bar{y}$. Finally for $i < j$ we should apply (2.33). Thus we take

$$\bar{x} = \langle y'_1, \ldots, y'_{i-1}, y_i, y'_{i+1}, \ldots, y'_{j-1}, y_i + 1, y'_j, \ldots, y'_{n-1} \rangle$$

and $x = y_i$ where $y'_k = y_k$ for $y_k < y_i$ and $y'_k = y_k + 1$ for $y_k > y_i$. Extracting y_i, replacing it by $y_i + 1$ and decreasing those components which are greater than y_i we again obtain $\bar{y}$. This way, for each pair (i, j), we have constructed a different input data $(x, \bar{x})$ such that *delete* produces the permutation $\bar{y}$.   ∎

2.4   The digital search

Let us consider an alphabet consisting of M symbols and a set U of all words over this alphabet. In a digital search, as in Section 2.3, we deal with finite subsets of U and elements of U. The main idea of the digital search is based on an M-ary tree structure. Such a tree represents a finite subset A of U in the following way. Each internal node of this tree has M sons labelled by the symbols of the alphabet. An internal node represents the set of all words which have a prefix defined by the sequence of labels lying on the path from the root to this node. Finally, each leaf represents either an element x of A or **nil**.

Consider, for example, an alphabet $\{a, b, \$\}$ where symbol $\$$ is used only to mark the end of a word, and a set A consisting of the words: *ab, abb, baba, aa, abab*. For this set we obtain the 3-ary tree presented in Figure 2.6. Symbol $\$$ is introduced to distinguish a word from its proper prefix, for instance, *abb* from *ab*. Moreover, each word $x \in A$ is situated in such a leaf that the path from the root to this leaf defines the shortest prefix that distinguishes x from the other elements of A.

We shall now describe some algorithms operating on M-ary trees. As in Section 2.3 we could define the three basic operations *member*, *insert* and *delete*, however *delete*(x, A) is not easily implemented in M-ary trees. Thus we shall discuss only the operations *member*(x, A) and *insert*(x, A).

It is easy to design the operation *member*(x, A). One should read the symbols creating a word x, one by one, and follow simultaneously the corresponding path on the tree representing the set A. If a leaf with value x is reached, the answer is *true*. If a leaf with another value $y \neq x$ or with the value **nil** is reached, then the answer is *false*. Note also that according to the special meaning of $\$$, the search for x always ends on a leaf. The formal definition of this algorithm is left as an exercise.

Rather more difficult to design is *insert*(x, A). First, of course, one must search for x in the same manner as in *member*(x, A). If x is found, then there is nothing to do. Otherwise there are two possibilities. Either a leaf is **nil** or it has another value $y \neq x$. In the first case x simply replaces **nil**. In the latter case the smallest prefix that distinguishes x from y should be found and the corresponding new path should be constructed. The details of this algorithm is also left as an exercise.

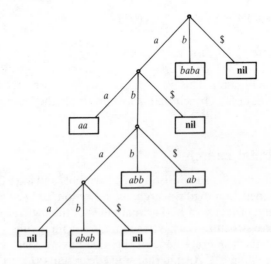

Figure 2.6 A tree representing a set $\{ab, abb, baba, aa, abab\}$

To begin the probabilistic analysis of a digital search consider a set A with n elements that are words of any length. What is the probability that k words ($k \leqslant n$) among these n words have a given prefix x? If the length of x is l, it is natural to assume that x appears with probability M^{-l}, since there are M^l different words of length l over the alphabet with M symbols. Thus assuming Bernoulli's distribution we have k successes, each one with the probability M^{-l}, and $n - k$ failures, each one with the probability $1 - M^{-l}$. Thus we have

$$q_{nkl}^x = \binom{n}{k} M^{-lk}(1 - M^{-l})^{n-k} \tag{2.34}$$

which is the probability that the word x of length l appears exactly k times as a prefix in n words of set A.

To construct a probabilistic model that satisfies (2.34) we note that it should admit words of unbounded length. In particular, when the special symbol \$ is used for marking the end of a word, the probability that x does not appear as a prefix is not equal to $(1 - M^{-l})$, since in this way we do not count words shorter than l. Why then do we assume (2.34)? First of all there is a probabilistic model which satisfies (2.34) and approximates practical situations. Secondly, using (2.34) we can estimate the average cost of the considered algorithms.

Let us construct first a probabilistic model that satisfies (2.34). Consider the simple case when $M = 2$. We want to deal with unbounded binary words such that (2.34) holds. To do so, we take any random variable $X, 0 \leqslant X < 1$, which has a uniform distribution in $[0, 1)$. Every value of X can be represented as an infinite binary word $0 . b_1 b_2 b_3 \ldots$. Since the assumed distribution is uniform, $Pr(X < 0.5) = Pr(X \geqslant 0.5) = 0.5$, so $Pr(b_1 = 0) = Pr(b_1 = 1) = 0.5$. The same holds for any b_i, $i \geqslant 1$, and it proves that (2.34) holds. In a similar way one can construct such a model for $M > 2$.

To continue the probabilistic analysis of the digital search let us denote by r_{nl}^x the probability that in a set A of size n at least two words have the same prefix x. Thus from (2.34) we get

$$r_{nl}^x = \sum_{k \geqslant 2} q_{nkl}^x$$

$$= \sum_{k \geqslant 2} \binom{n}{k} M^{-lk}(1 - M^{-l})^{n-k}$$

$$= \sum_{k \geqslant 0} \binom{n}{k} M^{-lk}(1 - M^{-l})^{n-k} - (1 - M^{-l})^n - nM^{-l}(1 - M^{-l})^{n-1}$$

$$= (M^{-l} + 1 - M^{-l})^n - (1 - M^{-l})^n - nM^{-l}(1 - M^{-l})^{n-1}$$

$$= 1 - (1 - M^{-l})^n - nM^{-l}(1 - M^{-l})^{n-1}$$

Denote by a_{nl} the average number of internal nodes lying at level l in an M-ary tree representing a set A. Since there are M^l words of length l that can be prefixes, we have

$$a_{nl} = M^l r_{nl}^x = M^l(1 - (1 - M^{-l})^n) - n(1 - M^{-l})^{n-1} \qquad (2.35)$$

Summing a_{nl} over $l \geqslant 0$ we obtain a formula for the average number of internal nodes in an M-ary tree. Let us denote this value by A_n. Then

$$A_n = \sum_{l \geqslant 0} a_{nl} = \sum_{l \geqslant 0} M^l(1 - (1 - M^{-l})^n) - n(1 - M^{-l})^{n-1}$$

$$= \sum_{l \geqslant 0}\left(M^l\left(1 - \sum_{k \geqslant 0}\binom{n}{k}(-1)^k M^{-lk}\right) - n\sum_{k \geqslant 0}\binom{n-1}{k}(-1)^k M^{-lk}\right)$$

$$= \sum_{l \geqslant 0}\left(\sum_{k \geqslant 1}\binom{n}{k}(-1)^{k+1} M^{-l(k-1)} - n\sum_{k \geqslant 0}\binom{n-1}{k}(-1)^k M^{-lk}\right)$$

$$= \sum_{l \geqslant 0}\left(\sum_{k \geqslant 2}\binom{n}{k}(-1)^{k+1} M^{-l(k-1)} - n\sum_{k \geqslant 1}\binom{n-1}{k}(-1)^k M^{-lk}\right)$$

$$= \sum_{k \geqslant 2}\binom{n}{k}(-1)^{k+1} \sum_{l \geqslant 0} M^{-l(k-1)} - \sum_{k \geqslant 1}\binom{n}{k+1}(k+1)(-1)^k \sum_{l \geqslant 0} M^{-lk}$$

$$= \sum_{k \geqslant 2}\binom{n}{k}(-1)^{k+1} \frac{M^{k-1}}{M^{k-1}-1} - \sum_{k \geqslant 1}\binom{n}{k+1}(k+1)(-1)^k \frac{M^k}{M^k-1}$$

$$= \sum_{k \geqslant 2}\binom{n}{k}(-1)^{k+1} \frac{M^{k-1}}{M^{k-1}-1} + \sum_{k \geqslant 2}\binom{n}{k}k(-1)^k \frac{M^{k-1}}{M^{k-1}-1}$$

$$= \sum_{k \geqslant 2}\binom{n}{k}(k-1)(-1)^k \frac{M^{k-1}}{M^{k-1}-1} \qquad (2.36)$$

It is not easy to give the exact asymptotic value of A_n (see Knuth (1973) Section 6.3). We shall try to estimate this value using the **binomial transform**. Namely, for a sequence f_k, $k \geqslant 0$, its binomial transform $\hat{f}_k$ is a sequence

$$\hat{f}_k = \sum_{i \geqslant 0}\binom{k}{i}(-1)^i f_i, \quad k \geqslant 0$$

Theorem 2.5

Let $\hat{f}_k$ be a binomial transform of f_k. Then the following equations hold:

$$\hat{\hat{f}}_k = f_k \quad \hat{k} = -\delta_{k1} \quad \widehat{\binom{k}{2}} = \delta_{k2} \quad \hat{1} = \delta_{k0}$$

(Where $\delta_{ij} = 1$ if $i = j$ and 0 otherwise; k denotes the series whose kth term is k, and so on.)

Proof To prove these equations let us apply the technique of generating functions. Namely, assuming that

$$F(z) = \sum_{k \geq 0} f_k \frac{z^k}{k!}$$

is an exponential generating function for f_k we immediately have that $\hat{F}(z) = F(-z)e^z$ is an exponential generating function for $\hat{f}_k$. Indeed we have

$$\hat{F}(z) = \sum_{k \geq 0} f_k \frac{(-z)^k}{k!} \sum_{k \geq 0} \frac{z^k}{k!} = \sum_{k \geq 0} \sum_{i=0}^{k} (-1)^i \frac{1}{i!(k-i)!} f_i z^k$$

$$= \sum_{k \geq 0} \left(\sum_{i=0}^{k} \binom{k}{i}(-1)^i f_i \right) \frac{z^k}{k!} = \sum_{k \geq 0} \hat{f}_k \frac{z^k}{k!}.$$

Thus $\hat{\hat{F}}(z) = \hat{F}(-z)e^z = F(z)e^{-z}e^z = F(z)$, which shows that $\hat{\hat{f}}_k = f_k$. Next by simple calculations we obtain

$$\sum_{k \geq 0} k \frac{z^k}{k!} = \sum_{k \geq 1} \frac{z^k}{(k-1)!} = ze^z$$

which shows that $\hat{F}(z) = F(-z)e^z = -ze^{-z}e^z = -z$ and $\hat{k} = -\delta_{k1}$. Similarly, because

$$\frac{1}{2}\sum_{k \geq 0} k(k-1) \frac{z^k}{k!} = \frac{1}{2}z^2 e^z$$

the corresponding $\hat{F}(z) = F(-z)e^z = \frac{1}{2}z^2 e^{-z}e^z = \frac{1}{2}z^2$ and we have

$$\widehat{\binom{k}{2}} = \delta_{k2}$$

Finally, for the last equation we immediately observe that $\hat{F}(z) = 1$ and $\hat{1} = \delta_{k0}$.   ∎

Another theorem helps to estimate A_n.

Theorem 2.6

Let f_n and g_n be two sequences such that $f_0 = f_1 = g_0 = g_1 = 0$. Then for $M \geq 2$ the condition

$$g_n = f_n + M^{1-n} \sum_{k \geq 0} \binom{n}{k}(M-1)^{n-k} g_k \qquad n \geq 2 \tag{2.37}$$

holds if and only if

$$g_n = \sum_{k \geq 2} \binom{n}{k}(-1)^k \hat{f}_k \frac{M^{k-1}}{M^{k-1}-1} \qquad n \geq 2 \tag{2.38}$$

holds.

Proof According to $\hat{\hat{f}}_k = f_k$ (Theorem 2.5) we can write (2.38) in the form $g_n = f_n + h_n$ where

$$h_n = \sum_{k \geq 2} \binom{n}{k} (-1)^k \hat{f}_k \frac{1}{M^{k-1} - 1} \tag{2.39}$$

Thus to show the equivalence of (2.37) with (2.38) it is sufficient to prove that

$$M^{1-n} \sum_{k \geq 0} \binom{n}{k} (M-1)^{n-k} g_k = h_n \tag{2.40}$$

Let us calculate the left-hand side of (2.40) in the following way:

$$M^{1-n} \sum_{k \geq 0} \binom{n}{k} (M-1)^{n-k} g_k = M^{1-n} \sum_{k \geq 0} \binom{n}{k} (M-1)^{n-k} (f_k + h_k)$$

$$= M^{1-n} \sum_{k \geq 0} \binom{n}{k} (M-1)^{n-k} \left(\sum_{i \geq 0} \binom{k}{i} (-1)^i \hat{f}_i \right.$$

$$\left. + \sum_{i \geq 2} \binom{k}{i} (-1)^i \frac{\hat{f}_i}{M^{i-1} - 1} \right)$$

$$= M^{1-n} \sum_{k \geq 0} \binom{n}{k} (M-1)^{n-k} \sum_{i \geq 0} \binom{k}{i} (-1)^i \hat{f}_i \frac{M^{i-1}}{M^{i-1} - 1}$$

$$= M^{1-n} \sum_{i=2}^{n} (-1)^i \hat{f}_i \frac{M^{i-1}}{M^{i-1} - 1} \sum_{k=i}^{n} \binom{n}{k} \binom{k}{i} (M-1)^{n-k} \tag{2.41}$$

The inner sum in (2.41) may be simplified as follows:

$$\sum_{k=i}^{n} \binom{n}{k} \binom{k}{i} (M-1)^{n-k} = \sum_{k=i}^{n} \binom{n}{k} \binom{k}{i} \sum_{j=0}^{n-k} \binom{n-k}{j} M^j (-1)^{n-k-j}$$

$$= \sum_{j=0}^{n-i} M^j \frac{n!}{i! j!} \sum_{k=i}^{n-j} \frac{(-1)^{n-k-j}}{(k-i)!(n-k-j)!}$$

$$= \sum_{j=i}^{n} M^{j-i} \frac{n!}{i!(j-i)!} \sum_{k=i}^{n-j-i} \frac{(-1)^{n-k-j+i}}{(k-i)!(n-k-j+i)!}$$

$$= \sum_{j=i}^{n} M^{j-i} \frac{n!}{i!(j-i)!} \sum_{k=0}^{n-j} \frac{(-1)^{n-k-j}}{k!(n-k-j)!}$$

$$= \sum_{j=i}^{n} M^{j-i} \frac{n!}{i!(j-i)!(n-j)!} \sum_{k=0}^{n-j} \binom{n-j}{k} (-1)^{n-j-k}$$

$$= \sum_{j=i}^{n} M^{j-i} \frac{n!}{i!(j-i)!(n-j)!} (1-1)^{n-j} = M^{n-i} \binom{n}{i}$$

which reduces (2.41) to

$$M^{1-n} \sum_{i=2}^{n} (-1)^i \hat{f}_i \frac{M^{i-1}}{M^{i-1}-1} M^{n-i} \binom{n}{i} = \sum_{i=2}^{n} (-1)^i \hat{f}_i \binom{n}{i} \frac{1}{M^{i-1}-1}$$

and by (2.39) completes the proof.   ■

Let us apply Theorem 2.6 to (2.36). Taking $\hat{f}_k = (k-1) + \delta_{k0}$, where the term δ_{k0} is added to ensure that $\hat{f}_0 = 0$, by Theorem 2.5 we get $f_k = \hat{\hat{f}}_k = 1 - \delta_{k1} - \delta_{k0}$ and by Theorem 2.6 we obtain

$$A_n = \begin{cases} 0 & n < 2 \\ 1 + M^{1-n} \sum_{k \geqslant 0} \binom{n}{k} (M-1)^{n-k} A_k & n \geqslant 2 \end{cases} \tag{2.42}$$

The average number of internal nodes in an M-ary tree defined by (2.42) helps us to estimate $E^-(n)$ and $E^+(n)$, that is, the average number of steps performed by $member(x, A)$ in an unsuccessful and a successful case, respectively. Indeed, turning back to (2.35) we see that $Ma_{nl} - a_{n(l+1)}$ is the average number of external nodes at level l, since Ma_{nl} is the average number of all nodes at level l. Thus

$$E^-(n) = \sum_{l \geqslant 0} (l+1) M^{-(l+1)} (Ma_{nl} - a_{n(l+1)})$$

$$= \sum_{l \geqslant 0} (l+1) M^{-l} a_{nl} - \sum_{l \geqslant 0} (l+1) M^{-(l+1)} a_{n(l+1)} = \sum_{l \geqslant 0} M^{-l} a_{nl}$$

$$= \sum_{l \geqslant 0} (1 - (1 - M^{-l})^n) - n \sum_{l \geqslant 0} M^{-l} (1 - M^{-l})^{n-1}$$

$$= \sum_{l \geqslant 0} \left(1 - \sum_{k \geqslant 0} \binom{n}{k} (-1)^k M^{-lk} \right)$$

$$- n \sum_{l \geqslant 0} \sum_{k \geqslant 0} \binom{n-1}{k} (-1)^k M^{-l(k+1)}$$

$$= \sum_{k \geqslant 1} \binom{n}{k} (-1)^{k+1} \frac{M^k}{M^k - 1} - n \sum_{k \geqslant 0} \binom{n-1}{k} (-1)^k \frac{M^{k+1}}{M^{k+1} - 1}$$

$$= \frac{1}{n+1} \sum_{k \geqslant 2} \binom{n+1}{k} (-1)^k \left(k - 2\binom{k}{2} \right) \frac{M^{k-1}}{M^{k-1} - 1}$$

Let $B_{n+1} = (n+1) E^-(n)$. For this variable we can apply Theorem 2.6. Let us take $\hat{f}_k = k - k(k-1) - \delta_{k1}$, then from Theorem 2.5 we have $f_k = k - \delta_{k1} - 2\delta_{k2}$ and by (2.37)

$$B_n = \begin{cases} 0 & n < 3 \\ n + M^{1-n} \displaystyle\sum_{k \geqslant 0} \binom{n}{k}(M-1)^{n-k}B_k & n \geqslant 3 \end{cases} \tag{2.43}$$

To estimate the asymptotic value of B_n we shall begin with the estimation of A_n. Suppose that

$$A_n = \frac{M(n-1)}{M-1} - \varepsilon_n \tag{2.44}$$

We shall show that $\varepsilon_n \geqslant 0$. Substituting (2.44) into (2.42) we obtain

$$\frac{M(n-1)}{M-1} - \varepsilon_n = 1 + M^{1-n} \sum_{k=1}^{n} \binom{n}{k}(M-1)^{n-k}\left(\frac{M(k-1)}{M-1} - \varepsilon_k\right)$$

which, after some simple calculations, gives

$$(1 - M^{1-n})\varepsilon_n = M - 1 - M(1 - M^{-1})^{n-1} + M^{1-n}\sum_{k=1}^{n-1}\binom{n}{k}(M-1)^{n-k}\varepsilon_k$$

Using the above equation we shall show by induction that $\varepsilon_n \geqslant 0$. For $n = 1$, $A_1 = 0$, so $\varepsilon_1 = 0$. Next $(1 - M^{-1}) \geqslant (1 - M^{-1})^{n-1}$ for $n \geqslant 2$, thus $M - 1 - M(1 - M^{-1})^{n-1} \geqslant 0$. The coefficient $(1 - M^{1-n})$ at ε_n is greater than 0, since $M^n > M$. This gives immediately that if $\varepsilon_k \geqslant 0$, $1 \leqslant k \leqslant n - 1$, then $\varepsilon_n \geqslant 0$ and immediately from (2.44) we have

$$0 \leqslant A_n \leqslant \frac{M(n-1)}{M-1} \tag{2.45}$$

Now we can focus our interests on estimating B_n. Suppose similarly to (2.44) that

$$B_n = \frac{nH_{n-1}}{\ln(M)} + \delta_n \tag{2.46}$$

and we try to prove that $\delta_n = O(n)$. Substituting (2.46) into (2.43) we obtain

$$\frac{nH_{n-1}}{\ln(M)} + \delta_n$$

$$= n + \frac{M^{1-n}}{\ln(M)}\sum_{k=1}^{n}\binom{n}{k}(M-1)^{n-k}kH_{k-1} + M^{1-n}\sum_{k=1}^{n}\binom{n}{k}(M-1)^{n-k}\delta_k$$

$$= n + \frac{n}{\ln(M)}\sum_{k=1}^{n-1}\binom{n-1}{k}(M-1)^{-k}H_k + M^{1-n}\sum_{k=1}^{n}\binom{n}{k}(M-1)^{n-k}\delta_k$$

$$\tag{2.47}$$

The whole problem consists in the first sum appearing in (2.47). Let us consider a general sum of the form

$$S_n(x) = \sum_{k=1}^{n} \binom{n}{k} x^k H_k \qquad x > 0$$

We shall show that

$$S_n(x) = (x + 1)^n (H_n - \ln(1 + x^{-1})) + \varepsilon_n \qquad \textbf{(2.48)}$$

where $0 < \varepsilon_n < 1/(n + 1)x$.

To prove that fact we shall begin with a recursive formula for $S_n(x)$:

$$S_{n+1}(x) = \sum_{k=1}^{n+1} \binom{n+1}{k} x^k H_k = \sum_{k=1}^{n} \binom{n}{k} x^k H_k + \sum_{k=1}^{n+1} \binom{n}{k-1} x^k H_k$$

$$= S_n(x) + \sum_{k=1}^{n+1} \binom{n}{k-1} x^k \left(H_{k-1} + \frac{1}{k}\right)$$

$$= S_n(x) + x \sum_{k=0}^{n} \binom{n}{k} x^k H_k + \sum_{k=1}^{n+1} \binom{n}{k-1} \frac{1}{k} x^k$$

$$= (x + 1)S_n(x) + \frac{1}{n+1} \sum_{k=1}^{n+1} \binom{n+1}{k} x^k$$

$$= (x + 1)S_n(x) + \frac{1}{n+1}((x + 1)^{n+1} - 1)$$

from which we immediately obtain

$$\frac{S_{n+1}(x)}{(x+1)^{n+1}} = \frac{S_n(x)}{(x+1)^n} + \frac{1}{n+1} - \frac{1}{(n+1)(x+1)^{n+1}}$$

and by direct induction

$$S_n(x) = (x + 1)^n \left(H_n - \sum_{k=1}^{n} \frac{1}{k(x+1)^k}\right)$$

Finally, by the expansion

$$\ln(1 + x^{-1}) = \sum_{k=1}^{n} \frac{1}{k(x+1)^k}$$

we obtain (2.48). Note that $S_{n-1}((M-1)^{-1})$ is the value of our first sum in (2.47). From (2.47) and (2.48) we have

$$\frac{nH_{n-1}}{\ln(M)} + \delta_n = n + \frac{nH_{n-1}}{\ln(M)} - n + \frac{n(1 - M^{-1})^{n-1}}{\ln(M)} \varepsilon_{n-1}$$

$$+ M^{1-n} \sum_{k=1}^{n} \binom{n}{k} (M-1)^{n-k} \delta_k$$

which, after some simple transformations, gives

$$\delta_n = M^{1-n} \sum_{k=1}^{n} \binom{n}{k} (M-1)^{n-k} \delta_k + \varepsilon'_n \qquad (2.49)$$

where

$$0 < \varepsilon'_n < \frac{(M-1)^2}{M \ln(M)}$$

since

$$\frac{n(1-M^{-1})^{n-1}}{\ln(M)} \varepsilon_{n-1} \leqslant \frac{M(1-M^{-1})^n}{\ln(M)} \leqslant \frac{(M-1)^2}{M \ln(M)}$$

Now using (2.49) we shall prove by induction that

$$0 \leqslant \delta_n \leqslant \frac{(M-1)^2 A_n}{M \ln(M)} \qquad (2.50)$$

For $n = 1$ we have $\delta_1 = B_1 - H_0/\ln(M) = B_1 = 0$ and (2.50) holds. From the inductive assumption and (2.49) we have

$$(1 - M^{1-n})\delta_n \leqslant \varepsilon'_n + M^{1-n} \sum_{k=1}^{n-1} \binom{n}{k} (M-1)^{n-k} \frac{(M-1)^2}{M \ln(M)} A_k$$

$$\leqslant \frac{(M-1)^2}{M \ln(M)} \left(1 + M^{1-n} \sum_{k=1}^{n-1} \binom{n}{k} (M-1)^{n-k} A_k \right)$$

But according to (2.42) the last sum may be replaced by $(1 - M^{1-n})A_n$, which gives the following estimations:

$$(1 - M^{1-n})\delta_n \leqslant \frac{(M-1)^2}{M \ln(M)} (1 - M^{1-n}) A_n$$

$$0 \leqslant \delta_n \leqslant \frac{(M-1)^2}{M \ln(M)} A_n$$

and using the estimation for A_n given by (2.45) we obtain

$$0 \leqslant \delta_n \leqslant \frac{(M-1)(n-1)}{\ln(M)}$$

which shows that $\delta_n = O(n)$ and our claim. From (2.46) we have

$$B_n = nH_{n-1}/\ln(M) + O(n) = n\log_M(n) + O(n)$$

Now taking into account that $E^-(n) = B_{n+1}/(n+1)$ we eventually reach our main target, that is to say

$$E^-(n) = \log_M(n) + O(1)$$

To estimate $E^+(n)$ let us introduce, as in the case of $E^-(n)$, a variable $B_n = nE^+(n)$, which defines the average cost of a search for all words in an M-ary tree of size n. Thus for this B_n we obtain a formula similar to that in (2.42)

$$B_n = \begin{cases} 0 & n < 2 \\ n + M^{1-n} \sum_{k\geq 0} \binom{n}{k}(M-1)^{n-k}B_k & n \geq 2 \end{cases}$$

since in (2.42) the term 1 represents the root when only the number of internal nodes was counted, and here n represents the root when the number of comparisons with this node is counted in the search for all n elements of A. To estimate B_n we can apply exactly the same technique as before, so we have the same asymptotic behaviour, that is

$$E^+(n) = \log_M(n) + O(1)$$

2.5 Searching in non-ordered sets

The searching problem in a non-ordered set does not differ very much conceptually from searching in an ordered set. This time the given set U is not necessarily ordered. Consequently there are no elementary operations able to test whether x is greater than y for x, $y \in U$. We can check only whether x is equal to y or not. Moreover, searching in a non-ordered set usually admits only two operations: *member*(x, A) and *insert*(x, A), where $x \in U$ and $A \subset U$, defined as in Section 2.3, that is, operation *delete*(x, A) is very seldom considered. A set A on which these two operations, *member*(x, A) and *insert*(x, A), are performed will be called a **catalogue**.

We start, as before, from the simplest algorithm called **sequential search**. The elements belonging to a set $A = \{x_1, \ldots, x_n\}$ are arranged in a linear list, as in Figure 2.2, however this time the elements $x_1, \ldots, x_n$ are not ordered. Thus, during the execution of *member*(x, A) or *insert*(x, A) the algorithm terminates when x is found or when the end of list is reached and a new element x is always added at the list end. We shall denote, as usual, by

$T^-(n)$ the random variable defining the cost of *member* in an unsuccessful case and by $T^+(n)$ the cost of *member* in a successful case, both being measured by the number of comparisons. The cost of *insert* differs from $T^-(n)$ only by a term of order $O(1)$, so its analysis reduces to that of *member*(x, A).

The probabilistic analysis of this algorithm was presented in Section 1.6. Thus we have

$$T^-(n) = n + 1, \quad E^-(n) = n + 1, \quad V^-(n) = 0, \quad D^-(n) = 0$$

and

$$E^+(n) = (n + 1)/2, \quad V^+(n) = (n^2 - 1)/12, \quad D^+(n) \cong 0.289n$$

The sequential search is evidently not very efficient. The most popular technique which enables us to speed up such a searching process is **hashing**. Suppose that instead of using a list for storing the elements of A we want to use an array $H[0 .. M - 1]$, where M is a certain chosen natural number. But how should we associate an item of H with an element x of U? The association is provided by the so-called **hash function**. It is a function $h: U \to \{0, 1, \ldots, M - 1\}$ possessing two important properties. First, the computation of $h(x)$ should be very fast, that is, it may require only a small number of elementary arithmetic operations. Moreover, h should distribute the elements of U as uniformly as possible, that is, h should take on each value from $\{0, 1, \ldots, M - 1\}$ with equal probability. Examples of good hash functions are provided by Knuth (1973). In what follows we assume that a hash function h is given.

Let us continue the algorithmic idea of the hash technique. We shall store the elements of a catalogue A in an array $H[0 .. M - 1]$. Now, for a given x we first compute $h(x) \in \{0, 1, \ldots, M - 1\}$. If position $H[h(x)]$ is empty, it means that $x \notin A$ and x may be stored at this position of H. If $H[h(x)]$ is occupied, then either $H[h(x)] = x$ or $H[h(x)] \neq x$. In the first case the searching process ends with the result *true*, in the second we encounter the so-called **collision problem**, that is, what action to take when $x \neq y$ and $h(x) = h(y)$.

For a hash function $h: U \to \{0, 1, \ldots, M - 1\}$ usually $|U| \gg M$, thus a lot of collisions may occur. The simplest technique which solves the collision problem is called **separate chaining**. It consists in maintaining in each entry $H[i]$, $i = 0, 1, \ldots, M - 1$ a linear list of elements $x \in A$ such that $h(x) = i$ (see Figure 2.7).

The algorithms implementing the idea of separate chaining are very simple, so we omit their formal definitions. Informally, the way in which *member*(x, A) and *insert*(x, A) are performed is reduced to a sequential search in the list $H[h(x)]$.

The probabilistic analysis of separate chaining may progress as follows. We start this analysis from the assumption that for a catalogue $A = \{x_1, \ldots, x_n\}$

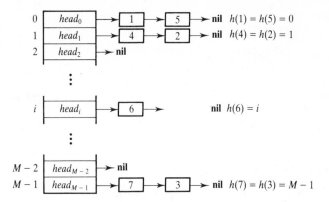

Figure 2.7   Example of a chained hash table $H[0 .. M-1]$.

the corresponding sequence of hash codes, $h_1 = h(x_1), \ldots, h_n = h(x_n)$, has the probability of occurrence $1/M^n$, that is, the probability that $h_i = j$ for $1 \leqslant i \leqslant n$ and $0 \leqslant j < M$ is $1/M$.

Let us consider $T^-(n)$. Assume that $h(x) = j$ when an unsuccessful search for x is performed. Denoting by p_{nk} the probability that the list $H[j]$ has length k we have

$$p_{nk} = \binom{n}{k}\left(\frac{1}{M}\right)^k\left(1 - \frac{1}{M}\right)^{n-k}$$

since the value j appears k times in a sequence $h_1, \ldots, h_n$ with the probability defined by the Bernoulli schema. Now we have

$$P_n^-(z) = \sum_{k \geqslant 0} p_{nk} z^{k+1}$$

which can easily be transformed to a simpler form

$$P_n^-(z) = \left(\frac{z}{M} + 1 - \frac{1}{M}\right)^n z$$

Thus differentiating $P_n^-(z)$ twice we have

$$P_n^{-\prime}(z) = \left(\frac{z}{M} + 1 - \frac{1}{M}\right)^{n-1}\left(\frac{nz}{M} + \frac{z}{M} + 1 - \frac{1}{M}\right)$$

$$P_n^{-\prime\prime}(z) = \left(\frac{z}{M} + 1 - \frac{1}{M}\right)^{n-2}\left(\frac{n-1}{M}\left(\frac{nz}{M} + \frac{z}{M} + 1 - \frac{1}{M}\right)\right.$$
$$\left. + \left(\frac{z}{M} + 1 - \frac{1}{M}\right)\left(\frac{n}{M} + \frac{1}{M}\right)\right)$$

which gives

$$P_n^{-\prime}(1) = \frac{n}{M} + 1 \qquad P_n^{-\prime\prime}(1) = \frac{n(n-1)}{M^2} + \frac{2n}{M}$$

From the above formulas we can calculate $E^-(n)$ and $V^-(n)$ as follows:

$$E^-(n) = P_n^{-\prime}(1) = \frac{n}{M} + 1$$

$$V^-(n) = P_n^{-\prime\prime}(1) + P_n^{-\prime}(1) - (P_n^{-\prime}(1))^2$$

$$= \frac{n(n-1)}{M^2} + \frac{2n}{M} + \left(\frac{n}{M} + 1\right) - \left(\frac{n}{M} + 1\right)^2$$

$$= \frac{n(M-1)}{M^2}$$

and denoting by $\alpha = n/M$, that is, the definition of table H, we immediately obtain

$$E^-(n) = \alpha + 1, \quad V^-(n) \cong \alpha, \quad D^-(n) \cong \sqrt{\alpha}$$

To estimate $E^+(n)$, that is, the average cost in a successful case, consider the function $nE^+(n)$. Its value is equal to the total number of steps performed when all n elements of A are searched for. But the list of length k contributes $\frac{1}{2}k(k+1)$ steps to the total. Consequently, since there are M lists, we have

$$nE^+(n) = M \sum_{k \geqslant 0} \frac{k(k+1)}{2} p_{nk}$$

and according to the definition of $P_n^-(z)$ we obtain

$$E^+(n) = \frac{M}{2n} \sum_{k \geqslant 0} k(k+1)p_{nk} = \frac{M}{2n} P_n^{-\prime\prime}(1) = \frac{n-1}{2M} + 1 \cong \frac{1}{2}\alpha + 1$$

It is also worth mentioning that when $M = 1$ we can obtain the formulas for $E^-(n)$ and $E^+(n)$, as in the case of the sequential search, because separate chaining reduces in this case to sequential search. The standard deviation $D^+(n)$ is, however, much harder to estimate, and moreover this calculation is not so instructive and important. It may be proved (see Knuth (1973), Exercise 6.4.37) that $D^+(n)$ is of order $O(M^{-0.5})$.

Separate chaining solves the problem of collision but wastes memory. Indeed, each stored element $x \in A$ requires an additional pointer, while not all entries of $H[0 .. M - 1]$ may be used. An elegant and still efficient technique which solves the collision problem without any additional memory is the so-called **linear open addressing**.

In linear open addressing all elements of a catalogue A are stored in an array $H[0 .. M - 1]$. The search for $x \in U$ starts from $H[h(x)]$ and goes through the consecutive entries of H in a cyclic manner, that is, for $i = h(x)$ it goes through $H[i]$, $H[i - 1]$, ..., $H[0]$, $H[M - 1]$, $H[M - 2]$, ... If during this search we encounter a free entry, it means that the search for x is unsuccessful, otherwise x had to be encountered before the first free entry and such a search is successful (see Figure 2.8). To guarantee the stop property of this algorithm, the array $H[0 .. M - 1]$ must not be filled up completely, in other words, at least one entry should be always left free.

We shall start the probabilistic analysis of this algorithm from an unsuccessful case (see Knuth (1973) Section 6.4). Let $f(M, n)$ denote the number of hash sequences $h_1, \ldots, h_n$ such that $H[0]$ remains free. Since the algorithm treats all entries of $H[0 .. M - 1]$ in the same way, $H[0]$ remains free with probability $1 - n/M$. There are M^n different hash sequences, so

$$f(M, n) = (1 - n/M)M^n$$

Next, denote by $g(M, n, k)$, where $0 < k < M$, the number of hash sequences $h_1, \ldots, h_n$ such that $H[0]$ remains free and $H[1], \ldots, H[k]$ are occupied and again $H[k + 1]$ remains free. Moreover, note that $f(k + 1, k)$

0	2
1	7
2	3
3	12
4	6
5	–

$\vdots$

$M - 4$	–
$M - 3$	10
$M - 2$	–
$M - 1$	11

Array $H[0..M - 1]$ after the sequence of insertions
$h(6) = 4,\ h(12) = 4,\ h(3) = 4,\ h(10) = M - 3,\ h(7) = 2,\ h(2) = 3,\ h(11) = 4$

Figure 2.8 Example of a hash table for linear open addressing.

denotes the number of hash sequences $h_1, \ldots, h_k, 0 \leqslant h_i < k + 1$, such that $H[0]$ remains free and $H[1], \ldots, H[k]$ are occupied, since it denotes that k elements are inserted into $H[0 .. k]$. Similarly $f(M - k - 1, n - k)$ denotes the number of hash sequences $h'_1, \ldots, h'_{n-k}, k + 1 \leqslant h'_i < M$, such that $H[k + 1]$ is free. Both hash sequences $h_1, \ldots, h_k$ and $h'_1, \ldots, h'_{n-k}$ may be merged into a single one in $\binom{n}{k}$ ways. Thus

$$g(M, n, k) = \binom{n}{k} f(k + 1, k) f(M - k - 1, n - k)$$

Let us denote by p_{nk} the probability that an unsuccessful search costs $k + 1$ steps. Since the algorithm treats all entries of array $H[0 .. M - 1]$ symmetrically we can assume that $h(x) = k$. How many hash sequences correspond to an unsuccessful case with the costs $k + 1$? Note that $g(M, n, k)$ denotes such a case when $H[k + 1]$ is free, $g(M, n, k + 1)$ denotes such a case when $H[k + 1]$ is occupied but $H[k + 2]$ is free, and so on. Since the number of all hash sequences is M^n we have

$$p_{nk} = M^{-n} \sum_{i=k}^{n} g(M, n, i) \tag{2.51}$$

From (2.51) we obtain

$$
\begin{aligned}
M^n E^-(n) &= M^n \sum_{k=0}^{n} (k + 1) p_{nk} = \sum_{k=0}^{n} (k + 1) \sum_{i=k}^{n} g(M, n, i) \\
&= \sum_{i=0}^{n} \sum_{k=0}^{i} (k + 1) g(M, n, i) = \sum_{i=0}^{n} g(M, n, i) \sum_{k=0}^{i} (k + 1) \\
&= \sum_{i=0}^{n} \binom{i + 2}{2} g(M, n, i) = \frac{1}{2} \sum_{k=0}^{n} (k + 1 + (k + 1)^2) g(M, n, k) \\
&= \frac{1}{2} \sum_{k=0}^{n} (k + 1) g(M, n, k) + \frac{1}{2} \sum_{k=0}^{n} (k + 1)^2 g(M, n, k) \tag{2.52}
\end{aligned}
$$

The first sum in (2.52) is equal to M^n. Indeed, we have

$$
\begin{aligned}
M^n &= M^n \cdot 1 = M^n \sum_{k=0}^{n} p_{nk} = M^n \sum_{k=0}^{n} M^{-n} \sum_{i=k}^{n} g(M, n, i) \\
&= \sum_{i=0}^{n} \sum_{k=0}^{i} g(M, n, i) = \sum_{k=0}^{n} (k + 1) g(M, n, k)
\end{aligned}
$$

Let us try to calculate the second sum in (2.52). Using the formulas for $f(M, n)$ and $g(M, n, k)$ we obtain

$$\sum_{k=0}^{n} (k+1)^2 g(M, n, k) = \sum_{k=0}^{n} (k+1)^2 \binom{n}{k} f(k+1, k) f(M-k-1, n-k)$$

$$= \sum_{k=0}^{n} \binom{n}{k} (k+1)^{k+1} (M-k-1)^{n-k-1} (M-n-1)$$

$$(2.53)$$

The sum appearing in (2.53) is a special case of a formula

$$s(n, x, y) = \sum_{k=0}^{n} \binom{n}{k} (x+k)^{k+1} (y-k)^{n-k-1} (y-n) \qquad (2.54)$$

since it is equal to $s(n, l, M-1)$. To find a simpler formula for $s(n, x, y)$ we shall apply Abel's binomial theorem.

Theorem 2.7

$$(x+y)^n = \sum_{k=0}^{n} \binom{n}{k} x(x-kz)^{k-1} (y+kz)^{n-k} \qquad z \neq 0$$

Proof   Consider first the case $x + y = 0$. Thus $y = -x$ and

$$\sum_{k=0}^{n} \binom{n}{k} x(x-kz)^{k-1} (-x+kz)^{n-k}$$

$$= x \sum_{k=0}^{n} \binom{n}{k} (-1)^{n-k} (x-kz)^{n-1}$$

$$= x \sum_{k=0}^{n} \binom{n}{k} (-1)^{n-k} \sum_{i=0}^{n-1} (-1)^i \binom{n-1}{i} x^i (kz)^{n-i-1}$$

$$= x \sum_{i=0}^{n-1} (-1)^i \binom{n-1}{i} x^i z^{n-i-1} \sum_{k=0}^{n} \binom{n}{k} (-1)^{n-k} k^{n-i-1}$$

$$= x \sum_{i=0}^{n-1} (-1)^i \binom{n-1}{i} x^i z^{n-i-1} \sum_{k=0}^{n} \binom{n}{k} (-1)^k (n-k)^{n-i-1}$$

The inner sums appearing in the above formula

$$\sum_{k=0}^{n} \binom{n}{k} (-1)^k (n-k)^m$$

are well known from combinatorics. They are called de Morgan numbers and designate the number of surjections from an m-element set on to an n-element set. However, in this case, all of them are equal to 0, because $m = n - 1, \ldots, 0$. Thus for $x + y = 0$ the right-hand side of Abel's formula is δ_{n0}.

Consider now a general case which we shall try to reduce to this special one. Substitute y by $x + y - x$. Then we have

$$\sum_{k=0}^{n} \binom{n}{k} x(x - kz)^{k-1}(x + y - x + kz)^{n-k}$$

$$= \sum_{k=0}^{n} \binom{n}{n-k} x(x - kz)^{k-1} \sum_{r=0}^{n-k} \binom{n-k}{r}(x + y)^r(-x + kz)^{n-k-r}$$

$$= \sum_{r=0}^{n} \binom{n}{r}(x + y)^r \sum_{k=0}^{n-r} \binom{n-r}{n-r-k} x(x - kz)^{k-1}(-x + kz)^{n-k-r}$$

because

$$\binom{n}{n-k}\binom{n-k}{r} = \binom{n}{r}\binom{n-r}{n-r-k}$$

Now the inner sum corresponds to the special case of Abel's formula and equals $\delta_{n-r,0}$. Consequently

$$\sum_{k=0}^{n} \binom{n}{k} x(x - kz)^{k-1}(y + kz)^{n-k}$$

$$= \sum_{k=0}^{n} \binom{n}{k} x(x - kz)^{k-1}(x + y - x + kz)^{n-k}$$

$$= \sum_{r=0}^{n} \binom{n}{r}(x + y)^r \delta_{n-r,0} = (x + y)^n \qquad \blacksquare$$

Using Abel's binomial theorem we shall prove the following recursive formula for $s(n, x, y)$:

$$s(0, x, y) = x$$
$$s(n, x, y) = x(x + y)^n + ns(n - 1, x + 1, y - 1) \qquad \textbf{(2.55)}$$

The boundary condition $s(0, x, y) = x$ follows directly from definition (2.54). Using the same definition we obtain

$$s(n, x, y) = \sum_{k=0}^{n} \binom{n}{k}(x + k)^{k+1}(y - k)^{n-k-1}(y - n)$$

$$= \sum_{k=0}^{n} \binom{n}{k} x(x + k)^k(y - k)^{n-k-1}(y - n)$$

$$+ \sum_{k=0}^{n} \binom{n}{k} k(x + k)^k(y - k)^{n-k-1}(y - n)$$

$$= x \sum_{k=0}^{n} \binom{n}{k}(x + n - k)^{n-k}(y - n + k)^{k-1}(y - n)$$

$$+ n \sum_{k=1}^{n} \binom{n-1}{k-1}(x + k)^k(y - k)^{n-k-1}(y - n) \qquad \textbf{(2.56)}$$

Now, if in Abel's binomial formula we replace x by $y - n$, y by $x + n$ and z by -1, the first term in (2.56) will be reduced to $x(x + y)^n$. Moving down by -1 the summation parameter k in the second term of (2.56) we obtain $ns(n - 1, x + 1, y - 1)$, which eventually proves (2.55).

We have already observed that (2.53) is equal to $s(n, 1, M - 1)$, which, according to the recursive formula (2.55), satisfies:

$$s(n, 1, M - 1) = M^n \sum_{k=0}^{n} (k + 1) \frac{(n)_k}{M^k}$$

where $(n)_k = n(n - 1) \ldots (n - k + 1)$. The above summation formula is a special case of

$$Q_r(n, M) = \sum_{k=0}^{n} \binom{r + k}{k} \frac{(n)_k}{M^k} \tag{2.57}$$

From (2.52) and (2.57) we immediately obtain

$$E^-(n) = \tfrac{1}{2}(1 + Q_1(n, M)) \tag{2.58}$$

Before we find the similar formulas for $E^+(n)$, $V^-(n)$ and $V^+(n)$, we shall prove a couple of facts concerning the functions $Q_r(n, M)$. They help us to deal with the summation forms akin to (2.58). Let us start this sequence of facts from

$$Q_r(n, M) = Q_{r-1}(n, M) + \frac{n}{M} Q_r(n - 1, M) \tag{2.59}$$

To prove (2.59) we can use definition (2.57) directly. Indeed, we have

$$Q_r(n, M) = \sum_{k=0}^{n} \binom{r + k}{k} \frac{(n)_k}{M^k}$$

$$= \sum_{k=0}^{n} \binom{r + k - 1}{k} \frac{(n)_k}{M^k} + \sum_{k=1}^{n} \binom{r + k - 1}{k - 1} \frac{(n)_k}{M^k}$$

$$= Q_{r-1}(n, M) + \sum_{k=0}^{n-1} \binom{r + k}{k} \frac{(n)_{k-1}}{M^{k+1}}$$

$$= Q_{r-1}(n, M) + \frac{n}{M} Q_r(n - 1, M)$$

which proves (2.59). By iterating (2.59) we immediately obtain

$$Q_r(n, M) = \sum_{k=0}^{n} \frac{(n)_k}{M^k} Q_{r-1}(n - k, M) \tag{2.60}$$

From (2.57) and (2.60) we have

$$\begin{aligned}
Q_r(n, M) &= \sum_{k=0}^{n} \frac{(n)_k}{M^k} Q_{r-1}(n - k, M) \\
&= \sum_{k=0}^{n} \frac{(n)_k}{M^k} \sum_{i=0}^{n-k} \frac{(n - k)_i}{M^i} Q_{r-2}(n - k - i, M) \\
&= \sum_{k=0}^{n} \sum_{j=k}^{n} \frac{(n)_j}{M^j} Q_{r-2}(n - j, M) \\
&= \sum_{j=0}^{n} \frac{(n)_j}{M^j} Q_{r-2}(n - j, M) \sum_{k=0}^{j} 1 \\
&= \sum_{j=0}^{n} \frac{(n)_j}{M^j} Q_{r-2}(n - j, M)(j + 1) \tag{2.61}
\end{aligned}$$

If we now apply (2.60) to (2.61), by the same technique as above, we obtain

$$Q_r(n, M) = \frac{1}{2} \sum_{k=0}^{n} (k + 1)(k + 2) \frac{(n)_k}{M^k} Q_{r-3}(n - k, M)$$

which, by observing that

$$k(k + 1) = 2 \frac{(k + 1)(k + 2)}{2} - 2(k + 1)$$

gives

$$2Q_r(n, M) - 2Q_{r-1}(n, M) = \sum_{k=0}^{n} k(k + 1) \frac{(n)_k}{M^k} Q_{r-3}(n - k, M) \tag{2.62}$$

The last equation concerning the functions $Q_r(n, M)$ has the following form:

$$\sum_{k=0}^{n-1} Q_r(k, M) = \frac{n}{r} Q_{r-1}(n - 1, M) + \frac{M}{r} (Q_{r-2}(n, M) - 1) \tag{2.63}$$

The proof of (2.63) needs the equation

$$\sum_{k=0}^{n-1} (k)_i = \frac{(n)_{i-1}}{i+1}$$

which can be easily shown by induction. By the above we obtain

$$\sum_{k=0}^{n-1} Q_r(k, M) = \sum_{k=0}^{n-1} \sum_{i=0}^{k} \binom{r+i}{i} \frac{(k)_i}{M^i} = \sum_{i=0}^{n-1} \binom{r+i}{i} \frac{1}{M^i} \sum_{k=i}^{n-1} (k)_i$$

$$= \sum_{i=0}^{n-1} \binom{r+i}{i} \frac{1}{i+1} \frac{(n)_{i-1}}{M^i}$$

$$= \frac{M}{r} \left(\sum_{i=0}^{n} \binom{r-1+i}{i} \frac{(n)_i}{M^i} - 1 \right)$$

$$= \frac{M}{r} (Q_{r-1}(n, M) - 1)$$

and using (2.59) we have

$$\frac{M}{r} (Q_{r-1}(n, M) - 1) = \frac{1}{r} (MQ_{r-1}(n, M) - M)$$

$$= \frac{1}{r} (nQ_{r-1}(n-1, M) + M(Q_{r-2}(n, M) - 1))$$

which proves (2.63).

Equation (2.63) for $r = 1$ gives

$$\sum_{k=0}^{n-1} Q_1(k, M) = nQ_0(n-1, M)$$

which enables us to calculate $E^+(n)$. Indeed, observe that the searched-for element could be inserted as a first one with the probability $1/n$, as a second one with the probability $1/n$ and so on. Moreover, for the linear hash algorithm inserted elements do not change their positions. Consequently, the average cost of searching in a successful case is

$$E^+(n) = \frac{1}{n} \sum_{k=0}^{n-1} E^-(k)$$

which shows that

$$E^+(n) = \tfrac{1}{2}(1 + Q_0(n-1, M)) \tag{2.64}$$

With $V^-(n)$ we proceed in a similar way to $E^-(n)$. Namely

$$M^n V^-(n) = M^n \sum_{k=0}^{n} (k + 1 - E^-(n))^2 p_{nk}$$

$$= M^n \sum_{k=0}^{n} (k + 1)^2 p_{nk} - M^n (E^-(n))^2$$

$$= \sum_{i=0}^{n} g(M, n, i) \sum_{k=0}^{i} (k + 1)^2 - M^n (E^-(n))^2$$

$$= \frac{1}{3} \sum_{k=0}^{n} g(M, n, k)(k + 1)^3 + \frac{1}{2} \sum_{k=0}^{n} g(M, n, k)(k + 1)^2$$

$$+ \frac{1}{6} \sum_{k=0}^{n} g(M, n, k)(k + 1) - M^n (E^-(n))^2 \qquad \textbf{(2.65)}$$

In (2.65) the third sum is equal to M^n and the second one is equal to $s(n, 1, M - 1)$. Both facts were proved in connection with (2.58). To find a simpler formula for the first sum we note that it is equal to $t(n, 1, M - 1)$ where

$$t(n, x, y) = \sum_{k=0}^{n} \binom{n}{k} (x + k)^{k+2} (y - k)^{n-k-1} (y - n)$$

and as it was in (2.55) we can prove that

$$t(n, x, y) = xs(n, x, y) + nt(n - 1, x + 1, y - 1)$$

Using this recursive equation we obtain

$$t(n, 1, M) = \sum_{k=0}^{n} (k + 1)(n)_k s(n - k, k + 1, M - k - 1) \qquad \textbf{(2.66)}$$

But from (2.55)

$$s(n - k, k + 1, M - k - 1) = M^{n-k} \sum_{i=0}^{n-k} (k + i + 1) \frac{(n - k)_i}{M^i}$$

$$= M^{n-k}(kQ_0(n - k, M) + Q_1(n - k, M))$$

Hence (2.66) by (2.61) and (2.62) reduces to

$$t(n, 1, M - 1) = M^n \sum_{k=0}^{n} k(k + 1) \frac{(n)_k}{M^k} Q_0(n - k, M)$$

$$+ M^n \sum_{k=0}^{n} (k + 1) \frac{(n)_k}{M^k} Q_1(n - k, M)$$

$$= M^n (3Q_3(n, M) - 2Q_2(n, M))$$

From (2.65) and taking everything together we obtain

$$V^-(n) = Q_3(n, M) - \tfrac{2}{3}Q_2(n, M) + \tfrac{1}{2}Q_1(n, M) + \tfrac{1}{6} - \tfrac{1}{4}(1 + Q_1(n, M))^2$$
$$= Q_3(n, M) - \tfrac{2}{3}Q_2(n, M) - \tfrac{1}{4}(Q_1(n, M))^2 - \tfrac{1}{12} \qquad (2.67)$$

Similarly to $V^-(n)$ it can be proved that

$$V^+(n) = \tfrac{1}{3}Q_2(n - 1, M) - \tfrac{1}{4}(Q_0(n - 1, M))^2 \qquad (2.68)$$

however this proof is left as an exercise.

The asymptotic values for $E^-(n)$, $E^+(n)$, $V^-(n)$ and $V^+(n)$ can be found by estimating $Q_r(n, M)$ with respect to the load factor $\alpha = n/M$. Let us expand the function $(n)_k = n(n - 1) \cdots (n - k + 1)$. It is a polynomial of degree k with first coefficient equal to 1 and the next one equal to $\binom{k}{2}$.

Thus

$$n^k - \binom{k}{2}n^{k-1} \leqslant (n)_k \leqslant n^k$$

and from (2.57)

$$\sum_{k=0}^{\infty}\binom{r+k}{k}\left(n^k - \binom{k}{2}n^{k-1}\right)\frac{1}{M^k} \leqslant Q_r(n, M) \leqslant \sum_{k=0}^{\infty}\binom{r+k}{k}\left(\frac{n}{M}\right)^k$$

For $\alpha < 1$ we have $\sum \alpha^k = 1/(1 - \alpha)$ and differentiating the series r times we obtain

$$\frac{1}{(1 - \alpha)^{r+1}} - \frac{1}{M}\binom{r+2}{2}\frac{\alpha}{(1 - \alpha)^{r+3}} \leqslant Q_r(n, M) \leqslant \frac{1}{(1 - \alpha)^{r+1}}$$

which shows that for large M and α not very close to 1 we have $Q_r(n, M) \cong (1 - \alpha)^{-(r+1)}$. Finally, we are ready to give the asymptotic formulas for the mean values and the standard deviations of the cost function of the analysed algorithm. From (2.58), (2.64), (2.67) and (2.68) we have

$$E^-(n) \cong \tfrac{1}{2}(1 + (1 - \alpha)^{-2})$$
$$E^+(n) \cong \tfrac{1}{2}(1 + (1 - \alpha)^{-1})$$
$$V^-(n) \cong \tfrac{3}{4}(1 - \alpha)^{-4} - \tfrac{2}{3}(1 - \alpha)^{-3} - \tfrac{1}{12}$$
$$V^+(n) \cong \tfrac{1}{3}(1 - \alpha)^{-3} - \tfrac{1}{4}(1 - \alpha)^{-2}$$

From $V^-(n)$ and $V^+(n)$ we can estimate the standard deviations, namely $D^-(n) < 0.86(1 - \alpha)^{-2}$ and $D^+(n) < 0.54(1 - \alpha)^{-1.5}$. This shows that the random variables $T^-(n)$ and $T^+(n)$ are not well concentrated around their mean values, especially when α is close to 1: for example, taking $\alpha = 0.9$ we have $E^-(n) \cong 60.5$, while $D^-(n) = 86$, and $E^+(n) \cong 5.5$, while $D^+(n) \cong 17$.

Knuth (1973) is a kind of bible for specialists in probabilistic analysis of algorithms. Most of the theorems, proofs and examples appearing in this chapter are taken from Knuth's book (we can only be exegetes in this context).

Sedgewick (1977) presents a deep analysis of *Quicksort* and this analysis was used as a basis for Section 2.2.

For more advanced mathematical techniques used for the analysis of algorithms, see Greene and Knuth (1981).

The reader who wishes to know how to construct good hash functions will find interesting results not only in Knuth (1973) but also in Carter and Weyman (1979).

SUMMARY

Key points covered in this chapter include:

- the permutation model for the sorting problem
- probabilistic analysis of *Insertionsort*
- probabilistic analysis of *Quicksort*
- probabilistic analysis of searching in ordered lists
- probabilistic analysis of binary search trees
- Hibbard's theorem
- probabilistic analysis of digital search
- probabilistic analysis of searching in non-ordered lists
- the method of hash functions
- probabilistic analysis of separate chaining
- probabilistic analysis of linear open addressing.

EXERCISES

2.1 Applying the theorems about the product of generating functions (Exercises 1.21 and 1.22), find the values of $E(n)$, $V(n)$ and $D(n)$ for a random variable $T(n)$ whose generating function $P_n(z)$ is

(a) $\prod_{k=1}^{n} \frac{(k-1)z + 1}{k}$ (b) $\prod_{k=1}^{n} \frac{1 + z + \cdots + z^{k-1}}{k}$

(c) $\prod_{k=1}^{n} \frac{z - 1 + k}{k}$

2.2   Using the results of Exercise 2.1 prove (2.5) and (2.6).

2.3   Prove that the algorithm *Select* from Section 1.9 has average time complexity $\Theta(n)$.

2.4   Prove that the worst-case time complexity of *Quicksort* is $\Theta(n^2)$.

2.5   Analyse the execution of the algorithm *Quicksort* for $a[1 .. n]$ with equal elements. Explain why the small repeat loops have the exit conditions $a[i] \geqslant v$ and $v \geqslant a[j]$, instead of $a[i] > v$ and $v > a[j]$.

2.6   Using the generating function $P_n(z)$ defined by (2.9), compute the distribution of a random variable defining the cost of *Quicksort* for $n = 5, 6$ and 7.

2.7   Solve the recursive equation (2.10) directly, that is, without the technique of generating functions.

2.8*   Since *Insertionsort* is the best sorting algorithm for short sequences, a good technique which improves *Quicksort* performance consists in using *Insertionsort* instead of recursive calling of *Quicksort* for $n \leqslant M$, where M is a given constant. Show that the average number of comparisons performed by such a modification of *Quicksort* is $(n + 1)(2H_{n+1} - 2H_{M+2} + 1) + \Theta(n)$ for $n > M$.

2.9   The term $\Theta(n)$ in the formula from the previous exercise includes the average total number of comparisons performed by *Insertionsort*. Prove that this value is of order $(M/6)(n + 1)$.

2.10   A good choice of the value of M in the algorithm from Exercise 2.8 may substantially increase the efficiency of *Quicksort* (in practice even up to 20%). Prove that the optimal value of M is 10, if we assume only the theoretical costs calculated in Exercises 2.8 and 2.9.

2.11   Write a Pascal implementation of the algorithm from Exercise 2.8 and run it on a computer. Try to estimate the optimal value of M according to the performed experiments and compare it with the theoretical result obtained in Exercise 2.10.

2.12   Write in Pascal the complete definition of the operations *member*, *insert* and *delete* for searching in ordered linear lists.

2.13   The algorithm which searches for an element in an ordered array $a[1 .. n]$ in $O(\log n)$ steps (see Exercise 1.16) is called *binary search*. Examine whether this method is useful for the implementation of all three operations *member*, *insert* and *delete*.

2.14 Perform the probabilistic analysis of the algorithm *binary* search, that is, estimate $E^-(n)$, $E^+(n)$, $D^-(n)$ and $D^+(n)$.

2.15 Write in Pascal the complete definition of the operation *delete* in binary search trees.

2.16 What is the probability that the operation *insert* performs exactly k comparisons during the insertion into an $n - 1$ element binary search tree?

2.17 Write in Pascal the complete definition of the operations *member* and *insert* in the case of a digital search.

2.18* Estimate $E^+(n)$ for an M-ary digital search in a similar way as was done for $E^-(n)$.

2.19 Write in Pascal the declaration of the operations *member* and *insert* in the case of a search in a non-ordered list.

2.20 Write in Pascal the complete definition of the hash chaining algorithms.

2.21 Prove that $D^-(n) \leqslant 0.5E^-(n)$ and $D^+(n) \leqslant 0.6E^+(n)$ hold for hash chaining algorithms.

2.22 Prove the recursive equation

$$t(n, x, y) = xs(n, x, y) + nt(n - 1, x + 1, y - 1)$$

where

$$t(n, x, y) = \sum_{k=0}^{n} \binom{n}{k} (x + k)^{k+2} (y - k)^{n-k-1} (y - n)$$

2.23 Prove formula (2.68) defining the variance $V^+(n)$ in the case of a linear open addressing.

Chapter 3
Optimality Considerations in Data Structures – Part 1

This chapter presents selected topics concerning the complexity of the dictionary problem. Three different solutions are considered and proved to be optimal in respective classes of algorithms. These solutions are: lists with move-to-front heuristic, self-adjusting binary search trees and biparental heaps (beaps).

3.1 Introduction

The optimality of algorithms and data structures is one of the main problems in the analysis of algorithms. One part of this problem is the construction of an algorithm or a data structure and the estimation of the number of operations which are executed. The other part of the optimality problem consists in finding a lower bound on the number of operations performed by any algorithm from a given class. This part is much harder and less understood; the number of related publications is relatively small as compared to the huge quantity of literature associated with the constructive part.

Several typical problems related to the optimality and lower bounds for algorithms operating on data structures will be considered. In this context one can speak about optimal data structures and lower bounds for the complexity of data structures. Some concrete and practically useful data structures are presented together with the proof of their optimality in corresponding classes of data structures. The topic is divided into two parts which are presented in this chapter and the next one.

In this chapter the complexity of the dictionary problem is analysed. The dictionary is a fundamental data structure. It supports sequences of the following operations: find an element in a set, insert or delete an element from a set (instead of 'element' and 'set' in computer science the terminology of 'record' and 'file' is also used).

In Section 3.2 a list solution for the dictionary problem is considered; it is given by the algorithm operating on the list of elements in such a way that at the moment of accessing an element it is moved to the beginning of the list. We also prove that the above solution of the dictionary problem is optimal in the class of list solutions of the dictionary problem. It is our first example of a self-organizing data structure. Such data structures adapt themselves to the input sequence of requests on-line. Frequently used elements are placed at the beginning of the list, which decreases the complexity of their access. Moreover, such a self-adjustment is done without the use of any auxiliary information, such as counters of the frequencies.

In Section 3.3 the solution of the dictionary problem by means of self-organizing binary search trees is presented. The accessed element is moved to the root of the tree by a sequence of rotations. In this way, frequently accessed elements stay near the root of the tree which guarantees fast access to them. It is proved that:

(1) The worst-case complexity of performing m operations is $O(m \log n)$, where n is the maximum cardinality of the set.

(2) Self-organizing binary search trees are optimal in the class of static solutions of the dictionary problem by means of binary search trees.

In Section 3.4 we consider a solution to the dictionary problem which uses the minimum possible amount of memory (only $O(1)$ auxiliary simple variables besides a table containing the elements of the set). The optimality (in the sense of time complexity) of the presented solution is proved in a certain class of solutions to the dictionary problem. The proof relies on the combinatorial theorem of Dilworth (1950).

3.2 Self-organizing lists

Let L be an infinite set with a relation ' $<$ ' of linear order. Throughout this chapter the elements of sets come from L. The **dictionary problem** is concerned with the design of a data structure supporting the execution of sequences of the following three types of operations (S is here a finite subset of L, and e is an element of L):

(1) *access* (e, S):: locate element e in the set S[†]

(2) *insert* (e, S):: insert element e into the set S

(3) *delete* (e, S):: delete element e from the set S

[†] Strictly speaking, this operation can only be defined in a computer implementation (at the abstract level one can only ask whether or not an element is present in the set S).

We assume that initially S is empty. The maximum cardinality of S will be denoted by n, and the number of operations in a given input sequence by m.

Now we shall define the class of list solutions to the dictionary problem and the cost of each of the operations. The solutions will be characterized by means of sequences of transpositions, that is, exchanges of adjacent elements in the list.

The set S is represented by a list.[†] The dictionary operations in the list representation are implemented according to the following schemes.

access (e, S)::
    searching: traverse the list S from the beginning until element e is encountered;

    transpositions: a number of transpositions of adjacent elements on the list is performed.

insert(e, S)::
    searching;
    insertion: e is appended to the end of the list S;
    transpositions.

delete(e, S)::
    searching;
    deletion: e is deleted from the list S;
    transpositions.

The implementation of the operations *searching, insertion,* and *deletion* is common to all list solutions. The only difference between any two list solutions is with respect to the implementation of the operation *transpositions*.

Our aim is to investigate what transpositions are to be made to minimize the total cost of the execution of a sequence of the operations: *access, insert,* and *delete* (a precise definition of the cost function will be given after considering some examples). The examples of solutions used in practice are:

(1) *elementary solution* B: no transpositions are made;

(2) *'move-to-front'* MF: when executing the operations *access* and *insert* the element involved is moved to the front of the list S (by performing a suitable number of transpositions moving this element to the front);

(3) *'transpose'* TR: when executing the operation *access* the element involved is moved one position towards the front of the list (performing one transposition), and when executing *insert* the element is placed before the last element of the list.

[†] By S we denote both a finite subset of elements and a data structure (e.g. a list, a tree etc.) representing the set S. The context will always determine uniquely the exact meaning of S.

(4) *'frequency counter'* FC: for each element e we remember how many times e was an argument of the operations *insertion* and *access*, that is, we maintain the frequency count for each element. The list S is always kept sorted with respect to the frequencies of elements.

For example, let us consider the results of performing the following sequence σ of operations:

insert $(1, S)$; *insert*$(2, S)$; *insert*$(3, S)$; *insert*$(4, S)$; *access*$(1, S)$;

access$(4, S)$; *access*$(3, S)$; *access*$(4, S)$; *access*$(2, S)$; *access*$(4, S)$.

We obtain the computations shown in Table 3.1.

We leave it as an exercise for the reader to program in Pascal the solutions described above.

The solutions MF, TR and FC are examples of data structures which adjust themselves to the input sequences of operations. This means that the elements frequently involved in the operations tend either to be in the initial part of the list S or to move towards the front of the list S. Access to these elements becomes faster and faster because the list adjusts itself to the frequencies of accessing the elements.

Let A be an arbitrary list solution to the dictionary problem. By the **cost** $COST_A(u)$ of a sequence $u = u_1, u_2, \ldots, u_m$ of operations in the solution A we mean the sum of costs of consecutive operations $u_i, 1 \leqslant i \leqslant m$. In turn, the cost of a single dictionary operation is defined to be the cost of all operations *searching*, *insertion*, *deletion* and *transpositions* performed during the execution of the dictionary operation involved.

The cost of the operation *searching* equals i, where i is the position on the list S of the element e (counting from the front of the list). The cost of the operations *insertion* and *deletion* equals 1. In order to define the cost of

Table 3.1 The computations of S produced by the four solutions.

B	MF	TR	FC
( )	( )	( )	( )
(1)	(1)	(1)	(1)
(1 2)	(2 1)	(2 1)	(1 2)
(1 2 3)	(3 2 1)	(2 3 1)	(1 2 3)
(1 2 3 4)	(4 3 2 1)	(2 3 4 1)	(1 2 3 4)
(1 2 3 4)	(1 4 3 2)	(2 3 1 4)	(1 2 3 4)
(1 2 3 4)	(4 1 3 2)	(2 3 4 1)	(1 4 2 3)
(1 2 3 4)	(3 4 1 2)	(3 2 4 1)	(1 4 3 2)
(1 2 3 4)	(4 3 1 2)	(3 4 2 1)	(4 1 3 2)
(1 2 3 4)	(2 4 3 1)	(3 2 4 1)	(4 1 3 2)
(1 2 3 4)	(4 2 3 1)	(3 4 2 1)	(4 1 3 2)

the operation *transpositions* we distinguish between two types of exchange of pairs of consecutive elements. An exchange is called **free** if it involves element e moving in the direction of the front of the list; otherwise, it is called **paid**. The cost of the operation *transpositions* is defined to be the number of paid exchanges performed during the execution of this operation. The reason for differentiating two kinds of exchange is that the cost related to free exchanges is covered already by the cost of the associated operation *searching* when all the elements preceding e on the list are visited.

It should be obvious that $COST_A(u)$ is proportional to the time of execution of u on a computer.

Now we shall prove a theorem about the optimality (within a constant factor) of the solution MF in the class of all list solutions.

Theorem 3.1

For each list solution A and each sequence of operations u the following holds:

$$COST_{MF}(u) \leqslant 2 \, COST_A(u)$$

Proof Let $u = u_1, u_2, \ldots, u_m$ be a sequence of dictionary operations. In the proof we shall apply the so-called **book-keeping** method for cost estimation. Let us consider the execution of u simultaneously in both the solutions A and MF. Assume that in MF the following lists are successively built:

$$S_0, S_1, \ldots, S_m$$

while in A

$$S'_0, S'_1, \ldots, S'_m$$

where S_0 and S'_0 are the initial empty lists, and S_i and S'_i are the lists after performing the ith operation u_i, for $1 \leqslant i \leqslant m$, in the methods MF and A, respectively.

Let S and S' be two lists containing the same elements. By an (S, S') **inversion** we mean a pair of elements e, e' such that

(1) e precedes e' in S'
(2) e follows e' in S

Let $C(S, S')$ denote the number of all (S, S') inversions.

Let t_i and t'_i denote the cost of u_i in the methods MF and A, respectively, and let $c_i = C(S_i, S'_i)$ for $0 \leqslant i \leqslant m$. The number c_i is called the **credit of the list** S_i. The number $v_i = t_i + c_i - c_{i-1}$ is called the **credit of the operation** u_i, $1 \leqslant i \leqslant m$.

Observe that

$$\sum_{i=1}^{m} v_i = \sum_{i=1}^{m} t_i + \sum_{i=1}^{m} (c_i - c_{i-1}) = \sum_{i=1}^{m} t_i + (c_m - c_0)$$

Since $c_0 = 0$ and $c_m \geqslant 0$ then

$$COST_{MF}(u) = \sum_{i=1}^{m} t_i = \sum_{i=1}^{m} v_i - c_m \leqslant \sum_{i=1}^{m} v_i \qquad (3.1)$$

Consequently, to estimate from the above the cost of the sequence u in the solution MF, it is sufficient to find an upper bound on the sum of credits associated with the consecutive operations in u.

Let us consider the case when $u_i = access(e, S)$. Assume that e is the jth element in S'_{i-1} and the kth element in S_{i-1}. Observe that $t_i = k$. Let p be the number of elements preceding e in S_{i-1} which appear after e in S'_{i-1} (see Figure 3.1).

The shift of e to the front of S_{i-1} changes by $-p + (k - 1 - p) = k - 1 - 2p$, the number of inversions with respect to e. Note that $k - p \leqslant j$, hence:

$$t_i + C(S_i, S'_{i-1}) - C(S_{i-1}, S'_{i-1}) = 2(k - p) - 1 \leqslant 2j - 1 \qquad (3.2)$$

Now consider the transformation of the list S'_{i-1} into S'_i by the operation u_i in the method A. One exchange of adjacent elements increases at most by 1 the number of (S_i, S^*) inversions where S^* is the consecutive list built by the solution A. Therefore the inequality (3.2) implies:

$$v_i = t_i + c_i - c_{i-1} = t_i + C(S_i, S'_i) - C(S_{i-1}, S'_{i-1})$$

$$= (t_i + C(S_i, S'_{i-1}) - C(S_{i-1}, S'_{i-1})) + C(S_i, S'_i) - C(S_i, S'_{i-1}))$$

$$\leqslant 2j - 1 + \text{the number of paid transpositions performed by } u_i \text{ in } A$$

$$\leqslant 2t'_i \qquad (3.3)$$

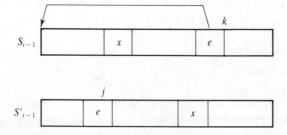

Figure 3.1   The lists S_{i-1} and S'_{i-1} in the proof of Theorem 3.1. The elements x which precede e in S_{i-1} and follow e in S'_{i-1} are counted.

In the cases when $u_i = insert(e, S)$ and $u_i = delete(e, S)$ it can be proved in a similar way that $v_i \leqslant 2t'_i$ (see Exercise 3.2). Hence by (3.1) it follows that

$$COST_{MF}(u) \leqslant 2COST_A(u)$$ ∎

Theorem 3.1 states that for every sequence of operations the method MF is, within a constant factor, at least as efficient as any other list solution. This also includes the list solutions which know a priori the distribution of frequencies of accesses to the elements.

None of the solutions B, TR and FC has this property. Specifically, Theorem 3.2 holds.

Theorem 3.2

The list solutions B, TR and FC are not optimal within a constant factor, that is, there is no constant $c > 0$ such that for every list solution A and for every sequence of operations u the following inequality holds:

$$COST_X(u) \leqslant cCOST_A(u) \quad \text{for} \quad X = \text{B, TR, FC}$$

Proof For the case $X = \text{B}$, see Exercise 3.4.

For the method TR, the counter-example is a sequence u consisting of n operations *insert* constructing a list of n elements, followed by $m - n$ operations *access* whose arguments are alternately the last two elements in the list. Assume that $m \geqslant n^2$. Then

$$COST_{TR}(u) = \sum_{i=1}^{n} i + (m - n)n = \tfrac{1}{2}n(n + 1)$$

$$+ (m - n)n \geqslant mn - \tfrac{1}{2}n^2 \geqslant (\tfrac{1}{2}n)m$$

and for $X = \text{MF}$

$$COST_{MF}(u) = \sum_{i=1}^{n} i + 2(m - n)$$

$$= 2m + \tfrac{1}{2}n(n + 1) - 2n \leqslant 2m + \tfrac{1}{2}n^2 \leqslant \tfrac{5}{2}m$$

For the method FC, the counter-example is the sequence u acting in the following way. Insert the first element into the list, then access this element $n - 1$ times. Next, insert the second element and access it $n - 2$ times, and so on. Finally, insert the nth element and access it $n - n$ times (no accesses). For such a sequence the method FC does not change the order of the list. It inserts only the current element at the end of the list. Hence $m = n(n + 1)/2$ and

$$COST_{FC}(u) = \sum_{i=1}^{n} (n + 1 - i)i = \tfrac{1}{2}(n + 1)n(n + 1) - \tfrac{1}{6}n(n + 1)(2n + 1)$$

$$= \tfrac{1}{6}n(n + 1)(n + 2) = \tfrac{1}{3}(n + 2)m$$

and for $X = $ MF

$$COST_{MF}(u) = \sum_{i=1}^{n} i + (m - n) = \tfrac{1}{2}n(n + 1) + (m - n) \leqslant 2m \qquad \blacksquare$$

Using Theorem 3.1 we shall show that all four solutions B, MF, TR and FC are optimal, within a constant factor, with respect to the worst-case cost as a function of n and m.

Theorem 3.3

Let A be an arbitrary list solution. Then

(1) if A is one of the solutions B, MF, TR or FC and u is a sequence of m operations on n elements, where $1 \leqslant n \leqslant m$, then

$$COST_A(u) = O(mn)$$

(2) $\max_{u} COST_A(u) = \Omega(mn)$

where the maximum is over all sequences u of m operations on n elements, $1 \leqslant n \leqslant m$.

Proof   First we assume that A is one of B, MF, TR or FC.

The cost of a single operation is $O(n)$ because the length of the list S is at most n. Hence the cost of any sequence of m operations is $O(mn)$.

On the other hand, we can construct a sequence requiring cost $\Omega(mn)$ in the following way. Let $m = 2n$. First we perform n operations *insert* which creates a list S of length n. Next we perform $m - n$ operations *access* always concerning the last element in the current list. Hence point (2) holds for $A = $ B, MF, TR and FC. By Theorem 3.1 method MF is optimal within the factor 2 in the class of all list solutions (also such list solutions that know the whole input sequence in advance). Hence point (2) holds for any list solution A. $\blacksquare$

Theorems 3.1, 3.2, and 3.3 give evidence of the optimality of some list solutions with respect to various functions of the cost. In the first case, it is the total function of the cost depending on the sequence u of operations; in the second case, it is the function of the worst-case cost depending on the number n of elements and the number m of operations in the input sequence u.

Theorem 3.1 is from the paper by Sleator and Tarjan (1985a), which also considers a closely related self-organizing data structure for the so-called **paging problem**. Assume that we are given an n-element set S, whose elements are called **pages** and also a natural number n_0, $1 \leqslant n_0 < n/2$ called the **capacity of internal memory**. The number $n - n_0$ is called the **capacity of external memory**. The paging problem is to design a data structure supporting the execution of sequences of operations of the following type ($S_0 \subseteq S$, $|S_0| = n_0$, p is a page in S):

p-$access(p, S_0)$:: as a result we obtain a subset $S'_0 \subseteq S$ such that $|S'_0| = n_0$ and $p \in S'_0$

The aim of the operation p-$access(p, S_0)$ is to obtain access to page p by placing it in the 'internal memory' S_0. The cost of p-$access(p, S_0)$ is the number $|S'_0 - S_0|$ which is equal to the number of pages fetched to the internal memory. The cost of a sequence of operations is defined as the sum of the costs of the consecutive operations in the sequence.

The basic solutions to the paging problem are of the following form:

if $p \in S_0$ then $S'_0 = S_0$ else $S'_0 = (S_0 - \{p'\}) \cup \{p\}$

where p' is one of the pages in S_0; in particular, in the solution

(1) LRU (Least Recently Used): p' is the page which has not been an argument of an operation p-$access$ for the longest time among the pages in S_0;
(2) FIFO (First-In First-Out): p' is the page which has stayed in S_0 for the longest time among the pages in S_0;
(3) MIN: p' is the page whose next p-$access$ is the latest among the pages in S_0.

The solutions LRU and FIFO are on-line solutions; the solution MIN is an off-line solution. Belady (1966) proved that MIN minimizes the cost of a sequence of the operations p-$access$ in the class of all solutions to the paging problem. Sleator and Tarjan (1985a) proved that the solutions LRU and FIFO are optimal solutions to the paging problem in the class of all on-line solutions (see Exercise 3.7).

3.3 Self-organizing trees

In this section we shall consider a solution of the dictionary problem in the class of binary search trees (as defined in Chapter 1, Example 1.15). The straightforward implementation of the dictionary problem by means of binary search trees is not the best one. The worst-case cost of performing the sequence u of dictionary operations is $\Theta(mn)$, so it is of the same order as in the case of list solutions.

Much more effective (asymptotically) is a solution using the so-called **AVL-trees**[†] for the set representation. An AVL-tree is a binary search tree satisfying the following conditions:

(1) **Balance condition**   For each node in the tree the difference between the heights of its subtrees is at most 1 (the height of the empty tree is defined to be -1).

(2) Each node v is assigned a balance factor $v.bal$ equal to the difference between the height of the left subtree and the height of the right subtree.

The operations $access(e, S)$, $insert(e, S)$ and $delete(e, S)$ start from the root of the AVL-tree and search for the place in the tree corresponding to the argument e, that is, they find a node at which e is stored (if e is present in the tree) or otherwise the element best approximating e, then in the cases of $insert$ and $delete$ the actual insertion or deletion is made. However, it can violate the balance condition (1) in the definition of AVL-trees. We go up to the root of the tree and on the way we make local restructurings of the tree (so-called **rotations**) to restore the condition (1). Simultaneously the balance factor is updated. The cost of performing a sequence u of operations in the solution based on AVL-trees is $O(m \log n)$. We shall not go into further detail about AVL-trees, but more can be found (for example) in the book by Knuth (1973). We shall consider another type of binary search tree more interesting from the point of view of optimality: self-organizing binary search trees.

The solution based on self-organizing binary search trees achieves a similar complexity (as AVL-trees) without using balance factors. Moreover, the algorithms are simpler and easier to program compared to AVL-trees. Self-organizing binary search trees adapt themselves dynamically to the frequencies of accesses to the elements. This means that the node containing the accessed element e is moved up to the root (this corresponds to moving e to the front of the list in the preceding section). Consequently, the elements that are more frequently accessed tend to appear closer to the root. We shall prove a theorem expressing the optimality of self-organizing binary search trees in the class of static (where only the operation $access$ is allowed) solutions of the dictionary problem on binary search trees.

We assume that for each node v in the tree the following attributes are defined:

- $v. item$ the element stored at v
- $v. left$ the pointer to the left subtree of v
- $v. right$ the pointer to the right subtree of v

[†] The abbreviation AVL comes from the initials of the authors Adelson-Velskij and Landis.

- $v.\ parent$ the pointer to the father of v or **nil** if v is the root (in the actual implementation it can be omitted)

The algorithms for the operations *access, insert,* and *delete* are based on the auxiliary operation *splay* described by the following specification:

$splay(e, S)$:: the binary search tree S is transformed into a binary search tree S' representing the same set of elements. If e is in S then the root of S' contains e, otherwise at the root of S' there is an element e' such that there is no element in S between the values e and e'.

We start with the explanation of how the operation *splay* can be used in implementing the dictionary operations.

The realization of *access*(e, S) consists in performing $splay(e, S)$; S contains e iff e is at the root of the resulting tree.

The operation *insert*(e, S) is realized as follows (see Figure 3.2). First $splay(e, S)$ is performed. If e is not in S then let S_1 and S_2 be the two subtrees of the root. A new root containing e is created, with pointers defined according to Figure 3.2. One of the pointers of the node containing e' is removed.

Similarly, the realization of the operation *delete*(e, S) is presented in Figure 3.3.

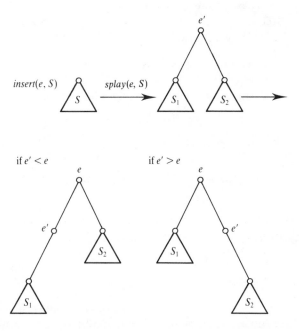

Figure 3.2 The implementation of the operation *insert* by means of *splay*.

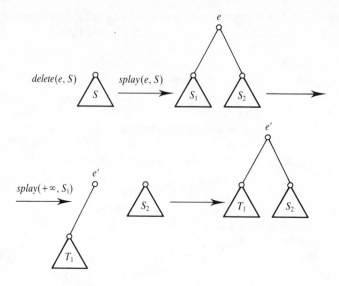

Figure 3.3   The implementation of the operation *delete* by means of *splay*.

In the algorithm for *splay*(*e*, *S*) described below, the basic elementary operation is a rotation. Specifically, if *S* is a binary search tree, and *y* is a node with a son *x* in *S* then by a **rotation in** *y* **with respect to** *x*, denoted by *rotate*(*x*, *y*), we mean the transformation of the tree *S* presented in Figure 3.4. The resulting tree is a binary search tree. In order to define the operation *splay* we need the following auxiliary operation:

> *splaying*(*x*): {*x* is a non-root node of the tree *S*}
>   **let** *y* = *x* . *parent*;
>   **if** *y* is the root **then** *rotate*(*x*, *y*)   {see Figure 3.5(a)}
>   **else**
>   **let** *z* = *y* . *parent*;
>   **if** both *x*, *y* are left sons or they are both right sons **then**
>   *rotate*(*y*, *z*), *rotate*(*x*, *y*)   {see Figure 3.5(b)}
>   **else** *rotate*(*x*, *y*), *rotate*(*x*, *z*).   {see Figure 3.5(c)}
> **end**

The following algorithm realizes the operation *splay*(*e*, *S*) as a sequence of operations *splaying*.

Algorithm 3.1   {*splay*(*e*, *S*)}

Find a node *x* such that *x* . *item* = *e* or (if *e* is not in *S*) there is no element of *S* between *x* . *item* and *e*; such a node can be found by traversing the tree from the root down to *x* (see Example 1.15);

(a)

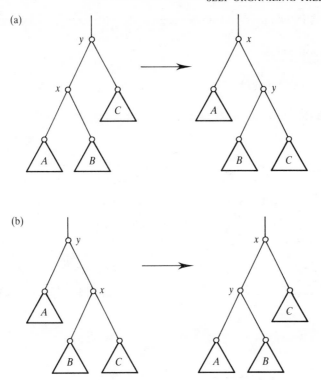

(b)

Figure 3.4 The rotation *rotate*(x, y) in y with respect to x: (a) in the case when x is a left son of y; (b) in the case when x is a right son of y.

while x is not the root **do**
    call splaying(x) $\{x$ goes up the tree$\}$
end

The action of the operation *splay* is illustrated in Figure 3.6.

Now we shall define the cost of a sequence u of operations. The cost of one operation *splay* is the number of executed (sub)operations *splaying* within this operation. The cost of a given dictionary operation is the total cost of all *splays* executed in this operation. Let $COST(u)$ denote the total cost of a sequence u of dictionary operations.

In the analysis of the complexity of self-organizing binary search trees, the book-keeping method (already encountered in the proof of Theorem 3.1) will be applied. We shall associate credits with operations, nodes and trees. First, several auxiliary notations will be introduced.

Assume that each node x is assigned a fixed positive real value called its **individual weight**, denoted by $iw(x)$. (In the following two alternative functions $iw(x)$ will be used.) Also with each node x we associate two parameters:

(1) The **total weight**

$$tw_S(x) = \sum_y iw(y)$$

where the summation is over all descendants y of x in S.

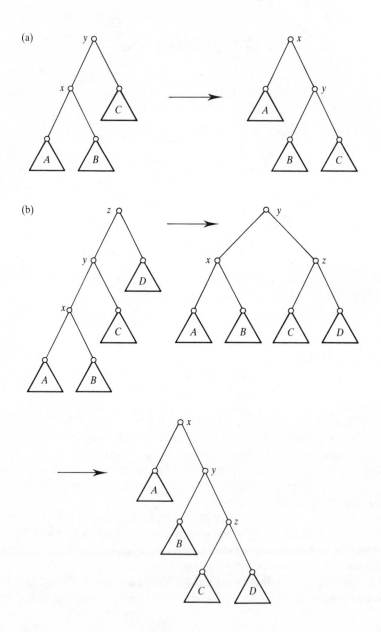

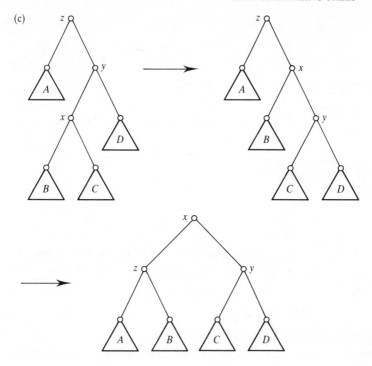

Figure 3.5 The operation *splaying* with respect to a node x: (a) y is the root and x is a left son (analogously if x is a right son); (b) x and y are both left sons (analogously if they are both right sons); (c) x is a left son and y is a right son (analogously if x is a right son and y is a left son).

(2) The **rank**

$$r_S(x) = \lfloor \log tw_S(x) \rfloor$$

The rank $r_S(x)$ of a node x in tree S is also called the **credit of x in S**.

We shall often make use of the following simple fact: if

$$tw_S(x) \leqslant tw_S(y)$$

for two nodes x and y in the tree S then

$$r_S(x) \leqslant r_S(y)$$

as well.

The value $C(S) = \sum_x r_S(x)$, where x ranges over all nodes in S is called the **credit of the tree S**.

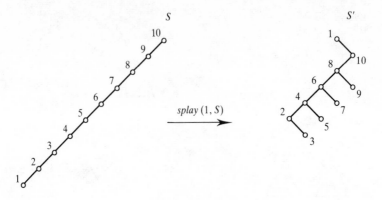

Figure 3.6 The effect of performing *splay*.

If f is one of the operations $splay(e, S)$, $access(e, S)$, $insert(e, S)$, or $delete(e, S)$, transforms the tree S into another tree S', has cost k, then the value

$$c(f) = k + C(S') - C(S)$$

is called the **credit of the operation** f.

Lemma 3.1 gives an estimation of the credit of the operation *splay*.

Lemma 3.1

If the operation $f = splay(e, S)$ transforms a binary search tree S into a binary search tree S', v is the root of S, and x is the root of S', then

$$c(f) \leqslant 3(r_S(v) - r_S(x)) + 1$$

Proof The proof applies the following property:

if nodes y and z in tree S are sons of a node t, and

$$r_S(y) = r_S(z) \text{ then}$$

$$r_S(t) \geqslant 1 + r_S(y) \tag{3.4}$$

Indeed, since $tw_S(y) \geqslant 2^{r_S(y)}$ and $tw_S(z) \geqslant 2^{r_S(z)}$ then

$$tw_S(t) \geqslant tw_S(y) + tw_S(z) \geqslant 2^{r_S(y) + 1}$$

Hence

$$r_S(t) = \lfloor \log tw_S(t) \rfloor \geqslant r_S(y) + 1$$

which proves the inequality (3.4).

If $v = x$ then Lemma 3.1 is evidently true. Let $v \neq x$. Assume that the operation f consists of k steps *splaying* (where $k > 0$) and that the ith *splaying* transforms a tree S_{i-1} into a tree S_i ($1 \leqslant i \leqslant k$). In particular $S_0 = S$ and $S_k = S'$. Assume also that nodes x, y_i and z_i are the arguments of the ith *splaying*, that is, x is a node that is moved to the root, y_i is the father of x in S_{i-1}, and z_i is the father of y_i in S_{i-1} (if y_i is already the root then $z_i = $ **nil**).

Let us partition the credit $c(f)$ of the operation f into the k *splaying* steps in such a way that the ith *splaying* is assigned the credit

$$c_i = 1 + C(S_i) - C(S_{i-1})$$

It is evident that

$$c(f) = \sum_{i=1}^{k} c_i$$

Since $r_S(v) = r_{S'}(x)$, to prove Lemma 3.1 it is sufficient to show that the following inequalities hold:

$$c_i \leqslant 3(r_{S_i}(x) - r_{S_{i-1}}(x)) \quad \text{for } 1 \leqslant i \leqslant k$$

and

$$c_k \leqslant 1 + 3(r_{S_k}(x) - r_{S_{k-1}}(x))$$

Let i be any integer such that $1 \leqslant i \leqslant k$. For simplicity we shall adopt the following auxiliary notations:

$$y = y_i \qquad r_y = r_{S_{i-1}}(y) \qquad r'_y = r_{S_i}(y)$$
$$z = z_i \qquad r_z = r_{S_{i-1}}(z) \qquad r'_z = r_{S_i}(z)$$
$$r_x = r_{S_{i-1}}(x) \qquad r'_x = r_{S_i}(x)$$

We shall consider three cases corresponding to the three possible forms of the ith *splaying* (see Figure 3.5).

Case 1 $i = k$ and $z_k = $ **nil**
We have $r'_x = r_y$. Hence it follows that

$$c_k = 1 + C(S_k) - C(S_{k-1}) = 1 + r'_x + r'_y - r_x - r_y$$
$$= 1 + r'_y - r_x \leqslant 1 + (r'_x - r_x) \leqslant 1 + 3(r'_x - r_x)$$

because $r'_y \leqslant r'_x$.

Case 2 $z_i \neq $ **nil** and both the nodes x and y are simultaneously either left or right sons.

We have $r'_x = r_z$. Hence

$$c_i = 1 + C(S_i) - C(S_{i-1}) = 1 + r'_x + r'_y + r'_z - r_x - r_y - r_z$$
$$= 1 + r'_y + r'_z - r_x - r_y \qquad (3.5)$$

If $r'_x > r_x$ then the formula (3.5) and the following inequalities $r'_y, r'_z \leqslant r'_x$ and $r_y \geqslant r_x$ imply that

$$c_i \leqslant 1 + r'_y + r'_z - r_x - r_y \leqslant 1 + 2(r'_x - r_x) \leqslant 3(r'_x - r_x)$$

It remains to consider the case $r'_x = r_x$. We obtain

$$r'_x = r_x = r_y = r_z$$

By applying (3.4) to the intermediate tree in Figure 3.5b it follows that

$$r'_z < r_x \qquad (3.6)$$

since if $r'_z = r_x$ then $r'_x > r_x$. Finally, the formulas (3.5) and (3.6) together with the inequality $r'_y \leqslant r'_x = r_y$ imply that

$$c_i = 1 + (r'_y - r_y) + (r'_z - r_x) \leqslant 1 + 0 - 1 = 0 = 3(r'_x - r_x)$$

Case 3 $z_i \neq$ **nil** and either x is a left son and y is a right son or vice versa. The proof proceeds as in Case 2. We have

$$r'_x = r_z, r'_y \leqslant r'_x, r'_z \leqslant r'_x, r_y \geqslant r'_y, r_z \geqslant r'_z, r_y \geqslant r_x$$

Now if $r'_x > r_x$ then

$$c_i = 1 + r'_y + r'_z - r_x - r_y \leqslant 1 + 2(r'_x - r_x) \leqslant 3(r'_x - r_x)$$

On the other hand if $r'_x = r_x$ then $r_x = r_y = r_z$. Next, it is easy to see that either $r'_y < r_y$ or $r'_z < r_z$. Indeed if $r'_y = r_y$ and $r'_z = r_z$ then $r'_y = r'_z$ and then by (3.4) it would follow that $r'_x > r'_z = r_z = r'_x$ (see Figure 3.5) which contradicts the proof assumption that $r'_x = r_x$. Therefore we obtain

$$c_i = 1 + (r'_y - r_y) + (r'_z - r_x) = 1 + (r'_y - r_y) + (r'_z - r_z) \leqslant 0 = 3(r'_x - r_x)$$

which completes Case 3 and the whole proof of Lemma 3.1.   ∎

Using Lemma 3.1 we shall prove two theorems characterizing the performance of self-organizing binary search trees.

Theorem 3.4

The cost of a sequence u of the operations *access*, *insert*, and *delete* in the solution of the dictionary problem by means of self-organizing binary search trees is $O(m \log n)$ where n is the maximal number of elements in the set S and m is the number of operations in u.

Proof Let $iw(x) = 1$ for each node x. Let S be a binary search tree containing at most n elements. Notice that $tw_S(x) \leqslant n$ and therefore $r_S(x) \leqslant \log n$ for each node in the tree S. Hence and by Lemma 3.1, the credit of each operation $splay(e, S)$ is at most $3 \log n + 1$. In implementing the dictionary operations by means of *splay* it follows that the credit of each operation $access(e, S)$ is also at most $3 \log n + 1$, and the credit of each operation $insert(e, S)$ is at most $4 \log n + 1$ (the credit associated with the whole tree S may increase by the credit of the new root, that is, by $\log n$). Also, the credit of each operation $delete(e, S)$ is at most $6 \log n + 2$ (the operation *delete* calls *splay* twice, and the remaining changes made to the tree S reduce at most the credit of the tree).

Let $u = u_1, u_2, \ldots, u_m$ be a sequence of dictionary operations. Denote by t_i the cost of the operation u_i, and by C_i the credit of the tree after performing the ith operation for $1 \leqslant i \leqslant m$. In addition, set C_0 to 0 (the credit of the empty tree). By definition it follows that

$$COST(u) = \sum_{i=1}^{m} t_i = \sum_{i=1}^{m} c(u_i) + C_0 - C_m \leqslant 6m \log n + 2m \qquad \blacksquare$$

Instead of starting the execution of a sequence u of dictionary operations from the empty tree, we could start from an arbitrary binary search tree S_0. If S_0 has at most n nodes then its credit is at most $n \log n$. From the proof of Theorem 3.4 the following corollary follows.

Corollary The cost of a sequence u starting from an arbitrary binary search tree S_0 is $O((m + n) \log n)$. □

Theorem 3.4 characterizes the cost of a sequence of operations as $O(m \log n)$ which means that 'on average' each operation costs $O(\log n)$. We say in such a case that the **amortized cost** of a single operation is $O(\log n)$. The worst-case cost of a single dictionary operation is $\Omega(n)$ (see Exercise 3.12). Note that in the solution using AVL-trees, the cost of all operations is $O(\log n)$ in the worst case. The advantages of self-organizing binary search trees are: lack of balance factors, simple algorithms and their optimality as explained below.

The **static dictionary problem** is as follows. A finite subset $S \subseteq L$ is given, $|S| = n$ and a sequence u consisting of m operations of the form $access(l, S)$, where e is in S. We are to give a data structure representing S and an algorithm for performing u. The static dictionary problem is a particular case of the general dictionary problem. Every solution of the general problem can be used to solve the static dictionary problem – in particular, self-organizing binary search trees.

By a **static solution** to the static dictionary problem we mean a solution to the static dictionary problem in which set S is represented by a fixed binary search tree, and the operation *access* is the ordinary operation *access* for the binary search tree. By $depth(x)$ we denote the depth of a node x in tree S. The cost of the operation $access(e, S)$ is defined as $depth(x) + 1$, where x is the node in S containing element e. The cost of a sequence u of the operations *access* is defined as the sum of the costs of the consecutive operations in the sequence u and is denoted by $COST_S(u)$.

Theorem 3.5

Let S and S_0 be two arbitrary binary search trees representing the same set of n elements, and let u be a sequence of the operations *access* concerning the given n elements. Then the cost of a sequence u starting from the tree S_0 in the solution by means of self-organizing binary search trees is

$$O(COST_S(u) + hn)$$

where h is the height of tree S.

Proof We can assume that both trees S and S_0 contain the same set of nodes. A node x (in both trees) is assigned its individual weight in the following way:

$$iw(x) = 3^{h - depth(x)}$$

(recall that $depth(x)$ denotes the depth of x in tree S).

Using induction on the depth of a node x it is straightforward to show that for each node x the following inequality holds:

$$3iw(x) \geqslant tw_S(x) \tag{3.7}$$

Denote by z the root of tree S. By (3.7) it follows that

$$3iw(z) \geqslant tw_S(z)$$

Hence

$$iw(x) = 3^{-depth(x)} iw(z) \geqslant 3^{-depth(x) - 1} tw_S(z)$$

and consequently

$$\log \frac{tw_S(z)}{iw(x)} \leqslant (\log 3)(depth(x) + 1) \tag{3.8}$$

Let S' be an arbitrary binary search tree with the same nodes as S and let v be the root of S'. By definition we obtain

$$r_{S'}(v) - r_{S'}(x) - 1 \leqslant \log \frac{tw_{S'}(v)}{tw_{S'}(x)} \leqslant \log \frac{tw_S(z)}{iw(x)}$$

Hence and by the inequality (3.8) it follows that

$$3(r_{S'}(v) - r_{S'}(x)) + 1 \leqslant 3(\log 3)(depth(x) + 1) + 4 \qquad \textbf{(3.9)}$$

Let us interpret both sides of the inequality (3.9). The left-hand side is an upper bound on the credit of the operation $access(e, S')$ in the solution using self-organizing binary search trees, where e is the element stored at node x. The right-hand side is proportional to the cost of the operation $access(e, S)$ in the static solution. It follows that the cost of a sequence u of the operation $access$ in the solution using self-organizing binary search trees is at most

$$3(\log 3)COST_S(u) + 4m + C(S_0) \qquad \textbf{(3.10)}$$

where $C(S_0)$ is the credit of the initial tree S_0.

Notice that $tw_{S_0}(x) \leqslant tw_S(z) \leqslant 3iw(z) = 3^{h+1}$ for each node x. Hence

$$r_{S_0}(x) \leqslant (\log 3)(h + 1)$$

and

$$C(S_0) = \sum_x r_{S_0}(x) \leqslant n(\log 3)(h + 1)$$

The last formula and the bound (3.10) imply the theorem. ∎

It follows from Theorem 3.5 that the execution time of a sequence of operations $access$ by means of self-organizing binary search trees is asymptotically not greater than the execution time of the same sequence of operations by the optimal binary search tree which is especially constructed for this specific sequence of operations. It is surprising that self-organizing binary search trees adjust themselves to an arbitrary frequency distribution not knowing this distribution in advance. However the 'learning' of this distribution during the execution of the operations takes time represented by a term $O(hn)$.

In the proofs of Theorems 3.1, 3.4, 3.5 and Lemma 3.1 the book-keeping method for cost estimation was used. It consists in allocating a credit to each operation (which is equal to its amortized cost). The operation pays its cost using the allocated credit. If the cost is smaller than the credit, the unused portion of the credit is deposited as the credit of the data structure. If the cost is greater than the allocated credit the operation can borrow the credit from the data structure. The data structure serves as a bank. Using this interpretation, it is obvious that the cost of the execution of a sequence of operations is equal to the sum of the credits allocated to the operations minus the difference in the amount of credits at the end and at the beginning of the whole process.

The material in this section on self-organizing binary search trees comes from the paper by Sleator and Tarjan (1983). A more refined and extended version can be found in Sleator and Tarjan (1985b).

In the paper by Sleator and Tarjan (1986) another example of a self-organizing data structure, the **self-organizing heap** is considered. The **mergeable priority queue problem** is to design a data structure supporting the execution of sequences of operations of the following three types (where S, S_1 and S_2 are finite subsets of set L, and e is an element of set L):

(1) *insert*(e, S):: insert element e into set S (we assume that e is not in S)

(2) *deletemin*(S):: delete the smallest element in set S (we assume that S is nonempty)

(3) *union*(S_1, S_2):: replace two disjoint sets S_1 and S_2 by their union $S_1 \cup S_2$

Any solution to the mergeable priority queue problem is called a **mergeable priority queue**. A **heap** is a binary tree whose nodes contain elements of set L and the following condition is satisfied: if a node v is a son of a node w then the element $v.item$ associated with node v is not less than the element $w.item$ associated with node w. In particular, the root of a heap contains the smallest element. Note that the Heapsort algorithm is based on this data structure (see, for example, Aho *et al.* (1974)). The best known mergeable priority queue is a **leftist tree** which is a special kind of a heap. A leftist tree is a heap satisfying the following conditions:

- Each node is assigned an additional attribute $v.length$ which is equal to the length of the rightmost path in the heap from v to a leaf.
- For each node v in the heap, every path from v to a leaf is of length at least $v.length$.

The cost of a sequence of m operations *insert*, *deletemin* and *union* on leftist trees is $O(m \log n)$ where n is the maximum number of elements in one heap. (Since the sorting problem can be reduced to the mergeable priority queue problem that solution is optimal.) The same cost is obtained by self-organizing heaps. They do not use any additional information in a node (besides $v.item$, $v.left$ and $v.right$). The fundamental operation is *union*(S_1, S_2). First, two rightmost paths in S_1 and S_2 are merged so that the resulting tree remains a heap. Next, we interchange left and right sons on the rightmost path (see Figure 3.7) to make it shorter. The proof that the cost of a sequence

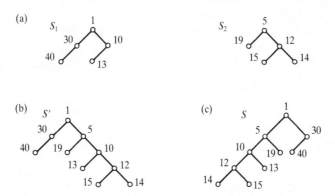

Figure 3.7   The operation $union(S_1, S_2)$: (a) two heaps S_1 and S_2; (b) heap S' resulting from the merging of the two rightmost paths in S_1 and S_2; (c) the final heap S resulting from the interchange of sons between vertices on the rightmost path in S'.

of m operations *insert*, *deletemin* and *union* is $O(m\log n)$ is the subject of Exercises 3.17–3.19.

3.4 Implicit data structures

The question of how to implement sets with the minimal space cost has a strong practical impact. A data structure which uses the minimal amount of additional storage is called an **implicit data structure**. A data structure which implements finite subsets of a set L is **implicit** if it uses $n + O(1)$ simple variables to implement an n-element subset S of L. As will be seen, the relative order of the values in such a data structure is implicit in the patterns in which the elements are retained, rather than explicit in pointers.

Let us consider the problem of implementing the dictionary using an implicit data structure. First, consider the general question of the existence of any implicit data structure. The answer to such a question is quite simple: take, for example, an ordered array. The time cost of *access* is in this case $O(\log n)$, while that of *insert* and *delete* is $O(n)$. Another example of an implicit data structure is the heap structure, described above, represented in an array (see Aho *et al.* (1974), pp. 87–92). The cost of *insert* is $O(\log n)$. The cost of *delete*, when the position of the deleted element is known, is also $O(\log n)$. However, the cost of the operation *access* is $O(n)$.

Examples of non-implicit data structures are trees such as binary search trees or AVL-trees. Each tree node requires, apart from a field for an element, at least two fields for pointers to its two sons.

The problem becomes non-trivial if we want to construct an implicit data structure which supports each of the dictionary operations in time which is strictly smaller than linear. Such a data structure is presented in this section.

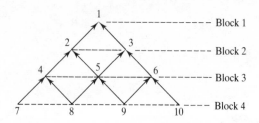

Figure 3.8   10-element beap consisting of four blocks. (Arrows show the order.)

We shall define an implicit data structure called a **beap** (biparental heap: each non-root node has two fathers) in which the cost of *access*, *insert* and *delete* is $O(\sqrt{n})$. Moreover, we shall prove that this data structure is optimal in a certain class of implicit data structures which includes heaps and beaps.

Without loss of generality we can assume that an implicit data structure implements a subset S in a one-dimensional array. Let us denote this array by $S[1 .. n]$. Beap resembles heap, but each node, besides having two **successors**, has two **predecessors** (see Figure 3.8). A formal definition of beap will be given after a number of preliminary definitions.

Array $S[1 .. n]$ is divided into parts called **blocks**. Block 1 consists of one element $S[1]$, block 2 consists of two elements $S[2]$, $S[3]$, and so on. Thus the ith block consists of i elements

$$S[i(i-1)/2 + 1], \ldots, S[i(i+1)/2] \qquad \text{if } i(i+1)/2 \leqslant n$$

or of $n - i(i-1)/2$ elements

$$S[i(i-1)/2 + 1], \ldots, S[n] \qquad \text{if } i(i-1)/2 < n < i(i+1)/2$$

Let $S(i, j)$ denote the jth element in the ith block, that is, $S(i, j) = S[i(i-1)/2 + j]$. Let the **height** of S be the number h of the last block, that is, the block which contains $S[n]$. Observe that

$$\tfrac{1}{2}h(h-1) < n \leqslant \tfrac{1}{2}h(h+1)$$

This immediately implies:

$$(h-1)^2 < 2n < (h+1)^2 \quad h = \lceil \sqrt{2n} \rceil \quad \text{or} \quad h = \lceil \sqrt{2n} \rceil - 1$$

which gives finally:

$$h = \sqrt{2n} + O(1) \tag{3.11}$$

Let us call the **domain of S** the following set R of pairs (i, j):

$$R = \{(i, j): \quad 1 \leqslant j \leqslant i \leqslant h, i(i-1)/2 + j \leqslant n\}$$

Array S is called a beap if for any non-root pair $(i, j) \in R$ the elements contained in the predecessors of (i, j) are less than the element stored at (i, j), where the predecessor and successor relations correspond to the respective relations in heaps and are defined as follows. Let us assume that (i, j) belongs to the domain R of beap S. If $(i - 1, j - 1) \in R$ then $S(i - 1, j - 1)$ is called a *predecessor* of $S(i, j)$, and symmetrically $S(i, j)$ is called a *successor* of $S(i - 1, j - 1)$. Similarly, if $(i - 1, j) \in R$, then $S(i - 1, j)$ is called a predecessor of $S(i, j)$, and symmetrically $S(i, j)$ is called a successor of $S(i - 1, j)$.

Now we shall present algorithms for the operations *access*, *insert*, and *delete* on a beap. Let S be an n-element beap.

For an element e not belonging to S the operation *insert*(e, S) is performed as in the case of a heap. First, e is stored in $S[n + 1]$. If e is smaller than any of its predecessors, then it is swapped with the greater one. This process is repeated until the inserted element becomes greater than both its predecessors.

```
function insert(e, S): beap;
var p, q: integer;
    {e ∉ S, |S| = n, i and j are non-local integer variables such that
       n = i(i − 1)/2 + j and 1 ⩽ j ⩽ i}
begin
    n := n + 1; S[n] := e;
    if j < i then j := j + 1 else begin i := i + 1; j := 1 end;
    {n = i(i − 1)/2 + j and 1 ⩽ j ⩽ i}
    while i ≠ 1 do
    begin
        p := i − 1;
        if 2 ⩽ j ⩽ p then
        begin
            {the case when both (i − 1, j − 1) and (i − 1, j) belong to R}
            if S(p, j − 1) < S(p, j) then q := j else q := j − 1
        end else
            {the case when exactly one of the pairs (i − 1, j − 1), (i − 1, j)
              belongs to R}
            if j = 1 then q := 1 else q := p;
        if e < S(p, q) then
        begin
            swap S(p, q) with S(i, j)
            i := p; j := q
        end else return S
    end;
    return S
    {element e has been inserted into beap S}
end
```

The cost of *insert* is proportional to the height h of beap S, so by (3.11) it is $O(\sqrt{n})$.

Let us assume that e belongs to beap S. So $e = S(i, j)$ for a certain element (i, j) of R. To delete e from S we first put in the place (i, j) the last element $x = S[n]$. The size of S is reduced by 1. Next, we correct beap S with e replaced by x. If x is smaller than one of its predecessors, then we swap x with the greater of them. We repeat this process until x becomes greater than both its predecessors. On the other hand, if x is greater than one of its successors, then we swap x with the smaller of them, and we repeat this process until x becomes smaller than both its successors. The cost of this algorithm is again proportional to the height of S, so by (3.11) it is $O(\sqrt{n})$. The complete algorithm for operation *delete* is left to the reader as an exercise (see Exercise 3.20).

Finally, let us consider the operation $access(e, S)$. All algorithms presented up to now have been traversing a beap vertically, as in the case of heap operations. To verify whether an element belongs to a beap, it is necessary to move horizontally. Fortunately, the width of a beap is $\sqrt{2n} + O(1)$, while the width of a heap was $O(n)$.

The searching process for element e starts from the rightmost position in beap S, that is, from the element $S(k, k)$ where k is a maximal number such that (k, k) belongs to the domain R of beap S.

We have $k = h - 1$ or $k = h$, since this position belongs either to the last or to the last-but-one block. We move through the beap in the way presented in Algorithm 3.2 (where the current position is designated by the pair (i, j)).

Algorithm 3.2

> $(i, j) := (k, k)$;
> **while** $e \neq S(i, j) \wedge (j > 1 \vee e > S(i, j)) \wedge (j > 1 \vee (i + 1, j) \in R)$
> **do**
> **if** $e < S(i, j)$ **then**
> 1: $(i, j) := (i - 1, j - 1)$
> **else**
> **if** $e > S(i, j) \wedge (i + 1, j) \in R$ **then**
> 2: $(i, j) := (i + 1, j)$
> **else**
> 3: $(i, j) := (i, j - 1)$;
> **if** $e = S(i, j)$ **then return** "$e = S(i, j)$" **else return** "$e \notin S$"
> **end**

It is better to analyse Algorithm 3.2 when array S is partitioned into rows and columns. Let us call the **rth row of S** the set

$$\{S(i, j): (i, j) \in R \text{ and } i - j = r - 1\}$$

for $1 \leqslant r \leqslant h$ and the *s*th **column of** *S* the set

$$\{S(i,j): (i,j) \in R \text{ and } j = s\}$$

for $1 \leqslant s \leqslant h$. Note that the *h*th column may be empty.

The statement labelled 1 in Algorithm 3.2 is interpreted as one move in a row of *S* (the corresponding column number is decreased). The statement labelled 2 is interpreted as a step in a column (the corresponding row number is increased). Finally, the statement labelled 3 is interpreted as a simultaneous move in a row and in a column (the column number is decreased, the row number is increased). Figure 3.9 provides an example of the operation *access* on a beap.

Observe that element *e* is searched for starting from position $S(k, k)$ belonging to the first row and the last column. Since at every step of the iteration either a column number decreases or a row number increases, the global number of iterations is less than or equal to $2h = 2\sqrt{2n} + O(1)$. This proves that the cost of Algorithm 3.2 is $O(\sqrt{n})$. What is left is to show that this algorithm correctly implements operation *access(e, S)*. To show it, let us consider the following condition:

$$e \in S \Leftrightarrow e = S(p, q)$$
$$\text{for some } (p, q) \in R, \ p - q \geqslant i - j \text{ and } q \leqslant j. \tag{3.12}$$

Condition (3.12) is an invariant of the iteration of Algorithm 3.2 (see Exercise 3.21). From this invariant we immediately obtain the correctness of operation *access* (see also Figure 3.10).

Thus we have proved Theorem 3.6.　■

Theorem 3.6

Beap is an implicit data structure implementing operations *access, insert* and *delete* on an *n*-element set *S* in cost $O(\sqrt{n})$.

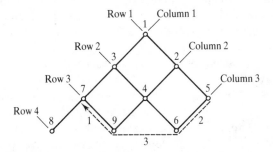

Figure 3.9 Beap with marked rows and columns. Dotted lines show the path of moves in the operation *access*(7, *S*). Below the dotted lines the labels corresponding to the statements in Algorithm 3.2 are given.

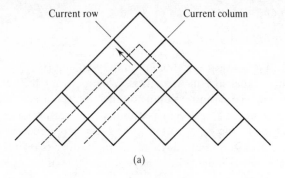

(a)

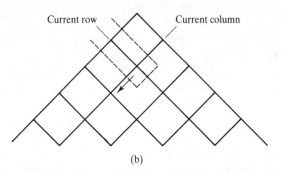

(b)

Figure 3.10 The area surrounded by dotted lines is eliminated: (a) after the execution of statement 1; (b) after the execution of statement 2. The direction of the step is denoted by the arrow.

We shall now show that beap is an optimal implicit data structure in the class of the so-called **rigid solutions** of the dictionary problem. Assume that the algorithms implementing dictionary may use only the information derived from the comparisons of elements in L. (The same assumption is made in the case of the sorting problem.)

We say that array $S[1 \ . \ . \ n]$ is **realized** in an implicit data structure if S may be obtained by a sequence of the operations *access*, *insert* and *delete*, starting from the empty set.

For every $n \geq 1$, let the symbol $\ll_n$ denote a partial order on the set $\{1, 2, \ldots, n\}$, that is, any relation which is non-reflexive and transitive. An implicit data structure is called **consistent** with the family of partial orders $\{\ll_n\}_{n \geq 1}$, if for every $n \geq 1$ the following two conditions hold:

(1) for every realized array $S[1 \ . \ . \ n]$ and for each $i, j \in \{1, 2, \ldots, n\}$

$$i \ll_n j \text{ implies } S[i] < S[j]$$

(2) for all arrays $S[1 .. n]$: if for each i, $j \in \{1, 2, \ldots, n\}$ $i \ll_n j$ implies $S[i] < S[j]$, then the array S is realized.

An implicit data structure consistent with a fixed family of partial orders is called a *rigid data structure*. The ordered array, heap and beap are examples of rigid data structures (see Figure 3.11). The meaning of the following theorem (Theorem 3.7) about the optimality of a beap structure is ambivalent: positive and negative. Positive, because it shows that beap is optimal in the class of all rigid data structures. Negative, because it implies that for rigidness we must pay with higher time complexity.

Theorem 3.7

For any rigid data structure let A_n denote the maximal number of comparisons necessary to perform the operation *access* in an n-element set $S[1 .. n]$, and let B_n denote the maximal number of assignments on variables $S[1], \ldots, S[n]$ necessary to perform a pair of operations: first *delete* and then *insert*. Then

$$A_n B_n \geqslant n$$

Proof Let the considered rigid data structure be consistent with the family $\{\ll_n\}_{n \geqslant 1}$ of partial orders in the set $\{1, 2, \ldots, n\}$. Let a_n denote the maximum number of independent elements in the set $\{1, 2, \ldots, n\}$ with respect to the relations $\ll_n$, and let b_n denote the length of the longest chain in the set $\{1, 2, \ldots, n\}$ with respect to $\ll_n$. Moreover, let X_n denote the minimal partition of the set $\{1, 2, \ldots, n\}$ into chains, that is, the partition with the minimum number of chains. For such an X_n denote by $x_n = |X_n|$ the number of chains in X_n, and denote by b'_n the length of the longest chain in X_n. We now apply the following theorem known as Dilworth's theorem (Dilworth, 1950):

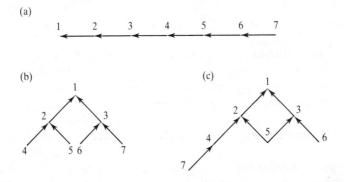

Figure 3.11 Partial order $\ll_7$ for: (a) ordered array, (b) heap, (c) beap.

In every partially ordered set the minimum number of chains covering the set of all elements equals the maximum number of pairwise incomparable elements.

$$a_n = x_n \tag{3.13}$$

which implies

$$a_n = x_n \geqslant \frac{n}{b'_n} \geqslant \frac{n}{b_n}$$

This gives

$$a_n b_n \geqslant n \tag{3.14}$$

Now it is sufficient to prove the following two inequalities:

$$A_n \geqslant a_n \tag{3.15}$$

and

$$B_n \geqslant b_n \tag{3.16}$$

Let us start from the proof of (3.15). Let $a = a_n$ and let $\{i_1, i_2, \ldots, i_a\}$ denote the set of the greatest cardinality with all elements independent with respect to $\ll_n$. Let X be the set of indices q such that $q \ll_n i_j$ for a certain j, $1 \leqslant j \leqslant a$. Note that for any j, $1 \leqslant j \leqslant a$, we have $i_j \notin X$.

Let us consider any array S and any element e satisfying the following four conditions:

(1) for any q_1, q_2, if $q_1 \ll_n q_2$, then $S[q_1] < S[q_2]$;
(2) for any $q \in X$, $S[q] < e$;
(3) for any q_1, q_2, if $q_1 \in X$ and $q_2 \notin X$, then $S[q_1] < S[q_2]$;
(4) for any $q \notin X$, $e < S[q]$.

Any array S satisfying (1)–(4) is realized according to condition (2) in the definition of consistency and (1) above. Moreover, let us note that conditions (1)–(4) impose some partial order on S. Namely, $S[q]$ for $q \in X$ is smaller than e, and e is smaller than the rest of S. Conditions (1)–(4) are consistent, since for no pair $q_1, q_2, q_1 \ll_n q_2, q_1 \notin X$ and $q_2 \in X$, is possible.

Next, we consider the computation of $access(e, S)$ for e, S satisfying (1)–(4). Such a computation ends with $e \notin S$. Since all indices in the set $\{i_1, i_2, \ldots, i_a\}$ are mutually independent, each comparison can determine only that $S[i_j]$ is not minimal in the set $Y = \{e\} \cup \{S[q]: q \notin X\}$. Thus, if during this computation less than a comparisons are performed, then there is at least one

$S[i_j]$ such that it is not known whether its value is minimal in Y. Let us replace $S[i_j]$ with e and repeat the same computation. This new computation performs the same comparisons and the results must be the same. Thus it ends with $e \notin S$. But this time $e \in S$, so in the original computation at least a comparisons were performed. This completes the proof of (3.15).

Our next claim is (3.16). Let $b = b_n$ and let $i_1 \ll_n i_2 \ll_n \ldots \ll_n i_b$ be the longest chain in $\{1, 2, \ldots, n\}$ with respect to $\ll_n$. It is clear that i_1 is minimal in $\{1, 2, \ldots, n\}$ with respect to $\ll_n$.

Let us consider an array S satisfying the following two conditions:

(1) for any q_1, q_2, if $q_1 \ll_n q_2$, then $S[q_1] < S[q_2]$;
(2) for every $1 \leqslant k \leqslant b, q \neq i_k$ and for every $1 \leqslant j \leqslant b$, if $S[q] < S[i_j]$, then $q \ll_n i_j$.

The values of $S[i_j]$ for $1 \leqslant j \leqslant b$ are possibly the smallest among the other values in S. Such an array S is realized by condition (2) of consistency of an implicit data structure with a family of partial orders. Thus S may be obtained as the result of the operations *access, insert* and *delete*. Let e be the greatest element in S. Consider the composition of operations:

$delete(S[i_1], S)$; $insert(e, S)$

Let us denote by $S'[q]$ a new value of $S[q]$. We have the following fact:

$$S'[i_j] \neq S[i_j] \quad \text{for every } j, 1 \leqslant j \leqslant b \qquad (3.17)$$

For $j = 1$ it is clear. Let us make an assumption that there exists a number $j, 2 \leqslant j \leqslant b$, such that $S'[i_j] = S[i_j]$. Consider the following sets of indices:

$X = \{q : 1 \leqslant q \leqslant n \text{ and } q \ll_n i_j\}$

$Y = \{q : 1 \leqslant q \leqslant n \text{ and } S[q] < S[i_j]\}$

$Y' = \{q : 1 \leqslant q \leqslant n \text{ and } S'[q] < S'[i_j]\}$

From the definition of S, $X = Y$. Since S' is realized, we have $X \subseteq Y'$. Moreover, from the definition of S' and from the assumption of the proof by contradiction Y' non $\subseteq Y$. Thus $Y = X \subseteq Y'$ non $\subseteq Y$, which is impossible. This proves (3.17). Consequently, during the execution of $delete(S[i_1], S)$ and $insert(e, S)$ each of $S[i_1], S[i_2], \ldots, S[i_b]$ changes its value. This proves that at least b assignments must be done during such a computation. This last observation ends the proof of (3.16) and the whole theorem.   ∎

Corollary Beap is an optimal rigid data structure with respect to the cost of the execution of a single operation *access, insert* and *delete*.   □

Note that Theorem 3.7 deals with the composition of *delete* with *insert*. Such a composition transforms an n-element set into an n-element set. Owing to this observation in the proof of Theorem 3.7 we are allowed to consider only one order $\ll_n$. Exercises 3.23 and 3.24 present a more general version of this theorem, where *insert* and *delete* are not coupled. However, some additional conditions must be satisfied by partial orders $\ll_n$ and $\ll_{n-1}$.

The proof of (3.15) is typical for lower bound estimations of selection and sorting problems where the number of comparisons is involved. Other examples of similar methods are presented by Knuth (1973), Reingold (1972) and Horowitz and Sahni (1978). Exercises 3.27 and 3.28 contain two examples of lower bounds for the number of comparisons.

Theorems 3.6 and 3.7 come from Munro and Suwanda (1980). In this paper there are also solutions to Exercises 3.25 and 3.26, which show how to construct non-rigid implicit data structures with a better product cost (the cost of *access* multiplied by the cost of *insert* or *delete*) than in a beap. The best known implicit dictionary was constructed by Munro (1984). It requires only $O(\log^2 n)$ time for each of the operations *access*, *insert* and *delete*.

SUMMARY

Key points covered in this chapter include:

- the list implementation of a dictionary
- move-to-front self-adjusting implementation
- the optimality of self-adjusting implementation
- self-adjusting binary search trees
- optimality among static solutions
- implicit data structures
- the optimality of beap among rigid solutions.

EXERCISES

3.1 Program the list solutions B, MF, TR and FC.

3.2 Complete the proof of Theorem 3.1.

3.3 Modify Theorem 3.1 for the case when the initial list S_0 is non-empty.

3.4 Complete the proof of Theorem 3.2.

3.5 Consider the following solution MH of the dictionary problem: while performing $access(e, S)$ and $insert(e, S)$ element e is moved half way to the front of the list. Prove that solution MH is optimal within the constant factor 4.

Let $F_A(u)$ denote the cost of a sequence of operations p-$access$ in a solution A of the paging problem.

3.6 Prove that for every on-line solution of the paging problem there exists a sequence u of operations p-$access$ such that

$$F_A(u) \geqslant n_0 F_{\text{MIN}}(u)$$

3.7 Prove that for every sequence u of the operations p-$access$ the following hold:

(a) $F_{\text{LRU}}(u) \leqslant n_0 F_{\text{MIN}}(u) + n_0$

(b) $F_{\text{MIN}}(u) \leqslant n_0 F_{\text{MIN}}(u) + n_0$

3.8 Consider the following solutions to the paging problem:

(a) LFU (Least Frequently Used) :: as the page p' for exchange take the page that has been accessed the least among pages in S_0;

(b) LIFO (Last In First Out):: as the page p' for exchange take the page that has been fetched from the external memory the most recently among the pages in S_0.

Prove that the solutions LFU and LIFO are not optimal within any constant factor in the class of all on-line solutions to the paging problem.

3.9 Design algorithms for the operations: $splay$, $access$, $insert$, and $delete$ on self-organizing binary search trees.

3.10 Consider the following operations on sets (S, S_1, S_2 are finite subsets of set L, all elements in S_1 are assumed to be smaller than all elements in S_2, e is an element in S):

$concatenate(S_1, S_2)$:: create the set $S_1 \cup S_2$
$split(e, S)$:: create two sets

$$S' = \{e' \in S : e' \leqslant e\} \quad \text{and} \quad S'' = \{e' \in S : e' > e\}$$

Using the representation of binary search trees express $concatenate$ and $split$ by means of $splay$.

3.11 Prove that the cost of m operations $access$, $insert$, $delete$, $concatenate$ and $split$ in the solution on self-organizing binary search trees is $O(m \log n)$.

3.12 Show that the cost of a single operation *access, insert* and *delete* in the solution on self-organizing binary search trees is $\Omega(n)$.

3.13 Using the fact that each operation *delete* is preceded by a unique operation *insert*, improve the bound on $COST(u)$ in Theorem 3.4.

3.14 Design a version of self-organizing binary search trees in which the elements are stored only in leaves. Prove the counterpart of Lemma 3.1.

3.15 Design a version of self-organizing binary search trees taking into account ranks of nodes (defined before Lemma 3.1).

3.16 Design a solution of the priority queue problem (the operations *insert* and *deletemin*) on self-organizing binary search trees.

3.17 Design a solution of the mergeable priority queue problem (*union* added) on self-organizing heaps. Express the operations *insert* and *deletemin* by means of *union*.

3.18* Define the weight of a node x in a heap S, $wt(x)$, as the number of all its descendants in S. A non-root node x is called **heavy** if $wt(x) > wt(x.parent)/2$, otherwise it is called **light**. The credit $c(S)$ of heap S is defined as the total number of heavy nodes being right sons. As the cost $t(f)$ of an operation $f = union(S_1, S_2)$ we adopt the sum of the lengths of the rightmost paths in S_1 and S_2. The amortized cost $c(f)$ of an operation $f = union(S_1, S_2)$ transforming heaps S_1 and S_2 into a heap S is defined as $c(f) = t(f) + c(S) - c(S_1) - c(S_2)$.
Prove that

$$c(f) \leqslant 3\log n + 1$$

where n is the total number of nodes in S.

3.19 Prove that the cost of a sequence of m operations *insert, deletemin* and *union* in the solution on self-organizing heaps is $O(m\log n)$, where n is the total number of elements in the heaps involved.

3.20 Design an algorithm for the operation *delete* on a beap.

3.21 Prove that the condition (3.12) is an invariant of the algorithm for the operation *access* on a beap.

3.22 Prove that an unordered list, ordered list, heap and beap are rigid data structures.

3.23* Assume that we are given a rigid data structure compatible with a family of partial orders $\{\ll_n\}_{n \geqslant 1}$ for which the following two conditions hold ($n \geqslant 2$):

(1) $\ll_{n-1} = \ll_n \cap \{1, 2, \ldots, n-1\} \times \{1, 2, \ldots, n-1\}$

(2) n is a maximal element in $\ll_n$

Let A_n denote the maximum number of comparisons required to carry out an operation *access* on an n-element set and let B_n denote that maximum number of assignments to indexed variables required to carry out an operation *delete* on an n-element set. Prove that

$$A_n(B_n + 1) \geqslant n$$

3.24 Formulate a counterpart of Exercise 3.23 with *insert* replacing *delete*.

3.25* By a **cyclic block** we mean an array $S[i \,..\, j]$ whose values satisfy the following condition:

there exists k, $i \leqslant k \leqslant j$, such that

$$S[k] < S[k+1] < \cdots < S[j] < S[i] < \cdots < S[k-1]$$

An array $S[1 \,..\, n]$ is called an **array of cyclic blocks** if the following two conditions are satisfied:

(1) Every block (in the sense of the definition given at the beginning of Section 3.4) is a cyclic block.

(2) All elements of block $i - 1$ are smaller than all elements of block i for $2 \leqslant i \leqslant h$, where h is the maximum block number (see Figure 3.12).

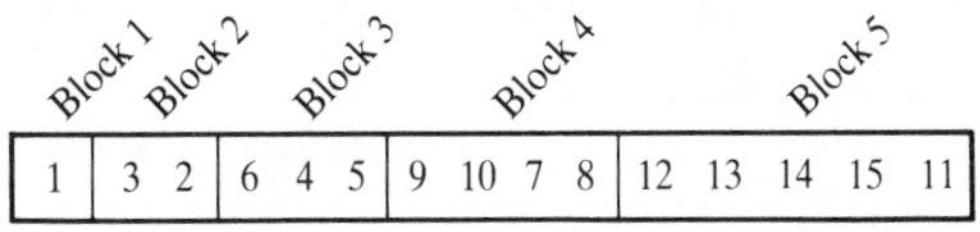

Figure 3.12   An example of an array of cyclic blocks.

Show that using arrays of cyclic blocks an operation *access* requires $2 \log n$ comparisons, operations *insert* and *delete* require $O(\sqrt{n} \log n)$ comparisons and assignments to indexed variables (n denotes the number of elements in the sets).

3.26* Design an implicit data structure based on beaps of cyclic blocks. Prove that each operation *access*, *insert* and *delete* can be performed in time $O(n^{1/3} \log n)$.

3.27 Prove that to merge two ordered sequences $a_1 < a_2 < \cdots < a_n$ and $b_1 < b_2 < \cdots < b_k, n \geqslant k$, at least $\log \binom{n+k}{k} \geqslant k \log(n/k)$ comparisons are required.

3.28* Assume that the elements of the set L can be manipulated only through the use of the identity relation '=' on L. Prove that to determine whether two sets $X, Y \subseteq L, |X| = |Y| = n$, are equal, at least $n(n+1)/2$ comparisons are required.

(*Hint*   Define a procedure (called an **oracle**) which, for any algorithm solving the problem in question, constructs a computation (specifying the results of comparisons) forcing the algorithm to perform at least $n(n+1)/2$ comparisons.)

Chapter 4
Optimality Considerations in Data Structures – Part 2

In this chapter we present three different concepts which use graph-theoretical means to model some aspects of computations: pointer manipulations, representations among data structures and space complexity. These concepts are: the graph-theoretical model of computations, embeddings and pebble games.

4.1 Introduction

This chapter is a continuation of Chapter 3. Here we present some results concerning the graph-theoretical models of data structures.

In Section 4.2 a graph-theoretical model of the computations common to data structures is presented. This model is based on pointer operations, hence it is also called a pointer machine model. In this graph-theoretical model, proof of a lower bound for a particular problem (that is, the lowest common ancestor problem, to be defined later) is presented.

In Section 4.3 we consider embeddings among fundamental data structures: lists, grids (arrays, tables) and binary trees treated as graphs. By an embedding we mean a representation of one data structure by another. The lower and upper bounds on the costs of embeddings are presented. A typical situation where embeddings play an important role is the representation of one type of memory by another, or in engineering design where systems with complex connection patterns are to be designed as simple arrangements

135

like grids or lines (such as VLSI chips or production lines in a factory). It is important that the elements which are functionally (logically) related be close to one another in the target arrangement.

In Section 4.4 a structural approach to the problems of space complexity is presented. The computations are modelled by computation graphs and the space complexity (number of memory locations used) corresponds to the number of pebbles needed in the so-called **pebble game**. In this game we move the pebbles through the graph in a certain way. One of the main phenomena in this area is the time–space trade-off: the less memory is used the more time is needed for the computation. Optimal pebbling methods for complete directed binary trees and pyramids are presented.

We show that the graph-theoretical approach, including the graph-theoretical model of computations, the theory of embeddings and the pebble games, provide general tools well suited for the unification of the variety of problems arising in the analysis of algorithms and data structures (especially in optimality considerations).

4.2   Graph programs – the lowest common ancestors problem

In this section we shall consider the problem known as the **lowest common ancestors problem**. Let V be an infinite set of objects called **vertices**. The problem is to design a data structure representing finite forests of trees over the set V and supporting the execution of sequences of the following types of operations (v and w denote vertices in the set V):

(1) $link(v, w)::$ make v a son of w provided that v and w are in distinct trees and that v is the root of a tree; we assume w to be the result of the operation

(2) $lca(v, w)::$ find the lowest common ancestor t of v and w provided that v and w are in the same tree; we assume t to be the result of the operation

We assume that initially the forest is empty.

For example, let V be the set of all natural numbers and

$$\sigma = link(1, 2),\ link(3, 1),\ link(4, 2),\ link(6, 5),\ link(7, 5),$$
$$link(5, 2),\ lca(3, 6)$$

The sequence σ builds the following forest

$$F = (\{1, 2, 3, 4, 5, 6, 7\}, \{(1, 2), (3, 1), (4, 2), (6, 5), (7, 5), (5, 2)\})$$

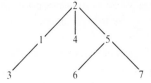

Figure 4.1   The tree built by the operations *link* in σ.

consisting of one tree (see Figure 4.1) and the last operation returns the result 2.

By *m* we denote the number of operations in the input sequence of operations and by *n* the total number of vertices present in the forests of trees under consideration, that is, appearing as arguments of operations in the input sequence. The current forest is denoted by $F = (W, T)$, where W is an n-element subset of V (the set of vertices of forest F) and $T \subseteq W^2$ (the set of edges of forest F). In addition, we assume that the execution of operations proceeds on-line, that is, the current operation has to be carried out completely without knowledge of any further operation in the input sequence and before starting the next operation.

If we represent a forest directly supplying each vertex with a link to its parent then each *link* and each *lca* requires $O(n)$ time implying a time complexity $O(nm)$ for a sequence of m operations. However, if we maintain an auxiliary array *JUMP* such that

$$JUMP[x, i] = \text{the vertex in the current forest that is the ancestor of } x$$
$$\text{distant from it by } 2^i$$

for all vertices x in V and $0 \leqslant i \leqslant \lfloor \log n \rfloor$, then it is possible to move along paths towards the root in time $O(\log n)$ instead of $O(n)$. The implementation based on *JUMP* has time complexity $O((m + n)\log n)$ (see Exercises 4.2 and 4.3).

In specific implementations we distinguish between two data structures: the actual forest defined by a sequence of *link* operations and the virtual representation (which may be a forest itself). The virtual representation has to be able to provide the correct answers to the operations *link* and *lca*. The elements of the actual forest are called vertices; the elements of the virtual representation are called **nodes**.

In general, the virtual representation of the actual forest is a graph. We shall introduce a formal graph-theoretical model of computations for which we shall prove that every algorithm for the lowest common ancestors problem requires $\Omega(m \log \log n)$ steps. In this model elementary operations are of the form: create a new node, move along an edge from one node to another and replace one edge by another. The access to nodes is facilitated by means of a fixed number of heads. All edges going out of a node are labelled with consecutive numbers. The precise definitions are given below.

Let k, j be natural numbers, $k, j \geqslant 2$. Let X be an infinite set of objects called nodes. One node is singled out as the **empty node** denoted by *nil*. By a (k, j)-**graph** we mean a system

$$G = (Z, E, \lambda, z_1, \ldots, z_k)$$

satisfying the following conditions:

(1) Z is a finite subset of X containing the empty node *nil*.
(2) $E \subseteq (Z - \{nil\}) \times Z$
(3) The pair (Z, E) is a directed graph such that the outdegree of each node is j except for the empty node *nil* whose outdegree is 0.
(4) $\lambda : (Z\text{-}\{nil\}) \times \{1, 2, \ldots, j\} \xrightarrow[\text{onto}]{} E$ such that if $\lambda(z, i) = e$, $1 \leqslant i \leqslant j$, then
    $e = (z, z')$ for some node z' in Z and i is called a **label** of edge e.
(5) For each $1 \leqslant i \leqslant k$, z_i is a node in Z; we say that the ith **head** of G **points to** node z_i.

Figure 4.2 presents an example of a $(2, 2)$-graph.
By a j-**graph** we mean a system

$$G = (Z, E, \lambda)$$

satisfying conditions (1)–(4) in the definition of a (k, j)-graph.

By a **graph instruction** we mean one of the following partial operations defined on (k, j)-graphs $(1 \leqslant p, q \leqslant k, 1 \leqslant s \leqslant j, r \geqslant 1)$:

(1) $p \leftarrow new$ Extend the current (k, j)-graph with a new node, say x, in the set $X - Z$. Direct all j edges going out from x to the empty node *nil*. Set the pth head at node x.

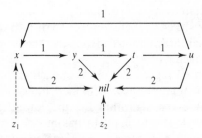

Figure 4.2   An example of a $(2, 2)$-graph: x, y, t, u are nodes and z_1, z_2 are heads.

(2) $p \leftarrow nil$ Set the pth head at the empty node *nil*.

(3) $p \leftarrow q$ Set the pth head at the node pointed to by the qth head.

(4) $p \leftarrow move_s(q)$ The instruction is defined only if $z_q \neq nil$. If $\lambda(z_q, s) = (z_q, z)$ for some node z in Z then set the pth head at z.

(5) $connect_s(p, q)$ The instruction is defined only if $z_p \neq nil$. In the current (k, j)-graph replace edge $\lambda(z_p, s) = (z_p, z)$ by the edge (z_p, z_q) (that is, $E := (E - \{(z_p, z)\}) \cup \{(z_p, z_q)\}$ and set $\lambda(z_p, s)$ to (z_p, z_q)).

(6) **if** $p <=> q$ **then goto** r If the pth head and the qth head point to the same node, then take as the next instruction for execution the rth instruction in the given sequence of instructions; otherwise take the instruction following the current one. If the obtained number of the next instruction exceeds the total number of instructions in the sequence then the computation terminates.

By a **graph program** we mean a finite sequence of graph instructions. The computation of a graph program consists in execution of consecutive instructions starting from the first; the computation may either terminate or be infinite or be aborted because of an undefined instruction. Algorithm 4.1 below shows an example of a graph program (each instruction is preceded by its number in the sequence).

Algorithm 4.1

1:   $2 \leftarrow 1$
2:   $2 \leftarrow move_1(2)$
3:   **if** $1 <=> 2$ **then goto** 6
4:   $connect_2(2, 1)$
5:   **if** $1 <=> 1$ **then goto** 2

The graph program defined by Algorithm 4.1 transforms the $(2, 2)$-graph in Figure 4.2 into the $(2, 2)$-graph presented in Figure 4.3.

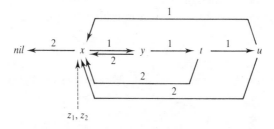

Figure 4.3   The result of applying Algorithm 4.1 to the $(2, 2)$-graph in Figure 4.2.

In the remainder of this section we shall assume that each application of an operation *link* or *lca* is implemented as a separate graph program. Therefore we can ignore instructions of type (6), and as the complexity measure we can simply adopt the number of instructions in the program.

Let us assume that the lowest common ancestors problem is being solved on-line on (k, j)-graphs by means of graph programs. Let $F = (W, T)$ be a forest of trees, $G = (Z, E, \lambda)$ $(G = (Z, E, \lambda, z_1, \dots, z_k))$ be a j-graph $((k, j)$-graph, respectively) and $f: W \xrightarrow{1-1} Z$ an embedding of F in G. We say that G **represents** F if, for each pair of nodes v and w in the same tree of forest F, the graph G contains a path either from $f(v)$ to $f(t)$ or from $f(w)$ to $f(t)$, where t is the lowest common ancestor of v and w (that is, the lowest common ancestor t can be computed in G from $f(v)$ and $f(w)$).

The following lemmas and theorem give a double logarithmic lower bound on the complexity of the operation *lca* in the model of graph programs. Let T_h denote a complete binary tree of height $h \geqslant 0$.

Lemma 4.1

For each natural number $h \geqslant 4$, for each 2-graph $G = (Z, E, \lambda)$ representing T_h there exist two leaves v and w in T_h such that if t is the lowest common ancestor of v and w in T_h then every graph program computing $f(t)$ starting from the $(k, 2)$-graph $G = (Z, E, \lambda, z_1, \dots, z_k)$, where $z_1 = f(v)$, $z_2 = f(w)$ and $z_i = nil$ for $3 \leqslant i \leqslant k$, performs at least

$$\log h - 2$$

graph instructions.

Proof Let q be the smallest natural number such that for each two leaves v and w in T_h if t is the lowest common ancestor of v and w in T_h then

$$\min(d_G(f(v), f(t)), d_G(f(w), f(t))) \leqslant q$$

where $d_G(x, y)$ denotes the distance from x to y in G.

To show the thesis of the lemma it is sufficient to prove that

$$q \geqslant \log h - 2 \tag{4.1}$$

The proof method for (4.1) is to estimate from above and below the following quantity:

$$Q = \sum_{v \text{ a leaf in } T_h} |Y(v)|$$

where $Y(v) = \{t \in T_h: d_G(f(v), f(t)) \leqslant q\}$. First we shall find an estimation from above. Since

$$|Y(v)| \leqslant 2^0 + 2^1 + \cdots + 2^q < 2^{q+1}$$

we have

$$Q \leqslant 2^h 2^{q+1} \tag{4.2}$$

Now we shall estimate Q from below. Let t be a node in T_h of height $i > 0$. Note that either for each leaf v in the left subtree of t or for each leaf v in the right subtree of t the following holds

$$t \in Y(v)$$

since otherwise the leaves v in the left subtree and w in the right subtree of t would exist, such that $t \notin Y(v)$ and $t \notin Y(w)$. That would mean that node $f(t)$ were not reachable from $f(v)$ and $f(w)$ in at most q steps, contrary to the definition of q. Hence t belongs to at least 2^{i-1} sets $Y(v)$ where v is a leaf in T_h. The overall contribution of nodes of height i to the sum Q is therefore at least $2^{i-1} 2^{h-i} = 2^{h-1}$. Hence we conclude that

$$Q \geqslant h 2^{h-1} \tag{4.3}$$

Combining the two estimates (4.2) and (4.3) we obtain that

$$h 2^{h-1} \leqslant 2^h 2^{q+1}$$

from which the desired inequality (4.1) follows.   ∎

We can show that $\Omega(m \log \log n)$ is the lower bound on the cost of the lowest common ancestors problem. This problem appears (as a practical problem) in compiler design: for example, in the code optimization and the analysis of the tree of prefixes in the programming language SIMULA 67. Unfortunately, there is a gap between the best known lower and upper bounds for the problem (in the graph-theoretical model and in the RAM model). The lower bound is $\Omega(m \log \log n)$ while the upper bound is $O(m \log n)$.

We leave to the reader (as Exercises 4.4 and 4.5) the proofs of the facts that the two restrictions appearing in Lemma 4.1 (that $j = 2$ and that the heads $z_3, \ldots, z_k$ point to the empty node) are not essential. Each solution to the least common ancestors problem on (k, j)-graphs can be simulated by a solution which satisfies the assumptions of Lemma 4.1 with preservation of the order of magnitude of the complexity. In other words, Lemma 4.2 holds.

Lemma 4.2

There are constants $c > 0$ and h_0 such that for every natural number $h \geqslant h_0$, for every j-graph G representing tree T_h and for every sequence of nodes x_1, $x_2, \ldots, x_{k-2}$ in G, there are two leaves v and w in T_h such that if t is the lowest common ancestor of v and w in T_h then every graph program computing $f(t)$, starting from the (k, j)-graph $G = (Z, E, \lambda, z_1, \ldots, z_k)$, where $z_1 = f(v)$, $z_2 = f(w)$, $z_i = x_{i-2}$ for $3 \leqslant i \leqslant k$, performs at least

$$c \log h$$

graph instructions.

From Lemma 4.2 our main theorem follows.

Theorem 4.1

Let m and n be integers, with $n \leqslant m$. There exists a sequence σ of m operations *link* and *lca* such that each on-line implementation of σ requires at least $\Omega(m \log \log n)$ graph instructions and $n \leqslant m$ is the total number of nodes in the forests of trees being built.

Proof Let $n \geqslant 8$, $h = \lfloor \log n \rfloor - 2$, $n' = 2^{h+1} - 1$. Note that

$$n' \leqslant \frac{n}{2} \leqslant \frac{m}{2} \quad \text{and} \quad 2^h \geqslant \frac{n}{8}$$

First let us perform a sequence of *link* operations creating tree T_h. This can be done by means of $n' - 1 \leqslant m/2$ *link* operations. Next, applying Lemma 4.2 we choose $m - (n' - 1) \geqslant m/2$ times an operation *lca* each requiring at least $c \log h$ graph instructions. Hence the execution of such a sequence of operations requires at least

$$(mc \log h)/2 \geqslant (mc \log \log n/8)/2 = \Omega(m \log \log n)$$

graph instructions.   ∎

Theorem 4.1 comes from Harel (1980) and Harel and Tarjan (1984). The model of graph programs was used earlier to prove a non-linear lower bound on the complexity of performing sequences of the operations *UNION* (combine two given disjoint sets) and *FIND* (find the name of the set to which a given element belongs) by Tarjan (1979), Tarjan and VanLeeuwen (1984) and Banachowski (1980). In Banachowski (1982) a general model of graph computations was defined and its basic properties were studied. Among others, it was proved that the complexity of an on-line execution of sequences of operations lies between $\Theta(n)$ and $\Theta(n \log n)$. Schonhage (1980) proved that multidimensional Turing machines can be simulated by graph programs in real time. Exercises 4.3–4.4 come from Aho *et al.* (1976).

4.3 Embeddings of data structures

In this section we shall consider representations of one data structure by another. By a data structure we mean here a static object (such as a linked list, grid or tree) with only one operation defined on the data structure: passing from one place to another adjacent place in the data structure. Under such assumptions a data structure can be identified with an undirected graph.

EXAMPLES _____

(1) The ***n*-element list** is a graph with a set of nodes

$$L = \{1, 2, \ldots, n\}$$

and a set of edges

$$E_L = \{(i, i + 1): 1 \leqslant i \leqslant n - 1\}$$

(see Figure 4.4(a)).

(a)

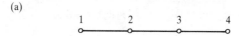

(b)

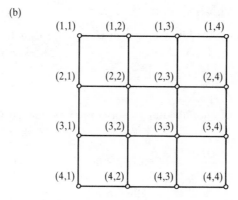

(c)

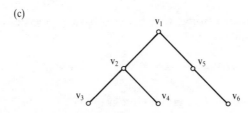

Figure 4.4 Data structures as undirected graphs: (a) the 4-element list, (b) the grid of size 4 × 4, (c) a binary tree with six vertices.

(2) The **grid of size $m \times p$** is a graph with a set of nodes

$$A = \{(i,j)\colon 1 \leqslant i \leqslant m,\ 1 \leqslant j \leqslant p\}$$

and a set of edges

$$E_A = \{((i,j),(k,s))\colon (i,\ j),(k,\ s) \in A \wedge |i - k| + |j - s| = 1\}$$

(see Figure 4.4(b)).

(3) An example of a binary tree with $n = 6$ nodes is shown in Figure 4.4(c). One node in a binary tree is distinguished, namely, its root. The set of nodes in a binary tree will be denoted by T and the set of edges by E_T.

Let $G = (V, E)$, $G' = (V', E')$ be two undirected graphs and $|V| \leqslant |V'|$. As before $d_G(v, w)$ denotes the distance between nodes v and w in G. By an **embedding** of G in G' we mean any 1–1 mapping

$$f\colon V \xrightarrow{\ 1\text{--}1\ } V'$$

The **worst-case cost** of an embedding f of G in G' is defined as the number

$$WCOST(f) = \begin{cases} \max_{(v,\ w) \in E} d_{G'}(f(v), f(w)) & \text{if } |E| > 0 \\ 0 & \text{otherwise} \end{cases}$$

The **dilation** of an embedding f of G in G' is defined as the number

$$DIL(f) = \sum_{(v,\ w) \in E} d_{G'}(f(v), f(w))$$

The **average cost** of an embedding f of G in G' is defined as the number

$$ACOST(f) = \begin{cases} \dfrac{DIL(f)}{|E|} & \text{if } |E| > 0 \\ 0 & \text{otherwise} \end{cases}$$

The following lemma brings together two basic properties of the cost functions $WCOST$ and $ACOST$.

Lemma 4.3

For every embedding f of graph G in graph G':

(1) $ACOST(f) \leqslant WCOST(f)$

(2) If there are nodes v and w in V and numbers $a, b > 0$ such that:

   (a) $d_G(v, w) \leqslant a$
   (b) $d_{G'}(f(v), f(w)) \geqslant b$

   then

   $$WCOST(f) \geqslant \frac{b}{a}$$

Proof Point (1) is obvious by the definitions. To prove (2) let $v = v_0$, $v_1, \ldots,\ v_s = w$ be the shortest path between nodes v and w, that is, $s = d_G(v, w) \leqslant a$. For each $0 \leqslant i < s$ consider the shortest path P_i in G' between $f(v_i)$ and $f(v_{i+1})$. The concatenation $P_0, P_1, \ldots, P_{s-1}$ is a path between $f(v)$ and $f(w)$. Hence

$$\sum_{i=0}^{s-1} d_{G'}(f(v_i), f(v_{i+1})) \geqslant b$$

Therefore there exists $0 \leqslant j < s$ such that

$$s d_{G'}(f(v_j), f(v_{j+1})) \geqslant \sum_{i=0}^{s-1} d_{G'}(f(v_i), f(v_{i+1})) \geqslant b$$

Finally we obtain

$$WCOST(f) \geqslant d_{G'}(f(v_j), f(v_{j+1})) \geqslant \frac{b}{s} \geqslant \frac{b}{a} \qquad \blacksquare$$

We shall analyse embeddings among fundamental static data structures: (linked) lists, grids and binary trees. (For completeness of presentation some theorems are quoted without proof.) First we shall deal with the problem of embedding a list in an arbitrary graph (hence in particular in a grid and a tree).

Theorem 4.2

For every $n \geqslant 1$, for every connected graph $G = (V, E)$, $|V| = n$, there is an embedding

$$f: L \xrightarrow{1-1} V$$

of an n-element list in the graph G such that:

(1) $WCOST(f) \leqslant 3$
(2) $ACOST(f) \leqslant 2$

Proof For $n = 1$ both the formulas (1) and (2) are obviously true. Assume that $n > 1$. The embedding f will be defined by means of the following algorithm.

1. Construct a spanning tree T for G.[†] Let v be the root of T.

2. Perform $\begin{cases} i := 1 \\ Linearize(v) \end{cases}$

where *Linearize(w)* is the following recursive procedure (w is a node of G, *depth(w)* as before denotes the depth of w in G).

Algorithm 4.2

```
procedure Linearize(w);
begin
  if depth(w) is even then
  begin
    f(i):= w;
    i:= i + 1
  end;
  let w₁, w₂, ..., wₖ be sons of node w;
  for j:= 1 to k do Linearize(wⱼ);
  if depth(w) is odd then
  begin
    f(i):= w;
    i:= i + 1
  end
end;
```

Figure 4.5 presents the embedding f for the 13-element list in a tree with 13 elements.

Considering all possible mutual positions of the nodes $f(i)$ and $f(i + 1)$ for $1 \leqslant i \leqslant n - 1$, we obtain

(1) $d_T(f(i), f(i + 1)) = 1 \Leftrightarrow depth(f(i))$ is even and $depth(f(i + 1))$ is odd

(2) $d_T(f(i), f(i + 1)) = 2 \Leftrightarrow depth(f(i))$ and $depth(f(i + 1))$ are of the same parity

(3) $d_T(f(i), f(i + 1)) = 3 \Leftrightarrow depth(f(i))$ is odd and $depth(f(i + 1))$ is even

Therefore

$$WCOST(f) \leqslant 3$$

[†] A tree $T = (V', E')$ is a spanning tree for a graph $G = (V, T)$ if $V = V'$ and $E' \subseteq E$.

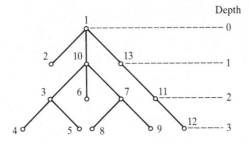

Depth

Figure 4.5 Embedding f of the 13-element list in a 13-node tree. Each node is labelled with a number which is the counter-image of that node at mapping f.

and

$$DIL(f) \leqslant 2(n-2) + 1 = 2n - 3$$

The last inequality holds because the nodes $f(1)$ and $f(n)$ have even and odd depths and therefore for $1 \leqslant i \leqslant n - 1$ the number of changes: $depth(f(i))$ even $\rightarrow depth(f(i+1))$ odd is greater by 1 than the number of changes: $depth(f(i))$ odd $\rightarrow depth(f(i+1))$ even. Consequently we obtain

$$ACOST(f) \leqslant \frac{2n-3}{n-1} \leqslant 2$$

Corollary The n-element list can be embedded in a grid of size $m \times m$ $(m^2 \geqslant n)$ and in any binary tree of n nodes with the worst-case cost not greater than 3 and the average cost not greater than 2.   □

Exercises 4.6 and 4.7 show that the numbers 3 and 2 in Theorem 4.2 cannot be lowered, that is, the embedding f defined above is optimal and can be constructed in linear time with respect to n.

Now we turn to the problem of embedding a grid of size $m \times m$ in the n-element list, where $n = m^2$. The case $m = 1$ is trivial – both the costs are equal to 0. Assume that $m > 1$. Consider the arrangement of elements of the grid row by row (see Figure 4.6). We obtain

$$WCOST(f) = m = \sqrt{n}$$

$$DIL(f) = m(m-1) * 1 + m(m-1) * m = (m-1)m(m+1)$$

$$ACOST(f) = \frac{(m-1)m(m+1)}{2m(m-1)} = \frac{m+1}{2} = \frac{1}{2}\sqrt{n} + \frac{1}{2}$$

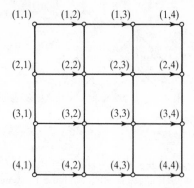

Figure 4.6   The linear arrangement of elements of the grid row by row.

Is there a better arrangement of a grid in a list? We shall show that there is no embedding f whose $WCOST(f)$ or $ACOST(f)$ would be of a lower order than $\sqrt{n}$.

Theorem 4.3

For every embedding f of the grid A of size $m \times m$ in the n-element list, where $n = m^2$, the following inequality holds:

$$WCOST(f) \geqslant \tfrac{1}{2}\sqrt{n} + \tfrac{1}{2}$$

Proof   Let v and w be nodes of grid A such that

$$v = f^{-1}(1) \quad \text{and} \quad w = f^{-1}(n)$$

Since $d_L(1, n) = m^2 - 1$ and $d_A(v, w) \leqslant 2(m - 1)$ it follows from Lemma 4.3 that

$$WCOST(f) \geqslant \frac{m^2 - 1}{2(m - 1)} = \frac{1}{2}m + \frac{1}{2} \qquad \blacksquare$$

The proof of the lower bound for the average cost is a little more complicated. First we shall show an auxiliary lemma which characterizes partitions of grids. For a graph $G = (V, E)$ and a subset $W \subseteq V$, by the **boundary** of W in G we mean the following set:

$$\partial W = \{w \in W : \text{there is } v \in V - W \text{ such that } (v, w) \in E\}$$

Lemma 4.4

Let A denote a grid of size $m \times m$ and let B be a non-empty subset of A such that

$$|B| \leqslant \tfrac{1}{2} m^2$$

Then

$$|\partial B| \geqslant \frac{1}{\sqrt{2}} \sqrt{|B|}$$

Proof   Denote by r and k the number of rows and the number of columns of A, respectively, which contain elements of B. Without loss of generality we can assume that $r \geqslant k$. Denote by r^* the number of rows of A, all of whose elements are included in B. Since

$$m r^* \leqslant |B| \leqslant \frac{m^2}{2}$$

we obtain

$$r^* \leqslant \frac{m}{2} \tag{4.4}$$

If $r^* = 0$ then $|B| \leqslant rk \leqslant r^2$ and

$$|\partial B| \geqslant r \geqslant \sqrt{|B|}$$

If $r^* > 0$ then $k = m$ and hence $r = m$. By (4.4) and the assumption $|B| \leqslant m^2/2$ it follows that

$$|\partial B| \geqslant r - r^* \geqslant m - \frac{m}{2} = \frac{m}{2} \geqslant \frac{1}{\sqrt{2}} \sqrt{|B|}$$

We conclude that in both cases the lemma holds.   ∎

Note that the lists can be partitioned into two disjoint sublists separated by only one edge. The difference in 'separability' between lists and grids accounts for the relatively big average cost of any embedding of a grid in a list.

Theorem 4.4

For every embedding f of a grid A of size $m \times m$ in an n-element list L, where

$n = m^2$ and $m > 1$ the following holds:

$$ACOST(f) \geqslant \frac{1}{23}\sqrt{n}$$

Proof Denote by D_i for $1 \leqslant i \leqslant n$, the following set:

$$D_i = \{f^{-1}(j): 1 \leqslant j \leqslant i\}$$

Let $M = m^2/2$. Applying Lemma 4.4 we have that for $i \leqslant M$

$$|\partial D_i| \geqslant \sqrt{\frac{i}{2}}$$

Hence using the interpretation of the integral as an area we obtain

$$DIL(f) = \sum_{(v,\,w)\in E_A} d_L(f(v), f(w))$$

$$= \sum_{\substack{1 \leqslant i < j \leqslant n \\ (f^{-1}(i),\, f^{-1}(j))\in E_A}} (j - i)$$

$$= \sum_{\substack{1 \leqslant i < j \leqslant n \\ (f^{-1}(i),\, f^{-1}(j))\in E_A}} \sum_{k=i}^{j-1} 1 \geqslant \sum_{k=1}^{n-1} |\partial D_k| \geqslant \frac{1}{\sqrt{2}} \sum_{k=1}^{\lfloor M \rfloor} \sqrt{k} \geqslant \frac{1}{\sqrt{2}} \int_0^{\lfloor M \rfloor} \sqrt{x}\,dx$$

$$= \frac{1}{\sqrt{2}} \frac{2}{3} \lfloor M \rfloor^{3/2} \geqslant \frac{4\sqrt{2}}{23} M^{3/2} \geqslant \frac{2}{23} m^3$$

Hence

$$ACOST(f) \geqslant \frac{\frac{2}{23}m^3}{2m(m - 1)} \geqslant \frac{1}{23} m \qquad\blacksquare$$

Notice that although both the lower and upper bounds are of the same order they differ significantly in coefficients.

Now let us consider the problem of the embedding of a grid in a complete binary tree. It is not difficult to devise such an embedding. Let A be a grid of size $m \times m$, $n = m^2$, and let T be a complete binary tree of height $h = 2\lceil \log m \rceil$. First, assume that $n = 2^{2k}$ for some $k \geqslant 0$. The algorithm for embedding A in T is recursive.

(1) If $k = 0$ then A is of size 1×1 and the single element of the grid is mapped into the single element of the tree.

(2) If $k > 0$ then we divide A into four subgrids A_1, A_2, A_3, A_4 of size $m/2 \times m/2$ (as shown in Figure 4.7(a)) and we map the subgrids recursively into the subtrees T_1, T_2, T_3, T_4 of tree T of height $2(k-1)$ (as shown in Figure 4.7(b)).

Let f denote the embedding under consideration. Since T is of height $2k = \log n$ we obtain

$$WCOST(f) \leqslant 2\log n$$

Now we shall estimate $DIL(f)$. Let a_k denote the value $DIL(f)$ for $n = 2^{2k}$. From the construction above, it follows the following recursive formula for a_k:

$$\begin{cases} a_0 = 0 \\ a_k \leqslant 4a_{k-1} + 2(2^k)2(2k) \end{cases}$$

Hence

$$\begin{cases} a_0 = 0 \\ a_k \leqslant 4a_{k-1} + 8k2^k \end{cases}$$

By induction it is easy to show that

$$DIL(f) = a_k \leqslant 16m^2 - 8m\log m - 16m$$

Therefore we have

$$ACOST(f) \leqslant \frac{16m^2 - 8m\log m - 16m}{2m(m-1)} = 8 - \frac{4\log m}{m-1} \leqslant 8$$

Note that every grid can be first expanded to the grid of size

$$2^{\lceil \log m \rceil} \times 2^{\lceil \log m \rceil}$$

(a)   (b)

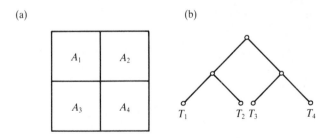

Figure 4.7 The partition (a) of the grid A, (b) of the tree T. The elements of A_i are mapped into T_i.

increasing the number of elements at most by

$$\frac{2^{2\lceil \log m \rceil}}{m^2} = 2^{2\lceil \log m \rceil - 2\log m} < 4 \text{ times}$$

and then the expanded grid can be embedded by the construction described above in the complete tree of height $h = 2\lceil \log m \rceil$. Our investigations end with the following theorem.

Theorem 4.5

There exists an embedding of a grid of size $m \times m$ into a complete binary tree of height $h = \lceil \log m \rceil$ such that

(1) $WCOST(f) = \Theta(\log m)$
(2) $ACOST(f) = \Theta(1)$

Now we shall show that the upper bounds in Theorem 4.5 are also lower bounds. Our argument, as in Theorem 4.4, will be based on the difference in 'separability' for grids and trees. It is difficult to partition arrays while trees are easily separable (in the sense of few edges between the resulting parts of the partition). The separability property for trees is expressed by the following lemma.

Lemma 4.5

Let T be a binary tree, D a subset of the set T, $|D| = n$. There is a subtree T^* of T such that

$$\left\lfloor \frac{n}{4} \right\rfloor \leq |T^* \cap D| \leq \frac{n}{2} \tag{4.5}$$

Proof We can assume that $n \geq 4$. Let h be the largest natural number such that each subtree of height h contains at most $\lfloor n/4 \rfloor - 1$ nodes in set D. Consequently, there is a subtree T^* of height $h + 1$, which contains at least $\lfloor n/4 \rfloor$ nodes in D. Since the subtrees of T^* contain at most $\lfloor n/4 \rfloor - 1$ nodes in D, T^* contains at most $1 + 2(\lfloor n/4 \rfloor - 1) = 2\lfloor n/4 \rfloor - 1 \leq \lfloor n/2 \rfloor$ nodes in D. ∎

Exercise 4.11 shows that the inequalities in Lemma 4.5 cannot be written as

$$\frac{n}{4} \leq |T^* \cap D| \leq \frac{n}{2}$$

Applying Lemmas 4.4 and 4.5 we shall show the following lower bound on the worst-case cost of an embedding of a grid in a binary tree.

Theorem 4.6

For every embedding f of a grid A of size $m \times m$ in a binary tree T, $|T| \geqslant n = m^2 > 1$ the following inequality holds:

$$WCOST(f) \geqslant \tfrac{1}{2}\log n - 2$$

Proof   Let $D = f(A)$. By virtue of Lemma 4.5 there is a subtree T^* of T such that

$$\left\lfloor \frac{n}{4} \right\rfloor \leqslant |T^* \cap D| \leqslant \frac{n}{2}$$

Let $B = f^{-1}(T^*)$. Hence

$$\left\lfloor \frac{n}{4} \right\rfloor \leqslant |B| \leqslant \frac{n}{2}$$

By Lemma 4.4 we have for $n \geqslant 4$

$$|\partial B| \geqslant \frac{1}{\sqrt{2}}\sqrt{|B|} \geqslant \frac{1}{\sqrt{2}}\sqrt{\left\lfloor \frac{n}{4} \right\rfloor} \geqslant \frac{1}{4}\sqrt{n}$$

Each node in grid A belonging to the boundary ∂B is connected by an edge with some node in the set $A - B$. On the other hand in tree T all the images of the nodes in ∂B are in the subtree T^*, and all the images of the nodes in the set $A - B$ in the remaining part $T - T^*$ (see Figure 4.8). Notice that every path connecting pairs of nodes, one in T^*, the other in $T - T^*$ must pass the root of the subtree T^*. Let k be the maximum distance of the root of the subtree T^* from the nodes $v \in f(\partial B)$. We obtain

$$2^0 + 2^1 + \cdots + 2^k \geqslant |\partial B| \geqslant \tfrac{1}{4}\sqrt{n}$$

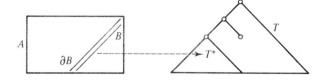

Figure 4.8   The set ∂B is mapped into the subtree T^*.

and therefore

$$2^{k+1} \geqslant \tfrac{1}{4}\sqrt{n}$$

Finally we obtain

$$WCOST(f) \geqslant k + 1 \geqslant \log \tfrac{1}{4}\sqrt{n} = \tfrac{1}{2}\log n - 2 \qquad \blacksquare$$

We shall now consider the problem of embedding a binary tree in a list. The algorithm f for embedding an n-vertex binary tree T in the n-element list is recursive. If $n = 1$ then the single element of the tree is mapped into the single element of the list. If $n > 1$ then by means of Lemma 4.5 ($D = T$) we first find a subtree T^* of T such that

$$\lfloor n/4 \rfloor \leqslant |T^*| \leqslant n/2$$

The graph $T - T^*$ is obviously a binary tree. Now we embed recursively T^* in the list $L_1 = \{1, 2, \ldots, |T^*|\}$ and $T - T^*$ in the list $L_2 = \{|T^*| + 1, \ldots, n\}$. Figure 4.9 presents the embedding of the complete binary tree with 7 nodes in the 7-element list.

We now obtain Theorem 4.7.

Theorem 4.7

For the embedding f defined above, the following two equalities hold:

(1) $WCOST(f) = O(n)$
(2) $ACOST(f) = \Theta(\log n)$

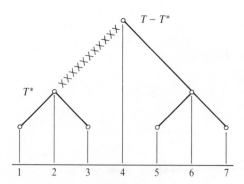

Figure 4.9 The embedding of the complete binary tree in the 7-element list. A partition can be chosen so that the embedding is a projection on the x-axis.

Proof Point (1) is evident. Now let us denote by a_n the maximum overall dilation $DIL(f)$ of the embedding f of an n-node binary tree in the n-element list. Since only one edge connects the subtrees T^* and $T - T^*$, we have the following recursive formulas:

$$\left\{ \begin{array}{l} a_1 = 0 \\ a_n \leqslant \max_{[n/4] \leqslant i \leqslant n/2} (a_i + a_{n-i}) + (n-1) \quad \text{for } n > 1 \end{array} \right.$$

On every recursive level the component $(n - 1)$ contributes at most $n - 1$ in total. Since there are $O(\log n)$ levels of recursion we obtain

$$a_n = O(n \log n)$$

Hence

$$ACOST(f) = \frac{DIL(f)}{n-1} = O(\log n)$$

Moreover, for the complete binary tree of height h

$$DIL(f) = \sum_{i=0}^{h-1} 2^{h-i} 2^i = h2^h$$

and

$$ACOST(f) \geqslant \frac{h2^h}{2^{h+1} - 2} = \Omega(\log n)$$

This completes the proof of point (2).   ∎

The following theorem shows that the embedding f defined above is optimal within a constant factor for the measure $ACOST$.

Theorem 4.8

For every embedding f of the complete n-node binary tree in the n-element list the following hold:

(1) $WCOST(f) \geqslant \dfrac{n-1}{2 \log n}$

(2) $ACOST(f) = \Omega(\log n)$

Proof Point (1) follows from Lemma 4.3. The proof of point (2) is outside the scope of this book and can be found in Yordanski (1976).   ∎

The lower bound in Theorem 4.8 point (1) is also an upper bound as Theorem 4.9 states.

Theorem 4.9

For every $n \geqslant 2$ and for every n-node binary tree T there exists an embedding f of tree T in the n-element list such that

$$WCOST(f) = O\left(\frac{n}{\log n}\right)$$

Proof   The proof can be found in Diks (1985). The proof in the case when T is the complete binary tree is left to the reader as an exercise (see Exercises 4.13 and 4.14).   ∎

To complete our goal of analysing mutual embeddings among the three basic data structures of lists, grids and binary trees, it remains only to consider the problem of embedding binary trees in grids. The algorithm for embedding an n-node binary tree in a grid of size $m \times m$ $(m^2 \geqslant n)$ is recursive. We divide T into two subgraphs T_1 and T_2 and A into two subgrids A_1 and A_2, and then we recursively embed T_1 in A_1 and T_2 in A_2. The main problem is how to divide both T and A evenly. The next three lemmas deal with this problem.

Lemma 4.6

For every natural number k, $1 \leqslant k \leqslant n$, for every n-node binary tree T there is a partition of T into two disjoint subgraphs $T = T_1 \cup T_2$ such that

(1) $|T_1| = k$
(2) the number of edges connecting T_1 and T_2 is at most

  $c \log n$

  where

  $$c = \frac{1}{\log (6/5)}$$

Proof   First we find a node v in T such that after removing it T breaks into two or three subtrees, each with at most $\lfloor n/2 \rfloor$ nodes. We start from an arbitrary node w in T and then carry out Algorithm 4.3.

Algorithm 4.3

> **repeat**
>> let $T_1, T_2, \ldots, T_s$ $(1 \leqslant s \leqslant 3)$, $|T_1| \geqslant |T_2| \geqslant \cdots \geqslant |T_s|$ be the trees which result from removing w from T;
>> **if** $|T_1| \leqslant \lfloor n/2 \rfloor$ **then return** w;
>> let w' be the node in T_1 which is connected to w;
>> $w := w'$
>
> **end** (see Figure 4.10).

The proof of Lemma 4.6 is by induction on n. For $n = 1$, it is obvious. Now let T be an n-node binary tree, where $n \geqslant 2$. By means of Algorithm 4.3 we find a 'central' node v. Let $D_1, \ldots, D_s$, $|D_1| \geqslant |D_2| \geqslant \cdots \geqslant |D_s|$, $1 \leqslant s \leqslant 3$, be the trees resulting from removing v from T. There are two possible cases. If $k \leqslant |D_1|$ then by the induction hypothesis there exists a partition $D_1 = D_1' \cup D_1''$ of tree D_1 such that $|D_1'| = k$ and the number of edges connecting D_1' with D_1'' is at most $c \log|D_1|$. We define

$$T_1 = D_1' \quad \text{and} \quad T_2 = T - D_1'$$

Obviously $|T_1| = k$ and the number of edges between T_1 and T_2 is at most

$$c \log|D_1| + 1 \leqslant c \log\frac{n}{2} + \frac{1}{\log(6/5)} \leqslant c \log n$$

The other case is when $k > |D_1|$. Then we apply the induction hypothesis to the tree $D^* = T - D_1$ with $k' = k - |D_1|$. If follows that there exists a partition $D^* = D_1^* \cup D_2^*$ such that $|D_1^*| = k'$ and the number of edges between D_1^* and D_2^* is at most $c \log(n - |D_1|)$. We define

$$T_1 = D_1 \cup D_1^* \quad \text{and} \quad T_2 = T - T_1$$

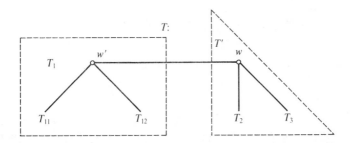

Figure 4.10 Finding a 'central' vertex in tree T. Since $|T_1| > \lfloor n/2 \rfloor$, $|T'| \leqslant \lfloor n/2 \rfloor$. Moreover $|T_{11}| < |T_1|$ and $|T_{12}| < |T_1|$.

Obviously $|T_1| = k$ and the number of edges connecting T_1 with T_2 is at most

$$c \log(n - |D_1|) + 1 \leqslant 1 + c \log\left(n - \frac{n-1}{3}\right) \leqslant 1 + c \log\left(\frac{n(3 - \frac{1}{2})}{3}\right)$$

$$= c \log n + 1 - c\frac{1}{c}$$

$$= c \log n$$

since

$$|D_1| \geqslant \frac{n-1}{3} \quad \text{and} \quad n - 1 \geqslant n/2 \qquad \blacksquare$$

As a result two subgraphs T_1 and T_2 arise which are forests of binary trees. Note that Lemma 4.6 remains valid if T is a forest of binary trees. Namely, if T consists of s trees $D_1, D_2, \ldots, D_s$ then we apply Lemma 4.6 to the tree D_i with

$$k' = k - \sum_{j=1}^{i-1} |D_j|$$

where i is the smallest number such that $1 \leqslant i \leqslant s$ and $\sum_{j=1}^{i} |D_j| \geqslant k$. Therefore we have the following lemma.

Lemma 4.7

For every natural number k, $1 \leqslant k \leqslant n$, for every n-node forest T of binary trees, there exists a partition of T into two node-disjoint forests of trees $T = T_1 \cup T_2$ such that

(1) $|T_1| = k$
(2) The number of edges connecting two subgraphs T_1 and T_2 is at most

$$c \log n$$

where

$$c = \frac{1}{\log(6/5)}.$$

Square grids can easily be divided into four approximately equal square subgrids. There is a kind of rectangular grid that can easily be divided into two approximately equal parts which are similar (in geometrical shape) to the grid being partitioned. By a **grid of order n** we mean a rectangular grid with the set of nodes A defined as follows (x, y, i, j denote natural numbers):

(1) If $n = 1$ then $A = \{(x, y)\}$.
(2) If $n > 1$ then

$$A = \{(i, j): x \leqslant i < x + 2\sqrt{n-1}, \, y \leqslant j < y + 2\sqrt{2(n-1)}\}$$

or

$$A = \{(i, j): x \leqslant i < x + 2\sqrt{2(n-1)}, \, y \leqslant j < y + 2\sqrt{n-1}\}$$

Lemma 4.8

For every grid A of order n the following two conditions are satisfied:

(1) $|A| \geqslant n$
(2) If $n > 1$ then A contains two node-disjoint subgrids of order $\lfloor n/2 \rfloor$ and $\lceil n/2 \rceil$, respectively.

Proof It is straightforward to see that the lemma holds for $n < 4$. Now assume that $n \geqslant 4$. Then

$$|A| \geqslant \lfloor 2\sqrt{n-1} \rfloor \cdot \lfloor 2\sqrt{2(n-1)} \rfloor$$
$$\geqslant (2\sqrt{n-1} - 1) \cdot (2\sqrt{2(n-1)} - 1) \geqslant \sqrt{n-1} \cdot \sqrt{2(n-1)} \geqslant n$$

Let us cut grid A of order $n > 1$ into halves along the longer side (of length $2\sqrt{2(n-1)}$). Because

$$\frac{1}{2}2\sqrt{2(n-1)} = 2\sqrt{\frac{n-1}{2}}$$

$$2\sqrt{n-1} = 2\sqrt{2\left(\frac{n-1}{2}\right)}$$

$$\left\lfloor \frac{n}{2} \right\rfloor - 1 \leqslant \left\lceil \frac{n}{2} \right\rceil - 1 \leqslant \frac{n-1}{2}$$

the halves contain grids of order $\lceil n/2 \rceil - 1$ and $\lfloor n/2 \rfloor - 1$, respectively. ∎

The algorithm for an embedding f of an n-node binary tree T into a grid A of order n is recursive. If $n = 1$ then the single node of T is mapped into the single element of A. For $n > 1$ we apply Lemma 4.7 to find a partition $T = T_1 \cup T_2$ into two disjoint forests of trees T_1 and T_2 such that

$$|T_1| = \lfloor n/2 \rfloor \quad \text{and} \quad |T_2| = \lceil n/2 \rceil$$

and the number of edges connecting T_1 with T_2 is at most $c \log n$, where $c = 1/(\log(6/5))$. We now apply Lemma 4.8 to find in A two disjoint subgrids A_1 and A_2 of orders $\lfloor n/2 \rfloor$ and $\lceil n/2 \rceil$, respectively, satisfying the conditions (1) and (2) in Lemma 4.8. We embed recursively T_1 in A_1 and T_2 in A_2. Observe that the maximum distance between nodes in grid A is at most

$$2\sqrt{n-1} + 2\sqrt{2(n-1)} \leqslant 5\sqrt{n}$$

Denote by a_n the maximum overall dilation $DIL(f)$ of the embedding under consideration. We obtain the following recursive formula for a_n:

$$\begin{cases} a_1 = 0 \\ a_n \leqslant a_{\lfloor n/2 \rfloor} + a_{\lceil n/2 \rceil} + 5c\sqrt{n}\log n \end{cases}$$

To find the order of magnitude of a_n it is sufficient to solve the above equations for n being powers of 2, $n = 2^k$ for $k \geqslant 0$ (see Exercise 1.19). We obtain

$$\begin{cases} a_{2^0} = 0 \\ a_{2^k} = 2a_{2^{k-1}} + 5ck2^{k/2} \quad \text{for} \quad k > 0 \end{cases} \tag{4.6}$$

Applying induction on k we obtain that

$$a_{2^k} \leqslant \begin{cases} c' & \text{if} \quad k < k_0 \\ c'(2^k - k^2 2^{k/2}) & \text{if} \quad k \geqslant k_0 \end{cases} \tag{4.7}$$

for some constants c' and $k_0 > 0$. Hence it follows that

$$DIL(f) = a_n = \Theta(n - \sqrt{n}(\log n)^2) = \Theta(n)$$

and consequently

$$ACOST(f) = O(1)$$

Thus we come to Theorem 4.10.

Theorem 4.10

For every n-node binary tree T there is an embedding f of T in a grid of size $m \times m$, where $m = \lceil 2\sqrt{2(n-1)} \rceil$ such that

$$ACOST(f) = O(1)$$

Note that for the embedding f defined above

$$WCOST(f) = O(\sqrt{n})$$

Theorem 4.11 shows that we can do better.

Theorem 4.11

For every n-node binary tree T there is an embedding f of T in a grid of size $m \times m$, where $m = O(\sqrt{n})$ such that

$$WCOST(f) = O(\sqrt{n}/\log n)$$

Moreover that embedding is optimal within a constant factor.

Proof   The proof of the first part can be found in Ruzzo and Snyder (1981). The second part follows directly from Lemma 4.3.   ∎

The subject matter presented in this section comes from the following papers: Rosenberg and Snyder (1978) (Theorem 4.2), Lipton *et al.* (1978) (Theorems 4.4 and 4.6), Yordanski (1976) (Theorems 4.7, point (2) and 4.8 point (2)), Diks (1985) (Theorem 4.9), Sheidvasser (1974) (Theorem 4.10) and Ruzzo and Snyder (1981) (Theorem 4.11). Let us turn attention to our main method for the construction of embeddings. We have constructed algorithms for embeddings by means of the divide-and-conquer method. The basis was the possibility of partitioning the underlying graphs into subgraphs separated appropriately from one another. Some further applications of this technique can be found in the papers by Lipton and Tarjan (1979, 1980). Exercises 4.16 and 4.17 come from Lipton and Tarjan (1980). We say that a graph $G = (V, E)$, $|V| = n$, has a **separator** s, where s is a natural number 1 through n, if there is a partition of set V into pairwise disjoint subsets $V = V_1 \cup V_2 \cup V_3$ such that

(1) There are no edges between nodes in V_1 and V_2.

(2) $|V_1|, |V_2| \leqslant \frac{2}{3}n$

(3) $|V_3| \leqslant s$

For example, lists and trees have separator 1; the n-element grid and also every planar n-node graph has separator $O(\sqrt{n})$. Exercise 4.16 expresses a general property of graphs whose separator is smaller than $O(n)$. Namely, if every n-node graph in some class of graphs has separator $O(n/(\log n)^{2+\varepsilon})$ for some $\varepsilon > 0$, then every such graph can be embedded in a binary tree with average cost $O(1)$. An inverse relationship also holds (see Exercise 4.17). There is a constant $c > 0$ such that if a graph $G = (V, E)$ can be embedded in a binary tree with average cost $p > 0$ then G has separator $cpm/\log n$, where $n = |V|$, $m = |E|$.

It is also possible to consider the **space cost** of embeddings. If f is an embedding of $G = (V, E)$ in $G' = (V', E')$ then its space cost is defined to be

$$SCOST(f) = \frac{|V'|}{|V|}$$

The embeddings presented in this section are of low space cost, namely $O(1)$. Exercises 4.18–4.20 contain examples where space costs are of a higher order than $O(1)$. They come from Hong *et al.* (1983). Exercises 4.13 and 4.14 come from Diks (1985), and Exercise 4.15 from Rosenberg and Snyder (1978).

Besides 'static' embeddings (as presented in this section) 'dynamic' embeddings between data structures have also been considered. In the latter case a data structure is equipped with an automaton which can move along edges between nodes. Dynamic embedding reduces to a simulation of one automaton by another. Loui (1983) showed that t steps on a tree can be simulated by

$$O\left(\frac{t^{1 + 1/d}}{\log t}\right)$$

on a d-dimensional grid and that the simulation is optimal. Reischuk (1982) showed that, vice versa, t steps on a d-dimensional grid can be simulated by $O(t5^{d \log^* n})$ on a tree (where $\log^* n = \min\{i \geqslant 1 : \log^{(i)} n \leqslant 1\}$, $\log^{(0)} = 0$ and $\log^{(i + 1)} n = \log(\log^{(i)} n)$ for $i \geqslant 0$).

4.4 Pebbling

Various algorithmic problems can be reduced to the following **pebbling** problem. We are given a **dag** (directed acyclic graph) $G = (V, E)$, a node v of G and a set of pebbles. We wish to put a pebble on v using the following rules:

(1) We can put a pebble on v provided each predecessor[†] of v in G is marked with a pebble.

(2) We can remove a pebble from a node (provided it has been marked with a pebble).

For example, let us consider the dag in Figure 4.11. It represents the arithmetic expression $((x + y) - (y * z))$. Pebbling of the node labelled '$-$'

[†] By a **predecessor** of v in G we mean any node w in G such that $(w, v) \in E$. By a **successor** of v in G we mean any node z in G such that $(v, z) \in E$.

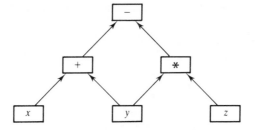

Figure 4.11 The dag of the arithmetic expression $((x + y) - (y * x))$. The vertex labelled '$-$' can be pebbled by applying the following steps:

(1) put pebble on x;   (5) put pebble on z;
(2) put pebble on y;   (6) put pebble on $*$;
(3) put pebble on $+$;   (7) remove pebble from y;
(4) remove pebble from x;   (8) put pebble on $-$.

according to the rules (1) and (2) corresponds to the evaluation of the expression using a fixed number of registers. Each pebble corresponds to a register. Thus the number of pebbles corresponds to the number of registers (that is, the space complexity) and the number of steps corresponds to the time required to evaluate the expression (that is, the time complexity).

We shall consider the problem of pebbling for two specific classes of dags: a complete binary tree and a **pyramid**, under the assumption that all edges are directed towards the root. A pyramid of height h is a directed graph corresponding to a beap (see Section 3.4 and Figure 4.12) consisting of the full $h + 1$ blocks. It follows that the pyramid of height h has exactly $((h + 1)(h + 2))/2$ nodes.

The algorithm for the pebbling of a complete binary tree T of height $h(n = |T| = 2^{h+1} - 1)$ is as follows:

(1) If $n = 1$ then we put a pebble on the only node of T.

(2) If $n > 1$ then let T_1 and T_2 be the left and the right subtree of the root of T, respectively:

   (2.1) We pebble recursively the root of T_1.

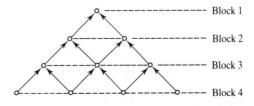

Figure 4.12 A pyramid of height 3 consisting of 4 blocks.

(2.2) We remove all the pebbles from the nodes in T_1 except for the root of T_1.

(2.3) We pebble recursively the root of T_2.

(2.4) We remove all the pebbles from the nodes in T_2 except for the root of T_2.

(2.5) We put a pebble on the root of T.

It is easy to see that the presented algorithm consists of $2n - 3$ pebbling steps and uses $h + 2$ pebbles (for $h > 0$). Exercise 4.21 asks for the change in the algorithm to obtain $2n - h - 2$ pebbling steps.

An algorithm for the pebbling of the pyramid P of height h ($n = |P| = ((h + 2)(h + 1))/2$) consists in processing the nodes block by block, starting from the block of the leaves and ending at the block of the root. Putting pebbles on the nodes of block i we remove them from block $i + 1$ for $1 \leqslant i \leqslant h$. It is easy to see that for $n > 1$ the presented solution consists of $2n - 3$ pebbling steps (n steps for putting a pebble and $n - 3$ steps for a removal) and uses $h + 2$ pebbles (the last block has $h + 1$ nodes and we need one additional pebble for the first node on the next block).

Now we shall show the optimality of the given solutions with respect to the number of pebbles used.

Theorem 4.12

(1) To pebble the root of a complete binary tree T of height h ($h > 0$) it is necessary and sufficient to use $h + 2$ pebbles.

(2) To pebble the root of a pyramid P of height $h(h > 0)$ it is necessary and sufficient to use $h + 2$ pebbles.

Proof We have already shown that the given numbers of pebbles are sufficient.

The proof that the given numbers are necessary is the same in both cases. Let $X = T$ or P. Let us consider any pebbling algorithm for X and the following property of the process of pebbling:

Each path from a leaf to the root in X contains a node marked with a pebble.   **(4.8)**

Property (4.8) does not hold at the beginning of the process of pebbling but it holds at the end (the root itself contains a pebble). Let us consider the pebbling step, at which dag X achieves the property (4.8) and continues to possess it after that step. The step in question consists in putting a pebble on some leaf v of X. Let us consider the path $S = v_h, v_{h-1}, \ldots, v_0$ in X, where v_0

is the root of X and $v_h = v$. There is a set $\{S_i\}_{0 \leqslant i < h}$ of paths from leaves to the root satisfying the following two conditions:

(1) The common part of S and S_i is $v_i, \ldots, v_0$.

(2) The common part of S_i and S_j for $i \neq j$ is included in S.

By the definition of the pebbling step, each path S_i contains a node which does not belong to S and which is marked with a pebble. It follows that after the pebbling step in question there are at least $h + 1$ pebbles on the nodes of X.

At this moment two cases are possible. Either X contains at least $h + 2$ pebbles placed on its nodes or exactly $h + 1$ pebbles. For the second case let us consider the next pebbling step. It can only be a step consisting in putting a pebble on a node (otherwise the property (4.8) would not hold) which gives the total of $h + 2$ pebbles. ∎

For the general case we have the following theorem (whose proof is outside the scope of this book).

Theorem 4.13

Let d be an integer and Γ a class of dags with the in-degree of nodes at most d. For every dag G in Γ and each node v in G it is possible to pebble v using $O(n/\log n)$ pebbles where n is the number of nodes of G. The given number of pebbles is also necessary, that is, for each n there is an n-node dag G in Γ and a node v such that to pebble v, $\Omega(n/\log n)$ pebbles are needed.

The material presented in this section comes from the following three papers: Paterson and Hewitt (1970) (Theorem 4.12(1)), Cook (1974) (Theorem 4.12(2)) and Paul *et al.* (1977) (Theorem 4.13). Further research was concerned mainly with the trade-off between the number S of pebbles and the number T of pebbling steps required to pebble nodes of dags. Note that:

(1) Each n-node dag can be pebbled in $O(n)$ steps using n pebbles (we can pebble the nodes in topological order, that is, consistent with the partial order defined by the edges).

(2) If a dag G with n nodes can be pebbled using S pebbles then G can be pebbled using S pebbles in

$$ T \leqslant \sum_{0 \leqslant k \leqslant S} \binom{n}{k} \leqslant 2^n $$

pebbling steps.

The reader is referred to the paper by Lengauer and Tarjan (1982) for further information about the time–space trade-off mentioned above.

The most important application of Theorem 4.13 is the following result due to Hopcroft *et al.* (1977):

Each deterministic Turing machine of time complexity $t(n)$ can be simulated by a deterministic Turing machine of space complexity $t(n)/\log t(n)$.

Important applications of the technique presented in this section are the results concerning the trade-off between time and space required to implement linear recursion, FFT, matrix multiplication and multiplication of integer numbers (see Lengauer and Tarjan (1982)).

Exercise 4.25 presents an application of Theorem 4.12 to showing that recursion is stronger than flow diagrams (programs with finite number of variables) (see Paterson and Hewitt (1970) and Manna (1974)).

SUMMARY

Key points covered in this chapter include:

- the graph-theoretical model of computations
- the lower bound of the lowest common ancestors problem
- embeddings among lists, trees and grids
- lower and upper bounds on the cost
- pebble games
- optimal pebbling for complete binary trees and pyramids.

EXERCISES

4.1 Design an algorithm for the lowest common ancestors problem. What is its time complexity?

4.2* Consider the problem of finding the depth of nodes in trees. Namely, design a data structure supporting on-line execution of sequences of operations of the following two types (F is a forest of trees over a set V of nodes, v and w are nodes in F):

  $link(v, w)$:: defined as in Section 4.2

  $depth(v)$:: find the depth of v in the current forest F

Initially, forest F consists of n 1-node trees. What is the time complexity of your solution? Using the data structure for the *FIND–UNION* operations on disjoint sets (see Aho *et al.* (1974), Section 4.7) design a data structure which supports the on-line execution of m operations *link* and *depth* in time $O((n + m) \log^* n)$.

4.3* Using the table $JUMP$ as explained in Section 4.2 design an algorithm for the lowest common ancestors problem whose time complexity is $O((m + n) \log n)$.

4.4 Prove that the assumption $j = 2$ is not essential in the proof of Lemma 4.1.

4.5 Prove that the assumption in Lemma 4.1 that the heads $z_3, \ldots, z_k$ point to *nil* is not essential.

4.6* Prove that for every embedding f of an n-element list $(n \geqslant 3)$ in a complete binary tree of height h, $n = 2^{h+1}$, the following hold:

(a) $WCOST(f) \geqslant 3$

(b) $ACOST(f) \geqslant 2 - \dfrac{2h}{n-1}$

4.7 Prove that the embedding f defined in the proof of Theorem 4.2 can be found in time $O(n)$.

4.8 By a **cyclic n-element list** we mean a graph with a set of nodes $L = \{1, 2, \ldots, n\}$ and a set of edges

$$E_L = \{(i, i + 1): 1 \leqslant i \leqslant n - 1\} \cup \{(n, 1)\}$$

How will Theorem 4.2 and Exercises 4.6 and 4.7 change if a list is replaced by a cyclic list?

4.9 By an **n-element star** we mean a graph with a set of nodes $V = \{1, 2, \ldots, n\}$ and a set of edges

$$E_S = \{(1, i): 2 \leqslant i \leqslant n\}$$

Determine optimal embeddings among lists, cyclic lists and stars with respect to

(a) the worst-case cost

(b) the average cost

4.10 Consider the class of all n-node graphs $(n \geqslant 1)$.

(a) Which graph can be embedded with the lowest cost in the remaining graphs in that class?

(b) In which graph can all the remaining graphs be embedded with the lowest cost?

4.11 Prove that the inequality (4.5) in Lemma 4.5 cannot be written as

$$\frac{n}{4} \leqslant |T^* \cap D| \leqslant \frac{n}{2}$$

4.12 Complete the proof of Theorem 4.10 showing that (4.7) gives a solution to the inequality (4.6).

4.13* By a **k-partition** of a graph $G = (V, E)$ we mean any partition of V into l pairwise disjoint non-empty subsets $V_1, V_2, \ldots, V_l$ such that

(a) $|V_i| \leqslant k$ for $1 \leqslant i \leqslant l$

(b) For every edge $(v, w) \in E$ if $v \in V_i$ then $w \in V_{i-1} \cup V_i \cup V_{i+1}$ (assuming $V_0 = V_{l+1} = \varnothing$).

Prove that if graph G has a k-partition then there is an embedding f of G in the $|V|$-list such that

$$WCOST(f) \leqslant 2k - 1$$

4.14* Prove that there is an embedding f of a complete binary tree with $n = 2^{h+1} - 1$ nodes in an n-element list such that

$$WCOST(f) = O(n/\log n)$$

(*Hint*   Using Exercise 4.13 show that a complete binary tree of height h has $s(n)$-partition where $s(n) = \min\{2^s : (s + 2)2^s \geqslant n\}$)

4.15 Let $f : V \to V'$ be an embedding of a graph $G = (V, E)$ in a graph $G' = (V', E')$. Denote by $max(G)$ the maximum degree of a node in G and by $avedeg(G) = |E|/|V|$ the average degree of a node in G. Prove that

(a) $WCOST(f) \geqslant \dfrac{\log(maxdeg(G))}{\log(maxdeg(G'))}$

(b) $ACOST(f) \geqslant \dfrac{\log(avedeg(G))}{\log(maxdeg(G'))} - 3$

4.16* Let k be a natural number and Γ a class of graphs satisfying the following three conditions:

(1) Γ is closed under the operation of a subgraph.

(2) For every graph G in Γ every node v in G has the degree bounded from above by k.

(3) For every $n > 0$ every n-node graph G in Γ has separator $O(n/(\log n)^{2+\varepsilon})$ for some constant $\varepsilon > 0$.
Prove that every graph G in Γ can be embedded in a binary tree with the average cost $O(1)$.

4.17* Let $f: G \to T$ be an embedding of a graph $G = (V, E)$, $|V| = n$, $|E| = m$, in a binary tree with the average cost p. Prove that there is a partition of set V into pairwise disjoint subsets $V = A \cup B \cup C$ such that

(1) There is no edge between nodes in A and B.

(2) $|A|, |B| \leqslant \frac{2}{3}n$

(3) $|C| \leqslant cmp/\log n$ for some constant $c > 0$.

(*Hint* Consider an appropriate partition of T such that for the counterimages at f the conditions (1) and (2) hold.)

4.18* Prove that for every embedding f of an n-element list in a complete binary tree, if

$$WCOST(f) = 1$$

then

$$SCOST(f) = \Omega\left(\frac{2^{n/2}}{n}\right)$$

4.19* Design an embedding f of a complete ternary tree T of height h, $n = |T|$, in a complete binary tree such that

(a) $WCOST(f) = 2$

(b) $SCOST(f) = O(n^{\log_3 4 - 1})$

4.20* Prove that there exists a constant $c > 0$ such that for infinitely many pairs of natural numbers h, h' where

$$|T(h)| \leqslant |B(h')|$$

$T(h)$ is the complete ternary tree of height h, and $B(h')$ is the complete binary tree of height h', for every embedding f of tree $T(h)$ in tree $B(h')$ the following holds:

$$WCOST(f) \geqslant c \log \log h$$

4.21 Modify the algorithm for the pebbling of a complete binary tree of height h ($n = 2^{h+1} - 1$) so that it performs $2n - h - 2$ pebbling steps for $h > 0$.

4.22 How many pebbles are required to pebble the nodes of the following dags: (a) list; (b) grid; (c) star; (d) binary tree with nodes connected on each level. (See Figure 4.13 for examples of graphs of type (c) and (d).)

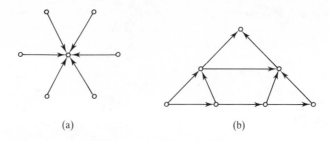

Figure 4.13   (a) 7-node star (b) a binary tree with nodes connected on each level.

For Exercises 4.23–4.25 let $G = (V, E)$ be a dag, $|V| = n$ and $B(v)$ a set of predecessors of v in G.

4.23* Prove that the call $depth\_first\_pebble(v, \varnothing)$, where

> **procedure** $depth\_first\_pebble(v, T)$;
> **begin**
> **for** $u \in B(v)$ **do**
> **if** u is not marked with a pebble
> **then** $depth\_first\_pebble(u, T \cup B(v))$;
> put a pebble on v;
> remove pebbles from nodes in the set $V - (T \cup \{v\})$
> **end**

pebbles a node v in dag G. Find a class of dags for which $depth\_first\_pebble$ requires $\Omega(n)$ pebbles.

4.24* Prove that the call $level\_pebble(V, v, \varnothing)$, where

> **procedure** $level\_pebble(S, v, T)$;
> **begin** $\{v \in S\}$
> **if** each node w in $B(v)$ is marked with a pebble
> **then** put a pebble on v
> **else**
> **begin**
>
>   divide set S into two disjoint non-empty subsets S_1 and S_2 such that:
> $S = S_1 \cup S_2$ and
>   if $u \in S_2$ and $(u, w) \in E$ then $w \in S_2$;
>   let C be the set of nodes u such that:
> $u \in S_1$ and
>   there is an edge $(u, w) \in E$ with $w \in S_2$;
>   **for** $u \in C$ **do**
>   **if** u is not marked with a pebble

      then *level_pebble*$(S_1, u, T \cup C)$;
      level_pebble$(S_2, v, T \cup C)$;
      remove pebbles from the nodes in $V - (T \cup \{v\})$
    end
  end

pebbles a node v in dag G. Find a class of dags for which *level_pebble* requires $\Omega(n)$ pebbles.

4.25* Prove that there does not exist a flow diagram (that is, a program composed of simple variables, function and relation symbols, **begin** . . . **end**, **if** . . . **then** . . . **else** . . . and **while** . . . **do** . . .) equivalent to any interpretation of the following recursive scheme:

$$z = F(a)$$

where

$$F(y) = \textbf{if } p(y) \quad \textbf{then} \quad f(y) \quad \textbf{else} \quad h(F(g_1(y)), F(g_2(y)))$$

and a is a constant, p is a 1-argument predicate symbol, g_1 and g_2 are 1-argument function symbols, and h is a 2-argument function symbol.
(*Hint*   Find an interpretation of symbols a, p, g_1, g_2, and h such that the computation of a flow diagram can be interpreted as the pebbling of a dag.)

Chapter 5
Reducing the Complexity by Analysis of Algorithms – Part 1

In this chapter we describe how to produce an efficient algorithm from its analysis. The idea of the dynamic simulation of an algorithm is presented using the string-matching problem.

5.1 Introduction

One of the main consequences of the analysis of algorithms is the production of more efficient algorithms. By an efficient algorithm we mean one whose complexity is small. In this chapter two types of complexity measure are considered: space and time complexity.

The main issue of this chapter is the simulational aspect of the analysis of algorithms. The analysis of algorithms is employed here to improve efficiency: for a given algorithm A simulate it by (transform it into) a more efficient algorithm B.

Two general methods of simulation are presented: **dynamic** and **algebraic simulation**. Several other useful methods for algorithm optimization are also demonstrated. All of them show the analysis of algorithms at work.

Usually when designing an algorithm for a given problem one starts with the most natural and straightforward algorithm A which certainly works. The first issue is correctness. However, generally such a 'naive' initial algorithm is not efficient. Nevertheless in many situations it contains the basic components of much more efficient constructions.

173

In the process of analysis we reach a better understanding of the structure, properties and invariants of algorithm A. This knowledge can be used to improve A, yielding an efficient algorithm B; the latter is usually much more complicated but its correctness will follow in general from the correctness of the initial simple algorithm A.

This method of efficient algorithm design is an advanced version of the stepwise refinement method whose main task is the production of algorithms in a structured way. In our case we are not satisfied when an algorithm just solves a given problem correctly. We need an algorithm whose complexity is small. This is achieved by further successive improvements and the main tool here is the analysis of algorithms.

In the stepwise refinement method one starts with a 'rough' structure of the algorithm and produces the final version by successive refinements which give a series of intermediate partly specified algorithms. These refinements and the improvements of complexity can be interweaved and mutually dependent. Sometimes the analysis of the algorithm at an intermediate stage shows the way to further refinements, in some situations it also turns attention to the mathematical (or other) properties of the input problem which can help to improve efficiency.

The initial or intermediate (partly specified) algorithm A can be thought of as a meta-algorithm A. It can serve as a common structure for several algorithms: each of these can be viewed as a (completely specified) instance of A. The efficiency can be obtained at the level of the meta-algorithm A. It is also easier to analyse such a general algorithmic scheme because it allows one to disregard details irrelevant to complexity.

The methods described here are not universal, and unfortunately there are no universal ready-recipes or theories to produce efficient algorithms automatically. We describe several informal principles, which are part of algorithmic methodology. We believe that one method of learning to design efficient algorithms is to look at the process of designing various existing ones. We also have to look at the general principles and general constructions which not only show relations between these algorithms but also help to design algorithms of a similar structure. Our main interest in this chapter is thus not the final product (an efficient algorithm) but rather the process of its formation, and this process is closely related to the analysis of algorithms.

We have chosen a group of algorithmic problems related to the properties of texts (words) and the recognition of context-free languages. Some of these problems are practical and some are only of a theoretical nature. However, in our opinion, all the problems presented provide algorithmically ample material and are very well suited for practising the design of efficient algorithms.

Our purpose is also to present several algorithms which are interesting enough to deserve a place of their own in the education of people interested in the design of efficient algorithms.

There are several other algorithmic areas in which the analysis of algorithms plays an important role in the design of more and more efficient algorithms: for example, problems related to maximal flows in networks, or maximal matchings in graphs.

The area of textual and context-free recognition problems has been chosen for several important reasons. First of all, it is algorithmically very rich, and at the same time scarce in the current book literature. Secondly, it is related to the theory of formal languages and automata, one of the most advanced theories in computer science, rich in interesting constructions and algorithms, and at the same time rather self-contained. Many ideas, initially purely theoretical, have practical applications. The ideas related to the string-matching problem are a typical example.

However, the main reason for our choice is that the algorithms to be presented are not a chaotic collection of independent examples. They are closely related to one another, and methods and constructions of a general nature play an important role here. We also have an opportunity to show the reader several important algorithmic concepts, tools and methods: stack, recursion, non-determinism, tabulation method, dynamic simulation and algebraic simulation (composition system) method.

The key role, from the point of view of further improvements on an algorithm, is played by the type of the information it gathers and the way this information is used. In the process of algorithm analysis we may sometimes observe a piece of information not fully applied in the algorithm or one not exploited at all, though implicitly present in the algorithm.

A general method of producing an efficient algorithm is **dynamic simulation**. We improve the time complexity of an algorithm by optimizing the use of information (this usually leads to an increase of space complexity). In this way the algorithm A is transformed into an algorithm B, where B behaves similarly to A, but makes much better use of information than A and works faster. Some parts of the computation of A are omitted because of information gathered by the algorithm. Dynamic simulation consists in such a transformation of algorithm A into B.

The main feature of dynamic simulation is that we preserve the main structure of the simulated algorithm: the sequence of operations in algorithm B is essentially a subsequence of that in A.

Another type of simulation is also possible; we call it **algebraic simulation**. We construct a kind of algebraic system whose elements are subcomputations of the simulated algorithm. The operation is the composition of subcomputations. We start with a set of generators – constant-sized subcomputations.

We thus obtain an algebraic system which we call a **composition system**. In the case when the computation structure of the given algorithm A is tree-like, the algebraic system corresponds to tree-cutting operations. Algebraic simulation is of an analytical nature, we apply a kind of a surgery and cut computations of the initial algorithm into separate pieces. We have to investigate the analytical structure of the algorithm.

The algebraic simulation of an initial algorithm A consists in finding the algebraic closure of the set of generators. We shall see that the final algorithm B does not usually reflect the order of the steps performed by A and, at first glance, could look rather theoretical. Our example of such a simulation will concern context-free grammars treated as non-deterministic recursive algorithms. A nice feature of algebraic simulation is that it works well in the presence of non-determinism. Another useful feature is that it is well suited to parallel computations as we shall see in Chapter 9.

Time complexity is the main complexity measure discussed in this chapter. However, we are also interested in space complexity. In this case instead of gathering useful information we are interested in deleting parts of information. It can happen that we have to change the way the algorithm makes use of information because of some losses of information (as a result of small memory). Usually this leads to an increase in time complexity.

The most interesting algorithms are the ones which are effective regarding both time complexity and space complexity: when a decrease in time complexity does not cause a big increase in space complexity.

Hence in this and the following chapters we present the simulational (or transformational) aspect of the analysis of algorithms. For a given algorithm A we want to simulate it by a faster algorithm $B1$ or by an algorithm $B2$ which uses less memory. Both $B1$ and $B2$ can be treated as versions of A.

A major part of this chapter is devoted to the string-matching problem. In this problem particularly, the analysis of information gathered by the algorithm and application of the general philosophy of dynamic simulation allows one to obtain many interesting and effective algorithms. The string-matching problem is an important practical problem. We discuss only the simplest type of patterns in string-matching: a single one-dimensional string pattern with no errors allowed. Also, only one aspect (that related to the analysis of algorithms) of string-matching is considered. Certainly the full story of string-matching deserves a separate monograph. In this book the string-matching problem just gives us an opportunity to discuss algorithmic techniques.

In Chapter 6 the second important problem is discussed: the context-free recognition.

Context-free grammars are a typical example of non-deterministic recursive algorithms. An analysis of recursion from the complexity point of view is given in the framework of dynamic and algebraic simulation. Our aim is not to present part of the theory of parsing. The main topic here is the treatment of recursion and the demonstration of two types of simulation applied to recursive algorithms. Context-free grammars provide us only with good material for discussing recursion.

In this chapter we show how efficient algorithms can be derived using the dynamic simulation approach together with the analysis of algorithms.

The string-matching problem is particularly suited for such algorithmic engineering.

Assume that we are given two texts x and y represented by tables

x: array$[1 .. m]$ of char, y: array$[1 .. n]$ of char

where we assume that $n > m$. The text x is called the **pattern**.

Let $z[i .. j]$ denote the subword $z[i + 1]z[i + 2] ... z[j]$, for $i < j$. (We start with the symbol on position $i + 1$ for convenience.) The string-matching problem consists in checking if x occurs in y as a subword, in other words, checking if $x = y[i .. i + m]$ for some position $0 \leqslant i \leqslant n - m$.

Such positions i are called **matches**. The size of the problem is n.

In practical applications we are also interested in finding all such matches i. However, here we restrict ourselves to the decision version of the string-matching problem and so will only be interested in the existence of a match. This will simplify the algorithms and we do not miss much from the point of view of the analysis of algorithms. The modification computing all matches is in most cases straightforward. Simplification of the exposition in many cases will be at the expense of implementation details. Hence our algorithms are not executable code.

Also, two simplifying programming constructs are assumed. The output of the algorithm is realized through an instruction return *true*. The execution of this instruction causes the algorithm to stop and output that the text satisfies the required property. If the algorithm stops (at the last **end**) and the output *true* is not produced then we assume automatically that the output is *false*.

The second assumption is as follows: if, during the verification of a certain logical condition, the algorithm attempts to read out of the range of a table then automatically the value of the condition being checked is set to *false* and the algorithm continues.

The most natural structure of the string-matching algorithm is as follows:

for $i := 0$ **to** $n - m$ **do**
    check if $x[0 .. m] = y[i .. i + m]$

We obtain two distinct 'naive' algorithms by implementing the 'check' operation in two different ways (see Figure 5.1).

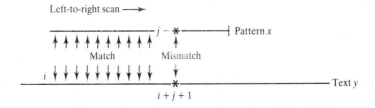

Left-to-right scan $\longrightarrow$

Figure 5.1   A situation in the naive algorithm.

The first way is the left-to-right scan of the pattern, symbol by symbol. The second way is the right-to-left scan. We introduce an auxiliary variable j to point to positions of the pattern.

The first naive algorithm is as follows:

Algorithm 5.1   {left-to-right scan}

> **begin** {texts x, y are stored in arrays}
> $i := 0$;
> **while** $i \leqslant n - m$ **do**
>   **begin**
>   1: {check if $x[0 .. m] = y[i .. i + m]$}
> $j := 0$; **while** $x[j + 1] = y[i + j + 1]$ **do** $j := j + 1$;
>   **if** $j = m$ **then** return *true*;
>
>   {invariant 1: $x[0 .. j] = y[i .. i + j]$}
>
>   2: {$i := i + shift$} $i := i + 1$;
>   **end**;
> **end** of algorithm.

Let us make a first attempt at analysing this algorithm. Its correctness is obvious. The time complexity $T(n)$ is dominated by the number of executed symbol comparisons '$x[j + 1] = y[i + j + 1]$?' Generally in this chapter we will measure the time complexity in string-matching algorithms by the number of symbol comparisons performed. It is easy to see that $T(n) = O(n^2)$. On the other hand for $n = 2k$, $x = a^{k-1}b$ and $y = a^n$ the number of comparisons is $(n/2 + 1)n/2$. Hence the time complexity of the algorithm is exactly of order n^2.

We could end the analysis with that conclusion, however the analysis of the algorithm should also involve its other properties, not only its complexity. A useful property of Algorithm 5.1 is the invariant which is named invariant 1. This expresses the fact of gathering certain information related to the variable j.

Let us examine how the algorithm uses this information. At the beginning of instruction 1 we set j to zero, and the information represented by j is wasted. It turns out that an application of information represented by j leads to a linear time algorithm. This will be discussed in the next section.

The second way of checking the condition '$x[0 .. m] = y[i ... i + m]$' leads to the following naive algorithm.

Algorithm 5.2   {right-to-left scan}

> **begin** {x, y are stored in tables}
> $i := 0$;

while $i \leqslant n - m$ **do**

  begin

    1: $\{$check if $x[0 .. m] = y[i .. i + m]\}$

      $j := m$; **while** $x[j] = y[i + j]$ **do** $j := j - 1$;

      if $j = 0$ **then** return *true*;

    $\{$invariant 2: $x[j .. m] = y[i + j .. i + m]\}$

    2: $\{i := i + shift\}$ $i := i + 1$;

  end;

end of algorithm.

The complexity of this algorithm is quadratic; we leave it to the reader as an exercise to find input data for which Algorithm 5.2 makes a quadratic number of symbol comparisons.

This algorithm, just as the previous one, makes no use of the information related to the invariant given in the text of the algorithm. We show later how to derive a linear time algorithm using this information.

In this way we obtain two distinct linear time algorithms for the string-matching problem. The first will be a version of Algorithm 5.1 and the second a version of Algorithm 5.2. In the derivation of these linear time algorithms we shall see the analysis of algorithms at work.

It is quite surprising that the two linear time algorithms differ substantially though their initial versions (Algorithms 5.1 and 5.2) seem to differ only in a technical detail (the direction of scanning the pattern).

5.2 Dynamic simulation of Algorithm 5.1

We shall now try to apply the information which Algorithm 5.1 gathers when performing instruction 1. At the moment of terminating the execution of this instruction, we know that invariant1 is preserved. We also have the text symbol $sym = y[i + j + 1]$. Moreover, we know that $x[j + 1] \neq y[i + j + 1]$. Using this information we analyse the maximal value of a safe shift s. A shift s is *safe* iff it guarantees (without knowing the remaining part of text y, beyond position $i + j + 1$) that there is no match at positions preceding position $i + s$.

A big shift allows one to omit some parts of the text and reduce the number of comparisons. Observe that $s \leqslant j + 1$ because we know nothing about the part of y beyond position $i + j + 1$.

If, after the shift, the pattern starts at position $i + s$ then it satisfies a certain condition *Cond* depending on s and j (see Figure 5.2). As a safe shift s we can take the minimal s for which this condition holds. For technical reasons, instead of expressing a suitable condition in terms of s we shall express it in terms of the value $p = \max\{0, j - s\}$.

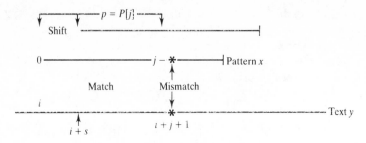

Figure 5.2   The shift of the pattern.

Let us look at Figure 5.2 which represents the situation when the pattern starts at position $i + s$. If we use all of the information then our condition *Cond* is:

$x[0 . . p]$ is a suffix of $x[0 . . j]$ and $((x[p + 1] = sym)$ or $(s = j + 1))$

A second possibility is to use only part of the information (the value of j and the fact that $y[i + j + 1] \neq x[j + 1])$, then our condition *Cond* could be:

$x[0 . . p]$ is a suffix of $x[0 . . j]$ and $((x[p + 1] \neq x[j + 1])$ or $(s = j + 1))$

The third possibility is to use only the value of j.

Hence it can be seen that the method of optimal use of information is rather informal, and several options are possible. In our case both options are essentially equivalent. When improving Algorithm 5.2 we shall see that one bit of information (the last mismatch) dramatically changes the complexity. Hence the principle of optimal use of information can have quite a distinct form even in the case of very similar algorithms (Algorithms 5.1 and 5.2).

We have to choose one of the three types of information. Full information complicates the efficient computation of the shift but saves more comparisons.

We shall start with the weakest information (the value of j). We denote the corresponding condition by $Cond(p, j)$:

$Cond(p, j) = (x[0 . . p]$ is a suffix of $x[0 . . j])$

Assume that $Cond(0, j)$ always holds.

We know that if the pattern starts at position $i + s$ and $j > 0$ then it should satisfy $Cond(j - s, j)$.

Now for $j > 0$ we can define the safe shift as a minimal $s > 0$ such that $p = j - s$ satisfies $Cond(p, j)$. For $j = 0$ we take $s = 1$.

An alternative definition of the safe shift is

$$s = \max(1, j - P[j])$$

where

$$P[j] = \max\{0 \leqslant p < j : Cond(p, j)\} \quad \text{for} \quad j > 0$$

Assume by definition $P[0] = 0$.

The table P is called the **failure function**. The name 'failure' comes from the situation when this function is used – it is applied in a situation such that the supposed match starting at position i fails at position $j + 1$ of the pattern.

Observe now that after executing the instruction $i := i + s$ the following invariant is preserved: $x[0 .. p] = y[i .. i + p]$. Hence we can start the execution of instruction 1 with $j = p$. In this way we save p redundant comparisons (we know in advance that their value is *true*). Hence, using the failure function P, we obtain the following version of Algorithm 5.1 (see also Knuth *et al.* (1977)).

Algorithm 5.3   {dynamic simulation of Algorithm 5.1}

```
begin {a version of the Knuth–Morris–Pratt algorithm}
i := 0; p := 0;
while i ≤ n − m do
   begin
      1: {check if x[0 .. m] = y[i .. i + m]}
         j := p; while x[j + 1] = y[i + j + 1] do j := j + 1;
         if j = m then return true;

         {invariant 1: x[0 .. j] = y[i .. i + j]}

         p := P[j];   s := max{1, j − p};
      2: {i := i + shift} i := i + s;
      end;
end of algorithm.
```

We can show that the number of symbol comparisons in the algorithm does not exceed $2n$. Each time we check the equality $x[j + 1] = y[i + j + 1]$ the value of $i + j$ increases by one if the answer is positive. The value of $i + j$ does not decrease at the moment of making the symbol comparison. Its maximal value is n. Hence we have at most n positive tests. On the other hand the number of negative tests is obviously not greater than n (at most one in each iteration). Hence the total number of symbol comparisons does not exceed $2n$. In fact, this bound can be decreased to $2n - m$ by a closer examination.

Up to now we have not considered the cost of computing the failure function $P[j]$. An interesting feature of Algorithm 5.2 is that it needs the values of $P[j]$ and at the same time it can be used to compute them. Assume that initially all entries of table P contain a special value *nil*, which represents an unknown value. Let us now analyse the behaviour of Algorithm 5.2 in a very special case when $x = y$, and when the following modification concerning the range of the variable i is assumed: initially $i = 1$ (previously 0) and the maximal value of i is m (previously $n - m$).

Of course the algorithm will not return *true*, but now we are not interested in finding a match (because there is no match of x against x at any position different from the initial one) and therefore the instruction containing 'return true' can be eliminated.

Invariant 1 is now equivalent to $Cond(j, i + j)$. Observe that in the course of Algorithm 5.3 the value of $i + j$ will be equal to each of the numbers $1, 2, \ldots, m$ at the moment of checking the condition '$x[j + 1] = y[i + j + 1]$?' At that moment invariant 1 is preserved. Hence $P[k] = p$, where p is the value of j at the first moment when $i + j = k$. It is now enough to modify the algorithm by checking if the value of $P[i + j]$ is computed (different from *nil*) when performing a symbol comparison.

If $P[i + j] = nil$ then we perform $P[i + j] := j$. Technically this can be implemented by inserting such a statement before the **while** instruction and after each symbol comparison. The values of $P[k]$ are computed directly from the definition because in this situation $Cond(j, i + j)$ is equivalent to invariant 1.

After this modification the following algorithm results. Observe that in this algorithm each value of $P[k]$ is computed before it is needed.

Algorithm 5.4   {computation of the failure function P, a version of Algorithm 5.3, initially $P[i] = nil$ for each i, and $x = y$}

```
begin
i := 0; p := 0;
while i ≤ m do
  begin
  1: j := p; if P[i + j] = nil then P[i + j] := j;
     while x[j + 1] = y[i + j + 1] do
        begin j := j + 1; if P[i + j] = nil then P[i + j] := j end;
     {Cond(i, i + j)}
     p := P[j];   s := max{1, j − p};
  2: {i := i + shift}   i := i + s;
  end;
end of algorithm.
```

The time complexity of Algorithm 5.4 is of the same order as that of Algorithm 5.3 since one algorithm is a version of the other and the same complexity analysis can be applied. Hence we know that the failure function can be precomputed in linear time. In this way we have proved the following theorem.

Theorem 5.1

The string-matching problem can be solved in $O(n)$ time.

Our algorithm for the computation of the failure function is different from the one presented in the classical paper of Knuth–Morris–Pratt. Now we discuss the derivation of the latter algorithm – an alternative linear time computation of the table P.

Here we can observe that there are many different ways to obtain an efficient algorithm for the same problem. We show how the analysis of a simple type of recursion can be applied.

We start with a table $P1$ similar to P. The value of $P[j]$ gives the number of symbols in the pattern x and the text y which agree after the shift when only information j is used. The information j means 'the value of j at the point when the mismatch is discovered'. However, in Algorithm 5.2 we have also disregarded the information about the symbol $y[i + j + 1] = sym$. Let us now apply this information to define another version of the shift.

Consider the minimal safe shift s making use of the whole information (j, sym). Let $P1(j, sym)$ be the number of symbols in x and y which agree after performing that shift. More formally:

$$P1(j, sym) = \max\{0 \leqslant k \leqslant j : k = 0 \text{ or}$$

$$(x[0 .. k - 1] \text{ is a suffix of } x[0 .. j] \text{ and } x[k] = sym)\}$$

There is the following close relation between the failure function P and the function $P1$:

$$P[j] = P1(j - 1, x[j]) \quad \text{for } j \geqslant 1$$

The advantage of the function $P1$ is that it can be simply defined and computed recursively:

$$P1(j, sym) = \textbf{if } j = 0 \textbf{ then } 0 \textbf{ else}$$

$$\textbf{if } x[P1(j - 1, x[j]) + 1] = sym \textbf{ then } P1(j - 1, x[j]) + 1$$

$$\textbf{else } P1(P1(j - 1, x[j]), sym)$$

How to compute $P1$ efficiently? The first approach is to try the recursive algorithm given above. However, the worst-case complexity is not linear (we leave it to the reader to find the worst-case input data). The direct recursive computation of $P1$ takes non-linear time because it can happen that the value of *P1* for the same argument x is computed a linear number of times (instead of just once). Hence the algorithm makes a lot of redundant computations.

However, there is a very simple general method of dealing with recursive algorithms to improve their efficiency by omitting redundant recomputations. It is called the **tabulation method**, and is a special type of dynamic simulation. The computed values of the recursive function are stored in a table, and whenever the algorithm tries to compute the function for an argument x it first looks at the table of stored results. Assume that initially the auxiliary table *Tab* contains only undefined values *nil*. We introduce here another programming construct – the conditional assignment. Its meaning is obvious.

Algorithm 5.5   {initially *Tab* contains only values *nil*}

```
function P1( j, sym);
begin
if Tab[ j, sym] = nil then
    begin
    Tab[ j, sym]:= if j = 0 then 0 else
                    if x[P1( j − 1, x[ j]) + 1] = sym then
                        P1( j − 1, x[ j]) + 1
                    else P1(P1( j − 1, x[ j]), sym);
    end;
P1 := Tab[ j, sym]
end of algorithm.
```

The above algorithm has linear time complexity. The tabulation method can also be used to obtain an iterative version. An iterative version is easy to design if we know the order of the arguments to which the function is applied. In our case we can order the arguments (j, sym) in such a way that if $j1 < j2$ then $(j1, sym) < (j2, sym')$. Instead of the function *P1* we can take the table with the same name and tabulate the computed results in this table. Algorithm 5.6 is thus produced.

Algorithm 5.6

```
begin
for each symbol sym do P1[0, sym]:= 0;
for j:= 0 to m − 1 do
    for each symbol sym do
        P1[ j, sym]:=
                    if x[P1[ j−1, x[ j]] + 1] = sym then P1[ j−1, x[ j]] + 1
                    else P1[P1[ j − 1, x[ j]], sym]
end.
```

In this way we have a linear time computation of $P1$ and also of table P, because $P[j] = P1[j-1, x[j]]$ for $j \geqslant 1$. However, the complexity depends on the size of the alphabet. If the alphabet is not of constant size then the algorithm is no longer linear time. The main cause is the large size of the table Tab. The size of Tab can be reduced as follows. Instead of tabulating $P1[j]$ we only tabulate the values of $P[j]$ which appear implicitly in the algorithm. To this end we try to modify the iterative version of function $P1$. First, observe that the recursive definition of $P1$ can also be written as follows:

$(*)$ $P1(j, sym) = $ if $j = 0$ then 0 else

$$\text{if } x[P[j] + 1] = sym \text{ then } P[j] + 1 \text{ else } P1(P[j], sym)$$

We know that $P[j] = P1(j-1, x[j])$ for $j \geqslant 1$.

Let us apply the tabulation method (iterative version) to the failure function with the last recursive definition $(*)$ of $P1$.

Algorithm 5.7

> **begin**
> $P[0] := 0;$
> **for** $j := 1$ **to** m **do** $P[j] := P1(j-1, x[j]).$
> **end**.

It turns out that this algorithm has linear time complexity independently of the size of the input alphabet. To understand why this is so we eliminate recursion. The recursion of type $(*)$ is a particular case of **linear recursion**, that is, one with only one recursive call (which will be executed) on the right side of the recursive equation defining the function. The equation $(*)$ can be rewritten in a more general form:

$$f(x) = \text{if } p(x) \text{ then } c(x) \text{ else } f(a(x))$$

where p, c and a are functions computable in constant time. The recursion of this form can be replaced by the following iterative version:

> **function** $f(x);$
> **begin**
> **while** not $p(x)$ **do** $x := a(x);$
> $f := c(x)$
> **end**.

We now introduce the function $P2_{sym}(j) = P1(j-1, sym)$. This function can be defined by means of a linear recursive function $f(x)$ with $x = j$.

The function a is $P[j]$ and the condition p is $(j = 0$ or $x[P[j] + 1]$ $= x[j])$.

We introduce the variable t to shorten the description.

Algorithm 5.8

```
begin
P[0] := 0; P[1] := 0; t := 0;
for j := 2 to m do {iterative version of P2_{x[j]}(j)}
   begin
   while (t > 0) and (x[t + 1] ≠ x[j]) do t := P[t];
   if x[t + 1] = x[j] then t := t + 1; P[j] := t;
   end
end.
```

After replacing recursion by its iterative version and with cosmetic simplification, Algorithm 5.7 is transformed into the algorithm presented above.

The complexity of this algorithm is linear. It is enough to show that the number of executed statements $t := P[t]$ is linear. We apply the so-called **store principle**: the number of deletions from an initially empty store is not greater than the total number of insertions. The variable t will be interpreted as the number of items in the store.

Initially $t = 0$ and the store is empty. Each time we execute $t := P[t]$ at least one element is deleted because $P[t] < t$ for $t > 0$. However, the total number of inserted items does not exceed m; in each iteration the value of t is increased at most by one and we have $m - 1$ iterations. This proves that the total time complexity of Algorithm 5.8 is linear. The size of the input alphabet does not intervene here.

The failure function can be used to solve the string-matching problem in a more direct way. Take the text $w = x\$y$ and compute the failure function P for this text. Then x occurs in y iff for some position j to the right of $\$$ we have $P[j] = |x|$.

To end this section we show two simple applications of string matching and the computation of the failure function. The first is the computation of a lexicographically maximal suffix of a given text x (denoted by $maxsuf(x)$). Assume that we have a linear order ' $<$ ' in the input alphabet. Our algorithm for the maximal suffix will be a version of Algorithm 5.8.

For $j = 1, \ldots, n$ we will compute the maximal suffix $x[k .. j]$ of text $x[0 .. j]$. The following invariant will be preserved:

$x[k .. j] = maxsuf(x[0 .. j])$ and the initial segment of the table P is the failure function for the text $x[k .. j]$

The algorithm is based on the following combinatorial property of maximal suffixes:

if $x[r .. j-1] = maxsuf(x[0 .. j-1])$ and $x[s .. j] = maxsuf(x[0 .. j])$ then $x[s .. j-1]$ is simultaneously a suffix and a prefix of $x[r .. j-1]$

Hence $|x[s .. j-1]| = P^q[j-1]$ for some integer q, where P^q is the qth iteration of P treated as a function. This property helps to find a suitable position s. The table P is computed in the same way as in Algorithm 5.8, the main difference being that the computation is performed for a dynamically changing pattern $x[k .. j]$. However, the next pattern does not differ much from the preceding one: owing to the property stated above, the next pattern is a prefix of the preceding one with one extra symbol $x[j]$. Hence only one entry of table P is to be changed (the one corresponding to the last position of $x[k .. j]$, that is, $P[j-k]$). If a position in $x[k .. j]$ has index t then it has index $t' = k + t$ in the whole text.

The interpretation of the variables is:

$x[k .. j-1]$ is the best suffix so far and t is the length of the longest prefix of $x[k .. j-1]$ which is a proper suffix of $x[k .. j-1]$

The modified Algorithm 5.8 is derived from Algorithm 5.5 (by algorithm analysis) and looks as follows:

Algorithm 5.9   {computation of maximal suffix, a version of Algorithm 5.1}

```
begin
    P[0] := 0; P[1] := 0; k := 0; t := 0;
    for j := 2 to m do
    begin
        t' := t + k;
        while (t > 0) and (x[t' + 1] ≠ x[j]) do
        begin
            if x[j] > x[t' + 1] then {x[j − 1 − t .. j] > x[k .. j−1]} k := j − 1 − t;
            t := P[t]; t' := t + k
        end;
        if x[t' + 1] = x[j] then t := t + 1 else t := 0; P[j − k] := t;
        if x[j] > x[k + 1] then {x[j] = x[j − 1 .. j] > x[k .. j−1]} k := j − 1
    end
    return {maxsuf = } x[k .. m];
end.
```

Correctness follows from the preservation of the invariants (placed in the text of the algorithm) in each iteration.

Observe that if we remove all updates of k (except the first statement setting k to zero) then the algorithm will compute table P for the whole text x.

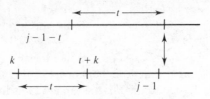

Figure 5.3   Computation of $maxsuf(x[0 \mathrel{..} j])$, $x[k \mathrel{..} j - 1] = maxsuf(x[0 \mathrel{..} j - 1])$.

However, in this case it will not return the correct maximal suffix. One could say that the updates of k are a side effect of the computation of the function P.

The linearity of time complexity is proved in a similar way as for Algorithm 5.5 using the store principle. Again the value of t can be interpreted as the number of items in a store. We leave the details to the reader.

The next problem related to string matching concerns cyclic shifts of texts. If $x = a_1 \ldots a_n$ then we denote by $x^{(k)}$ the text $a_{k+1} \ldots a_n a_1 \ldots a_k$. This is the **cyclic shift** of x by k symbols. We say that two words are **cyclic equivalent** (and write $x \cong y$) iff $x^{(k)} = y^{(s)}$ for some k, s. Denote by $maxshift(x)$ the lexicographically maximal shift of x.

Assume (to the end of this section) that $|x| = |y|$. String matching can be applied directly to check the cyclic equivalence of x and y because of the following obvious fact:

$x \cong y$ iff x occurs in yy as a pattern

Cyclic equivalence is also reducible to the computation of maximal shift because:

$x \cong y$ iff $maxshift(x) = maxshift(y)$

Finally, the maximal shift can be computed using the algorithm for maximal suffixes. Let $z = maxsuf(xx)$, then $maxshift(x)$ equals the prefix of length $|x|$ of z.

All these methods for checking cyclic equivalence use $O(n)$ space. However, there is a simple constant-space linear-time algorithm for this problem.

Suppose that we are to check the cyclic equivalence of texts x and y of size n. Let

$D1 = \{1 \leqslant k \leqslant n: x^{(k-1)} > y^{(j)} \text{ for some integer } j\}$

$D2 = \{1 \leqslant k \leqslant n: y^{(k-1)} > x^{(j)} \text{ for some integer } j\}$

We use the following fact:

if $D1 = \{1, 2, \ldots, n\}$ or $D2 = \{1, 2, \ldots, n\}$ then x, y are not cyclic equivalent

In the algorithm below we assume $w = xx$ and $u = yy$. The invariant is $[1 .. i] \subseteq D1$ and $[1 .. j] \subseteq D2$.

We recall our technical assumption that if we are out of the range of a table when checking a boolean condition then the value of this condition is set to *false* and the algorithm continues.

Algorithm 5.10

```
begin
    i := 0; j := 0;
    while (i < n) and (j < n) do
        begin
            k = 1;
            while w[i + k] = u[j + k] do k := k + 1; if k > n then return true;
            if w[i + k] > u[j + k] then i := i + k else j := j + k;
            {invariant}
        end;
    return false
end.
```

The algorithm returns *true* iff x and y are cyclic equivalent. The time complexity is linear. The maximal number of symbol comparisons is executed for $x = 111 \ldots 1201$ and $y = 1111 \ldots 120$. We leave to the reader the exact computation of the number of comparisons done for this data.

5.3   Efficient simulation of Algorithm 5.1 using small memory

We now consider the space complexity and time complexity together. By space complexity we mean the size (number of registers) of auxiliary memory. We do not count the memory needed to store the tables representing the pattern x and the text y. It is assumed that these input tables are read-only and cannot be modified.

In this section we show how to reduce the auxiliary table P used in Algorithm 5.3 without substantial increase in time complexity. When deriving Algorithm 5.3 from the naive Algorithm 5.1 a key role is played by the information gathered by the algorithm and by the table representing the failure function P.

Now we would like to apply a kind of dynamic simulation to the naive algorithm with more careful use and storage of information. Usually this leads to more advanced algorithms.

The key idea is to use an 'approximate' formula for the value of the shift of the pattern (instead of the table P which gives the shift exactly but requires linear size memory).

Let us investigate when it is easy to eliminate the table without a big loss in efficiency. Such a reduction is especially simple if the values of the entries of the table are given by a simple formula involving little information. In fact, for many patterns x the value of $P[j]$ can be given by such a formula. For technical reasons instead of $P[j]$ we consider here the values of $Shift(j) = j - P[j]$, for $j \geqslant 1$.

An example of an extremely simple pattern x which does not require a table for $Shift$ is $x = a^m$. In this case $Shift(j) = j - 1$. Another simple pattern is $x = (abcd)^{m/4}$. Also here the values of $Shift(j)$ and $P[j]$ are given by a simple formula which can replace the table P in Algorithm 5.3.

We offer yet another, much more interesting example, of a family of patterns. These are given by the **Fibonacci words** fib_k. The Fibonacci words are defined similarly as Fibonacci numbers, with addition replaced by the concatenation:

$$fib_1 = b, \quad fib_2 = a, \quad fib_{k+1} = fib_k \, fib_{k-1}$$

Hence $fib_3 = ab, fib_4 = aba, fib_5 = abaab, fib_6 = abaababa$.

Observe that each fib_k, for $k > 1$, is a prefix of the next word. Hence instead of many words we can consider one infinite Fibonacci word Fib such that each (finite) Fibonacci word is its prefix. The table P need be defined only for this word.

The Fibonacci words have many interesting properties. If we cut off the last two symbols of a Fibonacci word then we obtain a symmetric word (palindrome).

Let the operation C consist in interchanging the last two symbols of a word. Then

$$fib_k \, fib_{k+1} = C(fib_{k+1} \, fib_k)$$

Hence any two consecutive Fibonacci words 'almost' commute. Using the above property of Fibonacci words it can be proved that if the pattern is a Fibonacci word then

$$P[j] = j - F_{q-1} \quad \text{for} \quad F_q \leqslant j + 1 < F_{q+1}$$

where F_q is the qth Fibonacci number.

The following inequalities follow from this formula:

$$P[j] \leqslant 2j/3 \quad \text{and} \quad Shift(j) > j/4$$

We say that a pattern x is **very simple** iff $Shift(j) > \lfloor j/4 \rfloor$. Hence Fibonacci words are examples of very simple patterns. For very simple patterns we can use this as a rough estimate of the shift in Algorithm 5.3. We therefore obtain Algorithm 5.11

Algorithm 5.11   {pattern is very simple, $Shift(j) > j/4$}

```
begin
  i := 0;
  while i ≤ n − m do
    begin
      j := 0; while x[j + 1] = y[i + j + 1] do j := j + 1;
      if j = m then return true;
      {i := i + shift}   i := i + max{1, ⌊j/4⌋};
    end;
end algorithm.
```

Correctness follows from the inequality $Shift(j) > j/4$ for $j > 0$. Observe that we partly waste information contained in the value of j because in each iteration we first set j to zero. However, j is used to make bigger shifts. This is enough to guarantee the linearity of time complexity.

This shows that when we reduce the memory some information is usually wasted. Fortunately in this case this waste does not change the order of time complexity (though it increases the constant coefficient).

The linearity of time complexity follows here by a similar argument to that in the analysis of Algorithm 5.3. Here, instead of the sum $i + j$, we consider the sum $4i + j$. We leave the full analysis to the reader.

We cannot expect every pattern to be very simple. For example pattern *aaaaa* is not very simple. However, it turns out that each pattern has a property which allows us to reduce space complexity efficiently. The pattern *aaaa* is not very simple because it has a non-empty prefix of the form v^4. Generally, each pattern which is not very simple has a prefix of this form.

Let us examine a situation when a pattern x satisfies $Shift(j) = j − P[j] \leqslant \lfloor j/4 \rfloor$ for some $j > 0$. Take the prefix v of x of length $Shift(j)$. The word v has the following properties:

(1) v^4 is a prefix of x.

(2) v is a prime word (it is not a power of a shorter word).

The second property follows from the fact that $P[j]$ is the *maximal* length of a proper suffix of $x[0..j]$ which is also a prefix of x. If v is not a prime word then it is easily seen that $P[j]$ is not maximal.

A word v satisfying (1) and (2) is called a **basic prefix** of x. Hence a pattern is very simple iff it contains no basic prefix. We say that a pattern is **simple** iff it contains at most one basic prefix. If x is simple then an easy modification of the last algorithm gives a linear-time constant-space algorithm.

First we need some technical definitions related to periodicity. An integer p is a **period size** of the word w iff $w[i] = w[i + p]$ whenever values of $w[i]$ and $w[i + p]$ are defined. Observe that one word can have many period sizes. Denote by $period(x)$ the minimal period size of x. The word z is a period of w

iff z is a prefix of w and $|z|$ is a period size of w. The p-continuation of w is the maximal k such that $w[0 . . k]$ has period size p.

Assume that x has only one basic prefix v of length r. Let R be the $|v|$-continuation of x. It is easy to prove that:

if $Shift(j) \leqslant \lfloor j/4 \rfloor$ then $j \in [4r \ldots R]$

if $j \in [4r \ldots R]$ then $Shift(j) = r$, $P[j] = j - r$

Hence we can apply two types of shift, the exact shift r for $j \in [4r \ldots R]$ and the approximate shift $\lceil j/4 \rceil$ for other values of j. The key point is that for all j with the exact shift applied we need only one register to store the same shift r.

We apply an approximate version $G(j)$ of function $Shift(j)$:

$$G(j) = \text{if } j \in [4r \ldots R] \text{ then } r \text{ else } \lceil j/4 \rceil$$

If $j \in [4r \ldots R]$ then after making the exact shift we know that the next value of j can be set to $j - r$. This saves $j - r$ symbol comparisons. For other values of j we have to lose some information related to j by resetting j to zero (because the shift is only approximate). However, the complexity remains linear. The algorithm is presented below.

Algorithm 5.12   {version of Algorithm 5.3, instead of table P we know only values of r and R, x is a simple pattern, it has at most one basic prefix}

```
begin
i := 0; j := 0;
   while i ≤ n − m do
   begin
      while x[ j + 1] = y[i + j + 1] do j := j + 1;
      if j = m then return true;
      if j ∈ [4r ... R] then begin i := i + r; j := j − r end
                     else begin i := i + ⌈ j/4⌉; j := 0 end;
   end
end.
```

Correctness is obvious, similarly to Algorithm 5.3. Time complexity is linear because $4i + j$ does not decrease when observed at the moment of making symbol comparisons. The maximal value of $4i + j$ is $O(n)$. On each positive symbol comparison this value increases by one. Hence the number of such comparisons is $O(n)$. In each iteration there is at most one negative symbol comparison. Hence the total number of symbol comparisons is $O(n)$.

The space complexity is $O(1)$. We only have to remember a few integers: $i, j,$ r and R.

However, we have to precompute the values of r and R. If we know that x is a simple pattern then the computation of r and R in linear time and constant space can be done just as the computation of the table P in Algorithm 5.4. This algorithm was a version of Algorithm 5.3. Similarly, a time–space efficient algorithm computing parameters r and R can be designed as a version of Algorithm 5.12. We leave the design of such an algorithm as an exercise. Also instead of the decision version we can have a version of Algorithm 5.12 computing all occurrences of the pattern in the text y. All this proves the following lemma.

Lemma 5.1

If we know that x is a simple pattern then we can find all occurrences of x in y in $O(n)$ time using only $O(1)$ additional memory.

The main drawback of this lemma is that not all patterns are simple. For example, the pattern $x = aaaabaaaabaaaabaaaab$ has two basic prefixes: a and $aaaab$.

Let $z_1 = aaaa$ and $z_k = (z_{k-1} b)^4$. The pattern $x = z_k$ has at least $\log_5(m)$ distinct basic prefixes, where $m = |x|$. Using the theoretical machinery (concerning prefixes and periods) developed below one can show that the maximal number of distinct basic prefixes is logarithmic for each pattern.

Using this fact it is possible to design a linear-time string-matching algorithm which uses $O(\log n)$ memory to store parameters r and R for each of the logarithmically many basic prefixes. We also leave that as an exercise.

However, it is always possible to reduce the string-matching problem to the case of simple patterns because of the following surprising combinatorial theorem.

Theorem 5.2   (pattern decomposition theorem)

(1) Each pattern x has a decomposition $x = vw$ such that w is a simple pattern and $|v| \leqslant 2\ period(w)$.

(2) Such a decomposition can be found in linear time and with $O(1)$ additional memory.

Later we only prove the first part of this theorem, but the full proof can be found in Galil and Seiferas (1981). First we show its application. The importance of $period(w)$ is expressed by Lemma 5.2.

Lemma 5.2

There are at most $n/period(w)$ occurrences of the word w in the text y of length n.

Proof Two distinct occurrences cannot be closer than *period*(w). This implies the assertion.   ∎

Theorem 5.3

There is a linear-time constant-space algorithm for the string-matching problem.

Proof We describe informally the construction of such an algorithm. Assume that we have a decomposition of the pattern x into subwords vw according to the decomposition theorem.

The string-matching algorithm from Lemma 5.1 is applied to the pattern w and text y. Whenever we find an occurrence of w in y we check whether this occurrence is preceded in y by v. We use here a 'naive' algorithm and make $O(|v|)$ steps per occurrence of w.

According to Lemma 5.2 there are at most $O(n/period(w))$ occurrences of w in y. Hence our total time complexity is of order $|v|\,n/period(w)$. It is $O(n)$ because $|v| \leqslant 2period(w)$ due to the decomposition theorem. Additional memory is $O(1)$. This completes the proof.   ∎

The last part of this section is optional. It is devoted to the proof of the first part of the decomposition theorem. We believe that this theorem is of such fundamental importance that its proof deserves presentation. The first part concerns the existence of a good decomposition. The second part (effective construction of the decomposition) is a kind of implementation of the existence proof: we refer the reader to the paper of Galil and Seiferas (1981). The reader who is not deeply interested in the combinatorics of string-matching can pass directly to the next section.

Let $\gcd(i, j)$ denote the greatest common divisor of integers i and j. The proof of the decomposition theorem is based on the following 'periodicity lemma'.

Lemma 5.3

If the word w has two periods of sizes $p1$ and $p2$, and if $|w| \geqslant p1 + p2$ then w has a period of size $\gcd(p1, p2)$.

Proof We leave the proof of the following simple claim to the reader.

Claim If $p1 > p2$ then w has a period of size $p1 - p2$.
    Let us look more closely at Euclid's algorithm for $\gcd(p1, p2)$.

$x_1 := p1;\ x_2 := p2;$

while $x1 \neq x2$ do {invariant: w has periods of sizes $x1, x2$}

    if $x1 > x2$ then $x1 := x1 - x2$ else $x2 := x2 - x1$ {invariant}

It follows from our claim that the algorithm preserves the given invariant. Let $x1'$ be the last value of $x1$. After termination the invariant says that w has a period of size $x1' = \gcd(p1, p2)$. This completes the proof. ∎

Lemma 5.4

Assume that the word w has two prefixes of the form u^k, v^k, where $p1 = |u|, p2 = |v|, p2 > p1$ and the words u, v are prime. Then $p2 > (k-1)p1$.

Proof The proof is by contradiction. Assume that $p1 < p2 \leqslant (k-1)p1$. Then $p1 + p2 \leqslant k\, p1$. The word $w[0 .. p1 + p2]$ has periods of sizes $p1$ and $p2$, hence it also has a period of size $p = \gcd(p1, p2)$. Hence v has a full period of size $p < p2$. The word v is not prime. This contradicts the assumption of the lemma and completes the proof. ∎

We now introduce the partial operation '$//$' of cutting the word. If $u = vu'$ then $u//v = u'$.

Lemma 5.5

If the word w is prime then there is a decomposition $w = w_1 w_2$ such that for each word w' the word $w_2 w^3 w'$ has no basic prefix shorter than w.

Proof First we observe that if $w_2 w^3 w'$ has a basic prefix z shorter than w then $|z| < |w|/2$. This follows from Lemma 5.4 and the fact that the word $w_2 w_1$ is also prime (as a cyclic shift of a prime word w, the proof is left to the reader).

Take $v = w_2 w_1$, $u = z$, $k = 3$ and apply Lemma 5.4. We have $|u| < 2|v|$ and z is contained in $w_2 w^3$. Hence the decomposition (and its existence) does not depend on w'. In the proof we can take any word w': to make the proof easier we take $w' = www \ldots$ (w' is a 'very' long word consisting of several copies of w; we can treat w' as an infinite word to omit the problem of specifying its length).

Let $v = ww'$. We execute the following algorithm:

$z :=$ shortest basic prefix of v;
while $|z| < |w|$ **do**
  begin $v := v//z$; $z :=$ shortest basic prefix of v **end**.

If this algorithm terminates then the final value of v is of the form $w_2 www \ldots$. The word w_2 is the required suffix of w. The decomposition is $w = w_1 w_2$, where w_1 is the prefix of w of length $|w| - |w_2|$. Hence it is enough to prove that the algorithm above has the halting property.

First, observe that the lengths of the values of z are non-decreasing. Indeed, suppose that $|z_{i+1}| < |z_i|$ for two consecutive values of z. Applying Lemma 5.4 again, we obtain $|z_{i+1}| < |z_i|/2$.

Hence $(z_{i+1})^4$ is a prefix of a word v starting with three copies of z_i. At the moment of taking z_i as the shortest basic prefix of v the word z_{i+1} was a shorter basic prefix of v. We have a contradiction. This proves that the lengths of z are non-decreasing.

These lengths are bounded from above by the length of w. Hence if the algorithm does not halt then it loops with $z = z_i = z_{i+1} = z_{i+2} = \ldots$, where $|z_i| < |w|$. This implies that the initial word v has two distinct periods w and z such that $|w| + |z| \leqslant |v|$. It follows from the periodicity lemma (Lemma 5.3) that w has a full period of size $\gcd(|w|, |z|)$ and w is not a prime word.

This contradicts the assumptions of the lemma. Hence we have proved finally that the algorithm stops and the required decomposition exists. This completes the proof of the lemma.   ∎

5.3.1   Proof of part (1) of the decomposition theorem

We now present an algorithm finding the required decomposition vw of the pattern x.

If $w_1 w_2$ is a decomposition of w from Lemma 5.5 then set $f(w) = |w_1|$. This function is well defined for prime words w.

Algorithm 5.13   {computing a decomposition of the pattern x of length m}

> **begin**
> $s := 0$;
> **while** $x[s \ldots m]$ is not a simple word **do**
> > **begin**
> > $z :=$ the second (with respect to length) basic prefix of $x[s \ldots m]$;
> > $s := s + f(z)$;
> > > $\{s \leqslant 2|z|, period(x[s \ldots m]) \geqslant |z|\}$
> > **end**;
> {the required decomposition of x is $x = vw$, where}
> $v := x[0 \ldots s]$; $w := x[s \ldots m]$
> **end**.

Observe that in the algorithm we always have $f(z) \geqslant 1$ because z is the second basic prefix and z^3 contains a basic prefix shorter than z. Hence the algorithm halts (the value of s cannot exceed m). In the resulting decomposition the word w is simple.

However, we also have to prove that $|v| \leqslant 2 \, period(w)$, which is an important property of the decomposition. This inequality follows from the invariant formulated in the text of Algorithm 5.13. It is enough to prove that this invariant is preserved in the algorithm. The invariant holds after the first iteration, because then $s = f(z) \leqslant |z|$.

We now prove the second part of the invariant: the inequality

$$period(x[s \,.\, .\, m]) \geqslant |z|.$$

Assume that the inequality is false. Let

$$z1 = x[s \,.\, .\, s + |z|] \quad \text{and} \quad p = period(x[s \,.\, .\, m])$$

We have $|z1| < p$. The word $z1$ is prime (as a cyclic shift of the prime word z) and $z1^3$ is a prefix of $x[s \,.\, .\, m]$. However, $z1^3$ now has periods $|z1|$ and p. It follows from the periodicity lemma that $z1$ has a full period of size $\gcd(p, |z|)$ and $z1$ is not prime.

We have a contradiction, because $z1$ is a prime word. This proves that the second part of the invariant always holds.

We next prove the first part of the invariant: the inequality

$$s \leqslant 2|z|$$

Let $s1$ and $s2$ be two consecutive values of s and $z1$, $z2$ be two corresponding values of z. It is enough to prove the implication:

$$s1 \leqslant 2|z1| \Rightarrow s2 \leqslant 2|z2|$$

Observe that $s2 \leqslant s1 + |z2|$ and, because of Lemma 5.4,

$$|z1| \leqslant |z2|/3$$

Hence if $s1 \leqslant 2|z1|$ then

$$s2 \leqslant s1 + |z2| \leqslant 2|z1| + |z2| \leqslant 2|z2|/3 + |z2| \leqslant 2|z2|$$

Hence the first part of the invariant is preserved. Therefore the decomposition vw satisfies the requirements of the decomposition theorem. In this way we have proved the first (existential) part (1) of the pattern decomposition theorem. ∎

The proof of part (2) is very technical but its general idea is simple. Although part (1) is existential its proof has been constructive. We have given an algorithm for finding the decomposition. Now we have to implement this algorithm to work in linear time and in $O(1)$ additional space. The main point is the careful implementation of the algorithm from Lemma 5.5 and the computation of the function $f(z)$. Also we have to check whether the word is simple in linear time and small memory.

We omit the tedious details of the implementation. We refer readers to the paper of Galil and Seiferas (1981). Remember that we count only the additional space complexity. The tables containing the pattern x and text y are not counted in this case, they are only read. The additional memory is $O(1)$. Galil and Seiferas have shown that only five additional registers suffice.

5.4 Dynamic simulation of Algorithm 5.2

Our second naive algorithm for the string-matching problem was Algorithm 5.2. It differs from Algorithm 5.1 in the direction of scanning the pattern (right to left). We show that this algorithm can be transformed into a linear time algorithm just as Algorithm 5.1 was.

The basic tools are again algorithm analysis and dynamic simulation.

We optimize the use of information in the algorithm and try to increase the shift of the pattern. The information gathered by the algorithm is of three types:

(1) Information that the mismatch symbol is $sym = y[i+j]$.
(2) Information that the $j-1$ last symbols of x match.
(3) Information about the mismatch: $x[j] \neq y[i+j]$.

Let s be a value of the shift of the pattern such that there is a possibility that an occurrence of the pattern starts at position $i+s$. Let $position(a)$ be the last position of the symbol a in the pattern; if a does not occur then $position(a) = 0$. For example if $x = aaba$ we have $position(b) = 3$, $position(a) = 4$ and $position(c) = 0$.

Depending on the type of information used the shift satisfies the condition:

$cond1(s, sym)$ $j - s \leqslant position(sym)$, where $sym = y[i+j]$

$cond2(s, j)$ for each $j < k \leqslant m$ $(s \geqslant k)$ or $(x[k-s] = x[k])$

$cond3(s, j)$ $(s \geqslant j)$ or $(x[j-s] \neq x[j])$

As a shift s we take a minimal value of s satisfying a given condition. Such a shift is safe in the sense that we are sure that the pattern does not start at positions preceding $i + s$ (owing to the minimality of s). Figure 5.4 presents the shift satisfying the second condition.

Information of type (1) is very weak but in many cases it reduces time complexity considerably. Let

$shift1(j, sym) = \min\{s \geqslant 1 : (s = 1) \text{ or } (cond1(s, sym))\}$

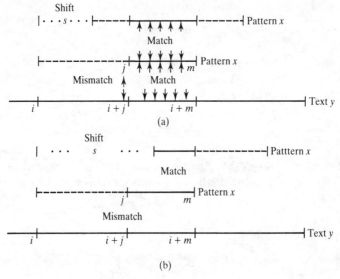

Figure 5.4   (a) $s < j$, (b) $s \geqslant j$.

Consider the following example: $x = a^{100}$, $y = (ab)^{1000}$. In this case we have $shift\,1(j, b) = j$.

Let us examine the behaviour of Algorithm 5.2 if we take $shift\,1$ as a *shift* of i (instead of 1). After the first execution of instruction 1 we have $i = 0, j = 100$ and $sym = b$. At that moment the *shift* is 100. After the next execution of instruction 1 we have $i = 100$ and the situation repeats. In this way we examine only 20 symbols in y.

This is the most important property of algorithms derived from Algorithm 5.2: in some cases they examine only a small part of the text. On the other hand, all algorithms derived from Algorithm 5.1 in the preceding section were inspecting roughly $n - m$ symbols of y. In our example $n - m = 1900$. The number 20 is a considerable improvement. The difference can grow with n.

Information related to *cond*1 is especially useful in the case of big alphabets. Here there is much probability that the symbol *sym* does not occur in the pattern at all and the shift is very large, as in the example above. The use of *cond*1 is an example of a so called *heuristic*: a method which improves the algorithm in many cases but there is no guarantee that it always does. The next example shows that the heuristic related to information of type (1) sometimes does not work well.

Take $x = ba^{m-1}$ and $y = a^{2m-1}$, where $n = 2m - 1$. In this case $position(a) = m$ and $shift\,1(j, a) = 1$. The algorithm will execute m^2 symbol comparisons, hence its complexity is quadratic in n.

We have to use information of types (1) and (2) to improve the time complexity for all possible inputs. Define

$d1(j) = \min\{s \geqslant 1: cond2(s, j)\}$

$d2(j) = \min\{s \geqslant 1: cond2(s, j) \text{ and } cond3(s, j)\}$

If we replace the instruction $i := i + 1$ in Algorithm 5.2 by $i := i + d2(j)$ then we obtain the following algorithm called the Boyer–Moore algorithm (see Boyer and Moore (1977)).

Algorithm 5.14 {Boyer–Moore algorithm, dynamic simulation of Algorithm 5.2 by using information related to j}

begin
$i := 0$;
while $i \leqslant n - m$ **do**
   begin
1:   $j := m$; **while** $x[j] = y[i + j]$ **do** $j := j - 1$;
       if $j = 0$ **then** return *true*;
2:   $\{i := i + shift\}$ $i := i + d2(j)$;
     end;
end of algorithm.

It seems that the difference between the shifts $d1(j)$ and $d2(j)$ is very small, in fact it concerns just a single mismatch. Observe that a similar situation occurred in the process of improving Algorithm 5.1. We had a choice between restricted information related to part of matched symbols only and fuller information related to the mismatch. It so happened that in Algorithm 5.1 the use of any of those pieces of information gave a linear time algorithm.

Surprisingly, in the situation of improving Algorithm 5.2 the use of information without mismatch (shift $d1(j)$) gives a quadratic algorithm, while inclusion of a small piece of information related to the mismatch guarantees the linearity of time complexity.

This is the second interesting phenomenon of the Boyer–Moore algorithm (the first was that in many cases the algorithm scans only a small portion of the text).

The difference between employing $d1$ and $d2$ can be clearly seen on the following example:

$x = cababababa, \quad y = aaaaaaaaaababababa$

Assume that our shift is $d1(j)$. Let us look at how the algorithm works for the given strings. Initially $i = 0, j = 10$. After the execution of instruction 1 we have $j = 9$ (mismatch: $x[9] \neq y[9]$) and $d1(9) = 2$. Hence the next value of i is 2.

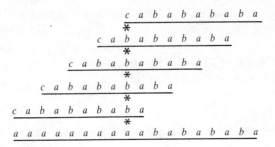

Figure 5.5   The history of the algorithm using the shift $d1$.

After the second execution of instruction 1 we have $i = 2, j = 7$. The next value of i is 4 because $d1(7) = 2$.

In this way the consecutive values of i are 0, 2, 4, 6, 8 and those of j are 9, 7, 5, 3,1. The total number of comparisons is 30. The history of the algorithm is illustrated in Figure 5.5.

Let us now look at the behaviour of the Boyer–Moore algorithm for the same strings. The shift is $d2(j)$. We have $d2(9) = 8$. Hence after the first iteration $j = 9$, $i = 0$ and the shift equals 8; this is much more than when applying $d1$. The next value of i is $i + 8 = 8$.

In the next iteration we perform 10 symbol comparisons and terminate the algorithm with the negative result (no match). Altogether we do only 12 symbol comparisons while the similar algorithm applying shift $d1$ does 30 comparisons.

It can be seen that the Boyer–Moore algorithm performs a linear number of operations, while its $d1$ version does a quadratic number of operations (see Exercise 5.22). Generally, the Boyer–Moore algorithm has linear time complexity. This is very surprising in view of the fact that the algorithm 'forgets' about the matched parts of the text: a symbol in the same position in y can be inspected many times (in fact a logarithmic number of times).

Hence it is not surprising that the proof of the linearity of time complexity is nontrivial. Therefore we omit the proof in this book. A very clean presentation of the proof of the following theorem can be found in Guibas and Odlyzko (1980) and with a slightly bigger coefficient in Knuth *et al.* (1977). Recently a new proof was given by Cole (1990), see Exercise 5.29.

Theorem 5.4

The Boyer–Moore algorithm performs at most $4n$ symbol comparisons. A symbol in the same position in the text y is inspected at most a logarithmic number of times.

We have restricted ourselves to the decision version of the string-matching problem. A more advanced version is to find all matches of the pattern in the text. Transformation of the decision algorithm into that advanced version was trivial for the algorithms in the preceding section, but it is not so for the Boyer–Moore algorithm. Suppose that the algorithm, instead of returning the result and stopping at the first match, reports this match and continues. This would give the following algorithm.

Algorithm 5.15   {a version of the Boyer–Moore algorithm}

begin
$i := 0$;
while $i \leqslant n - m$ **do**
  begin
1:   $j := m$; **while** $x[j] = y[i + j]$ **do** $j := j - 1$;
       if $j = 0$ **then** write (i);
2:   $\{i := i + shift\}$ $i := i + d2(j)$;
    end;
end of algorithm.

Consider the following example:

   $x = a^m$ and $y = a^{2m}$, $n = 2m$

The Boyer–Moore algorithm outputs *true* after inspecting the first m symbols of y. Then it stops. Only m comparisons are done.

    However, the situation is quite different for Algorithm 5.15. Observe that $d2(0) = period(x)$. In our example $d2(0) = 1$. Hence the algorithm performs $m(m + 1)/2$ symbol comparisons. This proves that the straightforward modification of the decision version of the Boyer–Moore algorithm gives an algorithm with quadratic behaviour. Observe that such bad behaviour occurs when the pattern has a short period.

    Again we use the dynamic simulation approach. Let us examine what information gathered by the algorithm can help to reduce the complexity. The algorithm forgets about the matched part of the text, this (wasted) information is most relevant when the match is reported. Hence let us remember whether for the last value of i the operation write(i) was performed. This information will be stored in a variable *info*.

    Suppose that for a given value of i we report a match (execute write(i)). Then the shift is $d2(0) = period(x) = p$. The value of *info* is set to *true* and the next value of i is $i0 + p$. We start to check the match ending at position $i0 + p$. However, if we inspect only the last p symbols with positive result then we need not check the other symbols because we already know that there is a match ending at position $i0 + p$. We report a match. We have saved $m - p$ comparisons.

    Hence using such limited information we can save many comparisons. In fact the complexity of the algorithm is reduced from quadratic to linear.

Let us introduce a variable l limiting (from below) the value of j. If the value of $info$ is true then we set l to $m - p$ since only pattern symbols at positions m, $m - 1, \ldots, m - p$ are to be inspected.

If $info = false$ then l is set to zero. We obtain a version of the algorithm from Galil (1979).

Algorithm 5.16 {dynamic simulation of Algorithm 5.15}

```
begin
i:= 0; info:= false;
while i ≤ n − m do
   begin
1:   if info then l:= m − p else l:= 0;
        j:= m; while j > l and x[j] = y[i + j] do j:= j − 1;
        if j = l then begin write(i); info:= true end else info:= false;
2:   {i:= i + shift}   i:= i + d2(j);
   end;
end of algorithm.
```

Algorithm 5.16 shows that a very small piece of information can change the complexity of the algorithm considerably. We have observed this phenomenon before when applying $d2(j)$ instead of $d1(j)$ in the Boyer–Moore algorithm: information about one mismatch was responsible for changing the quadratic behaviour to a linear one. In Algorithm 5.16 this is even more visible; the variable $info$ contains only one bit of information.

Theorem 5.5

Algorithm 5.16 reports all matches in linear time.

Proof Correctness follows from the correctness of Algorithms 5.2, 5.14 and 5.15. We started with an obviously correct naive Algorithm 5.2, and each of the subsequent algorithms was a simple refinement of the preceding one. (This shows that dynamic simulation is a useful method also from the point of view of correctness.)

By matches we mean here the position i at which an occurrence of the pattern starts and the instruction write(i) is executed. Denote by cost($i1, i2$) the time the algorithm takes from the start with $i = i1$ to the end after executing the whole iteration with $i = i2$. The key to the analysis of the algorithm is the following obvious claim:

cost$(i1, i2) = O(m + i2 − i1)$ if there is no match for intermediate positions $i1 < i < i2$

Let $i_1, i_2, \ldots, i_k$ be the sequence of the consecutive values of i in the algorithm. We partition this sequence into segments of two types:

(1) A maximal segment of consecutive matches excluding the first possible match $i = 0$; call such a segment a **matching chain**.

(2) A segment starting with $i = 0$ or with a position following the last position in some chain and ending with the first match or (if there is no match) with the last possible i; call such segment a **working chain**.

Let p be the period size of x. Then two consecutive positions in a chain differ by p. For example, assume i takes the following sequence of consecutive values:

0, 7, 10, 13, 16, 19, 23, 25, 29, 30, 33, 36, 39, 41, 45

Assume that matches are at positions 13, 16, 19, 30, 33, 36, 39. Then the sequence of i's is partitioned into two matching chains

(16, 19) and (33, 36, 39)

and three working chains

(0, 7, 10, 13), (23, 25, 29, 30) and (41, 45).

We analyse separately the time spent by the algorithm in matching chains and in working chains.

Let $i1$ and $i2$ be the first and last positions in a chain. Then, according to the claim, the cost of a working chain is proportional to m + length of chain, while the cost of a matching chain is just proportional to its length. The sum of all lengths is $O(n)$. Hence the total cost of matching chains is linear and the total cost of working chains is $O(n + rm)$, where r is the number of working chains.

It is enough to analyse the number r of working chains. We claim that this number is always $O(n/m)$. Let p be the period size of x. If p is large ($p > m/2$) then any two consecutive matches are at a distance of at least $m/2$. There are only $O(n/m)$ matches and also $O(n/m)$ working chains.

Suppose now that $p \leqslant m/2$. Assume that $i_s, i_t, \ldots, i_q$ is the sequence of consecutive i's, where i_s is the last match of some chain and i_q is the matching position ending the working chain $i_t, \ldots, i_q$. Now it is easy to see that the length of this chain is greater than $m/2$ (if not, then positions $i_s, \ldots, i_q$ should be included in the matching chain containing i_s). Hence intermediate working chains are long.

This proves that $r = O(n/m)$. Hence the total complexity is of order $n + rm = O(n + mn/m) = O(n)$. This completes the proof of the theorem.

■

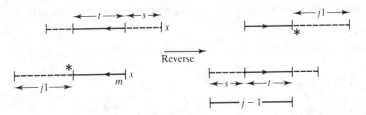

Figure 5.6 Table $d2$ is computed using the algorithm for the table $P1$ (failure function) for the reversed pattern.

To end this section we show how to compute efficiently the table $d2$. We derive a linear time algorithm by analysing Algorithm 5.8 for the computation of the failure table P. The resulting algorithm is non-trivial. The initial version given in Knuth *et al.* (1977) was incorrect; one possible case was missing. A correct version is given in Rytter (1980).

Let $x = a_1 a_2 \ldots a_m$. Let $x1$ be the reverse of x, that is, $x1 = a_m a_{m-1} \ldots a_1$.

Let us examine the behaviour of Algorithm 5.8 for the pattern $x1$. Let $P1$ be the table P computed for this pattern. Observe that at the moment when Algorithm 5.8 starts executing the instruction $t := P1[t]$ the following invariant holds:

$$x1[0..t] = x1[j-1-t..j-1] \quad \text{and} \quad x1[t+1] \neq x1[j]$$

We use the correspondence between x and $x1$ and reformulate the invariant. Position i in $x1$ corresponds to position $m - i + 1$ in x. Hence we obtain the following version of the invariant:

$$x[m-t..m] = x[m-t-s..m-s] \quad \text{and}$$
$$x[m-t] \neq x[m-t-s] \quad \text{where } s = j - t - 1$$

Observe now that this invariant is equivalent to:

$j1 > s$ and $cond2(s, j1)$ and $cond3(s, j1)$, where $j1 = m - t$

Hence at the moment when Algorithm 5.8 starts executing instruction $t := P1[t]$ we know that $d2[j1] \leqslant s$. On the other hand it can be proved that if a position $j1$ satisfies $j1 > s$ (and $s = d2[j1]$) then the situation described above should occur at a certain moment when the algorithm starts executing the instruction $t := P1[t]$.

This gives the following partial algorithm for the computation of $d2[j1]$ for those $j1$ which satisfy $d2[j1] < j1$. In this algorithm we use table $P1$ instead of P; table P will correspond to pattern x, while $P1$ corresponds to $x1$.

Algorithm 5.17   {a version of Algorithm 5.8 applied to the reverse $x1$ of x}

```
begin
for j1 := 1 to m do d2[j1] := m {maximal possible value of shift d2}
P1[0] := 0; P1[1] := 0; t := 0;
for j := 2 to m do
  begin
  while (t > 0) and (x1[t + 1] ≠ x1[j]) do
    begin
    s := j − t − 1; j1 := m − t;
    {invariant: s < j1, cond2(s, j1), cond3(s, j1)}
    d2[j1] := min{d2[j1], s};
    t := P1[t];
    end;
  if x1[t + 1] = x1[j] then t := t + 1
  else
    {t = 0, x[m] ≠ x[m − j + 1]} d2[m] := min{d2[m], j − 1};
  P1[j] := t
  end
end.
```

The values of $d2[j1]$ computed in this algorithm can be incorrect for $j1$ with $d2[j1] \geqslant j1$. For example, if $x = aaaa$ then the table $d2$ computed by the above algorithm will be $d2 = [4, 4, 4, 4]$, while the true table $d2$ is $[1, 2, 3, 4]$.

Observe that in the case $j \leqslant s$ we do not check the condition $cond3(s, j)$ because $j - s \leqslant 0$. In this case our condition (related to the computation of $d2[j]$) is reduced to the equality

$$x[s \, .. \, m] = x[0 \, .. \, m - s] \, ..$$

Hence $x[s \, .. \, m]$ is simultaneously a prefix and a suffix of x. Notice now that all such values of s (satisfying the condition above) occur in the course of executing the following instruction:

$$t := P[m]; \text{ while } t > 0 \text{ do begin } s := m - t; t := P[t] \text{ end.}$$

It is enough to complete this instruction with suitable modifications of $d2$. Then Algorithm 5.17 together with such an additional part gives a complete algorithm for the computation of $d2$.

We remove text $x1$ from Algorithm 5.17 replacing $x1[k]$ by $x[m - k + 1]$ for each k. The following algorithm computes all entries of $d2$.

Algorithm 5.18   {a complete algorithm computing $d2$}

```
begin
for j1 := 1 to m do d2[j1] := m {maximal possible value of shift d2}
P1[0] := 0; P1[1] := 0; t := 0;
```

for $j := 2$ **to** m **do**
  begin
  while $(t > 0)$ **and** $(x[m - t] \neq x[m - j + 1])$ **do**
    begin
    $s := j - t - 1; j1 := m - t;$
    $d2[j1] := \min \{d2[j1], s\};$
    $t := P1[t];$
    end;
  if $x[m - t] = x[m - j + 1]$ **then** $t := t + 1$
  else
    $\{t = 0, x[m] \neq x[m - j + 1]\}$ $d2[m] := \min \{d2[m], j - 1\};$
  $P1[j] := t$
  end

$\{$computing $d2[j]$ for all j satisfying $d2[j] \geqslant j\}$

compute table P using Algorithm 5.8;
$t := P[m]; q := 1;$
while $t > 0$ **do**
begin
  $s := m - t;$
  for $j := q$ **to** s **do** $d2[j] := \min \{d2[j], s\};$
  $q := s + 1; t := P[t]$
end
end of algorithm.

The complexity of this algorithm is of the same order as that of Algorithm 5.8. The computation of $d2$ shows a close relationship between Algorithms 5.1, 5.2 and their derivatives. The table $d2$ used in right-to-left scan string-matching is computed using the table P which was related to the left-to-right scan.

SUMMARY

Key points covered in this chapter include:

- dynamic simulation
- string-matching with a left-to-right scan of patterns
- string-matching with a right-to-left scan of patterns
- algorithms for problems related to string matching
- maximal suffixes
- the cyclic equivalence of texts.

EXERCISES

5.1 Give the exact formula (in terms of n and m) for the maximal number of symbol comparisons performed in Algorithm 5.2.

5.2 Give similar estimates for Algorithms 5.3 and 5.9.

5.3 How many symbol comparisons are done by Algorithm 5.10 for texts v, w of length n where $u = 11 \ldots 1201$ and $w = 111 \ldots 120$?

5.4 Construct a linear time algorithm which tests if a given text starts with the word of the form zz, where $|z| > k$ for a fixed integer k.

5.5 A similarity problem for convex polygons: assume we have two convex polygons represented by sequences of their consecutive vertices (in clockwise order). Design an algorithm to test the similarity of these polygons in linear time.
(*Hint* Compute the sequences of angles between consecutive sides for each polygon; what is the relation between the similarity and the cyclic equivalence of words?)

5.6 Two-dimensional string-matching: given two-dimensional tables x, y of characters, check if x is a subtable of y in time linear with respect to the size of the input data.

5.7 Find a formula for the function $Shift(j)$ for the pattern $x = (abcd)^{m/4}$.

5.8 Prove that if x, y are two consecutive Fibonacci words then $C(xy) = yx$, where the operation C interchanges the last two symbols.

5.9 Construct a linear-time constant-space algorithm which checks if a given text is a Fibonacci word.

5.10 Let the pattern x be the kth Fibonacci word and F_q be the qth Fibonacci number. Prove that $P[j] = j - F_q$ for $q \leqslant k$ and $F_q \leqslant j - 1 < F_{q+1}$.

5.11 Prove that if pattern x is a Fibonacci word then $Shift(j) \geqslant j/3$.

5.12 Prove that Algorithm 5.11 works in linear time for very simple patterns.

5.13 Design a linear time algorithm constructing a table P' similar to P, the only difference being that information about a mismatch is also considered. $P'[j]$ is the minimal proper suffix of $x[0 \ldots j]$ of length k which is a prefix of x, such that $x[k+1] \neq x[j+1]$. Suppose we use P' in place of P in string-matching algorithms. Does that reduce the number of comparisons?

5.14 Prove Lemma 5.1.

5.15 Assume that a pattern x is simple. Construct a linear-time algorithm finding all the occurrences of x in the text.

5.16 Construct a linear-time constant-space algorithm which finds the length r of the first basic prefix and its continuation R ($x[0 .. r]$ is a period of $x[0 .. R]$, and R is maximal with this property).

5.17 Prove that each pattern of length n has $O(\log n)$ basic prefixes. What is the constant factor?

5.18 Write a full algorithm for finding a pattern in a text if the decomposition uv of the pattern (according to the decomposition theorem) is given.

5.19 Write a full algorithm which finds a decomposition $x = uv$ (satisfying the requirements of the decomposition theorem) in linear time and constant space.

5.20 Prove that if a text of length n has periods p and q, where $p + q \leqslant n$, $p > q$, then it also has a period of size $p - q$.

5.21 Prove that the text vw is prime iff wv is prime.

5.22 Give a formula for the number of symbol comparisons performed in the modified versions of Algorithm 5.2 when the shift is $d2$ ($d1$) and the input data is $x = ca(ba)^k$ and $y = a^{2k+2}(ba)^k$.

5.23 Suppose that $i2 - i1 \leqslant m/2$, where m is the length of the pattern. Prove that if $i1$ and $i2$ are two consecutive occurrences of the pattern x in the text then $i2 - i1 = period(x)$.

5.24 Construct a linear time algorithm tabulating the values of the function $d1(j)$.

5.25 Let $Sub(x)$ be the set of all subwords of the text x. This set can be represented succinctly by a directed rooted acyclic graph G denoted by $dawg(x)$. ($dawg$ is an abbreviation for directed acyclic word graph.) The edges of G are labelled by symbols of the input alphabet. The label of a path is the concatenation of labels of its consecutive edges. The graph G represents $Sub(x)$ in the following sense: $Sub(x)$ equals the set of all words which are labels of paths in G starting at the root.

Prove that we can construct a $G = dawg(x)$ such that the size of G is $O(n)$.

(*Hint*   A subword z leads from the root to a node which corresponds to the set of all positions ending an occurrence of z in x. Hence the number of nodes equals the number of such sets of end positions of occurrences of a given subword. These sets satisfy the non-overlapping property: if two of them are not disjoint then one is contained in the other. Prove that each family of subsets of $\{1, 2, \ldots, n\}$ satisfying the non-overlapping property contains at most $2n$ subsets.)

5.26 Suppose you are given $G = dawg(y)$. How does this help to check if pattern x occurs in y? How do you use the graph G to find the lexicographically first subword of x?

5.27 Assume you are given $G = dawg(x)$. Compute the cardinality of $Sub(x)$ in linear time.

5.28 In the Boyer–Moore algorithm we check the occurrence of the pattern from right to left. Suppose we are given $G = dawg(x^R)$. Then we can find a right-to-left string in y starting at position i which is an element of $Sub(x)$. If this text has length smaller than $|x|/2$ then we can jump to position $i + |x|/2$. Prove that the average complexity of such a string-matching algorithm is sublinear.

5.29* In one iteration Algorithm 5.14 scans the part $y[i + j - 1 \,.. \, i + m]$ of the text y and then makes the shift $s = d2(j)$. If $j = 0$ then assume formally that $s = m$, in this case the algorithm stops. Let k be the minimal period size of $x[m - s \,.. \, m]$ which divides s (the full period). Prove that if $m - j > 3k$ then the part $y[i + j + k - 1 \,.. \, i + m - 2k]$ of the text is scanned in this iteration for the first time, see Cole (1990). Hence at most $3s$ symbols are scanned for the second time. If we sum this over all iterations then we have the bound $3n$. The sizes of parts scanned in each iteration for the first time give together at most n. This implies the bound $4n$ on the total number of comparisons.

Chapter 6
Reducing the Complexity by Analysis of Algorithms – Part 2

This chapter presents the idea of algebraic simulation of algorithms and the use of the composition systems. The analysis of algorithms related to the recognition of context-free languages is also performed here.

6.1 Introduction

We now continue the subject of Chapter 5, but here we are mainly concerned with the analysis of recursion and non-determinism in polynomial time algorithms. The main issue is not finding upper bounds for the complexity of specific problems, but finding techniques leading to such upper bounds.

We analyse a class of algorithms for problems related to the recognition of formal languages. The main features of such algorithms are recursion (or the workings of a stack) and non-determinism. Hence we analyse the mechanism of both recursion and non-determinism.

Let I be an Input alphabet. I is a finite set of elements called symbols or letters. A word over I is any sequence whose elements are symbols contained in I. A **formal language** L is any subset of I^*, where I^* is the set of all words over I. Any language can also be thought of as a property of words. Our interest focuses on the **syntactic properties** of words.

There is no exact definition of what the syntactic properties are. Roughly speaking, they are properties described by using simple operations on words: concatenating words, reversing, substituting a word for a part of another word (which corresponds to the mechanism of grammars) and so on.

The **recognition problem** for a given language L is:

verify the membership $x \in L$

The size of the problem is the length n of x. We assume here that the description (for example a grammar) of L is of a constant size.

Many decision problems can be presented as language recognition problems. It is sufficient to encode inputs to the problem by words, then the problem reduces to the membership problem for the language L consisting of all encodings of inputs with output *true*. For example, the membership in the set L of (decimal, say) representations of prime numbers can be thought of as checking primality. In this example the language L and the property 'the word is a representation of a prime number' can be informally identified. In this sense, the primality test can be reduced to the recognition problem for the language of all primes given in binary or decimal notation.

Dynamic simulation was presented in Chapter 5. This chapter presents the **algebraic simulation** method. It consists in constructing a composition system corresponding to the algorithmic problem. It is especially successful when improving recursive and non-deterministic algorithms. The main algorithmic problem in Chapter 5 for demonstrating algorithmic techniques was string matching; here it is **context-free** recognition.

We believe that the class of context-free languages is the most interesting class of formal languages from the algorithmic point of view. They are described using a syntactic mechanism of grammars.

There are two main features of **context-free grammars** which make them especially interesting in the analysis of algorithms. These are: non-determinism and recursion. Both are very strong algorithmic tools, used in a variety of algorithms.

A context-free grammar can be treated as a non-deterministic recursive algorithm. This algorithm can be viewed as a starting point for the design of an efficient algorithm. The recognition algorithm can then be thought of as a simulation of this algorithm. The techniques used in such simulations also apply to many other problems related to recursion and/or non-determinism, see Rytter (1985b). Hence context-free recognition can be thought of as a generic problem.

Context-free grammars seem very technical, but they provide a useful tool for the syntactic recursive definition of textual properties. Formally, a context-free grammar is given by a 4-tuple

$$G = (V_N, V_T, P, S)$$

where:

V_N is a finite alphabet of **non-terminal symbols** (syntactic variables);

V_T is a finite alphabet of **terminal symbols**;

P is a set of **syntactic rules (productions)**;

$S \in V_N$ is a starting non-terminal symbol.

We always assume that the terminal and non-terminal alphabets are disjoint sets. Denote their union by V. V is called the **dictionary** of the grammar.

Each syntactic rule (in short, rule) is of the form $A \rightarrow z$ where z is a word over the dictionary of the grammar and $A \in V_N$. Such a rule means that each occurrence of the non-terminal A in some word may be replaced by z.

We write $x \Rightarrow y$ iff x, y are of the form $x = uAv$, $y = uzv$, $A \rightarrow z$ is a rule of the grammar and u, v are some words. The relation '$\Rightarrow$' is the **one-step syntactic derivation (generation)**.

Let $\Rightarrow$* be the reflexive and transitive closure of the relation $\Rightarrow$. The language $L(G)$ generated by the grammar G is:

$$L = \{x \in V_T^* : S \Rightarrow {}^* x\}$$

In the examples below terminal symbols will be written with lower-case letters and non-terminal ones with upper-case letters. Assume also the following convention: a set of rules with the same left side

$A \rightarrow z1,\ A \rightarrow z2,\ \ldots,$

can be written as

$A \rightarrow z1 \,|\, z2 \,|\, \ldots$

For example, look at the context-free style definition of palindromes. Assume that our alphabet is $\{a, b\}$ and the language is the set P of symmetric words of even length. We can say that a text x has the property P iff $x \in P$. This property can be defined recursively: x has property P iff either (a) or (b), where:

(a) $x = aa$ or $x = bb$;

(b) $x = aya$ or $x = byb$, where y has property P.

Hence we have a sequence of alternatives which is reflected in the grammar. It can be written as a grammar:

$S \rightarrow aa \,|\, bb \,|\, aSa \,|\, bSb$

The text $x = abaaba$ is in this sense an even palindrome because we have a derivation:

$$Sa \Rightarrow Sa \Rightarrow abSba \Rightarrow abaaba$$

A straightforward recursive algorithm corresponds to the grammar above:

if $x = aa$ or $x = bb$ then return *true* else if the first and last symbols are distinct then return *false* else cut off these symbols and apply the algorithm recursively

Every context-free grammar G which does not use the empty word (it does not appear in any production) can be easily transformed into a grammar G' in the so-called Chomsky normal form: rules are of the form $A \to BC$ or $A \to a$.

Hence assume for simplicity that the considered grammars are in such a form. The grammar is called **unambiguous** iff for each terminal word x there is at most one derivation tree of x from the starting non-terminal. We assume also that the grammar contains no useless symbols (which do not appear in any derivation of a terminal word from the starting non-terminal). Then there is at most one derivation tree of any word x from any non-terminal symbol.

If the original grammar G is unambiguous then so is the Chomsky-like version G'.

The string-matching problem and problems related to symmetries in texts are also problems of recognition of particular context-free languages. For example, the context-free language corresponding to the string-matching problem is:

$$L = \{x\$y^R \colon x \text{ is a subword of } y\}$$

This language is context-free. However, observe that the complement of this language and the language $L' = \{x\$y \colon x \text{ is a subword of } y\}$ are not context-free (the complement of L' is not context-free either). Also, languages related to symmetries in texts discussed in Section 6.6 (languages of prefix palindromes, palstars and even palstars) are context-free. It is worth observing here that the recognition algorithms considered in Section 6.6 are linear-time algorithms, while algorithms for general context-free recognition are of an order higher than quadratic.

The linear time complexity of problems for prefix palindromes and palstars suggests that there could be a linear time recognition algorithm for general context-free languages. This is a very strong conjecture. In fact, the complexity of context-free recognition is not fully understood despite the very long history of the problem. The best lower bound is linear, the best upper bound is more than quadratic. The methods for particular languages considered in Section 6.6 suggest that combinatorics on texts could be a key to further improvement.

6.2. Time-efficient recognition of general context-free languages – algebraic simulation method

We shall now construct a kind of algebraic system, called a **composition system**, whose elements are subcomputations of a simulated algorithm or 'parts' of a syntactic generation. The operation is the composition of smaller subcomputations or smaller generations into bigger ones. We start with a set of generators – constant-sized subcomputations or generations.

A composition system is given by a 4-tuple

$$S = (N, T, \otimes, s)$$

where:

N is a finite set of elements of the system (the **carrier**);

$T \subseteq N$, the set of **initial elements** (**generators**);

$\otimes$ is a binary operation of **composition**, its arguments are elements of N and its values are subsets of N;

$s \in N$ is a **goal element**.

Let $closure(T)$ denote the closure of T with respect to the operation $\otimes$: the smallest set $X \supseteq T$ such that $x \otimes y \subseteq X$ for each $x, y \in X$. The composition system S is called **solvable** iff $s \in closure(T)$. We interpret '$z \in x \otimes y$' as 'z is a possible composition of x and y'. There are many possible elements composed of x and y because of non-determinism.

Composition systems are also called path systems. They were investigated in Cook (1970) and Gurari and Ibarra (1980).

Assume we have a grammar G and an input text x of length n. Our problem is to check if $x \in L(G)$. We can treat G directly as a non-deterministic recursive algorithm. Each non-terminal A can be treated as a recursive funtion $A(i)$. Its value is any position j such that $A \Rightarrow *x[i \mathrel{.\,.} j]$. In particular there may be no such j and the set of possible values may be empty.

In the preceding chapter we assumed that the execution of the return statement outputs a value and stops the execution of the whole algorithm. We assume here that the return statement in the body of a given function F returns a value v (executes $F := v$) and stops the execution of this particular call of F, but does not stop the execution of the whole algorithm. For example, consider the following grammar G:

$S \to BS \,|\, AB \,|\, AC, \ C \to SB, \ A \to a, \ B \to b$, with $x = aababb$

Then the corresponding functions are:

```
function S(i);
begin
goto choice (1, 2, 3);
1: j := B(i); j := S( j); return j;
2: j := A(i); j := B( j); return j;
3: j := A( j); j := C( j); return j;
end;

function C(i);
begin j := S(i); j := B( j) return j end;

function A(i);
if x[i + 1] = a then return i + 1 else failure;

function B(i);
if x[i + 1] = b then return i + 1 else failure.
```

The instruction **goto** choice(1, 2, 3) non-deterministically jumps to one of the labels 1, 2, 3. Recall that the return value statement outputs the result and stops the whole algorithm. The *failure* instruction corresponds to an error (a non-deterministic path of the computation which leads to no result). The outcome of a non-deterministic function is the set of all values y such that there is a computation path returning y.

A subcomputation is a triple (A, i, j) such that j is a value which can be returned in the call $A(i)$. For a given grammar G in Chomsky normal form and for an input text x, we now construct a composition system $S(G, x)$.

Elements of $S(G, x)$ are triples (A, i, j), where $A \in V_N$, $0 \leqslant i < j \leqslant n$. Such triples are potential subcomputations, but some of them may correspond to no computation. The triples corresponding to correct subcomputations are called **realizable**.

We would like to define a set T of generators and a composition operation $\otimes$ in such a way that the set of realizable elements will equal *closure*(T). Hence our system should simulate the composition of larger subcomputations from smaller ones.

The generators correspond to atomic subcomputations (one-step subcomputations at the 'bottom' level of recursion). Define

$$T = \{(A, i, i + 1): A \to x[i + 1], A \in V_N\} \text{ and } s = (S, 0, n)$$

The operation $\otimes$ is defined as follows:

$$\text{if } j1 \neq j2 \text{ then } (A, i, j1) \otimes (B, j2, j) = \varnothing$$
$$(B, i, k) \otimes (C, k, j) = \{(A, i, j): A \to BC\}$$

Now we can easily prove the following fact:

$(A, \quad i, \quad j) \in closure(T) \Leftrightarrow j$ is a possible outcome of the call $A(i) \Leftrightarrow A \to *x[i .. j]$

Lemma 6.1 trivially follows from our definitions.

Lemma 6.1

The composition system S corresponding to the grammar G and input text x is solvable iff x is generated by the grammar.

For example, consider the grammar

$G: S \to SS \,|\, a \,|\, b$

and text $x = aba$. Then our system $S = (N, T, \otimes, s)$ is:

$N = \{(S, 0, 1), (S, 0, 2), (S, 0, 3), (S, 1, 2), (S, 1, 3), (S, 2, 3)\}$

and

$T = \{(S, 0, 1), (S, 1, 2), (S, 2, 3)\}, \quad s = (S, 0, 3)$

In this case $closure(T) = N$. The system is solvable because $s \in closure(T)$.

Hence the recognition problem for context-free languages is reduced to the solvability of the corresponding composition systems. The solvability problem is mainly concerned with the computation of $closure(T)$.

There is another way from context-free grammars to composition systems by means of **derivation trees**. A derivation tree for an input text x is a syntactic tree (syntactic in the sense that its nodes are labelled by non-terminals and terminals). The leaves read from left to right form the text x. Each internal node has a non-terminal label. If the label of a given node is A and its sons (left-to-right) are labelled B and C then we require that $A \to BC$ is a rule of the grammar.

Figure 6.1 shows a derivation tree for $x = aababb$ in our example grammar G:

$S \to SS \,|\, AB \,|\, AC, \; C \to SB, \; A \to a, \; B \to b$

The $\otimes$ operation now corresponds to the composition of syntactic trees. If we have two trees $T1, T2$ whose roots are labelled B and C, and if there is a rule $A \to BC$ then we can join $T1$ and $T2$ to form a bigger tree T with root labelled A, whose sons are B and C. The drawback here is the size of the set of all potentially possible syntactic trees. However, in the compositions only roots and leaves are relevant.

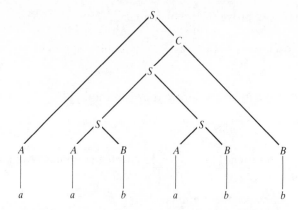

Figure 6.1   A derivation tree for text $x = aababb$ in G.

All trees with the same root label and with the same string encoded by leaves can be identified. The triple (A, i, j) represents any syntactic tree with root labelled A and leaves (left-to-right) labelled with consecutive symbols of the subword $x[i \,.\,.\, j\,]$.

We can see that the reduction of the amount of data is sometimes the crucial factor in complexity. Suppressing information related to the 'interiors' of trees reduces the size of the composition system from exponential to quadratic. This is in sharp contrast to the methods of Chapter 5 where the key point was to gather and use as much information as possible. Here our construction 'forgets' part of the information. This is further evidence that the optimization of information is an important method in the design of algorithms.

The natural informal algorithm to compute $closure(T)$ is to start with the set of generators and apply $\otimes$ until no new elements are added. Then we return *true* iff $s \in closure(T)$. Each newly created element will be called an **active element**. These elements (when composed with previously generated elements) can produce new active elements. Active elements will be placed on the stack $STACK$, and the set of non-active elements is denoted by R. For each active element u we generate all elements from $u \otimes v$ or $v \otimes u$ for $v \in R$.

Define

$$u \otimes R = \{z: z \in u \otimes v \text{ for some } v \in R\}$$

$$R \otimes u = \{z: z \in v \otimes u \text{ for some } v \in R\}$$

The operations POP and $PUSH$ refer to the pushdown store $STACK$. Initially R and $STACK$ are empty.

Algorithm 6.1   {testing solvability of the composition system}

> **begin**
> **for** each $u \in T$ **do** $PUSH(u)$; {all generators are active}
> **while** $STACK \neq \emptyset$ **do**
> > **begin**
> > $u := POP$; **if** $u = s$ **then** return $true$;
> > $insert(u, R)$;
> > > **for** each $z \in u \otimes R \cup R \otimes u$ **do** $\{z \in closure(T)\}$
> > > > **if** $z \notin R \cup STACK$ **then** {z is a new element} $PUSH(z)$
> > **end**;
> > {the goal element s was never taken from the stack}
> > return $false$
> **end**.

Lemma 6.2

Algorithm 6.1 returns $true$ iff the corresponding composition system is solvable.

Proof   It is obvious that each element z placed on the stack is in $closure(T)$. Hence if the algorithm returns $true$ then s is an element of $STACK$ and $s \in closure(T)$. This proves that the answer $true$ is correct.

We still have to prove that answer $false$ is correct. We have to prove the following implication:

$$z \in closure(T) \Rightarrow z \text{ is placed on the stack}$$

Let $size(z)$ be the minimal size of a tree generating z from the generators T. We prove the implication above by induction on $size(z)$. Elements of size one are generators and they are placed on the stack in the first statement in the algorithm.

Assume that $z \in closure(T)$ and z is of size greater than one. Then there are $v1$ and $v2$ of smaller size whose composition contains z. It is enough to prove that the following situation happens at the moment when instruction $u := POP$ is being executed:

$$(u = v1 \text{ and } v2 \in R) \text{ or } (u = v2 \text{ and } v1 \in R) \tag{6.1}$$

At this moment $z \in u \otimes R \cup R \otimes u$, and afterwards z will be inserted into $STACK$ if it is not already in R. However, if $z \in R$ then it must have been placed on the stack earlier.

The situation corresponding to condition (6.1) should happen. Using the inductive hypothesis (the sizes of $v1$ and $v2$ being smaller than $size(z)$) we know that $v1$ and $v2$ will appear on the stack. Therefore both will be inserted into R.

If the order of the insertions is $(v1, v2)$ then the situation ($u = v2$ and $v1 \in R$) will occur. Otherwise, the situation ($u = v1$ and $v2 \in R$) will occur. Hence (6.1) will be satisfied at some moment and z will be placed on the stack. This completes the proof. ∎

Let us assume that the sizes of $u \otimes v$ in the composition systems considered are bounded by a constant. This is true for the system $S(G, x)$ corresponding to the input text x and grammar G. The size of the system is the number r of its elements. Hence the size of $S(G, x)$ is $O(|x|^2)$.

A straightforward implementation of the $u \otimes R$ operation has $O(r)$ complexity. The set R can be represented by a list, and computation of $u \otimes R$ can consist in scanning this list and computing $u \otimes v$ for each $v \in R$. This gives a recognition algorithm for context-free languages of $O(n^4)$ time complexity, since the size of the system in this case is $O(|x|^2)$. However, in this case the complexity can be reduced by a factor of n.

Let us assume that our composition system S is $S = S(G, x)$, where G is a context-free grammar in Chomsky normal form and x is an input text of length n. The size of the problem is n. We analyse the general meta-algorithm (Algorithm 6.1) when applied to S. This will show how to create an efficient algorithm from a general algorithmic scheme by analysing specific properties of the input data.

The operation $u \otimes R \cup R \otimes u$ can be replaced by $R \otimes u$ if we place the initial elements on $STACK$ in a suitable order. Generally, such a replacement could make an algorithm incorrect, but in the case of context-free recognition it is possible.

Indeed, the initial elements of $S(G, x)$ are of the form $(A, i, i + 1)$. Suppose that elements with the highest value of i are pushed first. Then the following invariant is preserved in the algorithm:

if (A, i, j) is closer to the top than (B, k, l) then $j \leqslant l$

Moreover the second invariant will hold:

if $(A, i, j) \in STACK$ and $(B, k, l) \in R$ then $l \leqslant j$

Hence whenever we pop an element u from the stack then $u \otimes R = \varnothing$. Hence $u \otimes R \cup R \otimes u$ can be replaced by $R \otimes u$. This observation simplifies the algorithm.

However, the most costly operation is the computation of $R \otimes u$. The crucial point is to optimize this operation. To this end we partition set R into sets $R_j, j = 1 \ldots n$, where

$$R_j = \{(A, i, j') \in R : j' = j\}$$

Now $R \otimes (A, p, q)$ can be replaced by $R_p \otimes (A, p, q)$. Hence the cost of $R \otimes u$ is reduced from n^2 to n. The total complexity is reduced from n^4 to n^3.

Another simplification consists in elimination of the tests $z \notin R \cup STACK$. They are replaced by $z \notin R$. This can be achieved by inserting each element into R at the moment of pushing it onto the stack. The partition of R into R_j is simply implemented by the following table:

$$TAB[i,j] = \{A \in V_N : (A, i, j) \in R\}$$

Then R_j corresponds to the jth column of this table. Initially $STACK = \varnothing$ and each entry of TAB contains an empty set. In this way we obtain Algorithm 6.2.

Algorithm 6.2   {context-free recognition}

begin
    for $i := n - 1$ **downto** 0 **do**
        for each $A \in V_N$ such that $A \to a_{i+1}$ **do**
            begin $insert(A, TAB[i, i + 1])$; $PUSH((A, i, i + 1))$ **end**;
    while $STACK \neq \varnothing$ **do**
        begin
            $(A, i, j) := POP$; **if** $(A, i, j) = (S, 0, n)$ **then** return *true*;
            for $k := 0$ **to** $i - 1$ **do**
            for each $B \in TAB[k, i]$ and C such that $C \to BA$ **do**
                if $C \notin TAB[k, j]$ **then**
                    begin $insert(C, TAB[k, j])$; $PUSH((C, k, j))$ **end**
    end;
    {goal element $s = (S, 0, n)$ was never taken from the stack}
    return *false*
end.

Hence we have proved theorem 6.1.

Theorem 6.1

Each context-free language can be recognized in $O(n^3)$ time.

Algorithm 6.2 can be simplified. In fact, it is possible to remove the stack and use only TAB. The element (A, i, j) can only be generated by using compositions of elements of the form (B, i, k) and (C, k, j).

Let the size of the triple (A, i, j) equal $j - i$. Hence each element is generated as a composition of elements of smaller size.

Let R_s be the set of all generated elements of size at most s. We have $R = R_n$. The set T of initial elements equals R_1. We can compute the sets R_s in the order $s = 1, 2, \ldots, n$. Assume that R_{s-1} is computed; to check if $(A, i, j) \in R_s$ we only have to inspect the membership in R_{s-1} for all triples of the form (B, i, k) and (C, k, j).

There is only a linear number of such triples. This immediately gives a cubic time algorithm, since there is a quadratic number of triples (A, i, j) to consider. This type of algorithm was constructed in Younger (1967).

The above can be written more simply. Let us introduce the following operation on sets of non-terminals:

$$S1 \# S2 = \{ A: A \to BC \text{ for some } B \in S1, C \in S2 \}$$

Then we have the formula:

$$TAB[i, j] = \bigcup_{i < k < j} TAB[i, k] \# TAB[k, j] \qquad (6.2)$$

The whole algorithm is now:

compute $TAB[i, i + 1] = \{ A: A \to a_{i+1} \}$ for each i;

for (i, j) in increasing order with respect to $(j - i)$ do

apply the formula (6.2)

The algorithm can be rewritten in a still more abstract way. We can define the multiplication $\#$ of matrices whose elements are sets of terminals. Instead of the usual operations $+$ and $*$ we use $\cup$ and $\#$. Initially we compute all $TAB[i, i + 1]$. Other elements of table TAB contain empty sets. Then the algorithm is:

repeat $n - 1$ times
   $TAB := TAB \cup TAB \# TAB$

However, for general composition systems Algorithms 6.1 and 6.2 cannot be considerably simplified. This is because generally we have no order on the set of elements of the system which would allow us to simplify the computation. In our case (context-free recognition) we have the computation order corresponding to the ordering of the sizes of elements of the system (the size of (A, i, j) is $j - i$).

The cubic time complexity for recognition of context-free languages is not the best possible result. It is readily seen from the last algorithm that the recognition problem has something to do with matrix multiplication. In fact it is possible to reduce the time complexity to $\mathcal{O}(BM(n))$, where $BM(n)$ is the time to multiply boolean matrices, see Valiant (1975) and Graham and

Harrison (1976). It is known that $BM(n) = O(n^{2.5})$. The exponent 2.5 can be decreased at the cost of more and more complicated algorithms. However, it is not known whether boolean matrix multiplication can be done in quadratic time.

These upper bounds are not completely satisfactory in view of the fact that the best lower bound known is linear. In the last section of this chapter we shall see examples of non-trivial context-free languages with linear recognition functions. However, the corresponding algorithms are not instances of the general meta-algorithm for testing solvability of composition systems.

Hence the general meta-algorithm does not always produce the best algorithms, though it produces reasonably efficient ones in a simple, general way. However, we shall see that this general approach through composition systems is especially useful when considering space complexity and parallel computations.

To end this section we show how an algorithm for another problem (not related to texts) can be derived from the meta-algorithm for composition systems.

Suppose we want to compute the transitive closure B^+ of an $n \times n$ boolean matrix B. This is equivalent to computing the transitive closure of a directed graph corresponding to B. This graph has nodes $1, 2, \ldots, n$, and there is an edge from i to j iff $B[i, j] = true$.

The transitive closure of a graph results from adding to it all edges (i, j) such that there is a path from i to j in the original graph. Hence $B^+[i, j] = true$ iff there is a path from i to j in the initial graph corresponding to B.

Let us construct a composition system $S(B) = (N', T', \otimes, s')$, where

$$N' = \{(i, j): 1 \leqslant i, j \leqslant n\} \cup \{s'\}, \quad T' = \{(i, j): B[i, j] = true\}$$

and s' is a special element which cannot be generated. (The element s' is of no importance, because we are interested in computing all generated elements and not in generating a particular one.)

The $\otimes$ operation is defined as follows:

$$(i, k1) \otimes (k2, j) = \text{if } k1 = k2 \text{ then } \{(i, j)\} \text{ else empty set}$$

Observe now that $B^+[i, j] = true$ iff $(i, j) \in closure(T')$. Hence the computation of the transitive closure of B is equivalent to the computation of all elements generated in $S(B)$.

The algorithm is an instance of the general Algorithm 6.1. The set R is represented by the current value of a boolean matrix A:

$$A[i, j] = true \text{ iff } (i, j) \in R$$

Similarly to Algorithm 6.2 it is convenient to insert an element into R at the moment of pushing it onto the stack. Then checking the condition

$z \notin R \cup STACK$ can be replaced by checking $z \notin R$. The latter condition is equivalent to $A[i,j] = false$. After termination $A = B^+$.

We obtain the following non-standard algorithm computing transitive closure:

Algorithm 6.3   {computing the transitive closure of a boolean matrix B}

> **begin**
> $A := B$;
> **for** each (i,j) such that $A[i,j] = true$ **do** $PUSH((i,j))$;
> **while** $STACK \neq \emptyset$ **do**
>> **begin**
>> $(i,j) := POP$;
>> {test $(i,j) = s'$ is redundant}
>> **for** $k := 1$ **to** n **do**
>> **begin**
>>> **if** $A[k,i]$ and not $A[k,j]$ **then** {(k,j) is a new element}
>>>> **begin** $A[k,j] := true$; $PUSH((k,j))$ **end**;
>>> **if** $A[j,k]$ and not $A[i,k]$ **then** {(i,k) is a new element}
>>> **begin** $A[i,k] := true$; $PUSH((i,k))$ **end**
>> **end**
>> **end**;
> return $B^+ = A$
> **end**.

In the algorithm we have implemented the operation $u \otimes R \cup R \otimes u$. Can we replace $u \otimes R \cup R \otimes u$ by $R \otimes u$ as in Algorithm 6.2? We claim that this is possible if initially elements (pairs (i,j)) are placed on the stack in a suitable order. The modification of the algorithm is left as an exercise; the resulting algorithm is slightly simpler and shorter.

An operation similar to transitive closure is the computation of all elements accessible from a given initial element. One can construct a composition system such that operations of composition are unary; one element can generate all its successors in one step. Formally this can be written as:

$$v \otimes v = \{u: \text{there is a directed edge from } v \text{ to } u\}$$

The only initial element is the starting node u_0. Then an algorithm similar to Algorithm 6.3 can be derived as an instance of the meta-algorithm (Algorithm 6.1). The cost will be proportional to the size of the graph (number of edges plus number of nodes). If $STACK$ is a pushdown store then the order of the generated elements will be the depth-first-search order. If we replace $STACK$ by a queue then we obtain a variation of the breadth-first search. Both these types of traversing a graph can be viewed as a process of generation of elements from a single initial generator.

6.3   Unambiguous composition systems

A context-free grammar is called **unambiguous** iff for each string of terminals there is at most one derivation tree corresponding to the generation of this string from the starting non-terminal S. After making a suitable reduction of the grammar (removing useless non-terminals) this definition is slightly changed: for each string z of symbols over the dictionary of the grammar and for each non-terminal A there is at most one derivation tree of z rooted at A. Hence we can deal with this (stronger) definition. A context-free language is unambiguous iff it is generated by an unambiguous context-free grammar.

The concept of unambiguity is easily generalized for composition systems (see also Rytter (1982)).

A composition system S is unambiguous iff each element of the system has at most one generation tree from the generators T. The following fact is easy: if a context-free grammar G is unambiguous then the composition system corresponding to G and to any terminal word x is also unambiguous.

If the composition system considered is unambiguous then Algorithm 6.1 can be simplified. We need not check if $u \in R \cup STACK$. This gives Algorithm 6.4.

Algorithm 6.4   {testing solvability of an unambiguous composition system}

>**begin**
>>**for** each $u \in T$ **do** $PUSH(u)$; {all generators are active}
>>**while** $STACK \neq \emptyset$ **do**
>>>**begin**
>>>$u := POP$; **if** $u = s$ **then** return *true*;
>>>$insert(u, R)$;
>>>**for** each $z \in u \otimes R \cup R \otimes u$ **do** $PUSH(z)$
>>>**end**;
>>return *false*
>**end**.

It is not completely trivial to check that this algorithm is correct for unambiguous systems. For arbitrary systems it is incorrect. If we take $N = \{a, b\}$, $T = \{a\}$, $s = b$ and $a \otimes a = \{a\}$ then Algorithm 6.4 will never stop.

Lemma 6.3

Let S be an unambiguous composition system $(N, T, \otimes, s)$. Then

(1) Algorithm 6.4 stops.
(2) Its time complexity is $O(|N|)$ if the cost of computing $z \otimes R \cup R \otimes z$ is $O(|z \otimes R \cup R \otimes z| + 1)$ and the cost of *insert* is $O(1)$.

Proof   The algorithm stops because each element is pushed onto the stack at most once, because of unambiguity. The number of pushes executed is $O(|N|)$ and each generated element (a member of $z \otimes R \cup R \otimes z$) is pushed onto the stack. Hence the total cost of all operations $z \otimes R \cup R \otimes z$ executed is proportional to the number of pushes. Therefore it is $O(|N|)$, because the number of pushes is linear. This completes the proof.   ∎

Let us use this lemma to construct an efficient recognizer of unambiguous context-free languages. We have here a data structure problem. The set R should be implemented in such a way that the *insert* and *generate* operations are computed efficiently (satisfying the assumptions of lemma 6.2(2)).

We represent R by a vector SET of sets:

$$SET[A, j] = \{i : (A, i, j) \in R\}$$

Each element of this vector is a set represented by a linear list of its elements. The operation $insert((A, i, j), R)$ now corresponds to $insert(i, SET[A, j])$.

We obtain the following algorithm as an instance of Algorithm 6.4.

Algorithm 6.5   {recognition of unambiguous context-free languages in Chomsky normal form}

> **begin**
> **for** $i := n - 1$ **downto** 0 **do**
>   **for** each $A \in V_N$ **do if** $A \to a_{i+1}$ **then** $PUSH(A, i, i + 1)$;
> **while** $STACK \neq \varnothing$ **do**
>   **begin**
> $(A, i, j) := POP$; **if** $(A, i, j) = (S, 0, n)$ **then** return *true*;
> $insert(i, SET[A, j])$;
>   **for** each $C, B \in V_N$ such that $C \to BA$ **do**
>   **for** each $k \in SET[B, i]$ **do** $\{(B, k, i), (A, i, j) \in R\}$
> $PUSH(C, k, j)$;
>   **end**;
> return *false*;
> **end**.

Hence Lemma 6.2 implies Theorem 6.2.

Theorem 6.2

Each unambiguous context-free language can be recognized in $O(n^2)$ time.

The stack can be eliminated from the algorithm just as in Algorithm 6.2, owing to the fact that we can choose a 'good' order of computation of $[A, j]$.

The order of the time complexity does not change. We leave this as an exercise for the reader.

As another application of unambiguous composition systems we derive a linear time simulation of two-way deterministic pushdown automata (2dpda's, for short). Context-free grammars can be treated as text algorithms with recursion, while 2dpda's can be treated as text algorithms using the mechanism of the stack. In fact these two kinds of text algorithms are conceptually equivalent because the mechanisms of recursion and the stack are similar.

Recursion is easier to understand. A stack can be used to implement the recursion and programming with the stack can be thought of as a lower level programming. However, such programming gives better access to the stack. One of the classical results in the theory of formal languages and automata is the equivalence of one-way non-deterministic pushdown automata and context-free grammars. 2dpda's are two-way pushdown automata, and their capability of two-way moves in the input texts makes them quite powerful. For example, the language $\{x\$y: x$ is a subword of $y\}$ is not context-free, while it is accepted by a 2dpda.

A 2dpda is a special type of a stack-manipulating algorithm acting on words. An input is a text x of length n with left and right endmarkers (so that the 2dpda can detect the boundary of the text).

The auxiliary data used by the 2dpda is very restricted. It consists of one integer variable i pointing to a position in the input text x, a stack (last-in first-out storage) of symbols and some other auxiliary data which needs only a constant number of bits. This small data is called the **state** and is denoted by s.

The state s can consist of several boolean variables (it is the 'finite control' of the 2dpda). The only actions related to i are decreasing or increasing i by one. The algorithm has access to the symbol $x[i]$. We assume that x is given as a read-only vector of characters. The automaton starts in some pre-designated state s_0 and returns *true* iff it ends in a special accepting state s_a. We refer the reader to Aho *et al.* (1974) for a more detailed definition of 2dpda.

Let S be the set of states of a given 2dpda A. The crucial point is that the size of S is bounded by a constant. At a given moment of the computation, A has access to the following information:

state s

symbol $x[i]$

top symbol Z of the stack

The possible actions of A are:

moving the pointer i

changing the state s

modifying the stack using *POP* or *PUSH* operations

The language accepted by a 2dpda A is the set $L(A)$ of all texts x for which A returns *true* (ends in state s_a) if started in state s_0 with the stack containing only the initial stack symbol Z_0. Without loss of generality we can assume that when A accepts, the height of the stack is one and $i = n$. Hence at the moment of acceptance the state and position in the input text are uniquely determined. Another technical assumption is that in each move A makes a push or a pop operation.

We leave to the reader as an exercise the construction of a 2dpda A such that $L(A) = \{x\$y: x \text{ is a subword of } y\}$.

Hence the string-matching problem can be reduced to the problem of simulation of a specific 2dpda. Assume we are given a 2dpda A and an input text x of length n. Let S be the set of states of A. A **surface configuration** (**configuration**, for short) of A is a triple (s, i, Z), where $s \in S$, $1 \leqslant i \leqslant n$ and Z is a stack symbol (Z in this context is supposed to be the top of the stack). Denote by K the set of surface configurations.

Observe that from the point of view of surface configurations 'push moves' are uniquely determined, and 'pop moves' are determined up to the new top-of-stack symbol.

A configuration $q \in K$ is a **pop configuration** iff the next move of A is a pop move, otherwise it is a **push configuration**. The predicate $POP(q)$ holds iff q is a pop configuration. Assume that the accepting configuration is a pop configuration.

For $p, q \in K$ we write $p \Rightarrow q$ iff A can start with configuration p with a one-element stack and after a non-zero number of moves the configuration will equal q and the stack will be one element. Moreover, we require that during the computation from p to q all intermediate stacks be of height at least two. Let $\Rightarrow^*$ denote the reflexive and transitive closure of $\Rightarrow$.

If $p \Rightarrow q$ then q is called a **successor** of p, if $p \Rightarrow^* q$ and $POP(q)$ then q is called a **terminator** of p. Observe that, because of the determinism of 2dpda A, each configuration p has at most one successor and at most one terminator.

We say that a pair of configurations $(p1, q1)$ is *below* the pair of configurations $(p2, q2)$ iff $p2$ results from $p1$ by a push move and $q1$ results from $q2$ by a pop move, and moreover the top symbols of the stack are the same in $p1$ and $q1$. Denote by $BELOW(p2, q2)$ the set of all such pairs $(p1, q1)$; see Figure 6.2.

Let us define the following composition system

$$S(A, x) = (N', T', \otimes, s')$$

where

$$N' = \{(p, q): q \text{ is either a successor or a terminator of } p\};$$

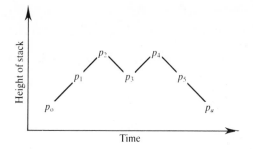

Figure 6.2 History of a computation of a 2dpda. p_is are surface configurations. p_3 is the successor of p_1 and p_5 is the terminator of p_1. The generators of the system are (p_2, p_2) and (p_4, p_4). The pair (p_0, p_a) is below (p_1, p_5).

$$T' = \{(p, p): POP(p)\};$$

$s' = (p_0, p_a)$, where p_0 is an initial configuration and p_a is an accepting configuration.

If r is not a successor of p then

$$(p, r) \in (p, q) \otimes (q, r)$$

iff (q is a successor of p, r is a terminator of q and $r \neq q$)

$$(p, q) \otimes (p, q) = BELOW(p, q)$$

Now the following facts can be easily proved:

$S(A, x)$ is solvable iff $x \in L(A)$

$S(A, x)$ is unambiguous

Now we apply Algorithm 6.4. However, for a set $R \subseteq N'$ we need a data structure satisfying the following assumptions:

for $z \in N'$ and $R \subseteq N'$ the cost of computing $z \otimes R \cup R \otimes z$ is $O(|z \otimes R \cup R \otimes z| + 1)$ and

the cost of $insert(z, R)$ is $O(1)$

We maintain two arrays TER and $PRED$. A set $R \subseteq N'$ is represented by these arrays as follows:

$PRED[q] = \{p: (p, q) \in R\}$ for all $q \in K$ such that not $POP(q)$

$TER[p] = \{q: (p, q) \in R$ and q is a terminator of $p\}$

Observe that entries of these arrays can contain empty sets; entries of *PRED* can contain sets of arbitrarily great (finite) cardinality while those of *TER* contain only sets of cardinality at most one.

The set $z \otimes R \cup R \otimes z$ is computed by the following function:

```
function generate(z, R); {R is represented by the arrays TER, PRED}
{z = (a, b)}
begin
result := empty_set;
if not POP(b) then
   for each c ∈ TER[b] do insert((a, c), result)
else
   begin
      for each c ∈ PRED[a] do insert((c, b), result);
      result := result ∪ BELOW(a, b)
   end;
return result;
end.
```

The operation *insert*$((a, b), R)$ can be implemented by the following statement:

```
if POP(b) then insert(b, TER[a]) else insert(a, PRED[b])
```

The insertions into entries of *TER* and *PRED* are easy because each time we insert new elements (we need not check if the element is already in the set), the sets $TER[p]$ and $PRED[p]$ can simply be implemented as linear lists.

The time complexity of computing $z \otimes R \cup R \otimes z$ and insertions into R satisfy the assumptions of Lemma 6.2. The automaton A accepts the input text x iff the pair (p_0, p_a) may be generated from the generators of the system $S(A, x)$. This implies Theorem 6.3.

Theorem 6.3

Assume that $L = L(A)$, where A is a 2dpda. Then L can be recognized in linear time.

6.4   Tabulation methods for recursive programs

The tabulation method is a kind of simple application of dynamic simulation. The outcomes of a recursive function are recorded in a table and whenever we start a recursive call the appropriate entry of this table is first inspected. If contains an already computed value then the function returns it saving a redundant computation of the function for the same argument again. Otherwise the function is computed and as a side effect the computed value is recorded in the table. This may speed up computation and improve time complexity, if the table look-up is done efficiently.

However, there is another virtue of the tabulation method. If we know in advance the order of the arguments for which the function will be computed then recursion can be totally removed and replaced by the computation of the entries of the table in a suitable order. Hence, the second benefit of the tabulation method is the removal of recursion. However, this is not always easily realizable as will be shown by the example of simulating 2dpda's using the tabulation method.

Let us assume that we are given a 2dpda A and an input text x of length n. As in the previous section, we consider the set K of (surface) configurations. Assume that A is loop-free (it always terminates its computations and has a move in each configuration with a non-empty stack). Let $TER(p)$ be the terminator of the configuration p. If A is loop-free then TER is well defined for each configuration p.

We define the following pop and push functions:

(1) $PUSHF(p) = q$ iff q results from p by a push move; the function is defined only for push configurations.

(2) $POPF(p, q) = r$ iff q results from p by a pop move and the top stack symbol in r is the same as in q; the function is defined only for pop configurations.

$POPF$ and $PUSHF$ are computable in $O(1)$ time.

Now TER can be written in a recursive way as follows:

function $TER(p)$; {returns the terminator of p}
begin
if $POP(p)$ **then** return p **else**
return $TER(POPF(p, TER(PUSHF(p))))$
end.

The function correctly computes the terminator of a given configuration if A is loop-free. However, its time complexity is generally exponential. We leave it to the reader as an exercise to find a 2dpda and a class of input texts for which the execution time of this function is exponential.

We now introduce a table TAB to store the computed values of the function and avoid recomputation of TER for the same argument. Assume that initially each entry of TAB contains a special 'no-value' information nil. The tabulation method gives the following version:

function $TER'(p)$; {returns the terminator of p}
begin
if $TAB[p] = nil$ **then**
$TAB[p] :=$ **if** $POP(p)$ **then** p **else** $TER'(POPF(p, TER'(PUSHF(p))))$;
return $TAB[p]$
end.

It can easily be seen that TER' correctly computes the terminators of configurations p. Its time complexity is proportional to the number of possible values of p, since for each p the function TER' is invoked at most once. Hence time complexity is linear.

This gives the linear time complexity of loop-free 2dpda's. The general case can be treated in the same way. We have to modify TER' to detect the moment when A loops (then the function returns *no terminator*).

To this end we introduce a table $ONSTACK(p)$ such that $ONSTACK(p)$ = *true* iff there is a call with parameter p which has not terminated. If $ONSTACK(p) = true$ and we call TER' with the same p then we detect at the same time that A loops. On the other hand if A loops then such a situation must take place. We leave the details to the reader.

Observe that there is no easy way to eliminate recursion from the algorithm for TER' (without replacing recursion by a stack).

A more general dynamic simulation of stack-manipulating programs was given by Rytter (1981b). For some special subclasses of deterministic pushdown automata more efficient simulation is possible, see Rytter (1981a, 1983). A survey on tabulation methods is given by Bird (1980). An efficient simulation of two-way non-deterministic pushdown automata is presented in Rytter (1985c).

Next we demonstrate the tabulation method for context-free grammars treated as recursive programs. We now assume that all grammars considered are non-left-recursive. This means that there is no derivation of the form

$$A \to {}^*Az$$

for any non-terminal symbol A and a string z. Fortunately, each context-free grammar G can easily be transformed into a non-left-recursive grammar G'. Moreover, if the original grammar G is unambiguous then G' is too.

In the transformation process we change the interpretation of recursive functions corresponding to non-terminals. Recall that in Section 6.2 we defined certain functions corresponding to non-terminals. The function $A(i)$ non-deterministically returns one (or none if there are none) value of j such that $A \to {}^*x[i \ . \ . \ j]$. Now for a non-terminal A let us define the deterministic recursive function $A'(i)$ whose value is the set of all those values j' which can be non-deterministically returned by $A(i)$.

Hence we eliminate non-determinism by dealing with the sets of possible values (this is similar to the powerset construction for determination of finite non-deterministic automata).

Consider again the same grammar as in Section 6.2:

$$S \to BS|AB|AC, \ C \to SB, \ A \to a, \ B \to b$$

The input text is $x = aababb$. This grammar is non-left-recursive. Now the corresponding functions are:

function $S'(i)$;
begin

    1: $set := B'(i)$; $result := \bigcup_{j \in set} S'(j)$;

    2: $set := A'(i)$; $result := result \cup \bigcup_{j \in set} B'(j)$;

    3: $set := A'(i)$; $result := result \cup \bigcup_{j \in set} C'(j)$;

    return $result$
end;

function $C'(i)$;
begin

    $set := S'(i)$; $result := result \cup \bigcup_{j \in set} B'(j)$; return $result$
end;

function $A'(i)$
    if $x[i + 1] = a$ **then** return $\{i + 1\}$ **else** return $\varnothing$;

function $B'(i)$;
    if $x[i + 1] = b$ **then** return $\{i + 1\}$ **else** return $\varnothing$;

Let us apply the tabulation method to functions S', A', B' and C'. We obtain the functions:

function $S'(i)$;
begin
if $Tab[S', i] = nil$ **then**
begin

    1: $set := B'(i)$; $result := \bigcup_{j \in set} S'(j)$;

    2: $set := A'(i)$; $result := result \cup \bigcup_{j \in set} B'(j)$;

    3: $set := A'(i)$; $result := result \cup \bigcup_{j \in set} C'(j)$;

    $Tab[S', i] := result$
end;
return $Tab[S', i]$
end;

function $C'(i)$;
begin
if $Tab[C', i] = nil$ **then**

begin

    $set := S'(i);\ result := result \cup \bigcup\limits_{j \in set} B'(j);$

    $Tab[C', i] := result$

end;

return $Tab[C', i]$

end;

function $A'(i)$;
begin
if $TAB[A', i] = nil$ **then**
begin
    if $x[i + 1] = a$ **then** $Tab[A', i] := \{i + 1\}$ **else** $Tab[A', i] := \varnothing$;
end;
return $Tab[A', i]$
end;

function $B'(i)$;
begin
if $Tab[B', i] = nil$ **then**
begin
    if $x[i + 1] = b$ **then** $Tab[B', i] := \{i + 1\}$ **else** $Tab[B', i] := \varnothing$;
end;
return $Tab[B', i]$
end.

(We have applied the tabulation method directly. However, the functions A' and B' could be considerably simplified by applying the method more carefully.)

In the same way we can transform any other non-left-recursive grammar G into an algorithm $Rec(G)$ consisting of recursive functions corresponding to non-terminals. We claim that such an algorithm recognizes texts of length n in $O(n^3)$ time in the case of general grammars, and in $O(n^2)$ time in the case of unambiguous context-free grammars. A more general transformation is presented in Rytter and Giancarlo (1987a).

The basic operation in the functions A', B' and C' is set-theoretic union. We have two possible representations of sets:

(1) vectorial representation by means of characteristic functions, or

(2) list representation.

In the first representation computing the union of two sets takes $O(n)$ time. The second representation is chosen for the case of unambiguous grammars, in which case the union of two disjoint sets $S1$ and $S2$ has a complexity proportional to the total size of these sets.

A given recursive function (corresponding to a non-terminal) is called at most once for each argument i because of tabulation. The cost of a given call is proportional to the cost of computing unions of $O(n)$ sets. This is $O(n^2)$ in the first representation. Multiplied by the number n of possible values of i this gives a cubic time complexity for the whole algorithm.

In the case of unambiguous grammars without useless non-terminals it can be proved that each operation of set union involves disjoint sets. Hence for a given i the cost is $O(n)$. The total cost is quadratic.

This shows that the transformation Rec of a grammar into a set of recursive functions automatically captures the property of unambiguity of the grammar.

The tabulation method can also serve to remove recursion. However, to do this we should know the order of the computation of the entries of Tab. Let $(X, i) \ll (X', i')$ mean that $Tab[X, i]$ should be computed before $Tab[X', i]$ (if $(X, i) \ll (X', i')$ does not hold then we know that $Tab[X, i]$ is not needed in the computation of $Tab[X', i']$).

For our example relation $\ll$ is defined as follows:

$(X, i) \ll (X', i')$ iff $(i > i')$ or $(i = i'$ and $X - \to *X')$, where $Y - \to X$ iff there is a production $X \to YZ$ for some $Z \in V_N$. In our grammar the relation $- \to$ is:

$$B - \to S; \; A - \to S; \; S - \to C$$

For example $(S, i) \ll (C, i)$ because of the rule $C \to SB$; when computing $Tab[C, i]$ we first call $S'(i)$ and compute $Tab[S, i]$.

Now we can remove recursion computing entries of Tab in order $\ll$. Algorithm 6.6 results:

Algorithm 6.6

> **begin**
> **for each** non-terminal X **do** $Tab[X, n] := \varnothing$;
> **for** pairs (X, i) in order $\ll$ **do**
> **if** $X = S$ **then**
>   **begin**
>
>   1: $set := Tab[B, i]$; $result := \bigcup_{j \in set} Tab[S, j]$;
>
>   2: $set := Tab[A, i]$; $result := result \cup \bigcup_{j \in set} Tab[B, j]$;
>
>   3: $set := Tab[A, i]$; $result := result \cup \bigcup_{j \in set} Tab[C, j]$;
>
> $Tab[S, i] := result$
>   **end**

else if $X = C$ **then**
   begin

$$set := Tab[S, i]; \ result := \bigcup_{j \in set} Tab[B, j]; \ Tab[C, i] := result$$

   end
else if $X = A$ **then**
   begin
      if $x[i + 1] = a$ **then** $Tab[A, i] := \{i + 1\}$ **else** $Tab[A, i] := \varnothing$;
   end
else
   begin
      if $x[i + 1] = b$ **then** $Tab[B, i] := \{i + 1\}$ **else** $Tab[B, i] := \varnothing$;
   end;
end.

In this way from a non-left-recursive grammar G we obtain an algorithm $Iter(G)$, which is an iterative version of the algorithm $Rec(G)$ consisting of recursive functions. $Iter(G)$ works by computing the sets $Tab[X, i]$ by expanding right sides of syntactic productions with non-terminal X on the left side.

$Iter(G)$ works in cubic time in the general case and in quadratic time in the case of unambiguous context-free grammars.

6.5   Algebraic simulation with small memory

In earlier sections we were mostly interested in time complexity and in the algorithm we collected as much information as possible. We stored the set of all elements generated up to a given moment. In this section we are concerned with space complexity, hence we will only store a small (of logarithmic size) subset of generated elements.

We say that a given composition system is **tree-like** iff there is a generation tree of each element $v \in closure(T)$ consisting of distinct elements of the system S. All the composition systems considered here are tree-like. In fact it would be enough (for considerations in this section) to assume an existence of a generation tree of a polynomial size (see Rytter (1985b)).

Observe that, in general, the system corresponding to a 2dpda A and an input text x is not tree-like. However, systems corresponding to context-free grammars are tree-like.

For an element $v \in N$ and a subset B of N define $\text{dist}(v, B)$ to be the minimal number of internal nodes (operations) of a generation tree of v from elements of $T \cup B$ (the minimal number of operations to generate v from $B \cup T$). If there is no such tree then define $\text{dist}(v, B)$ to be infinity. Hence $\text{dist}(v, \varnothing) = 0$ for each $v \in T$.

Lemma 6.4

Assume that $\text{dist}(v, B) = m$. Then there is $w \in N$ such that

$$\text{dist}(w, B) \leqslant 2m/3 + 1 \text{ and } \text{dist}(v, B \cup \{w\}) \leqslant 2m/3$$

Proof Let T be a tree with m internal nodes generating v from $T \cup B$. It is enough to show the existence of a node z such that the subtree T_z rooted at z has at most $2m/3 + 1$ internal nodes and the same is true for the tree T' resulting from T by replacing T_z by a leaf.

Let z be any node such that T_z has a minimal number of internal nodes among the subtrees having at least $m/3$ internal nodes. It is easy to see that z is the required node. Then w is an element whose generation tree is T_z. This completes the proof. ∎

We say that a composition system is **enumerative** iff its elements can be encoded by consecutive integers $1 \,.. \,|N|$. We require that the coding and decoding can be done using $O(1)$ additional (small) registers with a logarithmic number of bits each.

The triples (A, i, j) of the system corresponding to a grammar G can be easily encoded by consecutive integers. Hence the system $S(G, x)$ is enumerative. The notion of the enumerative system is a technical tool to enable one to list the elements of the system using small memory.

For $m > 4$ we have $2m/3 + 1 < m$. Let $Check(v, B)$ be the function which checks whether v can be generated from $T \cup B$ with at most four operations. It is easy to show that the value of $Check(v, B)$ can be computed in $O(1)$ additional space if we have a table storing elements of B.

We design a function $Test(v, B, t)$ which returns *true* iff v can be generated from $T \cup B$ with at most t operations $\otimes$.

```
function Test(v, B, t);
begin
var w: element of N;
if t ∈ T ∪ B then return true else if t < 4 then return Check(v, B);
for each w ∈ N do
    if Test(v, B ∪ {w}, 2t/3 + 1) and Test(w, B, 2t/3 + 1) then return true;
return false {if true has not been returned yet}
end.
```

Let us assume that the elements of a composition system are stored in a table. In our considerations we do not count memory needed to store this table – it is treated as an input.

Lemma 6.5

Test can check the solvability of a given enumerative tree-like composition system using $O(\log^2 n)$ additional memory, where $n = |N|$.

Proof Correctness follows from Lemma 6.4. The depth of recursion is $O(\log n)$. At each level of recursion we need memory to store the local variable w and the value of the parameter B. This last value needs logarithmic memory because $|B| = O(\log n)$. Hence the memory needed to store the stack of recursion is $O(\log^2 n)$. This completes the proof.   ∎

Let us reduce the space complexity of the algorithm by analysing the behaviour of *Test*. Most space is occupied by the sets B. However, if we look more closely at the recursion stack storing the values of B at each level then a certain regularity can be observed.

The B sets in consecutive recursive calls only differ by one element. Moreover, if insertions and deletions from B are organized in a stack manner (last-in, first-out) then the elements distinguishing the sets B are at the top of the stack. This suggests the following way of improving space complexity: remove the local parameter B, instead of that maintain a global set B implemented as a stack.

Algorithm 6.7 {testing solvability of a composition system using small memory}

```
begin
function Test1(v, t);
var w: element of N;
if t ∈ T ∪ B then return true else if t < 4 then return Check(v, B);
for each w ∈ N do
   if Test1(w, 2t/3 + 1) then
      begin
      PUSH(w, B); if Test1(v, 2t/3 + 1) then return true;
      POP(B);
      end;
return false {value true was not returned}
end;
B := empty stack;
return Test1(s, m)
end of algorithm.
```

Lemma 6.6

Algorithm 6.7 tests the solvability of a given path system using an at most logarithmic number of additional registers.

Proof Correctness follows from the correctness of *Test*. *Test*1 is a modification of *Test*. Space complexity is now logarithmic because B need not be separately stored at each level of recursion. This completes the proof.   ∎

As a corollary we obtain Theorem 6.4.

Theorem 6.4

Each context-free language can be recognized using only $O(\log n)$ additional integer registers (only $O(\log^2 n)$ additional bits).

In the case of deterministic context-free languages it is possible to construct a recognition algorithm working in $\log^2 n$ space and simultaneously in polynomial time. However the algorithm is much more complicated. We refer the reader to Braunmuhl *et al.* (1983) and Rytter (1985a). Braunmuhl *et al.* have given an algorithm using $\log^2 n$ tape, while the algorithm from Rytter uses $\log^2 n$ bounded pushdown store (which is a more restricted memory than the tape).

6.6   Context-free languages related to palindromes

The context-free languages considered in this section have some special combinatorial properties. This allows us to design efficient (linear time) recognition algorithms. It also demonstrates how the mathematical properties of the input data are used in the analysis and design of algorithms. The sources of the presented material are Galil and Seiferas (1978) and Manacher (1975).

The problems solved in this section are purely theoretical. However, they deserve presentation as very rich algorithmic material well suited for practising the analysis of algorithms.

A **palindrome** is a non-trivial symmetric word. A one letter word is symmetric, but its symmetry is not interesting and it is not a palindrome according to our definition. More formally, let x^R be the reverse of x. Then a palindrome is a word x such that $x = x^R$ and $|x| > 1$. The palindrome is even iff its length is even. For example, *kayak* is a palindrome and *retter* is an even palindrome.

Let P denote the set of all even palindromes over a given alphabet, and let P_1 denote the set of all palindromes. It is obvious that the recognition of palindromes can be done in linear time with a constant number of additional memory locations (each of logarithmic size). We shall now introduce more ambitious languages related to palindromes.

Let $\hat{L}$ be the set of all words with an element of L as a prefix, and let L^* be the set of all concatenations of elements of L. Each word in L^* is of the form $x = x_1 x_2 \ldots x_k$, where each x_i is a member of L.

We examine the complexity of recognizing the following languages:

- $\hat{P}$ (prefix palindromes)
- P^k for $k = 2, 3, 4$
- P^* (even palstars)
- P_1^* (general palstars)

An example of a palstar is $x = abbabaab$: it can be decomposed into the palindromes *abba*, *baab*. Observe that in this case the decomposition is unique, but generally we can have many distinct decompositions.

This absence of uniqueness is related to non-determinism. It is very easy to guess a decomposition and check its correctness. However, it is usually difficult to simulate such a non-determinism by deterministic means. At this stage we ask the reader to find a quadratic time algorithm for testing palstars, and then to compare that method with our route to a linear time algorithm.

A first approach to testing palstars is to simulate directly the non-deterministic linear time algorithm: such a direct simulation can consist in following all possible paths in a non-deterministic computation (using a kind of backtracking). However, this can lead to an exponential algorithm. The main point is to decrease the number of possibilities.

We start with an algorithm for $\hat{P}$. This language is much simpler than palstar testing. It is easy to write a quadratic time algorithm. This algorithm can then be transformed into a linear time one using the same general approach as in Section 6.5: dynamic simulation. In fact the initial algorithm will be very similar to Algorithm 5.1.

Let x be an input text of length n. We want to check if x starts with an even palindrome. The most natural algorithm consists in checking all prefixes of x. For a given prefix it is very easy to check if it is a palindrome in linear time. There are n prefixes, hence the total complexity is quadratic.

For $i = 1, 2, \ldots, n/2$ we check the equality $x[0 \ldots i] = x[i \ldots 2i]^R$. Just as in Algorithm 5.1 this leads to two possible algorithms depending on the direction of checking that equality. We introduce the following condition:

$$\text{symm}(i, j): x[i - j \ldots i] = x[i \ldots i + j]^R$$

Algorithm 6.8   {recognition of prefix palindromes, x is of even length}

```
begin
i := 1;
while i ≤ n/2 do
   begin
   1:  { check if x[0 .. 2i] is a palindrome }
       j := 0; while x[i − j] = x[i + j + 1] do j := j + 1;
       {x[0 .. i] is scanned right-to-left }
       if j = i then return true;
       { invariant: symm(i, j) and x[i − j] ≠ x[i + j + 1] and j < i}
   2:  { i := i + shift} i := i + 1
   end
end.
```

The algorithm outputs *true* iff the input text starts with an even palindrome. Look at the behaviour of the algorithm for $x = ba^{n-1}$. The number of operations is quadratic.

We now apply the dynamic simulation approach and try to transform this algorithm by optimizing the way it uses information. Just as in Algorithm 5.1 the wasted information is expressed by the value of j. Each time the next iteration starts j is set to zero and the information related to j is lost.

At this moment the similarity between simulations of Algorithms 5.1 and 6.8 ends. In Algorithm 5.1 it was enough to know the last value of j to speed up the algorithm. Now we have to record all preceding values of j (after each iteration) to make an improvement.

Let $Rad[i]$ be the value of j after the iteration for a given value of i. $Rad[i]$ is called the radius of the maximal even palindrome centred at i.

$$Rad[i] = \max\{j: \text{symm}(i, j)\}$$

To simplify our considerations let us assume that our text starts with a specially inserted unique leftmost symbol. Then the initial text contains a prefix palindrome iff $Rad[i] = i - 1$ for some i in the modified text.

After each iteration we place the value of j in $Rad[i]$. Hence when starting a new iteration we know $Rad[1], Rad[2], \ldots, Rad[i]$. We have the following surprising combinatorial fact which implies that we can easily compute some values of $Rad[i + k]$ without inspecting new symbols in the text.

Lemma 6.7

If $1 \leqslant k \leqslant Rad[i]$ and $Rad[i - k] \neq Rad[i] - k$ then

$$Rad[i + k] = \min\{Rad[i - k], Rad[i] - k\}$$

Proof We consider two separate cases.

(1) $Rad[i - k] < Rad[i] - k$ In this case the palindrome centred at $i - k$ with radius $Rad[i - k]$ is properly contained in the maximal palindrome centred at i. Hence if we reflect the palindrome centred at $i - k$ with respect to i we obtain the maximal palindrome centred at $i + k$. The radius of this palindrome is the same as that of the palindrome centred at $i - k$ due to symmetry. This completes the proof for case (1).

(2) $Rad[i - k] > Rad[i] - k$ Let $q = Rad[i] - k$. In this case symm$(i + k, q)$ holds since the symmetry of the palindrome centred at $i - k$ extends beyond the maximal palindrome centred at i and because $i + k$ is symmetric to $i - k$ with respect to i. Hence

$$Rad[i + k] \geqslant q$$

It is now enough to prove that $Rad[i + k] < q + 1$, which is equivalent to

$$x[i + k + q + 1] \neq x[i + k - q] \tag{6.3}$$

Observe that $i + k + q + 1 = Rad[i] + i + 1$, hence

$$x[i + k + q + 1] = x[i + Rad[i] + 1] \tag{6.4}$$

According to the definition of $Rad[i]$ as the maximal radius we have

$$x[i + Rad[i] + 1] \neq x[i - Rad[i]] \tag{6.5}$$

Hence the proof of the lemma reduces to the proof of

$$x[i + k - q] = x[i - Rad[i]]. \tag{6.6}$$

(because (6.3) follows from ((6.4), (6.5) and (6.6))).

Equation (6.6) follows from symmetries implied by palindromes centred at i and $i - k$. It is enough to make two suitable reflections. This completes the proof of the lemma. ∎

It follows from Lemma 6.7 that if we have computed the table Rad for all $i \leqslant i'$ then the value of $Rad[i' + k]$ for all $1 \leqslant k \leqslant Rad[i']$ such that $Rad[i' - k] \neq Rad[i'] - k$ can be found as

$$\min\{Rad[i' - k], Rad[i'] - k\}$$

We can take as a shift the minimal value of k for which $Rad[i' + k]$ cannot be computed using that formula but needs more symbol comparisons. After making the shift we need not start with $j = 0$, because we know that

$$\text{symm}(j', i + k) \text{ for } j' = \max\{0, Rad[i] - k\}$$

Hence we can start with $j = j'$; this saves j' symbol comparisons. Assume that $x[1]$ is a specially added leftmarker. Hence the condition $j = i$ for a prefix palindrome is now equivalent to $j = i - 1$.

Algorithm 6.9   {Manacher's algorithm, computes Rad, dynamic simulation of Algorithm 6.8, x is of even length, $x[1]$ and $x[n]$ are specially added end-markers}

begin
$i := 2; j := 0; Rad[1] := 0;$

```
while i ≤ n/2 do
  begin
  1:   {check if x[1 . . 2i − 1] is a palindrome}
       while x[i − j] = x[i + j + 1] do j := j + 1;
       if j = i − 1 then write(i) {prefix palindrome centred at i}
       Rad[i] := j;
       {compute Rad[i + k] for consecutive i + k for which a formula
         from the lemma applies}
       k := 1;
       while Rad[i − k] ≠ Rad[i] − k and k ≤ j do
       begin Rad[i + k] = min{Rad[i − k], Rad[i] − k}; k := k + 1 end;
       j := max(j − k, 0);
  2:   {i := i + shift} i := i + k
  end
end.
```

Theorem 6.5

The language $\hat{}P$ can be recognized on-line in linear time. The table Rad can be computed in linear time. We can compute the first prefix palindrome in time proportional to its length.

Proof Correctness of Algorithm 6.9 follows from the correctness of Algorithm 6.8 and Lemma 6.7.

We can estimate the complexity of the algorithm. The dominating operations are symbol comparisons – verification of $x[i − j] = x[i + j + 1]$. There is obviously a linear number of such comparisons with negative result. The number of successful comparisons is also linear as shown by the following argument.

Consider the value of $i + j$ at the moments of successful symbol comparisons. Each time we make such a comparison this value is immediately increased. On the other hand, this sequence of values is non-decreasing and its maximal value is n. Hence the number of successful comparisons does not exceed n. The total complexity is linear.

Let r be the length of the first prefix palindrome (assume that it exists). The first output is r. Up to the moment of producing this first output the algorithm does $O(r)$ comparisons. We can stop when producing the first output. This proves the last part of the theorem and completes the proof of the whole theorem.   ∎

Let $first(x)$ be the length of the minimal prefix even palindrome of x; if there is no such palindrome then define $first(x) = 0$. If $first(x) \neq 0$ then, according to the last theorem, $first(x)$ can be computed in $O(|first(x)|)$ time. Assume that the empty word is also a palstar.

An informal algorithm for testing even palstars can work as follows:

for each prefix palindrome z of the text **do**
begin
    cut off the prefix z;
    check if the remaining part of the text is an even palstar.
end.

Let us analyse this algorithm. Its inefficiency follows from the fact that there are many possible prefix palindromes z. It could happen that the text has a linear number of prefix palindromes.

Our simple analysis tells us that the key to an efficient algorithm is the reduction of the number of possibilities. Let us try to reduce the linear number of possibilities to only one possible prefix palindrome and consider only the first (smallest) prefix palindrome instead of all of them.

A naive algorithm for testing even palstars can now look as follows:

if x is non-empty **then** find the first even palindrome z and cut it off;
check if the remaining part of the text is an even palstar.

Let us introduce a variable s. The remaining part of the text is $x[s \, . \, . \, n]$. This text is empty iff $s = 0$. An iterative version of the naive algorithm above is Algorithm 6.10.

Algorithm 6.10   {recognition of even palstars, $|x|$ is even}

begin
    $s := 0$; {current text is $x[s \, . \, . \, n]$}
    while $s < n$ {non-empty text} **do** {cut off the first palindrome}
        begin
        $f := first(x[s \, . \, . \, n])$; **if** $f = 0$ **then** return *false* **else** $s := s + f$;
        end;
        return *true* {we have arrived at an empty word}
end.

The complexity is linear, this follows from the last theorem because the cost of computing f is $O(f)$ for $f > 0$. However, the correctness is non-trivial because it seems that our reduction of possibilities was rather 'naive'. Surprisingly, such a rough reduction gives a correct algorithm.

To prove this precisely we have to consider decompositions of a palstar into palindromes, and prove that there is always a decomposition starting with the smallest initial palindrome.

Assume that x is a non-empty even palstar. We shall introduce the following function:

$$parse(x) = \min\{k : x[0 \, . \, . \, k] \in P \text{ and } x[k \, . \, . \, n] \in P^*\}$$

Now the correctness of Algorithm 6.10 follows from Lemma 6.8.

Lemma 6.8

If x is an even non-empty palstar then $parse(x) = first(x)$.

Proof If follows directly from the definitions that $first(x) \leqslant parse(x)$. It is enough to prove the reverse inequality. Assume that

$$first(x) < parse(x)$$

Let $f = first(x)$, $p = parse(x)$. We consider two cases which are potentially possible (in fact we prove that they cannot occur).

Case 1 $p/2 < f < p$
In this case take the suffix z of $x[0 \ .. \ f]$ of size $f - p/2$ (see Figure 6.3). Then the even palindrome $z^R z$ is a suffix and a prefix of $x[0 \ .. \ f]$. It is also a prefix of the whole string x. Then $x[0 \ .. \ f]$ is no longer the smallest prefix palindrome because $x1$ is smaller. This contradicts the definition of $first(x)$. Hence case 1 cannot occur.

Case 2 $2 \leqslant f \leqslant p/2$
Let $x1 = x[0 \ .. \ f]$, $x2 = x[f \ .. \ p - f]$ and $x3 = x[p - f \ .. \ p]$. The words $x1$, $x2$, $x3$ are palindromes (except that $x2$ may be empty). Now there is a decomposition of x into palindromes starting with $x1$. The word $x1$ is a palindrome starting a decomposition and its length is less than p. This contradicts the definition of $p = parse(x)$ as the length of the shortest palindrome starting a decomposition. Hence case 2 cannot occur.

Cases 1 and 2 cover all possibilities. None of them can occur. Hence it is impossible that $first(x) < parse(x)$. This completes the proof of the lemma. ∎

As a corollary of Lemma 6.8 and Algorithm 6.9 we have Theorem 6.6.

Theorem 6.6.

Even palstars can be tested in linear time.

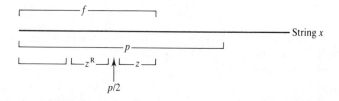

Figure 6.3   Impossibility of case 1.

Unfortunately the algorithm similar to Algorithm 6.9 does not work for arbitrary palstars (elements of P_1^*). We define:

$$Parse1(x) = \min\{k: x[0 \ .. \ k] \in P_1 \text{ and } x[k \ .. \ n] \in P_1^*\}$$

Let $first1(x)$ be the length of the minimal prefix palindrome of x; if there is no such palindrome then assume $first1(x) = 0$. The function $first1$ can be computed similarly to $first$ in time proportional to the length of the result (if it is non-empty).

The key to Algorithm 6.10 was a relation between $parse$ and $first$. Unfortunately it can happen that $parse1(x) \neq first1(x)$. Hence we cannot restrict the number of prefix palindromes examined to (the shortest) one. Fortunately, it turns out that we can restrict this number to three.

Take $x = bbabb$. For this text $parse1(x) = 5$, but $first1(x) = 2$. If we define $f = first1(x)$ and $p = parse1(x)$ then $p = 2f + 1$. For $x = abbabba$ we have $p = 2f - 1$ and for $x = aabb$ we have $p = f$.

Lemma 6.9

Let x be a non-empty palstar and $p = parse1(x), f = first1(x)$. Then

$$p \in \{f, 2f - 1, 2f + 1\}$$

Proof   We proceed similarly to the proof of Lemma 6.8. We exclude all other possibilities. The proof is by contradiction. Assume that p is not an element of $\{f, 2f - 1, 2f + 1\}$. Three cases are possible:

Case 1 $f < p < 2f - 1$

Case 2 $p = 2f$

Case 3 $p > 2f - 1$

We shall prove the impossibility of case 1 only. The proof for other cases is analogous. Assume that

$$f < p < 2f - 1$$

We derive a contradiction. Figure 6.3 applies to this case also. An initial palindrome shorter than $x[0 \ .. \ f]$ is thus found.

This contradicts the definition of $p = first1(x)$. Similarly cases 2 and 3 cannot occur.

This implies that $p \in \{f, 2f - 1, 2f + 1\}$ and that completes the proof of the lemma.   ∎

Hence the natural algorithm for testing arbitrary palstars may look as follows:

> let $f = first1(x)$;
> **for** each prefix palindrome z such that $|z| \in \{f, 2f - 1, 2f + 1\}$ **do**
> **begin**
> cut off the prefix z;
> check if the remaining part of the text is an even palstar.
> **end**.

Let $FIRST1[i + 1] = first1(i)$. Assume that we already know the table $FIRST1$ together with the table of radii of maximal palindromes. The latter allows us to compute in constant time the predicate

$$pal(i, j) = (x[i \mathbin{..} j] \text{ is a palindrome})$$

Let $palstar(i)$ be the boolean function returning *true* iff $x[i \mathbin{..} n]$ is a palstar.

> **function** *palstar* (i);
> **begin**
> **if** $i = n$ **then** *palstar* := *true* {empty *palstar*} **else**
> **begin**
> f := $FIRST1[i + 1]$; **if** $f = 0$ **then** *palstar* := *false* **else**
>   *palstar* := (*palstar*($i + f$) or (*pal*($i, i + 2f - 1$) and *palstar* ($i + 2f - 1$))
>   or (*pal*($i, i + 2f + 1$) and *palstar*($i + 2f + 1$)))
> **end**
> **end**.

The algorithm is recursive and has exponential time complexity when implemented in a straightforward way. The key to an improvement is the tabulation method.

Recall that this method consists in tabulating known values in a table. Assume that we have a table $Tab[i]$ and initially all its entries contain the value 'not computed'. We modify the recursive function *palstar* by using the tabulation method.

> **function** *palstar*(i);
> **begin**
> **if** $Tab[i] \neq$ 'not computed' **then**
> **begin**
> **if** $i = n$ **then** $Tab[i]$:= *true* {empty *palstar*} **else**
> **begin**
> f := $FIRST1[i + 1]$; **if** $f = 0$ **then** $Tab[i]$:= *false* **else**
> $Tab[i]$:= (*palstar*($i + f$) or (*pal*($i, i + 2f - 1$) and *palstar*($i + 2f - 1$))
>   or (*pal*($i, i + 2f + 1$) and *palstar*($i + 2f + 1$)))

end
end;
palstar := *Tab*[*i*]
end.

The computation of *palstar*(0) has linear time complexity. The algorithm outputs *true* iff *x* is a palstar. In recursive calls the values of *i* increase.

Hence we can remove recursion by replacing the function *palstar* by a table *PALSTAR* and computing this table from *n* down to 0.

Algorithm 6.11   {iterative computation of table *PALSTAR*}

begin
PALSTAR[*n*] := *true*;
for *i* := *n* − 1 **downto** 0 **do**
    begin
        f := *FIRST*1[*i* + 1];
        if *f* = 0 **then** *PALSTAR*[*i*] := *false* **else**
        PALSTAR[*i*] := (*PALSTAR*[*i* + *f*] or ((*pal*(*i*, *i* + 2*f* − 1) and
        PALSTAR[*i* + 2*f* − 1])) or ((*pal*(*i*, *i* + 2*f* + 1) and
        PALSTAR[*i* + 2*f* + 1]))
    end;
return *PALSTAR*[0]
end.

The algorithm has linear time complexity if *FIRST*1 is already computed. However, a linear time algorithm computing this table is non-trivial.

For each position *i* we compute the first odd and the first even palindrome starting at this position. Then *FIRST*1 [*i*] is the minimum of these values. We only show how to compute the first even palindromes. The computation of odd palindromes is similar.

Let *FIRST*[*i*] be the smallest length of an even palindrome starting at *i*. We say that a position *j* is in the range of the maximal palindrome centred at *i*, where *j* ⩽ *i*, iff *x*[*j* . . *i*] is contained in this palindrome (as interval). Denote the corresponding predicate by *inrange*(*j*, *i*). Given the table of radii of maximal palindromes this predicate can be trivially computed in constant time.

The computation of *FIRST* is based on the following obvious fact:

$$FIRST[j] = 2[i0 − j + 1), \text{ where } i0 = \min\{i : j \leqslant i \text{ and } inrange(j, i)\}$$

This suggests the following informal algorithm:

Scan text *x* from left to right (*i* = 1, 2, . . . , *n*)

for each examined position i compute the value of $FIRST[j]$

for all j such that $inrange(j, i)$ and $FIRST[j]$ not computed

Now we have an exercise in data structure design. A suitable data structure is needed for keeping all j for which $FIRST[j]$ is not computed. For a given i we want to list all j for which $FIRST[j]$ is computed according to centre i (the palindrome corresponding to $FIRST[j]$ is centred at i). Such a list should be computed in a time proportional to its length.

The required data structure is the stack (pushdown store) of positions j. Let the operations $PUSH(i)$ and POP have the usual meaning (the value of POP is a popped element of the stack). The value of the variable top is automatically the top element of the stack. We obtain the following algorithm by refining our informal algorithm given above.

Algorithm 6.12   {computation of $FIRST$}

begin
$PUSH(0)$; {0 is the bottom of the stack, it is never popped}
for $i := 1$ **to** n **do**
  begin
    $PUSH(i)$; {compute $FIRST[j]$ for j such that $inrange(i, j)$}
    while $inrange(\text{top}, i)$ **do**
      begin $j := POP$; $FIRST[j] := 2(i - j + 1)$ **end**
end;
{the remaining js are not in the range of any palindrome}
while top $\neq 0$ **do** $FIRST[POP] := 0$
end.

The algorithm computes table $FIRST$ in linear time. The table of first odd palindromes as well as the table $FIRST1$ can be computed similarly. This proves Theorem 6.7.

Theorem 6.7

We can test arbitrary palstars in linear time.

Next we investigate the problem of testing compositions of an arbitrary number of palindromes. We consider compositions of a fixed number k of even palindromes (for general palindromes the problem is solved similarly). It is known that testing P^k has linear time complexity for $k = 1, 2, 3, 4$. For $k = 5$ the existence of a linear time algorithm is an open problem. It is interesting that algorithms for palstars cannot be modified for P^k.

The recognition of P^2 can easily be done by a linear algorithm:

for $i = 2$ to $n - 2$ do

if $pal(0, i)$ and $pal(i, n)$ then return *true*

However, it is possible to precompute in linear time a data structure which allows one to check if $x[i .. j] \in P^2$ in constant time. We denote the corresponding predicate by $twopal(i, j)$.

The key to the efficiency of testing palstars were the properties of the smallest prefix palindromes; surprisingly for P^k this role is played by maximal palindromes. Let $MAXPAL[i]$ be the longest palindrome starting at i.

Lemma 6.10

(1) If $x \in P^2$ then $x = x_1 x_2$, where $x_1, x_2 \in P$ and (x_1 is the maximal prefix palindrome or x_2 is the maximal suffix palindrome).

(2) $MAXPAL$ can be computed in linear time.

(3) If $MAXPAL$ is computed for x and for its reverse then for each i, j such that either $i = 0$ or $j = n$ we can compute the predicate $twopal(i, j)$ in constant time.

We omit the proof of 1 and 2. Point 1 has a tedious text-combinatorial proof, and we refer the reader to Galil and Seiferas (1978).

The algorithm computing $MAXPAL$ can be constructed using the predicate $inrange(i, j)$ as in the algorithm for $FIRST$. This time we have to scan the text right to left.

Point 3 follows easily from 1 and 2.

Theorem 6.8

If $k \leq 4$ then the language P^k can be recognized in linear time.

Proof We only show an algorithm for the hardest case: $k = 4$. The tables $MAXPAL$ are computed for the text x and its reverse. Then we execute the statement

for $i := 2$ to $n - 2$ **do**
if $twopal(0, i)$ and $twopal(i, n)$ **then** return *true*

The complexity is linear, because checking the conditions $twopal(0, i)$ and $twopal(i, n)$ takes constant time for a given i. This completes the proof. ∎

We have defined the set P_1 of palindromes to be the set of symmetric strings of length greater than one. Similarly we can define the set P_k of k-

palindromes whose length is bigger than k. The notion of a palstar can also be generalized to **k-palstars**.

We introduce functions $first_k$ and $parse_k$ by the straightforward generalizations of $first1$ and $parse1$. Then Theorem 6.9 can be proved.

Theorem 6.9

If $x \in P_k^*$ then $parse_k(x) \in \{f, 2f-1, 2f-2, \ldots, 2f-k, 2f+1, \ldots, 2f+k\}$, where $f = first_k(x)$. The language P_k^* can be recognized in linear time for a given k.

Proof The proof is similar to that for palstars, where $k = 1$. We refer the reader to Galil and Seiferas (1978). ∎

To end this section consider the relation of palindromes to string matching. Let P be the failure table (considered in the string-matching problem) for the text $x\$x^R$. Then x has a prefix palindrome iff $P[|x\$x^R|] > 0$. This gives a very simple algorithm for the recognition of $\hat{}P_1$. However, this algorithm does not find the first prefix palindrome z in $O(|z|)$ time, which was the crucial point in linear time recognition of palstars.

SUMMARY

Key points covered in this chapter include:

- algebraic simulation
- composition systems for context-free grammars
- composition systems for two-way pushdown automata
- tabulation methods for context-free grammars
- tabulation methods for two-way pushdown automata
- reducing the space complexity
- context-free languages related to symmetries.

EXERCISES

6.1 Prove that if an unambiguous context-free grammar in Chomsky normal form has no useless non-terminals (each non-terminal is reachable from the starting one, and each terminal generates a terminal string) then the corresponding composition system is unambiguous.

6.2 Construct a composition system $S'(G, x)$ for a grammar G in Chomsky normal form and a text x such that $closure(T)$ contains only those triples (A, i, j) satisfying the following: there is a derivation of $x[0 . . i]Az$ from the starting non-terminal, where z is a word over the dictionary of G. Give examples of grammars G and texts x for which the number of such triples is much less than the total number of triples.

6.3 Define a composition system for any context-free grammar (not only for grammars in Chomsky normal form). As elements of the system take the triple $(A \to \alpha . \beta, i, j)$, where $A \to \alpha . \beta$ is a 'dotted' rule. Such a rule is of the form $A \to \alpha . \beta$, where $A \to \alpha\beta$ is a production. The triple $(A \to \alpha . \beta, i, j)$ can be interpreted as: there is a derivation from α to $x[i . . j]$ (however nothing is known about the derivation from β). Assume that $\gamma = B\gamma'$. Then the dotted rule $(A \to \alpha B . \gamma', i, j)$ can be composed from dotted rules $(A \to \alpha . \gamma, i, k)$, and $(B \to z ., k, j)$ for some z.

6.4 Let L be a language generated by a given linear context-free grammar G (right sides of productions contain at most one non-terminal). Construct an algorithm recognizing language L^* in $O(n^2)$ time. (Observe that the language P of palindromes is also generated by a linear grammar: P^* is the set of palstars.)

6.5 Consider the following **shuffling problem**: given three texts x, y and z, verify if x is a **shuffle** of y and z. The shuffle of two words y and z is any word which can be decomposed into two disjoint subsequences which gives words y and z. Reduce this problem to the solvability of a composition system.

6.6 Design a linear time algorithm which will be an instance of Algorithm 6.1 and which computes all nodes reachable from a given node in a directed graph. For a graph and a starting node define a suitable composition system.

6.7* We say that a context-free language H is the hardest context-free language iff for every context-free grammar G there is a homomorphism (coding) h such that

$$x \in L(G) \Leftrightarrow h(x) \in H$$

We introduce an operation $Nondet(L)$, which produces a non-deterministic version L' of a given language L over an input alphabet I. Two new symbols \$ and # are added to the input alphabet. Each word of L' consists of a sequence of component words $z_1, z_2, \ldots, z_k$ separated by \$s. Each component word consists of a sequence of words over the alphabet I (called choice words) separated by #s. The whole text is in L' iff we can choose from each component word z_i a choice word w_i such that $w_1 w_2 \ldots w_k \in L$.

Prove that the language $Nondet(D_2)$, where D_2 is the language of well-formed sequences of two types of brackets, is the hardest context-free language. Hence the time and space complexity of the recognition of any context-free language is at most that of recognizing the language $Nondet(D_2)$.

We refer the reader to Greibach (1973).

6.8 Prove that the language $Nondet(P)$, where P is the set of even palindromes, is the hardest linear context-free language. The time and space complexity of the recognition of any linear context-free language is at most that of recognizing $Nondet(P)$.

Similarly one can find the hardest deterministic context-free language. However, each deterministic context-free language can be recognized in linear time, hence the hardness in this case is only interesting with respect to space complexity.

6.9 Let T be a tree with m internal nodes. Let z be any node such that T_z has a minimal number of internal nodes among the subtrees having at least $m/3$ internal nodes. Prove that T_z rooted at z has at most $2m/3 + 1$ internal nodes and the same is true for the tree T' resulting from T by replacing T_z by a leaf.

6.10 Show that the value of $Check(v, B)$ can be computed in $O(1)$ additional space if we have a table storing elements of $T \cup B$.

6.11 What is the time complexity of Algorithm 6.6? Is it polynomial?

6.12 Construct a linear time algorithm computing the table of radii of maximal odd palindromes in a given text.

6.13 For a given integer K and a given text, compute in linear time the number of all subintervals of length greater than K containing palindromes.

6.14 Prove that cases (2) and (3) in the proof of Lemma 6.9 cannot occur.

6.15 Construct a linear time algorithm computing the table $FIRST1$.

6.16 Construct a linear time algorithm computing the table $MAXPAL$.

6.17 Prove Lemma 6.9.

6.18 Construct a linear time algorithm testing compositions of three palindromes. Construct an $O(n^2)$ time algorithm testing compositions of 100 palindromes.

6.19 Prove Theorem 6.9.

6.20 Construct a linear time algorithm testing k-palstars.

6.21 A two-way non-deterministic pushdown automaton (2npda) differs from the 2dpda by its capability to use non-determinism. In a given situation the automaton has a constant number of possible moves. It accepts the input text iff there is an accepting computation. Prove that each language accepted by a 2npda can be recognized in cubic time. For a given 2npda A and input text x construct a suitable composition system $S(A, x)$ and apply Algorithm 6.1.

6.22 Let $S(A, x)$ be the composition system corresponding to a 2dpda A and text x. Prove that system $S(A, x)$ is solvable iff $x \in L(A)$; prove also that $S(A, x)$ is unambiguous.

6.23 Assume that a 2dpda A has p two-way pointers in the input text and q one-way pointers. The two-way pointers can be moved one position left and right. One-way pointers can only be moved to the right. Let $L = L(A)$. Prove that L can be recognized in $O(n^{p+1})$ time (p, q are constants).

6.24* Construct a 2dpda A accepting the languages

$$L = \{1^n \colon n = k^2 \text{ for some } k\}$$

$$L' = \{1^n 2^{f(n)} \colon f(n) = 2^n, n \geqslant 1\}.$$

Recall that according to the definition A can detect the first and the last position.

6.25 Find a 2dpda and a class of input texts for which the execution time of the function *TER* (see Section 6.4) is exponential.

6.26 Give a complete description of a linear time version of function *TER'* (see Section 6.4) for the general 2dpda's (when A is not necessarily loop-free).

6.27 Eliminate the stack from Algorithm 6.4 by choosing a 'good' order of computation of $[A, j]$. The order of time complexity should not change.

6.28* Let L be a language accepted by a one-way deterministic pushdown automaton A. Prove that we can simulate A (recognize L) in polynomial time using only $O(\log n)$ additional memory (consisting of registers containing integers of logarithmic size).
(*Hint*   Associate with each (surface) configuration q a configuration q' which is the first configuration preceding (or equal to) q and on the same

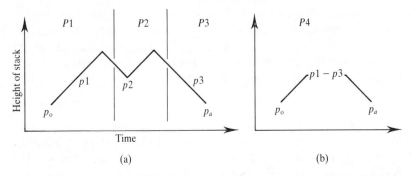

Figure 6.4   The history of the computation and the history with the shortcut.

level as q. We require that the stack between q' and q is not lower than at q and q'. Denote such a configuration by $F(q)$. Assume that we push onto the stack the triple $(q, F(q), height)$, where *height* is the current height of the stack and q is the current configuration. Hence on the top of the stack there are 'extended' configurations: triples $(q, F(q), height)$. We start with the 'extended' automaton A which always stores on the stack its extended configurations.)

We can simulate A on a given input text x of length n by partitioning the history of the computation into three smaller parts $P1$, $P2$ and $P3$, as indicated in Figure 6.4(a), each of size $n/3$. The simulation is described by a recursive procedure $SIM(q_0, t)$, which generates the sequence of all extended configurations which A can reach starting at q_0 in time t. Each configuration appears as a value of a global variable. The sequence can be much longer than t and some configurations can repeat many times, however all configurations of A in the time interval $[0 .. t]$ appear. The computation of A on x consists in simulating recursively three sub-computations of sizes smaller by a factor $2/3$:

(1) Simulate A in parts $P1$ and $P2$; compute the lowest configuration $p2$ in part $P2$ and $p1 = F(p2)$; record $p1$ and $p2$.

(2) At this moment in the additional memory we have the pair $(p1, p2)$. Simulate A in parts $P2$ and $P3$ starting at $p2$; compute the terminator $p3$ of $p2$; record that the terminator of $p1$ is $p3$, remove the information related to $p2$.

(3) At this moment in the additional memory we have the pair $(p1, p3)$. The whole computation is reduced to the smaller subcomputation $P4$ by assuming that A goes directly from $p1$ to $p3$, see Figure 6.4(b); simulate such a smaller subcomputation recursively by the same algorithm.

The depth of recursion is logarithmic, at each level we store a constant number of registers in additional memory. This memory consists of pairs (p, p'); each pair corresponds to a shortcut in the computation. It is easy to show that the time is polynomial by solving suitable recurrences for time complexity:

$$T(n) \leqslant 3T(2/3n) + c$$

Is it possible to apply such a method to each recursive or stack manipulating program? Observe that the number of steps of the simulated program should be small (for example, polynomial). The method does not apply to general 2dpda's since a 2dpda can have an exponential number of moves (see Exercise 6.24).

6.29 We are given an adjacency list representation of a directed graph. The list of neighbours of v is two-directional for each node v. Construct an algorithm checking whether the graph has a cycle. The additional memory should be of a constant size (few registers containing integers with logarithmic number of bits).

6.30 Suppose we know that an input graph is acyclic. Can we verify whether a node v can be reached from a node w with similar space complexity as in Exercise 6.29? What is the time complexity?

6.31 Consider the same problem, however remove the assumption about acyclicity. What is the space complexity?

6.32 Let L be a language generated by the grammar:

$S \to (S) \mid [S] \mid SS \mid () \mid [\ ]$

Construct a recognition algorithm using $O(1)$ additional small registers (with a logarithmic number of bits each). The input text is stored in the read-only table.

6.33* Let L' be a language generated by the grammar:

$S \to (S) \mid)S(\mid [S] \mid]S[\mid SS \mid () \mid [\ ] \mid)(\mid][$

Construct a recognition algorithm for L' using $O(1)$ additional small registers (with a logarithmic number of bits each). The input text is stored in the read-only table.

6.34* The deterministic two-way pushdown automaton with k input heads (2dpda(k), for short), is an extension of a one-head automaton. The surface configuration now includes all positions of the input heads. There are $O(n^k)$ such configurations. Prove that the 2dpda(k) can be simulated on a given input of length n in time and space complexity simultaneously proportional to the number of surface configurations reachable from the starting one. For example, the automaton from Exercise 6.23 has only $O(p^{+1})$ reachable configurations.

(*Hint* use the pyramidal structure, see Rytter (1983).)

Chapter 7
Analysis of Parallel Algorithms

The subject of this chapter is the analysis of parallel algorithms. Most of the algorithms discussed here have their sequential versions presented in Chapter 6. The crucial role of the combinatorics of trees in parallel algorithms is also demonstrated.

7.1 Introduction

The analysis of very fast parallel algorithms is closely related to an analysis of some combinatorial operations on trees. In this chapter we choose two representative groups of algorithms which allow us to see this relation and whose analysis is based on the combinatorics of trees. The algorithms considered are refinements of two simple meta-algorithms: Algorithm 7.1 and Algorithm 7.2.

The first representative group is related to the parallel computations of straight-line programs. Such programs are, roughly speaking, graphs whose nodes correspond to operations. The parallel complexity of these graphs depends on the structure of certain trees related to them. For example, graphs corresponding to the computation of expressions are trees. The computation of straight-line programs generalizes the evaluation of expressions.

The second group of algorithms is related to composition systems. The basic assumption about composition systems considered in this chapter is that they are tree-like. This means that the graphs of generation are trees. The parallel computations are based on this property.

The analysis of parallel algorithms for straight-line programs and composition systems shows the basic difficulties in analysing and constructing efficient parallel algorithms.

We are generally interested in very fast algorithms whose parallel time is polylogarithmic. A fast computation is possible mostly because the computation is tree-structured in a certain way. If the tree is of polynomial size and is balanced (of logarithmic height) then it is natural that the time is polylogarithmic. However, the main difficulty in the analysis of fast parallel algorithms is that the corresponding trees are generally not balanced or that they are too big. For example, in the parallel computation of expression trees the basic difficulty is their height, while in the computation of straight-line programs the difficulty is caused by the size of the tree structure of the computation graph.

Our model of parallel computations is a **Parallel Random Access Machine (PRAM)**. The PRAM is an idealized parallel computer (see Fortune and Wyllie (1978) and Gibbons and Rytter (1988)). The model essentially neglects any hardware constraints which a highly specific architecture may impose. All possible links between processors and memory locations are possible. This complexity of linkages is not physically realizable in present-day hardware.

On the other hand PRAMs are very attractive from the theoretical point of view, especially in the high-level design of efficient parallel algorithms. Most parallel algorithms in the literature are designed to run on PRAMs .

The PRAM consists of a number of processors working synchronously and using a common global memory. Elementary arithmetic operations are of constant time.

Essentially it is enough to extend the sequential programming languages by a 'parallel do' construction:

for each x in X **do in parallel** (action depending on x)

The action of such an instruction consists in assigning a processor to each x and performing corresponding (to x's) actions simultaneously. For example, if we have a vector of n variables then to compute the boolean 'or' we can write:

$result := false$;

for each $1 \leqslant i \leqslant n$ **do in parallel if** x_i **then** $result := true$;

As we can see in this example many processors can write a value into the same location at the same time. Such situations are called **write conflicts**. Similarly we can define **read conflicts**. Let the letters E, C, R and W stand for respectively 'exclusive', 'concurrent', 'read' and 'write'. We have four types of PRAM, **EREW**, **CREW**, **CRCW** and **ERCW** depending on the types of conflicts allowed (the last model ERCW is considered uninteresting).

Our computation of the 'or' function was on a CRCW PRAM in $O(1)$ time. It has been proved that if the write conflicts are not allowed then $O(\log(n))$ steps are needed to compute this function. Hence conflicts are unavoidable if a constant-time implementation is to be achieved. This also proves that the CRCW model is in one sense the most unrealistic, but it also permits the computation in $O(1)$ time of the string-matching problem and the maximal element of a vector.

In this chapter our model of the computation is the PRAM without write conflicts.

The most interesting class of problems from the point of view of parallel computation is the class called **NC**. This class name is an acronym for Nick (Pippenger)'s class. NC contains all problems which can be solved in poly-logarithmic ($\log^k n$ for some k) time with a polynomial number of processors. Problems which are in NC can be called well-parallelizable (see Cook (1983)).

Obviously any problem in NC admits a polynomial time-sequential algorithm (one processor can simulate step by step a polynomial number of processors). Hence NC is a subset of P (the class of sequentially feasible (polynomial-time computable) problems).

It seems (see Cook (1983)) that the main theoretical question in the complexity theory of parallel computations is: '$NC = P$?' It is a general belief that the answer to this question is negative. Hence the next interesting general problem is: which problems contained in P are in NC? The PRAM model is well suited to deal both with $P = NC$ and the classification problem, since PRAMs are simulated in polylogarithmic time (with a polynomial number of processors) on a bounded-degree network of processors. Such networks are considered as more realistic parallel computers. There are many such networks: perfect shuffle, cube connected, butterfly, and so on.

7.2 Expressions and straight-line programs

One of the simplest sequential computations well suited for parallelization is the parallel assignment statement:

$$(x_1, \ldots, x_n) = (val_1, \ldots, val_n)$$

Such a statement can be written to be executed in parallel as follows:

for each i do in parallel

$\quad x_i := val_i$

where val_i are constant-size expressions involving only constants.

The basic operation here is an assignment of a value to the variable. A straight-line program is a generalization of the parallel assignment statement.

It is a sequence of assignment statements:

$$x_1 := exp_1; \ x_2 := exp_2; \ldots, \ x_n := exp_n$$

where exp_i are constant-size expressions (which may include variables).

We assume that at most two variables occur in the expression exp_i, and all occurring variables x_j are with indices $j < i$ and that the size of each expression is $O(1)$. Hence in exp_1 there are only constants. For example, consider the following expression W:

$$2*(3*(x1 + x2) + 2*((2*x3) + 2)) + x4$$

with the values of $x1$–$x4$ given as follows:

$$x1 = 1, \ x2 = 2, \ x3 = 3, \ x4 = 4$$

The sequential computation can proceed by traversing in postorder the computation tree of the expression, the internal nodes of the tree corresponding to variables. The straight-line program P computing the expression W is

Program P;

$$x1 = 1, \ x2 = 2, \ x3 = 3, \ x4 = 4, \ x5 = 2*x3, \ x6 = x5+2, \ x7 = x2+x1$$
$$x8 = 3*x7+2*x6, \ x9 = 2*x8+x4$$

We assume that whenever we consider an expression then we know its computation tree. We refer the reader to Diks and Rytter (1990) and to Bar-on and Vishkin (1985) for efficient parallel transformations of expressions to corresponding trees. Both transformations work in $\log(n)$ time with $n/\log(n)$ processors. The Bar-on and Vishkin transformation works on a CREW PRAM and that of Diks and Rytter works on an EREW PRAM. Such a transformation is an example of a problem which imposes some difficulties for the EREW PRAM (as compared with a CREW PRAM). The presentation of parsing of expressions is beyond the scope of this book.

The computation graph $T = graph(P)$ of the straight-line program P is the directed acyclic graph whose nodes are variables relevant to the computation of x_n. The sons of a node (variable) x_i are variables occurring at a given moment on the right side of the equation defining x_i. x_n is the root of the computation graph. The computation graph includes only those nodes which can be reached from x_n.

Observe that the number of nodes of $graph(P)$ can be smaller than the size n of P (some variables (nodes) cannot be reached from the root).

In the case of straight-line programs computing expressions directly the computation graph T is a tree.

Although a straight-line program is a generalization of a parallel assignment statement, the same method of parallel computation does not work well in this case. We cannot simply write

for each _i_ do in parallel

$x_i := exp_i;$

since values of some variables occurring in the right sides are not known. However we use a similar idea.

The method of simultaneous substitutions generalizes the parallel implementation of the parallel assignment statement. We follow the material presented in Rytter (1990). An alternative parallel algorithm for expression evaluation can be found in Gibbons and Rytter (1989).

In each parallel step we try to evaluate or partly evaluate each of the variables x_i. In our parallel algorithm the basic operation is the substitution: the variable x can be replaced by its right side, afterwards all possible local reductions take place. Such an operation is denoted by subst(x). For example, after applying subst($x5$) to the right side for $x6$ we obtain $x6 = 2 * x3 + 2$. We replaced in expression $x5 + 2$ the variable $x5$ by subexpression (right side of $x5$) $2 * x3$.

The crucial notion is the safeness of the substitution. We use two different definitions for safeness: one in the case of straight-line programs computing expressions (when the graph of the straight-line program is a tree), and the second for the computation of general straight-line programs.

The general parallel meta-algorithm is very simple.

Algorithm 7.1   {main algorithm in this chapter}

repeat
    for each x_i **do in parallel**
        apply all safe substitutions to the right side of x_i.
  until x_n is computed.

The number n is the length of the sequential program. In our example $n = 9$.

We consider first the case when the computation graph is a tree. In this case we define the safeness of the substitution as follows.

First definition of safeness
The substitution subst(x) is safe if the right side for x contains at most one variable.

Let us look at our sequence of assignment statements after each iteration. In our example, initially substitutions involving the first six variables are safe.

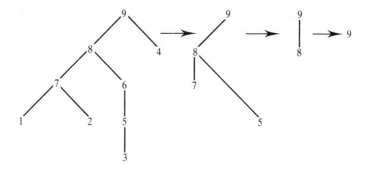

Figure 7.1   The sequence of computation graphs for the example straight-line program.

We show only the right sides of variables involved in the computation of $x9$ (corresponding to the nodes of the computation graph; recall that only nodes reachable from x_n are in this graph). After the first iteration

$P1$: $x5 = 6$, $x7 = 3$, $x8 = 3 * x7 + 2 * x5 + 4$, $x9 = 2 * x8 + 4$

After the second iteration

$P2$: $x8 = 25$, $x9 = 2 * x8 + 4$

After the third iteration

$P3$: $x9 = 54$

The sequence of computation graphs: $T0 = graph(P)$, $T1 = graph(P1)$, $\ldots$, $T3 = graph(P3)$ is shown in Figure 7.1. Observe that the sizes decrease by a factor at least $2/3$.

We shall prove later that this is always true. Hence the number of iterations is bounded by $\log_{3/2} n$.

We can use one processor for the manipulation on the right side of a given variable. The processor has to read right sides of some other variables in a given stage. There are no write conflicts. This proves Theorem 7.1.

Theorem 7.1

Algorithm 7.1 computes expressions (with operations $+$, $*$, $/$) in $O(\log n)$ time using n processors of a PRAM.

One of the crucial points is the following observation. Let us take the class F of functions f of the form $(ax + b)/(cx + d)$, where a, b, c and d are constants and $cx + d \neq 0$. Then F is closed under the composition.

The algorithm can be also applied in the case when $/$, $*$ and $+$ are any operations in an algebra with a carrier of a constant size. This guarantees that the manipulation of a given right side of the program can be performed in a constant time (we can keep a table representation of the function). For example, consider the problem of computing a maximal cardinality independent set in a tree. Now the operations are boolean operations *not*, *and*, and *or*. Every node of a tree corresponds to a boolean variable whose value is *false* if it is not in a computed independent set and *true* if it is. The values of leaves are *true*. If x has sons y and z then we write

$$x = not(y \ or \ z)$$

As another example consider the problem of the minimal cardinality dominating set in a tree: it is the minimal set X such that each node is in X or is a neighbour of a node in X. We can associate the values 0, 1 or 2 with the nodes in such a way that the value of a leaf is zero, the value of a node is 1 if it is not in a dominating set but is dominated by one of its sons contained in this set, and the value of a node is 2 if it is in the constructed dominating set. It is easy to write a straight-line program. We shall consider only binary trees with at least two nodes.

Generally, the graph of the computation is not a tree, instead it may be any directed acyclic graph. Assume that the operations are $+$ and $*$. The parallel complexity of the problem changes dramatically. The problem is now P-complete (the hardest problem to parallelize in the class of sequentially polynomial time computable problems).

However, if the degree of computed polynomials (assuming that constants correspond to input variables, and the leaves of the computation graph have degree one) is bounded by a polynomial then we can show that the straight-line program can be computed by an NC algorithm.

The algorithm is essentially the same as before (performing $O(\log n)$ iterations, each one consisting of all safe substitutions). The only difference is in the notion of safeness.

Second definition of safeness

The substitution is safe if the right side of the corresponding variable is of degree at most one (for example, $x1 + 2 * x2 + x6$).

However, the number of processors needed is now bigger than linear, though it is polynomial.

Theorem 7.2

Algorithm 7.1 with the second definition of safeness can be implemented to compute polynomial-degree straight-line programs in $\log^2 n$ time using n^3 processors.

The proof is postponed until the next section where we show that the number of iterations is bounded by $\log_{3/2}(n + d)$, where d is the degree. This is the crucial point.

The analysis of the number of iterations for the two different definitions of safeness is very similar.

Here we show in an example that one iteration can be reduced to matrix multiplication (hence it requires only $\log n$ time and n^3 processors).

Consider the following program P.

$x1 = 1$

$x2 = 2 * x1 + 2$

$x3 = 3 * x1 + 2 * x2 + 3$

$x4 = x1 + 3 * x2 + 2 * x3 + 2$

$x5 = (x1 + 2 * x2 + x4) * (2 * x1 + 3)$

The safe variables are $x1$–$x4$.

The vectorial representations of variables $x1$–$x5$ are given by vectors:

$(0, 0, 0, 0, 0, 1)$
$(2, 0, 0, 0, 0, 2)$
$(3, 2, 0, 0, 0, 3)$
$(1, 3, 2, 0, 0, 2)$
$(0, 0, 0, 0, 1, 0)$

If the variable is safe then the last component of its vector is a constant on the right side (zero if there is no constant). Other components correspond to constant coefficients at variables x_i. If the ith variable is non-safe then the ith component of its vector is 1, and all other components are zero.

Let A be an $(n + 1) * (n + 1)$ matrix whose ith row is the vector for x_i, if $i < n + 1$. The last row is $(0, 0, \ldots, 0, 1)$. Suppose that we want to perform simultaneously all safe substitutions on the right side of the variable $x4$. Then we compute

$(1, 3, 2, 0, 0, 2) * A = (12, 4, 0, 0, 0, 15)$

Hence after substitutions $x4 = 12 * x1 + 4 * x2 + 15$. We multiplied the vectorial representation of the right side of $x4$ by the matrix A.

A more complicated situation is when making substitutions on the right side of a non-safe variable. We can demonstrate it on the variable $x5$. The right side of $x5$ can be represented by two vectors representing linear forms of the factors.

$(1, 2, 0, 1, 0, 0)$ and $(2, 0, 0, 0, 0, 3)$

After multiplying both factors (in their vectorial form) by A we obtain

$$(1, 2, 0, 1, 0, 0) * A = (5, 3, 2, 0, 0, 7)$$
$$(2, 0, 0, 0, 0, 3) * A = (0, 0, 0, 0, 0, 5)$$

Hence after making all substitutions we have

$$x5 = (5 * x1 + 3 * x2 + 2 * x3 + 7) * 5$$

We made additionally scalar multiplication, because the degree of one factor has reduced to zero. Finally we have

$$x5 = 25 * x1 + 15 * x2 + 10 * x3 + 35$$

$x5$ becomes a safe variable. The new vectorial representation of the right side of $x5$ is

$$(25, 15, 10, 0, 0, 35)$$

After performing in parallel all such manipulations on the vectorial representations of the right sides of variables we update matrix A whose rows are the representations. For example, now the fourth row of A is

$$(12, 4, 0, 0, 0, 15)$$

and the fifth row is

$$(25, 15, 10, 0, 0, 35)$$

We can see that one iteration reduces to the multiplication of vectors by a matrix. This can be easily done in $\log n$ time with n^2 processors. We make $O(n)$ such operations, hence a cubic number of processors is sufficient.

7.3   The analysis of Algorithm 7.1

In this section we analyse the number of iterations executed by Algorithm 7.1. First, consider the case when the computation graph is a tree (of an expression) and the first definition of safeness is used. Let $T = graph(P)$. Now the variable is safe iff its corresponding node (in T) has outdegree at most one. We define $reduce(T) = T' = graph(P')$, where P' is the program resulting from P after one iteration of Algorithm 7.1.

The operation $reduce$ works on trees as follows (see Figure 7.2). Every edge leading to a leaf is deleted. Every edge leading from a node v to a node w with

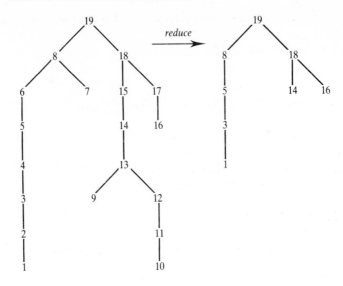

Figure 7.2 The chains in the first computation graph are: {6, 5, 4, 3}, {15, 14} and {12, 11}.

outdegree one is replaced by the edge $(v, son(w))$. The tree $reduce(T)$ consists of all nodes reachable from the root after performing all these operations on edges.

We denote by $|T|$ the number of nodes of T.

Lemma 7.1   (key lemma)

If $|T| > 1$ then $|reduce(T)| \leqslant (2/3)\,|T|$.

Proof Some nodes do not appear in $reduce(T)$ because they are not reachable from the root after changing the edges. We shall estimate how many nodes remain.

Let us define a chain as a maximal branch of nodes of outdegree one (we do not include the leaves in the chains). If such a branch has odd cardinality and ends at the node v whose son is a leaf then v is not included in the chain corresponding to this branch. The chains are illustrated in Figure 7.2.

We partition the set V of nodes of T into the subsets $V1$ and $V2$, where $V1$ is the union of all chains and $V2$ contains all remaining nodes. Now observe that at most half of the nodes in every chain remain.

If m is the number of leaves then $|V2| \leqslant 3m$, because the number of internal nodes with outdegree greater than one does not exceed m, the number of fathers of leaves is also not greater than m.

Every leaf or its father is removed, hence at most $(2/3)\,|V2|$ nodes remain in $V2$.

Together there remain at most

$$1/2|V1| + 2/3|V2| \leqslant 2/3(|V1| + |V2|) = 2/3n$$

nodes in *reduce*(T). This completes the proof.   ∎

Corollary   The number of iterations of Algorithm 7.1 in the case when *graph*(P) is a tree and the first definition of safeness is used is at most $\log_{3/2} n$.

☐

If *graph*(P) is not a tree and the first definition of safeness is used then the number of iterations can be linear (not polylogarithmic). For example, consider the straight-line program for computing Fibonacci numbers.

$$x_1 = 1, x_2 = 1, x_3 = x_1 + x_2, \ldots, x_n = x_{n-1} + x_{n-2}$$

Consider now the case when *graph*(P) is a general acyclic directed graph and the second definition of safeness is used. Outdegrees can be greater than two, and the outgoing edges (from * nodes) are partitioned into two sets: left and right sons (which may overlap). Assume that the operations are arithmetic + and *. Assume that initially each right side contains at most one operation.

The straight-line program computes a polynomial, assuming that the variables whose right sides are initially constants are input variables. For example, the straight-line program

$$P: x1 = 1, x2 = 2, x3 = x1 + x2, x4 = x1 * x3, x5 = x4 * x3$$

computes the polynomial $x1 * (x1 + x2)^2$. The input variables here are $x1$ and $x2$.

We denote by *deg*(P) the degree of such a polynomial. In our example $deg(P) = 3$. The computation graph of P is shown in Figure 7.3(a).

There is a possible alternative (equivalent) definition of the degree in terms of computation graphs. Let $G = graph(P)$. We define the degrees of nodes of G as follows. The degree of every leaf is one. The degree of a 'plus' node is the maximal degree of its sons. The multiplication nodes impose more complicated structures on their sons. The multiplication nodes correspond to variables whose right sides are of the form:

$$(a_1 x_1 + \cdots + a_k x_k) * (b_1 y_1 + \cdots + b_r y_r) + c$$

The sons of such a node are partitioned into left sons $(x_1, \ldots, x_k)$ and right sons $(y_1, \ldots, y_r)$. The degree of the node is the maximal sum of the degree of a left son and the degree of a right son.

The degree of P (and of G) is the degree of the root of G.

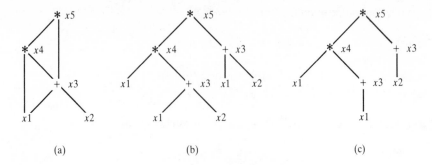

(a)   (b)   (c)

Figure 7.3 A computation graph G, its tree structure T and a subtree $T1$ from $sub(T)$.

One iteration of Algorithm 7.1 with the second definition of safeness corresponds to the following operation *reduce'* on G:

Every edge leading to a leaf is removed.
Every edge leading from a node v to a plus node w is replaced by edges leading from v directly to the sons of w.

If after such operations a multiplication node has only left, or only right sons then it becomes a plus node.

The graph *reduce'*(G) for the graph G in Figure 7.3(a) is presented in Figure 7.4(a).

We associate a tree T with every computation graph G: T is called the **tree structure** of G. The nodes of T correspond to paths of G starting at the root. A variable and an operator corresponding to a node in G (reached by the corresponding path from the root) is associated with every node. Multiplication nodes in T also impose the same structure (left, right) on their sons as nodes in G.

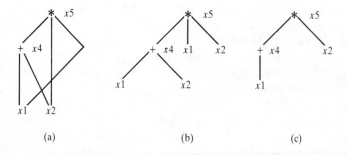

(a)   (b)   (c)

Figure 7.4 The graph $G' = reduce'(G)$, its tree structure T' and a subtree $T1'$ from $sub(T')$. Observe that $T1' = reduce(T1)$, where $T1$ is the tree from Figure 7.3(c). The right sons of node $x5$ in the first graph (a) are $x1$ and $x2$.

The tree structure of G from Figure 7.3(a) is presented in Figure 7.3(b).

We observe that the program P for the direct computation of Fibonacci numbers has degree one, however the tree structure of its computation graph has an exponential number of nodes.

Let T be the tree structure of a given computation graph G. By $sub(T)$ denote the set of all subtrees $T1$ of T rooted at the root of T and satisfying the following:

- If a node in $T1$ is a plus node then exactly one of its sons (in T) is in $T1$.

- If a node v in $T1$ is a multiplication node then exactly one of its left, and one of its right sons (in the sense of T) is in $T1$.

An example of a tree from $sub(T)$ is presented in Figure 7.3(c), for T in Figure 7.3(b).

We define $rank(G)$ to be the maximal size (number of nodes) of a subtree in $sub(T)$, where T is the tree structure of G. It can easily be seen that $deg(G)$ is the maximal number of leaves in a tree in $sub(T)$. The length of a path in G is at most n (number of nodes of G). Hence

$$rank(G) \leqslant |G| * deg(G)$$

Lemma 7.2

If $|G| > 1$ then $rank(reduce'(G)) \leqslant 2/3 \ rank(G)$

Proof Let $reduce'(G) = G'$ and let T' be the tree structure of G' and T be a tree structure of G. For every subtree $T1'$ in $sub(T')$ there is a subtree $T1$ in $sub(T)$ such that $T1' = reduce(T1)$.

In our example the subtree $T1$ for the subtree $T1'$ in Figure 7.4(c) is presented in Figure 7.3(c). Now the thesis follows from Lemma 7.1. This completes the proof.   ∎

Corollary   The number of iterations of Algorithm 7.1 with the second definition of safeness is at most $\log_{3/2} n + \log_{3/2}(deg(P))$.   □

Hence the parallel computation of the straight-line program P is fast if its degree is small. Can we compute efficiently in parallel the degree of P? The answer is probably not. It was proved that this problem is a so-called **P-complete problem.** This means that it is computable sequentially in polynomial time and its membership in NC implies that each problem computable sequentially in polynomial time is in NC.

The straight-line programs with boolean operations *or* and *and* (instead of $+$ and $*$) are called **boolean circuits.** The computation of boolean circuits is also a P-complete problem. However, the computation of such circuits with small degree is readily parallelizable.

7.4   Testing the solvability of composition systems

Let us assume that we are given a tree-like composition system $S = (N, T, \otimes, s)$ and we have to test its solvability in parallel. It is enough to compute the set $closure(T)$ consisting of elements generated from T. S is tree-like in the sense that the set of nodes of each generation tree of an element in $closure(T)$ from generators consists of pairwise distinct elements.

Assume that our composition system S is linearly ordered. This means that we have a linear order $<$ on set N such that for each $p \in q \otimes r$ we have $p > q$ and $p > r$.

A first approach to test if $s \in closure(T)$ is to construct a suitable polynomial-degree straight-line program which computes the answer. We construct the following straight-line program $SLP(S)$. It has two types of variables. The first type are variables x_p corresponding to each element p of N. The second type are variables $x_{p,q,r}$ corresponding to all triples p, q, r such that $p \in q \otimes r$.

For each $p \in T$ we write an assignment:

$$x_p = true$$

For each variable $x_{p,q,r}$ we write an assignment:

$$x_{p,q,r} = x_q \text{ and } x_r$$

For other variables x_p we write

$$x_p = \text{disjunction of } x_{p,q,r} \text{ over all } q, r$$

We treat operation *and* as $*$ and operation *or* as $+$. If S is tree-like and linearly ordered then $SLP(S)$ is a polynomial-degree straight-line program. We leave the proof of this fact to the reader.

Now we can apply a method from Section 7.3. This may prove, for example, that context-free recognition is in NC. However the number of processors is quite big. It is cubic with respect to the number of variables of $SLP(S)$. In the case of context-free grammars the corresponding composition systems have $O(n^3)$ triples (p, q, r) such that $p \in q \otimes r$. Hence in this case the number of processors is $O(n^9)$.

We now describe a completely different method which gives a polylogarithmic time algorithm with a smaller number of processors (see also Chytil *et al.* (1989)). The crucial point is the reduction of the problem to several applications of path computations in suitable directed graphs.

For a subset X of N denote by $Dep(X)$ a directed graph $D = (N, E)$ with marked nodes. This graph is called the **dependency graph** with respect to X. The set of edges of D is defined as follows:

$$E = \{(z, x): z \notin X \text{ and } z \in (x \otimes y \cup y \otimes x) \text{ for some } y \in X\}$$

All nodes $x \in X$ are marked. Denote by $Reach(D)$ the set of all nodes of D from which a marked node is reachable. All marked nodes are also in $Reach(D)$. Algorithm 7.2 computes the set of generated nodes:

Algorithm 7.2   {returns $X = closure(T)$; $n = |N|$}

> **begin**
> $X := T$;
> **repeat** $\lceil \log_2 n \rceil$ **times**
>   **begin** $D := Dep(X)$; $X := Reach(D)$ **end**:
> return X
> **end**.

Lemma 7.3

Assume that the composition system is tree-like. Let X be the set returned by Algorithm 7.2. Then $X = closure(T)$.

Proof It is obvious that $X \subseteq closure(T)$. We show that for each $x \in closure(T)$ we have $x \in X$.

Let H be a tree of generation of x from T. The proof is by induction with respect to

$$index(x) = \lceil \log(weight(x)) \rceil$$

where $weight(y)$ is the number of leaves in the subtree of H rooted at y.

We can show that after $index(x)$ iterations the element x is marked (is in X). Consider the heaviest branch B in H: a path from x down the tree turning always to the son with greater $weight$ (when both sons have the same $weight$ we can go to either of them). For each son $y \notin B$ of a node on this path we have $index(y) < index(x)$.

Hence all such nodes y are marked (and are in set X after the iteration $index(x) - 1$) by the inductive assumption. Hence the path B is in graph $Dep(X)$ when the $index(x)$ iteration starts. The last element of this path is in X. Hence in the $index(x)$ iteration there is a path from x to a marked element in graph D and x will be inserted into X. This completes the proof.   ■

Theorem 7.3

The solvability of the tree-like linearly ordered composition system $S = (N, T, \otimes, s)$ can be checked in $\log^3 |N|$ parallel time using $O(|N|^3)$ processors.

Proof The thesis follows from the fact that the operation *Reach* can be performed in $\log^2 |N|$ time with $O(|N|^3)$ processors. It can be reduced to the computation of transitive closure. This completes the proof.   ∎

Corollary Each context-free language can be recognized in $\log^3 n$ time using n^6 processors.   □

In fact the time can be reduced to $\log^2 n$ at the cost of more complicated algorithms (see Gibbons and Rytter (1988), and Rytter (1985b)). The first NC algorithm for context free recognition was given by Ruzzo (1979).

The directed acyclic graph D is said to have the unique path property iff for each of two nodes v and w there is at most one path from v to w.

Lemma 7.4

Assume that the directed acyclic graph D has the unique path property and let X be a set of marked nodes of D. Let m and n be the number of edges and nodes of D respectively.

We can then compute *Reach(D)* in logarithmic parallel time using $O(m + n)$ processors.

Proof We can assume that D is a binary graph (each node has at most two immediate successors called sons). It is easy to transform the graph to its binary version by adding $O(m)$ new nodes. This resembles the transformation of grammars to Chomsky normal form.

We can then construct a straight-line program P whose variables are nodes of D. For each non-leaf node v we write an assignment statement:

$v := v1$ or $v2$

where $v1$ and $v2$ are sons of v. Marked nodes (elements of X) are leaves: they have no sons. For each marked node v we write

$v := $ *true*

For non-marked leaves v we write $v := $ *false*.

We then have a straight-line program such that the final value of the element v is *true* iff $v \in Reach(D)$.

The crucial point is that we can apply the simultaneous substitution method with the first definition of safeness to the program P. Then after logarithmic time all nodes $v \in Reach(D)$ will have value *true*.

The simultaneous substitution method works in the same way for straight-line programs whose computation graphs are trees as it does for those with computation graphs satisfying the unique path property. This is so because for each variable the part of the graph relevant to the computation of this variable is a tree if the graph has the unique path property. This completes the proof.   ∎

Theorem 7.4

(1) Each unambiguous context-free language can be recognized in $\log^2 n$ time using n^3 processors.
(2) Each deterministic context-free language can be recognized in $\log^2 n$ time using n^2 processors.

Proof

(1) We can assume that the context-free grammar G has no useless non-terminals.

   Let $S = S(G, x)$ be the composition system corresponding to an input text x of length n and unambiguous context-free grammar G without useless non-terminals. Let X be a set of realizable elements of the system S. We leave to the reader the proof of the following claim.

   Claim   The graph $D = Dep(X)$ has the unique path property.

   Now point 1 follows from Lemma 7.4, because the number of edges is cubic and the graph D has in our case the unique path property.

(2) This point is proved in the same way. We refer the reader to Chapter 6 to recall the composition system associated with the deterministic push-down automaton. The graph D has now the unique path property and $|N| = O(n)$, $m = O(n^2)$.

   This completes the proof of the theorem.   ∎

To end this section we consider the following problem for a given context-free language L:

   check if $L \cap \{y: |y| = n\} = \varnothing$

For this problem we can construct the same composition system S' as $S(G, x)$ for some text x of length n except the set T of generators. Now let us define

$$T = \{(A, i, i + 1): 0 \leqslant i \leqslant n, A \to a \text{ for some symbol } a\}$$

The algorithms for the system S' work in the same way as for $S(G, x)$. We leave the remaining details to the reader as an exercise. An even simpler construction is possible relying on the fact that, for each context-free language L the language unary(L) is a regular language (unary(L) results by replacing each letter in words of L by the same letter a).

Two interesting results about parallel parsing are $\log(n)$ time recognition of deterministic languages (see Klein and Reif (1988)) and $\log(n)$ time recognition of unambiguous languages (see Rytter (1987a)). Each deterministic context-free language is also unambiguous. It was proved (see Rytter (1987b)) that parallel construction of the parse tree is essentially not harder than the recognition problem.

7.5 Weighted composition systems

Assume that for each p, q, $r \in N$ we are given the cost $weight(p, q, r)$ of applying the composition $q \otimes r$ to generate p in one step from q and r. Assume also that for each initial element $p \in T$ we are given its initial cost $init(p)$.

The cost $c(T')$ of the generation tree T' is the sum of weights $weight(p, q, r)$, taken over all elements p, q, r such that p is a father of q, r, plus the weights $init(p)$ of leaves of T'. For example, consider a system such that $N = [1 .. n]$ and $weight(p, q, r) = 1 + q + r$, $init(p) = p - 1$. Let T' be the generation tree of element 7 from the generators (see Figure 7.5). Then

$$c(T') = init(4) + init(5) + init(1) + init(2)$$
$$+ weight(7, 6, 2) + weight(6, 3, 1) + weight(3, 4, 5)$$
$$= 3 + 4 + 0 + 1 + 10 + 5 + 9$$

Let $cost(p)$ be the minimal cost of a generation tree of element p from initial elements (generators) of S. Assume we are given a linearly ordered tree-like composition system $S = (N, T, \otimes, s)$ and we have to compute $cost(p)$ for each element $p \in closure(T)$ in parallel.

A first approach is to construct a suitable polynomial-degree straight-line program which computes the required values. Let us construct a straight-line program $SLP(S)$. It has two types of variables. The first type are variables x_p corresponding to each element p of N. The second type are variables $x_{p,q,r}$ corresponding to all triples p, q, r such that $p \in q \otimes r$.

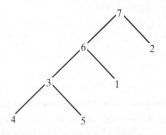

Figure 7.5 A generation tree of element 7.

For each $p \in T$ we write an assignment:

$$x_p = init(p)$$

For each variable $x_{p, q, r}$ we write an assignment:

$$x_{p, q, r} = x_q + x_r + weight(p, q, r)$$

For other variables x_p we write:

$$x_p = \text{minimum of } x_{p, q, r} \text{ over all } q, r$$

We treat operation $+$ as $*$ and operation min as $+$. If S is tree-like and linearly ordered then $SLP(S)$ is a polynomial-degree straight-line program. We leave the proof of this fact to the reader.

We can now apply a method from the previous section. The following fact follows from Theorem 7.2: The costs of all elements $p \in closure(T)$ can be computed in $\log^2(|M|)$ time using $O(|M|^3)$ processors if the system S is tree-like and linearly ordered, where M is the number of triples p, q, r such that $p \in q \otimes r$.

We can show how the computation of costs of weighted composition systems can be applied to the dynamic programming problems. The dynamic programming problem is given by a system of recurrence equations:

$$cost(i, j) = \min\{cost(i, k) + cost(k, j) + weight(i, k, j) : i < k < j\}$$

$$\text{if } i < j - 1 \qquad (7.1)$$

$$cost(i, i + 1) = init(i)$$

where $weight(i, j, k)$ and $init(i)$ are functions computable sequentially in $O(1)$ time.

In the case of the dynamic programming problem the corresponding composition system S consists of elements (i, j), where $0 \leqslant i < j \leqslant n$. The composition is defined as follows:

$$(i, k) \otimes (k, j) = \{(i, j)\} \quad \text{and}$$

$$weight((i, j), (i, k), (k, j)) = weight(i, k, j)$$

$$T = \{(i, i + 1) : 0 \leqslant i \leqslant n\}$$

The number M of triples p, q, r such that $p \in q \otimes r$ is here $O(n^3)$. It follows from the fact stated earlier that the dynamic programming problems can be computed in $\log^2 n$ time using n^9 processors by computing a suitable straight-line program.

We give three examples of dynamic programming problems. The first one is the optimal order of matrix multiplication.

Let us assume that we are given n matrices $M_1, M_2, \ldots, M_n$. The ith matrix is of the shape $r_{i-1} \times r_i$. The cost of multiplication of two matrices of shapes $k \times l$ and $l \times r$ is assumed to be klr. We would like to compute the cost of the optimal order of multiplying matrices M_i. It can be also thought as the cost of the optimal bracket structure of the sequence $M_1, M_2, \ldots, M_n$.

Now we can define $cost(i, j)$ as the cost of the optimal order to multiply the sequence $M_{i+1}, \ldots, M_j$. We have $init(i) = 0$ and $weight(i, k, j) = r_{i-1} r_k r_j$.

As the second example consider the optimum triangulation problem. We are given the nodes of a polygon and a distance between each pair of nodes. Our problem is to select a set of diagonals such that no two diagonals cross and such that the entire polygon is divided into triangles. The cost of the triangulation is the total length of all constructed diagonals.

Let the polygon be given by its nodes (in clockwise order) $v_0, v_1, \ldots, v_n$. Then we can define $cost(i, j)$ as the cost of triangulating the polygon $v_{i+1}, \ldots, v_j$. The dynamic programming recurrences can be written similarly as in the previous problem.

The third example is the computation of the minimal cost of a binary search tree for a given linearly ordered set of keys, where each key has a certain frequency of occurrence. We refer the reader to the book by Aho *et al.* (1974).

We now describe another method which gives a polylogarithmic time algorithm with a smaller number of processors, and which works in a way similar to testing the solvability of composition systems.

Assume that for each element p initially $COST(p)$ is set to infinity except for initial elements $p \in T$, for which $COST(p)$ is set to $init(p)$.

Let us assume that we have, at a given moment in the computation, a partially computed table $COST(p)$ for $p \in N$. Some of the entries contain the value infinity. For a given value of table $COST$ denote by $Dep'(COST)$ a directed graph $D = (N, E)$. This graph is called the **weighted dependency graph** with respect to $COST$. The set of edges of D is defined as follows:

$$E = \{(z, x) \colon z \in x \otimes y \cup y \otimes x \text{ for some } y \in N\}$$

$$weight(z, x) = \min\{leftmin, rightmin\}$$

where

$$leftmin = \min\{weight(z, x, y) + COST(y) \colon z \in x \otimes y\}$$

$$rightmin = \min\{weight(z, y, x) + COST(y) \colon z \in y \otimes x\})$$

We shall denote by $Reach'(D)$ the table $COST$ such that $COST(p)$ is the minimal cost of the path from p to an element of T in the weighted graph D (including the cost of that element).

Algorithm 7.3   {refinement of Algorithm 7.2, $n = |N|$}

begin
initially $COST(p) = init(p)$ for each $p \in T$;
repeat $\lceil \log_2 n \rceil$ **times**
    begin $D := Dep'(COST)$; $COST := Reach'(D)$ **end**;
return table $COST$
end.

Lemma 7.5

Assume that the composition system is tree-like. Let $COST$ be the table returned by Algorithm 7.3. Then $COST = cost$.

Proof   The proof is essentially the same as the proof of Lemma 7.3. We can prove that after $index(x)$ iterations $COST(x) = cost(x)$.   ∎

Let us assume that the graph D has s nodes. Then $Reach'(D)$ can be easily computed in $O(\log^2 s)$ time using $O(s^3)$ processors, by successive squaring of the matrix of weights of the paths in the graph. Hence Lemma 7.5 implies Theorem 7.5.

Theorem 7.5

We can solve the system of equations of a given dynamic programming problem in $\log^3 n$ time using $O(n^6)$ processors.

In fact, the time can be lowered to $\log^2 n$ at the cost of more complicated algorithms (see Rytter (1988b)), however the number of processors in the general case is essentially the same as that needed to multiply two matrices of size $n^2 \times n^2$.

In some special cases these general performance bounds can be improved: for example, the Huffman coding can be described in the framework of dynamic programming and then the number of processors can be considerably reduced.

As a final example we present an application of weighted composition systems to context-free recognition with errors. For two strings x, y of the same length n we define

$$dist(x, y) = |\{i: 1 \leqslant i \leqslant n, x[i] \neq y[i]\}|$$

In other words the distance between the strings is the number of positions on which these strings differ.

Suppose we are given a context-free grammar G and an input text x of length n. We can assume that there exists a text y of length n generated by G

(see the end of Section 7.4). The problem of context-free recognition with errors is to compute

$$cost(x, G) = \min\{dist(x, y): y \in L(G)\}$$

We add the weights to the generation rules of system S' (see the end of Section 7.4 for the definition of S').

$weight((A, i, j), (B, i, k), (C, k, j)) = 0$ for $A \rightarrow BC$

$init((A, i, i + 1)) =$ if $A \rightarrow x[i + 1]$ then 0 else 1

It is easy to see that $cost(x, G)$ equals the cost of the minimal generation of $(S, 0, n)$ in system S'. Hence Lemma 7.5 implies Theorem 7.6.

Theorem 7.6

We can solve the problem of context-free recognition with errors in $\log^3 n$ time using $O(n^6)$ processors.

We could consider a more difficult problem by defining the distance as the minimal number of edit operations between strings: operations delete, insert and change single symbol. The last theorem also holds if this more complicated distance is considered.

7.6 Height-reduction of composition systems

Finally, we sketch an alternative approach to the parallel computations on composition systems. Assume that we are given a tree-like composition system $S = (N, T, \otimes, s)$ and we have to test its solvability in parallel. It is possible to compute the set $closure(T)$ by a parallel algorithm using the idea of height reduction. Denote by $height(S)$ the minimal number t such that for each $x \in closure(T)$ there is a generation tree of height not exceeding t. Usually the exact computation of the number t is difficult, however it is easy to make a good approximation. Assume that we know an upper bound $height'(S)$ on $height(S)$ such that

$$height'(S) = O(height(S))$$

Algorithm 7.4   {returns $X = closure(T)$; $n = |N|$}

begin
$X := T$;
repeat $height'(S)$ **times**
(*) **for each** $x, y, z \in N$ **do in parallel**

if $z \in x \otimes y$ and $x, y \in X$ **then** add z to X;
return X
end.

Obviously the algorithm works in $O(height(S) \log(n))$ parallel time using a polynomial number of processors if we know the number $height'(S)$. The additional logarithmic factor at the time complexity is due to the fact that implementation of the instruction ($*$) on a parallel computer without write conflicts requires logarithmic time.

Let us analyse the time complexity of this algorithm on the composition system $S(G, x)$ related to the recognition of context-free languages. Unfortunately, for general context-free grammars, $height(S) = \Omega(n)$. The derivation trees may be 'skewed'. We know a good approximation $height'(n) = n$ of the exact height of $S(G, x)$.

We shall now investigate the question of the height reduction of system S. Lemma 6.3 suggests using an extension of the system by defining new elements of the form (x, B), where $B \subseteq N$. The object (x, B) can be treated as x with the set B of 'gaps' or 'holes'. The element (x, B) is realizable in the new system S' iff $x \in closure(T \cup B)$ in the original system. The original elements x are identified with $(x, \varnothing)$. The composition rules for new elements are the following:

$$(x, B) \in (x, B \cup \{y\}) \otimes (y, B) \tag{7.2}$$

The generators are the objects (x, B) such that x can be generated from a pair of elements in $T \cup B$ in one step.

The new system (with logarithmic height) is:

$$S' = (N', T', \otimes, S')$$

where $N' = \{(x, B): B \subseteq N, |B| \leqslant c \log(n)\}$, for a constant c (implied by Lemma 6.3). The goal element is $s' = (s, \varnothing)$. The element (x, B) can be identified with the statement

'$x \in closure(T \cup B)$'.

$T' = \{(x, B): x$ can be generated from $T \cup B$ applying at most one composition of the original system $S\}$.

Now $height(S') = O(\log n)$, due to Lemma 6.3. The size of the object (x, B) can be defined as the minimal number of nodes in a tree generating x from $T \cup B$, if $x \in closure(T \cup B)$. The size of x is the same as the size of $(x, \varnothing)$. Lemma 6.3 essentially says that each realizable object (x, B) of size m can be generated in one step from some objects of size at most $(2/3)m + 1$. This guarantees a logarithmic depth.

However, the number of processors is not polynomial, since the sets B are of logarithmic size. There are potentially $O(|N|^{\log n})$ such sets. Their number is somewhere between polynomial and exponential.

We therefore have the following data structure problem. The size of the

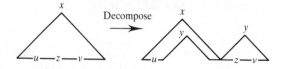

Figure 7.6   Decomposition into two smaller trees.

data structure consisting of the objects (x, B) is too big. We have to reduce it considerably and still guarantee that the height is logarithmic.

We can redefine rule (7.2) as follows:

$$(x, B) \in (x, B_1 \cup \{y\}) \otimes (y, B_2), \text{ for } B_1, B_2 \subseteq B \tag{7.3}$$

The crucial point is that now if we restrict the set of objects only to those (x, B) with $|B| \leqslant 3$ then the height is still logarithmic. This fact was observed in Ruzzo (1979) and it is based on the following simple observation: for each three distinct leaves u, z, v there is an internal node y such that exactly two of them are in the subtree rooted at y (see Figure 7.6).

We can then decompose $(x, \{u, z, v\})$ into trees $(x, \{y, v\})$, $(y, \{z, v\})$, see Figure 7.6. Such a decomposition can be unbalanced. However in the next stage we can decompose each of $(x, \{y, v\})$, $(y, \{z, v\})$ into balanced parts using Lemma 6.3. Now we can choose a good decomposition point, because our sets B are of size at most two and we can add one node to B. The invariant $|B| \leqslant 3$ will be satisfied.

The set of objects is now of a size bounded by a polynomial $P(n)$. In this way we have an NC algorithm working in $\log^2 n$ time. However, the degree of the polynomial $P(n)$ is not satisfactory. It can be reduced substantially by using the following fact observed in Rytter (1985b): it is enough to consider the objects B such that $|B| \leqslant 1$, the logarithmic depth of the system is preserved.

We can now write (x, y) instead of $(x, \{y\})$ and x instead of $(x, \varnothing)$. The pair (x, y) is a tree rooted at x with all leaves in T except leaf y. It can be treated as a tree x with the gap y. It can be also interpreted as an implication

$$y \in closure(T) \Rightarrow x \in closure(T)$$

The following rule is added:

if $x \in y \otimes z$ in S then $(x, y) \in z \otimes z$ and $(x, z) \in y \otimes y$ in the modified
system   (7.4)

This rule can be interpreted as follows:

$$(z \in closure(T) \text{ and } x \in y \otimes z) \Rightarrow (y \in closure(T) \Rightarrow x \in closure(T))$$

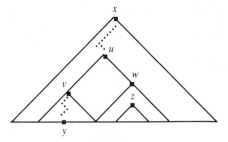

Figure 7.7   The structure of the tree (x, y); the tree rooted at x with the gap y. The node u is the first node from y to the root such that the size of the subtree rooted at u is at least $m/2$.

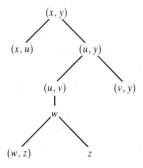

Figure 7.8   The generation of (x, y) from the smaller objects.

The proof of the fact that the logarithmic depth is sufficient follows from the decomposition illustrated in Figure 7.7. Let m be the size of the tree corresponding to (x, y). Let the node u be the first node from y to the root such that the size of the subtree rooted at u is at least $m/2$. This implies that the sizes of the objects (x, u) and (v, y) are bounded by $m/2$. Then the object (x, y) of the size m can be generated in constant time from the objects (x, u), (v, y), (w, z) and z, see Figure 7.8. Each of them is of a size bounded by cm, where c is a constant smaller than 1.

We refer the reader to Rytter (1985b). There, the operation of the height reduction of the composition system was called *bush*. The system *bush(S)* is a 'bushy' version of S. If S is a tree-like composition system then *bush(S)* is a system of logarithmic height and small size. The exact construction of the transformation and the number of processors needed in Algorithm 7.4 (in which S is replaced by *bush(S)*) are left to the reader (see Exercise 7.28).

For the composition systems corresponding to context-free recognition the bound $O(n^6)$ on the number of processors can be proved (with $\log^2 n$ time).

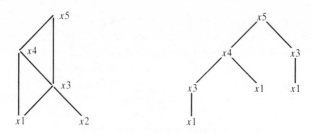

Figure 7.9   Assume that $val(x1) = true$ in the program P presented on the left. Then a generation tree in the system $S(P)$ is presented on the right. We have ignored the artificial \$-leaves. Observe that the degree of P equals the number of leaves in the presented tree.

If the composition system S is weighted then one can extend the operation *bush* to produce a weighted version of S with small height (see Exercise 7.30).

Our last observation concerns the relation between the parallel computation of straight-line programs and the solvability of composition systems. We showed how to reduce the solvability problem for tree-like composition systems to the computation of straight-line programs of a polynomial degree. Now we shall show a reverse reduction.

Assume we have a straight-line program P with boolean operations 'or' and 'and'. The operation 'and' is treated as a multiplication, and 'or' is treated as an addition. There are n boolean variables x_i for $i = 1 .. n$. Let us construct the composition system $S(P)$ whose universe contains all variables of P and in which the following equivalence holds:

$$x_i \in closure(T) \text{ in } S(P) \text{ iff } val(x_i) = true \text{ in } P$$

The set T of generators is the set of all input variables of P whose value is *true*. For two boolean variables x and y the value of $x \otimes y$ is the set of all z such that $z = x \wedge y$ in the program P. Let us introduce a special element \$. The value $x \otimes \$$ is the set of all variables z such that $z = x \vee y$ in the program P for some variable y. Let x_n be the output variable of P.

It is easy to see that if $val(x_n) = true$ and P has a polynomial degree then the tree of the generation of x_n in the system $S(P)$ is of a polynomial size if we disregard elements \$. In fact the number of leaves in each such tree (not counting \$-leaves) does not exceed the degree of P, see Figure 7.9.

Hence the computation of a given boolean straight-line program of polynomial degree is NC reducible to the solvability problem for a composition system whose generation trees have polynomial size. The algorithms for such systems are essentially the same as for tree-like systems. We leave the details to the reader.

We have analysed algorithms computing straight-line programs and testing composition systems. However, in our straight-line programs we assumed that they were of polynomial degree, and in composition systems we assumed that they were tree-like. If we remove these restrictions then both problems become P-complete. It is a general belief that P-complete problems are not in the class NC. This means that 'probably' there are no 'polylogarithmic time/polynomial number of processors' parallel algorithms for these problems. Anyway if it could be shown that such algorithms exist they would have a completely different structure than the algorithms presented in this chapter.

We refer the reader to Crochemore and Rytter (1990) for parallel algorithms related to problems considered in Chapter 5.

SUMMARY

Key points covered in this chapter include:

- the parallel computation of expressions
- the parallel computation of straight-line programs
- composition systems
- the solvability of the composition system
- the cost of the composition system.

EXERCISES

7.1 The prefix sum computation consists in computing all sums $a_1, a_1 + a_2$, $a_1 + a_2 + a_3, \ldots$ Implement the prefix sum computation in $\log(n)$ time using $O(n/\log(n))$ processors on an EREW PRAM.

7.2 Compute on a CRCW PRAM in $O(1)$ time the maximal element of a vector. Solve also the string-matching problem on a CRCW PRAM in $O(1)$ time. Minimize the number of processors.

7.3 Design an algorithm computing matrix multiplication in logarithmic time with a cubic number of processors. Is it possible to reduce the number of processors? Can we parallelize the sequential Strassen's algorithm (see Aho *et al.* (1974)) for matrix multiplication?

7.4 Implement efficiently the parallel operation of a safe substitution where the second type of safeness is assumed. Reduce the problem to matrix multiplication/addition.

7.5 What is the number of iterations of Algorithm 7.1 when a straight-line program computing Fibonacci numbers is processed according to the first definition of safeness. What is the degree of the straight-line program computing the nth Fibonacci number?

7.6 Let $reduce'(G) = G'$ and let T' be a tree structure of G' and T be a tree structure of G (see proof of Lemma 7.2). Prove that for every subtree $T1'$ in $sub(T')$ there is a subtree $T1$ in $sub(T)$ such that $T1' = reduce(T1)$.

7.7 Reduce the problem of computing a maximal cardinality independent set in a tree to the problem of expression evaluation.

7.8 Reduce the problem of the minimal cardinality dominating set in a tree to expression evaluation.

7.9 Prove that if the composition system S is tree-like and linearly ordered then $SLP(S)$ is a polynomial-degree straight-line program.

7.10 Transform in parallel a directed acyclic graph to its binary version adding $O(m)$ new nodes.

7.11 Prove that the simultaneous substitution method works in the same way for straight-line programs whose computation graphs are trees as for those with computation graphs satisfying unique path property.

7.12 Let $S = S(G, x)$ be the composition system corresponding to an input text x of length n and unambiguous context-free grammar G without useless non-terminals. Let X be a set of realizable elements of the system S. Prove the following claim: the graph $D = Dep(X)$ has the unique path property.

7.13 Consider the following problem for a given context-free language L:

check if $L \cap \{y : |y| = n\} = \emptyset$

Prove that this problem can be solved in $\log^3 n$ time with n^6 processors using a composition system similar to $S(G, x)$.

7.14 Assume that a graph D has s nodes. Prove that $Reach'(D)$ can be computed in logarithmic time using $O(s^3)$ processors by successive squaring of the matrix of weights of the paths in the graph.

7.15* Prove that the number of iterations of Algorithm 7.1 in the case when $graph(P)$ is a tree and the first definition of safeness is used is at most $\lceil \log_f n \rceil$, where f is the **golden ratio** $f = (1 + \sqrt{5})/2$. This is a slightly better bound than $\log_{3/2} n$ proved before.

7.16* Show that for infinitely many values of n there exists a tree with n nodes which requires $\lceil \log_f n \rceil + c$ iterations of Algorithm 7.1, where c is a constant. This shows that the bound given in Exercise 7.15 is optimal.

7.17 Show that each linear context-free language can be recognized in $\log^2 n$ time with a cubic number of processors (see also Rytter (1988a)).

7.18 Let $n = |N|$. Suppose we know in advance a bound $L(n)$ on the size of a generation tree for the goal element s, given that such a tree exists. What then is the parallel complexity of testing solvability of a given composition system? Before we considered only tree-like systems which satisfied $L(n) = n$.

7.19 Suppose that we have several composition operations in the composition system, for example one unary, one binary and one ternary operation. Their values are subsets of N. Generalize Algorithms 7.2 and 7.3 for the case of these more general composition systems. Assume that the systems are tree-like.

7.20 Let $n > 1$ be a power of two. Construct a tree T of size $3n - 1$ such that the size of $reduce(T)$ is $2n - 1$. The outdegrees of nodes of T should be bounded by two. This shows that the estimation given in Lemma 7.1 is asymptotically optimal.

7.21* The monotone planar circuit value problem (MPCVP): we are given a planar computation graph G of a boolean circuit with operations *or* and *and*; the problem consists in computing the value of the root.

We assume that G is given together with its planar embedding. Moreover, the set of nodes of G is partitioned into **layers**. The leaves are at the zero layer and the sons of nodes at layer l are at layer $l - 1$. All nodes in a single layer are of the same type: *or* nodes or *and* nodes.

Prove that the problem MPCVP is in NC.

(*Hint* Consider the following composition system. Its elements are triples (l, i, j) representing segments of consecutive nodes at layer l. The generators are triples $(0, i, j)$ such that the corresponding segment of leaf nodes is a maximal 'bottom' segment containing only inputs with value *true*. Define the operation of composition in such a way that $(l, i, j) \in closure(T)$ iff values of all nodes in the segment corresponding to (l, i, j) have value *true* and that the system is tree-like (see also Mayer (1987)).)

7.22* Consider the **longest common substring** problem: given two texts x and y find the length of the longest common subword of x and y. Design an efficient parallel algorithm for this problem.

(*Hint* Consider a composition system whose elements are triples (i, j, l). The triple (i, j, l) can be generated iff $x[i \mathbin{..} i + l] = y[j \mathbin{..} j + l]$. Generators are triples with $l = 1$. The triple (i, j, l) can be composed of triples (i, j, l') and $(i + l', j + l', l'')$, where $l' = \lfloor l/2 \rfloor$ and $l'' = \lceil l/2 \rceil$.)

7.23 We can modify Algorithm 7.1 as follows. Define two types of substitutions: **1-safe substitutions** and **0-safe substitutions**. One iteration of the algorithm consists in first performing all 1-safe substitutions and then all 0-safe substitutions. Let Algorithm 7.1′ be the obtained version of Algorithm 7.1. The substitution $subst(x_i)$ is 0-safe iff the right side for x_i contains no variables.

We have two definitions of 1-safe substitution:

First definition of 1-safeness
$subst(x_i)$ is 1-safe iff the right side for x_i contains exactly one variable

Second definition of 1-safeness
$subst(x_i)$ is 1-safe iff the right side for x_i has degree exactly one.

Prove that Algorithm 7.1′ with the first definition of 1-safeness does at most $\lceil \log_2 n \rceil$ iterations if the computation graph is a tree, and it does at most $\lceil \log_2(n + d) \rceil$ iterations with the second definition of 1-safeness for straight-line programs of degree d.

7.24 Assume that we are given a binary tree with leaves listed from left to right. Assume we know which node is a left son and which one is a right son of its father. Left leaves are leaves which are left sons, and similarly we define right leaves. If the tree consists of only one node (the root) then we do not consider this node as a leaf.

Define the operation of removal of a leaf v as follows: let v' be the brother leaf of v, remove v and $father(v)$. The node v' becomes the son of $father(father(v))$ of the same type as $father(v)$ was: left or right son.

Define one operation of *leaves cutting* to consist of two parallel steps: remove in parallel each second left leaf; remove in parallel each second right leaf.

Prove that after $\lceil \log_2 n \rceil$ leaves cutting operations only the root will remain. Applying this idea show how to compute an expression tree in $\log n$ parallel time using n processors of an EREW PRAM. (See also Gibbons and Rytter (1989).) Another algorithm was given by Miller and Reif (1985).

7.25 Show that $n/\log(n)$ processors are sufficient to compute an expression of size n in logarithmic time on an EREW PRAM.
(*Hint* Partition the sequence of leaves into subsegments of logarithmic size. Assign one processor to each segment (altogether $n/\log(n)$ processors). In each subsegment one processor performs all possible leaves cutting operations within this subsegment. Then the expression tree is reduced by a factor $\log n$ and the algorithm from Exercise 7.24 can be used (see also Gibbons and Rytter (1989)).)

7.26 Assume we are given a binary tree with numbers associated with the nodes of this tree. For a node v define *prefsum(v)* to be the sum of values associated with nodes on the path from v to the root. Compute all *prefsum(v)* values in logarithmic time using $n/\log(n)$ processors.

(*Hint*   Apply the leaves cutting operations from Exercise 7.24. Whenever we remove *father(v)* then we also add the value associated with *father(v)* to the remaining brother v' of v. After reducing the tree to one node (the root) we have to start the decompression phase and update the values of *prefsum(v)* of nodes v removed in the preceding phase which are now being reconstructed.)

7.27* Let L be the language of well-formed (nested and balanced) sequences of two types of brackets. Construct a parallel algorithm recognizing L in $\log(n)$ time using $O(n/\log(n))$ processors.

7.28* Let L be a language accepted by a one-way deterministic pushdown automaton A. Prove that L can be recognized in $O(\log n)$ time using a polynomial number of processors of CREW PRAM.

(*Hint*   Partition the computation of A on a given input text x of length n into segments of length 2^k for each k. Call them **k-segments**. Assume that each surface configuration p also includes an additional parameter $h(p)$, the (supposed) height of the stack.

At the kth iteration maintain two tables $NEXT_k$ and $PREDICT_k$ which satisfy the following invariant for each surface configurations p, q:

$NEXT_k[p]$ is the first surface configuration q in the k-segment after the k-segment of p which follows from p. Assume that the initial stack is one-element, see Figure 7.10. If there is no such configuration in the next k-segment then q is the terminator of p in the same k-segment as p.

$PREDICT_k[p, q] = r$, where r is the lowest configuration following q in its k-segment. We assume that the computation starts with q and the initial stack consists of the $h(q)$ bottom symbols of the stack which results if we start at p (with a one-element stack) and finish at $NEXT[p]$, see Figure 7.10.

One of the main difficulties here is that we use an 'implicit' stack. At the $(k + 1)$ iteration we compute in $O(1)$ parallel time the tables T_{k+1} and $NEXT_{k+1}$ (satisfying the invariant) knowing the tables $PREDICT_k$ and $NEXT_k$. See also Klein and Reif (1988).)

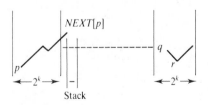

Figure 7.10

7.29* Define the following operation *bush* acting on composition systems. Let $S = (N, T, \otimes, s)$ be a tree-like composition system. Let $bush(S)$ be the system $(N'\ T';\otimes', s')$, where N' consists of pairs (x, y) of elements of N and of the pairs $(x, \varnothing)$, where $x \in N$ and $\varnothing$ is a special new element.
The composition $\otimes'$ is defined as follows:

$$(x, y) \otimes' (y, z) = \{(x, z)\}, \text{ for } x, y \in N \text{ and } z \in N \cup \{\varnothing\}$$

$$(x, \varnothing) \otimes' (x, \varnothing) = \{(z, y): z \in x \otimes' y \cup y \otimes' x\}$$

$$T' = \{(x, \varnothing): x \in T\}$$

The pair (x, y), where $y \neq \varnothing$, is interpreted as follows:

if $y \in closure(T)$ then $x \in closure(T)$

and the pair $(x, \varnothing)$ is interpreted as $x \in closure(T)$.

Prove that for each element $x \in closure(T)$ there is a generation tree for element $(x, \varnothing)$ in the system $bush(S)$ such that the height of that tree is logarithmic. (The operation *bush* was introduced in Rytter (1985b). The operation *bush* can be used to obtain a parallel algorithm testing tree-like composition systems. What is the number of processors of an NC algorithm obtained in this way?

7.30 We proved in Chapter 6 that each context-free language has a recognition algorithm of $O(\log^2 n)$ space complexity. Using the properties of the operation *bush* prove that one can assume that this additional space is very restricted: it consists only of $O(\log n)$ tape and one pushdown store of height $\log^2 n$. (See also Rytter (1985a).)

7.31 Let $S = (N, T, \otimes, s)$ be a weighted composition system. Show how to construct the weighted version of $bush(S)$, such that the derivation cost of the goal element in S is the same as the derivation cost of the goal element in $bush(S)$.

7.32* Give an $O(\log^2 n)$ parallel time algorithm for the shuffling problem (see Exercise 6.5) which uses only a quadratic number of processors.

Bibliography

Aho A. V., Hopcroft J. E. and Ullman J. D. (1974). *The Design and Analysis of Computer Algorithms*. Reading, MA: Addison-Wesley

Aho A. V., Hopcroft J. E. and Ullman J. D. (1976). On finding lowest common ancestors in trees. *SIAM J. Comp.*, 5, 115–32

Baase S. (1983). *Computer Algorithms: Introduction to Design and Analysis*. Reading, MA: Addison-Wesley

Banachowski L. (1980). A complement to Tarjan's result about the lower bound on the complexity of the set union problem. *Inf. Proc. Let.*, 11, 59–65

Banachowski L. (1982). *On pointer complexity of performing sequences of operations*. Rep. University of Warsaw, 114.

Bar-on I. and Vishkin U. (1985). Optimal parallel generation of a computation tree form. *ACM Trans. on Prog. Lang. and Syst.*, 7(2), 348–57

Belady L. A. (1966). A study of replacement algorithms for virtual storage computers. *IBM Sys. J.*, 5, 78–101

Bird R. (1980). Tabulation techniques for recursive programs. *ACM Comp. Surv.*, 12(4), 403–17

Blum M., Floyd R. W., Pratt V., Rivest R. L. and Tarjan R. E. (1972). Time bounds of selection. *J. Comp. Sys. Sci.*, 7, 448–61

Boyer R. and Moore J. (1977). A fast string searching algorithm. *CACM*, 20, 762–72

Braunmuhl B., Cook S., Melhorn K. and Verbeek R. (1983). The recognition of deterministic cfl's in small time and space. *Information and Control*. 56, 34–51

Carter Y. and Weyman M. (1979). Universal classes of hash functions. *J. Comp. Sys. Sci.*, 18, 143–54

Chytil M., Crochemore M., Monien B. and Rytter W. (1989). On the parallel recognition of unambiguous cfl's (to appear in *Theoretical Computer Science*)

Cole R. (1990). Tight bounds on the complexity of the Boyer–Moore pattern matching algorithm. In manuscript, New York University

Cook S. A. (1970). Path systems and language recognition. In *Proc. ACM Symp. Theory of Comp.*

Cook S. A. (1974). An observation on time–space trade-off. *J. Comp. Sys. Sci.*, 9, 308–16

Cook S. A. (1983). The classification of problems which have fast parallel algorithms. In *Proc. FCT '83*, Springer-Verlag.

Crochemore M. and Rytter W. (1990). Parallel computations on strings and arrays. In *Proc. of Symposium on Theoretical Aspects of Computer Science*,

Diks K. (1985). Embeddings of binary trees in lists. *TCS*, 36, 319–31

Diks K. and Rytter W. (1990). Optimal parallel computations on sequences of brackets. To appear in *Theoretical Computer Science*

Dilworth R. P. (1950). A decomposition theorem for partially ordered sets. *Ann. of Math.*, 51, 161–6

Fortune S. and Wyllie J. (1978). Parallelism in random access machines. In *Proc. ACM Symp. on Theoretical Comp. Science*, pp. 114–18

Galil Z. (1979). On improving the worst case running time of the Boyer–Moore string matching algorithm. *CACM* 22, 505–8

Galil Z. and Seiferas J. (1978). A linear time on-line recognition algorithm for 'palstars'. *J. ACM*, 25, 102–11

Galil Z. and Seiferas J. (1981). Time–space optimal string matching. In *Proc. ACM Symp. on Theory of Comp.*, pp. 106–13

Gibbons A. and Rytter W. (1988). *Efficient Parallel Algorithms.* Cambridge University Press.

Gibbons A. and Rytter W. (1989). Optimal parallel algorithms for the dynamic evaluation of expressions and applications to context-free recognition. *Information and Computation*, 81, 32–45

Graham S. and Harrison M. (1976). Parsing of general context-free languages. *Adv. in Comp.*, 14, 77–185

Greene D. and Knuth D. (1981). *Mathematics for the Analysis of Algorithms.* Boston: Birkhauser

Greibach S. (1973). The hardest context-free language. *SIAM J. Comp.*, 2, 304–10

Guibas L. and Odlyzko A. (1980). A new proof of the linearity of the Boyer–Moore string searching algorithm. *SIAM J. Comp.*, 9, 672–82

Gurari E. and Ibarra O. (1980). Path systems: constructions, solutions, applications. *SIAM J. Comp.*, 9, 348–74

Harel D. (1980). A linear time algorithm for the lowest common ancestors problem. In *Proc. 21st IEEE Symp. on Found. of Comp. Science*, pp. 308–19.

Harel D. and Tarjan R. E. (1984). Fast algorithms for finding nearest common ancestors. *SICOMP*, 13, 338–55

Hoare C. A. R. (1962). Quicksort. *Comp. Jour.*, 5, 10–15

Hong J. W., Mehlhorn K. and Rosenberg A. L. (1983). Cost tradeoffs in graph embeddings with applications. *J. ACM*, 30, 709–28

Hopcroft J., Paul W. and Valiant L. (1977). On time versus space. *J. ACM*, 24, 332–7

Horowitz E. and Sahni S. (1978). *Fundamentals of computer algorithms.* London: Pitman

Klein J. and Reif J. (1988). Parallel time $O(\log n)$ recognition of deterministic cfl's *SIAM J. Comp.* 17, 463–85

Knuth D. E. (1968). *The Art of Computer Programming.* Vol. 1. Reading, MA: Addison-Wesley

Knuth D. E. (1973). *The Art of Computer Programming.* Vol. 3. Reading, MA: Addison-Wesley

Knuth D. E., Morris J. and Pratt V. (1977). Fast pattern matching in strings. *SIAM J. Comp.*, 6, 323–50

Lengauer T. and Tarjan R. E. (1982). Asymptotically tight bounds on time–space trade-offs in a pebble game. *J. ACM*, 29, 1087–130

Lipton R. J., Eisenstat S. C. and De Millo R. A. (1978). Preserving average proximity in arrays. *Comm. ACM*, **21**, 228–31

Lipton R. J. and Tarjan R. E. (1979). A separator theorem for planar graphs. *SIAM J. Appl. Math.*, 36, 177–89

Lipton R. J. and Tarjan R. E. (1980). Applications of planar separator theorem. *SIAM J. Comp.*, 9, 615–27

Loui M. G. (1983). Optimal dynamic embedding of trees into arrays. *SIAM J. Comp.*, 12, 463–72

Manacher G. (1975). A new linear time on-line algorithm for finding the smallest initial palindrome of the string. *J. ACM*, 22, 346–51

Manber U. (1989). *Introduction to Algorithmics: A Creative Approach*. Reading, MA: Addison-Wesley

Manna Z. (1974). *Mathematical Theory of Computation*. New York: McGraw-Hill

Mayer E. (1987). *The Dynamic Tree Expression Problem*. Report STAN–CS–87–1156

Miller G. and Reif J. (1985). Parallel tree contraction and its applications. In *26th IEEE Symp. on Found. of Comp. Science*, pp. 478–89

Munro J. I. (1984). An implicit data structure for the dictionary problem that runs in polylog time. In *Proc. 25th IEEE Symp. on Found. of Comp. Science*, 369–74

Munro J. I. and Suwanda H. (1980). Implicit data structures for fast search and update. *J. Comp. Sys. Sci.*, 21, 236–50

Paterson M. S. and Hewitt C. E. (1970). Comparative schematology. In *Record of Proj. MAC Conf. Concurrent Syst. and Parallel Comp.*, pp. 119–28. ACM: New York

Paul W. J., Tarjan R. E. and Celoni J. R. (1977). Space bounds for a game on graphs. *Math. Sys. Theor.*, 10, 239–51

Pohl I. (1972). A sorting problem and its complexity. *Comm. ACM*, 15, 462–4

Reingold E. (1972). On the optimality of some set algorithms. *J. ACM*, 19, 649–659.

Reischuk R. (1982). A fast implementation of a multidimensional storage into a tree storage. *TCS*, 19, 253–66

Rosenberg A. L. and Snyder L. (1978). Bounds on the costs of data encodings. *Math. Sys. Theor.*, 12, 9–39

Ruzzo W. (1979). Tree-size bounded alternation. *J. Comp. Sys. Sci.*, 21, 218–35

Ruzzo W. and Snyder L. (1981). Minimum edge length planar embeddings of trees. In *VLSI System and Computations* (Kung H., Sproull B. and Steele G., eds.), pp. 119–123. Berlin: Springer-Verlag

Rytter W. (1980). A correct preprocessing algorithm for Boyer–Moore string searching. *SIAM J. Comp.* 9, 509–12

Rytter W. (1981a). An efficient simulation of deterministic pushdown automata with many one-way and two-way heads. *Inf. Proc. Lett.* 12, 234–7

Rytter W. (1981b). The dynamic simulation of recursive and stack manipulating programs. *Inf. Proc. Lett.*, 13(2), 58–63

Rytter W. (1982). Time complexity of unambiguous path systems. *Inf. Proc. Lett.*, 15, 102–4

Rytter W. (1983). Remarks on the pyramidal structure. In *Proc. CAAP'83*. Springer-Verlag

Rytter W. (1985a). On the recognition of context-free languages. *Lect. Notes in Comp. Science*, 208, 318–25. Berlin: Springer-Verlag

Rytter W. (1985b). The complexity of two-way pushdown automata and recursive programs. In *Combinatorial Algorithms on Words* (Apostolico A. and Galil Z. eds.), 341–56. Berlin: Springer-Verlag

Rytter W. (1985c). Fast recognition of push-down automaton and context-free languages. *Inf. and Control*, 67, 12–22

Rytter W. (1987a). $O(\log n)$ parallel recognition of unambiguous cfl's *Information and Computation*, 73, 75–86

Rytter W. (1987b). On the parallel complexity of parsing context-free languages. *Theoretical Computer Science*, 47, 315–21

Rytter W. (1988a). Parallel computation of paths as a grid graph. *Inf. Proc. Lett.* 29, 71–4

Rytter W. (1988b). On the parallel computation of dynamic programming problems. *Theoretical Computer Science*, 59, 297–307

Rytter W. (1990). On parallel evaluation of expressions and straight-line programs. *Computers and Artificial Intelligence*, 9, 427–39

Rytter W. and Giancarlo R. (1987a). Transformations of nondeterministic recursive programs to deterministic efficient ones. *Fundamenta Informaticae* X, 149–60

Rytter W. and Giancarlo R. (1987b) Optimal parallel parsing of bracket languages. *Theoretical Computer Science*, 53, 295–306

Schonhage A. (1980). Storage modification machines. *SIAM J. Comp.*, 9, 419–508

Schonhage A., Paterson M. and Pipinger N. (1976). Finding the median. *J. Comp. Sys. Sci.*, 13, 184–99

Sedgewick R. (1977). Analysis of Quicksort programs. *Act. Inf.*, 7, 327–55

Sedgewick R. (1988). *Algorithms* 2nd edn. Reading, MA: Addison-Wesley

Sheidvasser M. A. (1974). On the length and breadth of graph embeddings in lattices. *Probl. Kib.*, 29, 63–102.

Sleator D. D. and Tarjan R. E. (1983). Self-adjusting binary trees. In *Proc. ACM Symp. on Theory of Comp.*, 235–45.

Sleator D. D. and Tarjan R. E. (1985a). Amortized efficiency of list update and paging rules. *Comm. ACM*, 28, 202–8

Sleator D. D. and Tarjan R. E. (1985b). Self-adjusting binary search trees. *J. ACM*, 32, 652–86

Sleator D. D. and Tarjan R. E. (1986). Self-adjusting heaps. *SICOMP*, 15, 52–68

Tarjan R. E. (1979). A class of algorithms which require nonlinear time to maintain disjoint sets. *J. Comp. Sys. Sci.*, 17, 110–27

Tarjan R. E. and Van Leeuwen J. (1984). Worst-case analysis of set union algorithms. *J. ACM*, 31, 245–81

Valiant L. (1975). General context-free recognition in less than cubic time. *J. Comp. Sys. Sci.*, 10, 308–15

Williams J. W. J. (1964). Algorithm 232: Heapsort. *Comm. ACM.* 7, 347–8

Yordanski M. A. (1976). Minimal enumerations of tree nodes. *Probl. Kib.*, 31, 109–33 (in Russian)

Younger D. (1967). Recognition and parsing of context-free languages in cubic time. *Inf. and Control*, 10, 189–208

Index